Coyote

in the

Maze

Coyote in the Maze

tracking
Edward
Abbey
in a
world of
words

edited by

Peter

Quigley

the university
of utah press
salt lake city

03 02 01 00 99 98
6   5   4   3   2   1

LIBRARY OF CONGRESS CATALOGING-IN-PUBLICATION DATA

Coyote in the maze : tracking Edward Abbey in a world of words /
edited by Peter Quigley.
        p.   cm.
    Includes bibliographical references and index.
    ISBN 0-87480-563-5 (alk. paper)
    1. Abbey, Edward, 1927– —Criticism and interpretation.
2. Environmental protection in literature. 3. Environmental policy
in literature. 4. West (U.S.)—In literature. 5. Deserts in
literature. 6. Nature in literature. 7. Utah—In literature.
I. Quigley, Peter, 1951– .
PS3551.B2Z6   1998
813'.54—dc21   98-11872

CONTENTS

Heraclitean Fire, Bakhtinian Laughter, and the Limits of Literary Judgment

PETER

QUIGLEY

Life is fire, Eternal Fire.
Here burns a portion of the sun.
—Abbey, "A Maxim," *Earth Apples*
... serenity is for the gods, not becoming in a mortal.
—Abbey, *The Brave Cowboy*

Margins, Surfaces, and Centers

This collection was inspired by the wholesale dismissal of Edward Abbey in the arena of "serious" scholarship. This has been especially noticeable at some of the eco-literature conferences, where I have noticed intensely contradictory behavior regarding Abbey (and the concept of nature as well). He is frequently referenced, but discussed in corridors more so than on panels. Disturbingly, he is too often discredited with a scathing epithet or a knowing nod. It seems to me that we owe him much more than that.

Robinson Jeffers, a writer whom Abbey admired, was similarly dismissed by critics who were seduced by the dictates of New Criticism. Demanding short, dense poems, free of sociopolitical references, new critics found that Jeffers could not satisfy these requirements of form and content. "The Double Axe," an antiwar poem written in 1948, elicited a savage response from the press. At his death in 1962, fourteen years after this literary scandal, an uncharitable reviewer proclaimed that "it took his death to remind most readers that he had in fact still been alive" (qtd. in Karman 1995, 1–2). Only in the last

1

decade has Jeffers begun to emerge from almost complete obscurity. Looking back, we can see that what passed for the critics' aesthetic judgment now looks more like politically and ideologically charged rejection.

These fascinating forces of inclusion and exclusion can be seen swirling around Abbey within the current academic battles over ideological and aesthetic priorities. Collective appraisals easily form within academic power structures, and—hoping to please the popular direction of criticism, and perhaps thereby get attention, acceptance, and employment—young scholars too quickly assume the attitudes of their more secure and noted colleagues or mentors. Even those mentors who are supposedly questioning tradition do so, frequently, rather didactically. In this case, it has become fashionable to scoff at Abbey's work and so achieve a measure of acceptance in current discourse. But the result of exclusion has consequences beyond the academy. As Jim Cahalan has pointed out, Abbey has even remained "largely unknown in his native Western Pennsylvania" (1996, 92).

If only for his unique treatment of the desert—which goes beyond many superb passages that capture the lightning, juniper, red rock, glistening pines, and chasms—Abbey deserves consideration. The desert becomes a focal point for Abbey for one of the most classic literary reasons: tension. Tension between nature and culture, but also between the desert and other imagery. Other narratives full of admiration for and tribute to forest and ocean have preprogrammed us to appreciate these things. In other words, as constructionists say, these representations are cultural and political because they are ontologically prior to their associated objects. In *The New West of Edward Abbey,* Ann Ronald admits that the desert "draws me less than the powerful pull of a flowered mountain meadow" (1982, xiii). Structurally speaking, then, by focusing on the desert, its dangers, its inhospitable and formidable features, its heat, Abbey makes a literary gesture. The Russian formalists would have called this "making it strange," a point echoed in Scott Slovic's reminder that *The Monkey Wrench Gang* is "an artifact, a work of the imagination" (1992, 107).

Also, Abbey picks the desert, a buzzard, a snake, even in preference to humans (a bit he borrowed from Robinson Jeffers), partly because he isn't supposed to, because they do not fit conventional definitions of beauty and pleasure. "The desert which is his passion is loved because it is one of the last things which no one could want to own" (Wakoski 1989, 120). Abbey's willful embrace of the desert, his insistence on this choice with such force and defiance, lures us into believing that we are being led to answers. But neither Abbey nor the desert can give us the answers we seek. We may, however, under their influence become stronger, more flexible, more joyous, less arrogant. This makes Abbey's work sound like a literature that, as Matthew Arnold hoped, causes the reader to become a better person, but caution is necessary here. The critics in this volume also identify a disruptive energy in the writing, more akin to Nietzsche and Foucault than Arnold.

Terry Tempest Williams expresses similar sentiments in *Refuge* (1991) when she decides that nature provides no solid resting place, no answer, no way for her to give up her pain or her questions. Nature moves from a closed concept, a reconciling and finished place, to a concept, a principle, a space where conflict and opposition can reside. And from this lesson, from this "nature," she learns to accept death and change, and to oppose the apparent truth of patriarchal and capitalist systems; she becomes more fully aware of her vulnerability and, therefore, the intensity and fleeting beauty of her life.

By picking up on this quality in nature writing, many critics in this volume strike a different note than the modernist sensibility that dominates much "eco-crit" discourse now, and which served critics like Ann Ronald so well fifteen years ago. Ronald has done the only full-length study of Abbey, but he was to write for six more years and have three more books published: *The Fool's Progress* (1988), *Hayduke Lives!* (1992), and *Confessions of a Barbarian* (1994). Nevertheless, Ronald's *The New West of Edward Abbey* (1982) remains a landmark work. Particularly interesting are her insights regarding the use of irony and the manner in which she carries out a structural analysis. I also want to discuss her text as a means to draw attention to methodological shifts.

In *The New West* Ronald asserts that Abbey "undercuts western heroism" (1982, 17), yet her main focus is the way Abbey reworks the Western narrative and the genre of romance. Particularly demonstrative of the methodological biases that drive Ronald is her sense that Abbey's early work abdicates the "romancer's responsibility to offer a visionary alternative" (37). Insisting that Abbey *is* a romancer, and that he must be judged according to that structure, she also complains that Abbey "negates any alternatives" (36) and "offers no . . . option" (37). Irony and anarchy are the unfortunate substitutes one is forced to employ in a world that frustrates realization of the real, and Ronald quotes Northrop Frye to make the point that irony emerges when heroism and unity are foredoomed. In addition, these choices occur when "confusion and anarchy reign over the world" (228).

This is the existential modernist scene: the individual—the sacred unified self—faced with a world of chaos, chooses whatever tools are at hand to shore up these fragments and to express some small but significant testimony to identity and meaning. In Eliot's words, "damnation is salvation from the ennui of modern life, because it at least gives some significance to living" (qtd. in Sharpe 1990, 124). In this view, contradiction and anarchy become brave acts of defiance, unacceptance, and even defeat, but are not values in and of themselves.

Again and again in Ronald's analysis, anarchy is presented in a typically American fashion: negative, destructive, the last refuge of those without other options. Irony also violates one of the aesthetic principles that guide this modernist reading: unity and form. "Unlike the romance . . . irony possesses . . . no mythic pattern," Ronald says. She then quotes a 1972 text on criticism that describes irony as a "negative vision" that cannot "generate . . . a pattern of action" (1982, 213). In Abbey's view, according to Ronald, a civilization that treats nature so destructively "deserves no quarter. The only justifiable rejoinder, then, is anarchy" (77). Here anarchy—like irony, contradiction, multiple voices, and points of view—is identified as the unfortunate choice of a writer who would have had it otherwise. This continuing emphasis on the negative and unproductive qualities of anarchy, irony, and contradiction is visible even in the work of bright young scholars such as Scott Slovic, but it is not a sign of a positive pluralism or a radical democracy.

Much modernist methodology typically distinguishes between false consciousness and true, between authentic and inauthentic "experience," while all the time moving toward the reconciliation of opposites. New Criticism explained over and over how literature would save us from chaos, and Ronald argues that Abbey gradually approaches the point in his narrative where "rock-bottom" realities surface (89), supplanting the contradictory rhetoric. This, according to Ronald, is the alternative not apparent in the earlier writing. "An alternative universe is created," but unfortunately its "bedrock is one of paradox," which "delimits its potency" (88). The desire for certainty drives Ronald's critical narrative.

Although *The New West* is instructive and produces a good argument, Ronald's view requires sweeping aside the passage so important for many of the writers in this collection: "I am convinced now that the desert has no heart, that it presents a riddle which has no answer, and that the riddle itself is an illusion" (Abbey 1991, 273). Ronald dismisses this as a passing moment of rationality soon displaced by "the deep spirit of the place, he cannot displace the romance" (1982, 91). Ronald concludes by stating that Abbey produces a situation where "myth, vision, and reality become the same" (238).

Ronald's argument does important critical work: it validates the fact that Abbey can be discussed in areas such as genre, complexity, "the tradition," and development. However, because of the dictates of this critical period, Ronald's argument marginalizes and diminishes qualities of Abbey's work that now seem to have more interest to critics. Poststructural analysis, for instance, posits a much more interwoven and volatile sense of the possibilities of multiple genres (beyond settling on the Western or the romance for the structuring agents) and a much less static notion of language and reception; poststructuralism, finally, offers some alternative to moving a fictional or critical narrative toward closure, improvement, and clarity.

Abbey's focus on the desert has other intriguing dimensions, moving away from the romantic traditions of breakthrough, myth, discovery, utopia, and finality. Oddly enough, both Abbey and Jean Baudrillard find something central to America in the desert. In *America* (1986), Baudrillard finds speed, distance, and vacuity in the desert. Most assume that Abbey found quite dissimilar things, and it is true that he went to the desert in the Thoreauvian tradition—to slow down, to encounter the opposite of the city. On the other hand, many readers of Abbey, and some in this collection, find that he went to the desert and emerged closer to Baudrillard, not farther away. Abbey sounds like a student of simulacra when in *Desert Solitaire* he says he rejects absolute, essential, and transcendental realities. He is afraid that readers will complain that his book "fails to engage and reveal the patterns of unifying relationships which form the true underlying reality of existence. Here I must confess that I know nothing whatever about a true underlying reality, having never met any" (1991, xi). It is this strain in Abbey that offers a counter to another assumed truth about Abbey: that he was a cranky, didactic absolutist, fully in possession of an unmediated referent.

Literature and Cultural Work

One of the more impressive features of Abbey's work, in addition to his conscious disregard for satisfying what he considered unnecessary literary formalities, is the fact that he was and is read, and often, by many "untrained" readers. Jane Tompkins noted in *West of Everything* (1992) that unlike Hawthorne, writers in the nineteenth century such as Susan Warner were widely read. Tompkins was aiming her argument against the lingering assumption that a serious student of literature should not waste time on popular texts. In fact, to be popular, to be read, to be accessible were sure signs that a book lacked literary merit. Popular Culture Studies, New Historicism, Poststructuralism, and attacks on the notion of a modernist aesthetic hierarchy have altered this valuing system somewhat, but even Abbey himself embraced this notion, thinking his fiction was "literature" and his essays "just" prose.

The fact of the matter is that contrary to Auden's lament that poetry (or literature or painting) makes nothing happen (and many, such as Ransom at mid-century, thought that indeed it should not), it has been quite clear over the years that this is not the case with Abbey. As is well known, Abbey's writing spawned the formation of the radical environmental group Earth First!, which found itself the target of FBI infiltration in the '80s and a federal conspiracy trial in Prescott, Arizona, in the '90s. Less well known is the fact that Abbey has inspired a well-organized and active web site, designed and managed by a Swede (http://www.utsidan.se/abbey)!

What is it in Abbey's writing that attracts so many readers? Perhaps it is his willingness to say anything; he will speak when we are silent. Perhaps it is that Abbey lets us remain human and flawed while still ushering us into the beauty of the world. So many other nature writers seem to want so much from us, but Abbey laughs at himself, at human pretension, and at the literary industry. Still he remains reverent, poised, struck by "this monstrous and inhuman spectacle of rock and cloud and sky and space" (1991, 6). Also, Abbey aimed in a different direction with the scene and theme for his environmental messages. The character of Hayduke depicts an uneducated, damaged, exploited Vietnam vet brought up in the American school of crass commercialism and hard knocks. Although surely not a role model, Abbey allows this member of the working class to take up the privileged position of being a defender of nature and an articulator of resistance to power.

It is odd that the same folks who have entered the literary profession since the early 1980s arguing for a politically "relevant" canon and the methodologies "to do political work" are often those who have rejected Abbey's work in articles or have ignored him in their scholarship and omitted him from their syllabuses. Many of these scholars are drawn to a quieter, more complex treatment of language, sexuality, personality—all more thoroughly laden and subdued and muted. In environmental circles, they focus on the recently emerging and admirable eco-feminist writing or the elegant world of Gary Snyder and his Buddhist aesthetics and politics. Snyder's world is a cedar-scented place where tinkling chimes blow lightly in the breezes of the eternal void, where we chop wood and carry water. All of this is fine and indispensable work and should be read often. However, a more charitable, wide-ranging, vigorous, and eclectic criticism would embrace all writing that exhibits stylistic, aesthetic, or cultural significance. By not doing so, English departments will continue to be targets of accusations of narrowness and hypocrisy, which some richly deserve.

David Morris is one critic who does appreciate the different voice that Abbey brings to the environmental discussion, and he points to its value and its problematic: "the comic context suggests that to experience a reverence for nature one does not have to be—what is the word?—as 'decorous,' as 'genteel,' as 'distinguished' as the personae of Lopez and Eisley" (1993, 24). In reference to Dillard, Morris states that for Abbey, she "touches the sublimely reverent note too frequently" (24). Abbey does not provide the serenity sought by many readers (which is for the gods), but instead he courts disaster in language, philosophy, social scenes, politics, sexuality, and in literature.

Apart from some recent intelligent attention from writers such as Morris, Daniel Payne (whose *Voices in the Wilderness* [1996] offers a thirteen-page overview chapter), and Scott Slovic (*Seeking Awareness in American Nature Writing,* one chapter), Abbey's work has received little that can be called a fair, focused, or sustained treatment by scholars of American literature. Although Abbey is so often discussed in the halls of the Association for the Study of Literature and the Environment (ASLE) and at Western American Literature conferences, he is infrequently written about. A stark example of this irresponsible treatment recently came to my attention. In an anthology of writings about wilderness, the editor introduces a selection from *Desert Solitaire* by blithely identifying Abbey as "a self-styled agrarian anarchist and ecological terrorist" (Bergon 1994, 334). Well, without quibbling over what "self-styled" could possibly mean, the accusation of "terrorist," which Bergon delivers as though reading a shopping list, seems extraordinarily irresponsible. It has the confidence associated with the kind of "common knowledge" that starts with "As we all know. . . ." Had Bergon perhaps been more familiar with the degree to which Abbey labored over the distinction between saboteur and terrorist, he would have been more careful about applying the term with such apparent ease—and without the hint of qualification or, needless to say, documentation.

Genre and Style

The themes that drive many of the essays in this collection relate to postmodernism, Nietzsche, ambiguity, and contradiction. Those schooled in recent political criticism will recognize the vigor associated with a writer whose language, attitudes, and themes elicit such wide divergences of reactions and understandings. *And it is this very quality of being in-between*—of being opposed to growth and progress as defined by the engines of Enlightenment technoculture, and of being equally opposed to rigid antitechnological dogmatism—that interests me. Scott Slovic echoes this same point of view, saying that Abbey's writing "calls into question the very notion of a static ideology, whether pro-environment or pro-development . . . Abbey, it seems, delights in luring us to make a commitment to one ideology or another, to one mode of reading or another, only to pull the rug out from under our feet suddenly" (1992, 101). In *The Brave Cowboy,* Paul Bondi states, "I'll not be a slave to my own ideology" (1992, 112). Abbey himself once said, "It's hard for me to stay serious for more than half a page at a time" (qtd. in Lensink 1988, 27).

But Abbey can lose his focus on the satire of humanity to momentarily reveal the source of his contradictions, ambiguity, and humor: "the vast approach, from far beyond Andromeda, of the Lord of the Universe, Uranus, seeking out his bride, Gaia, green bosomed, brown thighed, rosy bellied, Earth" (1990, 223). This is the sense of vastness that he learned from Jeffers, what Jeffers called "Inhumanism." This groundlessness taught him to look at pomposity with satire and humor, and to respect the quiet hum of eternity embodied by the graceful, solemn calm of a floating buzzard. It is no longer the case that ambiguity or contradiction is easily ascribed to literary merit on the one hand or lack of a strong vision on the other. These were the mid-century choices of an eviscerated right-wing New Criticism wallowing in luxurious indecision, or a self-assured new left assuming the existence of an indisputable referent. Today, philosophical perspective has shifted toward the postmodern, and this new perspective, which leaves us with so much less certainty, opens passages into Abbey. The writers in this collection take advantage of this opening and discuss Abbey's use of contradiction and ambiguity in ways that have not been explored.

Diane Wakoski (1989) has correctly connected Abbey with Jeffers and a tradition of inhumanism, in which ambiguity and contradiction are used for specific sociopolitical reasons. This position denies human knowledge and experience as central, but far from simply being negative, it provides a critique of power that points toward sane living, a method that Snyder says results in "healing not saving" (1974, 6). Abbey calls this "civilization." As Wakoski points out, "Strangely, Abbey is no prophet of doom. Like the desert, he seems to offer philosophies which do not bring final answers but lead one to other questions" (1989, 120). Call it inhumanism, carnival, satire—call it what you will—Abbey's writing is part of a long tradition of taking the broadest, most expansive look at human nature and life.

So often when reading Abbey, one cannot help but think of Mikhail Bakhtin, of the genres of satire, scandal, comedy, carnival, irony. The motivation for such a representation is, finally, not to affront but, as Wakoski has pointed out, to affirm, to celebrate. Abbey's concentration on the life of the body in all of its delights and smells and processes can be seen as a part of Bakhtin's definition of carnival, which "brings together . . . the sacred and the profane, the lofty with the low, the great with the insignificant, the wise with the stupid. In addition, we are to find carnivalistic blasphemies, a whole system of carnivalistic debasings and bringings down to earth, carnivalistic obscenities linked with the reproductive power of the earth and the body, carnivalistic parodies on sacred texts and sayings" (1994, 123).

A celebration of reproduction appears constantly in Abbey's work, whether he is describing Gaia or the sexual longings of his characters. Parodies of the sacred and a concentration on the body define Abbey well, as evidenced by his frequently overdrawn characters. Like a Brueghel painting, they are grossly physical, heavy with weight of flesh on bone; they smell; they defecate; they belch; they laugh and jiggle; they are lusty; they are loving, lonely, desperate, and fulfilled.

Laughter, of course, is key. Abbey is not, however, simply in it for the cheap joke (well, not always). This politically oppositional and joyous laughter has a higher purpose, as described by Bakhtin:

> Carnivalistic laughter . . . is directed toward something higher—toward a shift of authorities and truths, a shift of world orders. Laughter embraces both poles of change, it deals with the very process of change, with crisis itself. Combined in the act of carnival laughter are death and rebirth, negation (a smirk) and affirmation (rejoicing laughter). This is a profoundly universal laughter, a laughter that contains a whole outlook on the world. Such is the specific quality of ambivalent carnival laughter. (1994, 127)

Of course, Bakhtin's final horizon is a celebration of "the people." Not the people of a strict and uniform communist state, but the people who embrace and embody the free, unencumbered expression of living, yearning, hopeful bodies.

While Bakhtin wrote under Stalin, Abbey's work emerged under McCarthy and Hoover. Like Bakhtin, Abbey was no misanthrope (as is sometimes claimed) but finally one who celebrated life in all of its diversity, perversity, and teeming polyphony. As Bakhtin says, "The category of the familiar contact is also responsible for the special way mass actions are organized" (1994, 123), and the cast of incredible characters at the Earth First! rendezvous in *Hayduke* suggests pure carnival:

> a motley crude Coxey's army of the malcontent, the discontent, the visionary, the vengeful revolutionist, the pipe-smoking field trained deep ecologist, the misty-eyes tree-hugging Nature Lover, the sober conservationist, the native American Earth Goddess, the mountain man in buckskin and fringes . . . the beer-drinking fun-loving gun-happy trailbusters in sweat-rich camouflage T-shirts and worn-out steel-sole jungle boots, the zealot eyed unisexual funhating sectarian Marxists in corduroy and workman shirts . . . misanthropic redneck pseudointellectuals steeped in Thoreau and Garrett Hardin, a few . . . macho mystics, three socio-feminist Furies. . . . (1990, 186)

This is not a dogmatic approach or a one-sided body slam from a didactic demagogue; this is a satirist celebrating humanity—and condemning humanity—for its vanity, its silliness, its irreverent diversity. From this perspective, complaints about Abbey's lack of decorum seem thin, but it is an important point because this lack of consistency disturbs people who want a systematic approach for use in doctrinaire positions.

Tracking Abbey in a Maze of Words

This volume opens with two sharply contrasting voices, both of them revealing regarding Abbey and the issues surrounding his work. Ed Twining, a friend of Abbey's and someone whom he thought understood his work, reviews what sympathetic readers will recognize as characteristic themes. Twining acknowledges the environmental importance of Abbey's work but attempts to push beyond—to the philosophy, the anarchism, the issues surrounding life in late modernism. SueEllen Campbell, drawing on newer traditions, also examines Abbey's work from a broad, encompassing perspective. No ideologue, Campbell offers criticism at its best: deeply inquisitive, erudite, playful, even suspenseful. Drawing on Derrida, Foucault, Baudrillard, and Haraway, Campbell's questions proliferate from Abbey's text in a masterful profusion, and her chapter points to several others in the collection whose authors find poststructural analysis particularly applicable to Abbey's work. Although Campbell and Twining stand somewhat opposed to one another—in tone, style, and method—from another perspective they are in full agreement regarding the energy and contemplation generated by Abbey's texts. While Campbell questions the way Abbey constructs nature and his experience there, Twining asks whether too many constructions on the part of critics have kept us from seeing Abbey more clearly and fairly.

Barbara Barney Nelson's chapter is delightful for the way she examines Abbey's treatment of the cow and discovers hidden layers of complexity. In fact, she identifies a plurality of voices that reveal a more inclusive side of Abbey: one more sympathetic towards cows, the third world, and other elements that he, supposedly, monolithically opposed. In "Edward Abbey's Cow," Nelson proves that the questions Abbey raised about modern and "apparently" superior ancient ways of living outnumbered his uncompromising and bold pronouncements.

The chapter by Tom Lynch echoes concerns similar to Campbell's. Moving instructively between Abbey's work and Native American authors, Lynch demonstrates where they share perspective, and where they depart. Lynch is particularly astute at showing how writers such as Luci Tapahonso, Simon Ortiz, Gary Snyder, and others identify nature as home, as a scene that suggests family, ancestors, and domestic ritual. Abbey, of course, omits much of this. Although Lynch recognizes that Abbey also referred to the desert as home, he is finally critical of the degree to which Abbey is part of a paradigm that sees the desert as exile and escape.

Werner Bigell, a German scholar teaching in Norway, closely examines the concept of nature as Abbey uses it for differing sociopolitical ends. By appropriating Abbey for environmental purposes, Bigell claims, critics have had to ignore the contradictions in his work. Bigell draws on poststructural thought and on critics such as Chaloupka, Foucault, and Derrida, as well as Norwegian eco-theorists such as Kvaløy, to theorize nature as a cultural space in Abbey. According to Bigell, "Protecting heterotopias such as wilderness does not mean protecting 'nature,' but protecting a cultural openness, both in space and signification."

From within the swirl of critical disagreements, Paul Lindholdt examines Abbey's place in the anti-machine, or neo-Luddite, tradition. In "Rage against the Machine," Lindholdt identifies several traditions that have bearing upon a proper understanding of Abbey's attacks on technology. In all, Lindholdt adds significantly to Abbey scholarship by tracing the development of opposition to machinery in his work, his life, and his style. Finally, Lindholdt examines all of Abbey's commentary in the context of autobiography.

Harold Alderman, Steven Norwick, and Bryan Moore all demonstrate the attraction Abbey has for political and philosophical thinkers. Norwick's chapter explores the many similarities between passages from Nietzsche and Abbey, while Alderman carefully examines several anarchist positions, looking for the closest tie to Abbey. Moore explores Abbey's use of rhetoric, while noting Abbey's objection to the topic. Drawing on Plato's definitions of rhetoric, Moore suggests that although language and words may indeed be volatile, they need not be without a sense of truthfulness and nobility. Moore connects what he calls "noble rhetoric" with Abbey's concern for the wilderness, and his examination of the various rhetorical elements in Abbey's work contrasts markedly with the analyses of language conducted by the poststructural critics in this collection.

David Rothman makes a counterclaim that Abbey was not so much relying on rational argument and philosophical discourse as he was on poetry. Rothman's important study looks deep into the legacy of the poetic past in *Desert Solitaire,* demonstrating that Abbey was a careful reader of other texts and highly conscious of the conversation he was carrying on with American literature. Abbey, according to Rothman, borrows from, argues with, and works in and around literally dozens of poets and philosophers, frequently without documenting them.

In *Against Nature: The Concept of Nature in Critical Theory* (1996) Steven Vogel points to the theoretical tension between social constructionists and those who cling to what he calls "the naturalistic fallacy" (9). According to Vogel, "There is no nature in itself. . . . The nature we encounter has no noumenal status nor even any noumenal correlate; it is something we constitute" (123). This positioning has earned poststructuralists a reputation for being against nature, of being urban Derrideans, and Claire Lawrence takes this important issue on in her chapter. Because nature writers must translate the "real" into words—an impossible task—Lawrence believes that they confront a special set of philosophic and artistic challenges. Making a compelling argument that Abbey was quite conscious of the problem of trying to "fit or contain the natural world in words," Lawrence positions herself with Bigell and other writers in the collection who counter the claim that Abbey was a naive realist. Lawrence also partially answers some of Campbell's questions concerning Abbey and his desire for the land. As do several other authors who contributed to this volume, Lawrence makes it clear that Abbey was aware of the historical framework of his approach to the land. She also makes a strong case that Abbey was aware that discourse, or naming, is a form of domination, but hopelessly unavoidable—another one of the strong tensions that inform his style and characterize his unique genre.

Genre is again the issue in Rebecca Raglon's chapter, "Surviving Doom and Gloom: Edward Abbey's Desert Comedies," which opens a much needed discussion. Raglon believes that Abbey's work allows us to challenge "the pious and moralizing tendency of some nature writers," and she connects Abbey to Joseph Meeker's notion that "comedy illustrates that survival depends upon man's ability to change himself rather than his environment, and upon his ability to accept limitations rather than to curse fate for limiting him."

In "Edward Abbey's Inadvertent Postmodernism: Theory, Autobiography, and Politics," William Chaloupka orchestrates a complex discussion that interweaves Abbey with Foucault, Haraway, Zizeck (an Eastern European), and other theorists to demonstrate how Abbey takes a postmodern turn that avoids the modernist stance of the Greens. In short, Abbey moves beyond a debilitating modernist metaphysics, therefore "politicizing situations that otherwise would have been plowed under in the rush to general, theological pronouncement." It is this intellectual base, Chaloupka says, that allowed Abbey to point away from the doctrinaire, modernist positionings of contemporary environmentalism.

My contribution to the collection, "The Politics and Aesthetics of a Hopeful Anarchism," focuses on two things: the use of ambiguity and contradiction for political ends, and the significance of Norway for Abbey and for American environmentalism.

James Papa explores the details of Abbey's attitudes toward national parks. Using Thoreau as a foil, Papa shows where Abbey and Thoreau converge and depart. At the same time, Papa carries on an instructive discussion concerning such policies as the Wilderness Act of 1964 and Abbey's own views. This essay gives a much needed historical and political context for Abbey's views of parks and how this affected his writing.

Although many authors in this volume discuss gender, Paul Bryant makes it the focus of "Edward Abbey and Gender." An established critic on Abbey, Bryant tackles this difficult and volatile issue and examines whether innuendo and rumor have persisted in place of fact regarding Abbey and his attitudes and actions. Carefully reasoned and anticipating disagreement, Bryant's chapter counters gossip with the record.

In what is, to my mind, the first serious treatment of Abbey's journals, David Morris discusses them as literary construction and as autobiography. He also compares Abbey with Emerson and Foucault, confronting the question of where the person or the author resides in language. This chapter has urgent importance for Abbey scholarship and reflects a great deal of intelligence. Morris has discovered something quite significant in the journals, and his wonderfully written analysis again points to the central issue of this collection: the amazing complexity at the heart of Abbey's writing.

David Rothenberg—naturalist, essayist, professor, editor, musician, translator, and friend of Arne Naess—loves the questions in Abbey more than the answers: "I would say that this is because he studied enough philosophy to get hooked on the idea that dilemma is worth more than solution." Rothenberg admires Abbey "because he did it. He turned away from the institutions that spawned him." It is this apparent straightforwardness that attracts many to Abbey.

Discord, ambiguity, upheaval, joyous undoing—all were guests invited to this campfire supper on Abbey's road. Abbey served up the strange, the sublime, the indecent—a concoction of moral outrage and cosmic laughter that we will not hear again soon. Indeed, what a strange note he sounded in the canyons of literature, environmental thought, and the personal lives of so many. As Rothenberg notes, "Like Socrates, he said just those things that would make him unpopular, while teaching the rest of us a thing or two. Only he died long before his time, and our loss grows deeper with each thinking year." Refusing serenity and engaging the rapids of thought and life, Abbey believed that "serenity is for the gods, not becoming in a mortal. Better to be partisan and passionate on this earth; be plenty objective enough when dead" (1992, 49). When things are settled, one has not the vigorous cacophony of democracy, but fascism. Like a multivoiced democracy, wilderness is diverse, but a clear-cut, like fascism, is a monoculture.

Abbey clearly knew that there is no final answer—"The desert says nothing"—but that there is also no escape from being provisionally partisan—"There is no way out of these difficulties" (1991, 270). He also sensed the danger and responsibility surrounding this activity of conceptualizing nature. Luc Ferry, in *The New Ecological Order* (1995), reminds us that Hitler enacted laws that protected animals and nature, and even restricted hunting, and he asks readers to contemplate the possible implications. Abbey, too, frequently sensed an unhealthy contempt for the human in some recent environmental positions and in what he called a mad rush for the romantically primitive, which was the Nazi trajectory. He could smell tyranny and hatred a long way off. As a counter, he celebrated the diversity in humanity and in nature. The voices that echo from the maze where we chase Abbey may not answer any ultimate questions, but like the frogs in *Desert Solitaire*, they sing "out of spontaneous love and joy . . . for love of their own existence, however brief it may be, and for joy in the common life" (1991, 143).

We will continue to honor Gary Snyder for giving us his vision of a city,

Preserved in seed from beginningless time.
a city crowded with books,

Thick grass on the streets,
a race of dark people
Wearing thin sandals, reading all morning in alleys. . . .

(1978, 47)

Abbey provides a vision that is equally profound. In the unpredictable process of life, destruction and creation are linked, and a striking mixed-race community floats out of Abbey's political and poetic imagination and hovers on an impossible horizon:

No matter, it's of slight importance. Time and the winds will sooner or later bury the Seven Cities of Cibola, Phoenix, Tucson, Albuquerque, all of them, under dunes of glowing sand, over which blue-eyed Navajo bedouin will herd their sheep and horses, following the river in the winter, the mountains in the summer, and sometimes striking off across the desert toward the red canyons of Utah where great waterfalls plunge over silt-filled, ancient, mysterious dams. (1991, 145)

It is time to honor Edward Abbey for his dreams, his anger, his courage, his craft, his joy, and, yes, his humanity.

Note

I would like to thank Gary Abbate for the loan of the books and for reminding me that most writing is for the enjoyment of readers, not academics. Thanks to David Morris for helping me think about the project in new ways. A special note of consideration goes out to Tim Hope, Anne Mette Soiland, and my other students in Norway who taught me so much in the Environmental Literature and Politics seminar at the University of Bergen. I would also like to thank my editor, Dawn Marano, who was always helpful and kept me buoyant. Thanks to Tim Hunt for suggesting University of Utah Press, and to Ed Leuders for encouragement and suggestions. I have also appreciated conversations with Donn Rawlins regarding his relationship with Edward Abbey. A special thanks goes out to Alexis Mills Noebels, who gave the manuscript first-class editing. And, as always, thanks to Polly, Daniel, and Dylan for unending, unconditional love and support. Most of all I would like to thank Edward Abbey for being wondrous, practical, romantic, difficult, angry, loving, humorous, critical, and outrageous.

Works Cited

Abbey, Edward. 1990. *Hayduke Lives!* New York: Little, Brown and Co.
———. [1968] 1991. *Desert Solitaire: A Season in the Wilderness.* Reprint, New York: Ballantine.

————. [1956] 1992. *The Brave Cowboy*. Reprint, New York: Avon.

Bakhtin, Mikhail. [1984] 1994. *Problems of Dostoevsky's Poetics*. Reprint, Minneapolis: University of Minnesota Press.

Baudrillard, Jean. 1988. *America*. London: Verso.

Bergon, Frank, ed. [1980] 1994. *The Wilderness Reader*. Reprint, Reno: University of Nevada Press.

Bishop, James. 1994. *Epitaph for a Desert Anarchist*. New York: Atheneum.

Cahalan, Jim. 1996. " 'My People': Edward Abbey's Appalachian Roots in Indiana County, Pennsylvania." *Pittsburgh History* (fall): 92–107.

Evernden, Neil. 1992. *The Social Creation of Nature*. Baltimore: Johns Hopkins University Press.

Ferry, Luc. [1992] 1995. *The New Ecological Order*. Trans. Carol Volk. Reprint, Chicago: University of Chicago Press.

Karman, Jim. 1995. *Robinson Jeffers: Poet of California*. Brownsville, Ore.: Story Line Press.

Lensink, Julie Nolte. 1988. "An Interview with Edward Abbey." In *Words From the Land: Encounters with Natural History Writing*, ed. Steven Trimble. Salt Lake City: Smith.

Morris, David. 1993. "Celebration and Irony: The Polyphonic Voice of Edward Abbey's Desert Solitaire." *Western American Literature* 28 (1): 21–32.

Payne, Daniel. 1995. *Voices in the Wilderness: American Nature Writing and Environmental Politics*. Hanover, N.H.: University Press of New England.

Ronald, Ann. 1982. *The New West of Edward Abbey*. Reno: University of Nevada Press.

Sharpe, William. 1990. *Unreal Cities*. Baltimore: Johns Hopkins University Press.

Slovic, Scott. 1992. *Seeking Awareness in American Nature Writing*. Salt Lake City: University of Utah Press.

Snyder, Gary. 1974. *Turtle Island*. New York: New Directions.

————. [1960] 1978. *Myths and Texts*. Reprint, New York: New Directions.

Tompkins, Jane. 1992. *West of Everything*. New York: Oxford University Press.

Vogel, Steven. 1996. *Against Nature: The Concept of Nature in Critical Theory*. Albany: State University of New York Press.

Wakoski, Diane. 1989. "Joining the Visionary 'Inhumanists.' " In *Resist Much, Obey Little: Some Notes on Edward Abbey*, ed. James Hepworth and Gregory McNamee. Tucson: Harbinger House.

Williams, Terry Tempest. 1991. *Refuge*. New York: Vintage.

The Roots of Abbey's Social Critique

EDWARD S.

TWINING

As time goes on, it's becoming clearer that Edward Abbey's novels and essays have greater heft than criticism of them has so far shown itself able to acknowledge. Popular since the publication of *The Brave Cowboy* in 1956, Abbey became a dynamic personal presence in the public drama over ecological conflicts after *Desert Solitaire,* published in 1968. In short, Abbey became a prominent voice in a centrally important American political struggle, still ongoing. That is more than enough for many people. As time goes on, though, and we look deeper into what has seemed Abbey's open and easy books, the Abbey we thought we knew fits less and less well into the seemingly obvious categories we have wanted to contain him in. He keeps spilling over them, running away.

The first problem is that this easy-voiced humorous populist— this lover of the common man (and woman) who spoke so fluent and natural a colloquial American English—more and more reveals himself as a master stylist whose surfaces have gulled us into believing his mind is as lyric and transparent as his voice. The politics he engaged with, and the drama of the politics implicit or explicit in Abbey's writing, have foregrounded themselves—perhaps inevitably, given the importance that ecological consciousness has increasingly assumed throughout the developed world in the last half century. Part of the fun, and the *relevance,* of Abbey has been his resonant, witty, and uncompromising voice in this centrally important discussion about the direction our burgeoning civilization is taking us. Abbey has been a leader. His voice has been a coherent, rational, and yet humorously

passionate one in defense of wilderness and against short-sighted destruction in the name of economic exploitation, promoting the realization that the natural world we Americans, especially, have been
lucky enough to inherit matters complexly and profoundly to us.
Charles Bowden perhaps said it best in identifying one of Abbey's
most distinctive accomplishments: "Ed Abbey invented the Southwest we live in. He made us look at it, and when we looked up again
we suddenly saw it through his eyes and sensed what he sensed—we
were killing the last good place" (1990, 164). It is certainly true that
Abbey has formulated images only inchoately present before, creating
a distinctive world that is part now of our collective American imagination; he has taken his place with John C. Van Dyke, Mary Austin,
Joseph Wood Krutch, and others as part of that small, distinguished
body of writers who have imaginatively created for us our now-shared
sense of the desert Southwest—and its transcendent value.

Underlying this numinous vision of the Southwest, however, is a
deeper nexus of ideas undergirding another valuation of nature altogether: underneath the dramatic politics of our time in defense of
wilderness are deeper philosophic tenets that have been present and
coherent throughout Abbey's writing career. His explicit defense of
anarchism is well known to readers, documented, for instance, in the
pithy four-page "Theory of Anarchy" in his last collection of essays,
published the year before his death (*One Life at a Time, Please*
[1988]). "Anarchy is democracy taken seriously," he wrote there
(26). Throughout his writing life, Abbey made it clear that he was a
realist, one who obdurately insisted on the unavoidable primary importance of the material world that manifests itself to our (unignor-
able) senses. In one of his journals he wrote, "The world is really
nothing but an idea in the mind of God, say the physicist-orientalist-
mystics. To which my response is: So what? Who cares? What difference does that make? We still have to live in the world of actual
daily experience, of all those hard objects and firm living bodies
that certainly *appear* to share the world with us. We are not alone"
(1994, 311).

But even Abbey's anarchist sympathies and principles—and his
obvious, insisted upon realism—obscure for many readers a deeper
philosophical seriousness and complexity, which is not to say that
either Abbey's anarchism or his realism are themselves superficial,
simple, or insignificant. Abbey is, first of all, a quintessential American
individualist, but his uniqueness reflects the options possible in his

time, which means that it takes into account the profoundly changed material circumstances of the American late twentieth century.

Let it be said simply: Abbey's writing registers major changes in the America of our time with clarity and force. The responsive chord Abbey struck with enthusiastic audiences from the beginning of his publishing career is doubtless at least partly attributable to this distinctive element in his writing. Readers have recognized that both his novels and his essays record substantive historic alterations in the material circumstances undergirding life in this country. But the novels and essays do more than that; they reveal the underlying human significance in those material changes, the profound alteration in the mental landscape all Americans perforce survey. Both material circumstances and mental landscape will alter even more significantly in the foreseeable future, and Abbey is supremely articulate in demonstrating the true character of our loss.

Certain fragments Abbey does attempt to shore against our ruins. He is in this sense a prophet for many of his readers; a prophet both because he foresaw and warned against the diminished future we are all in fact demonstrably rushing into, and because he inveighed against that as an evil in a positively Old Testament fashion. It cannot be stated too strongly: Abbey's writing is about the real world, our world, about historic changes taking place in his and our America, and his conviction that those changes are profoundly significant for us.

Abbey's mode as a writer had nothing to do with "magic realism" or any other contemporary experimental narrative and structural techniques—except movies, and that in a small way. Rather, Abbey wrote in both his novels and his essays as what he essentially was: a contemporary American product of the Enlightenment. He was a rationalist and, in a fundamental sense, a materialist. He insisted, first to last, on two inescapable propositions: that the world is real, and that it is knowable. Consequently, he insisted that human events and outcomes in this real, knowable world are largely controllable. Because they are so, he affirmed, we have the absolute and inescapable moral and civic responsibility to commit ourselves to shaping those outcomes. That assertion of civic responsibility is, of course, a conventional one, honored in this country for a long time indeed: it has been around on these shores at least since Paine and Franklin and Jefferson, and it has found literary expression in imaginative American writers from Thoreau to Twain to Abbey himself.

A basic fact underlying Abbey's concerns can be conveyed in one stark statistic: during his sixty-two-year life, from 1927 to 1989, America's population more than doubled—from about 122 million at the time of his birth, to more than 250 million at his death. During Abbey's lifetime the United States added more people than had previously accumulated here during the entire history of immigration to this country; more people, that is, than in the four hundred years of emigration from Europe and Africa and Asia (and likely more than in the previous ten—or is it twenty?—millennia). Of course, this phenomenal rate of growth continues, thanks to current governmental policies and the business considerations largely driving them. Legal immigration in the mid-1990s is adding just under a million people a year—900,000 officially. Best estimates for illegal immigration, the figure for which is understandably uncertain, adds some large fraction of another million every year. And, thanks to tax policies that encourage multichild families and promise to do so even more in the future, the "natural" increase from excess of births over deaths drives population growth in numbers that are absolutely higher every year. Two more doublings will give America the dubious boon of attaining China's population. At the actual rate of growth prevailing during Abbey's lifetime, and continuing unabated, Abbey's descendants, and ours, may soon live in a United States with a population of one billion people.

Everyone is familiar, too, with the explosion of technology in our time—and with at least some its consequences. The increase in general wealth since the Second World War—enabling burgeoning numbers of us to buy and use everything from recreational and "all-terrain" vehicles to high-tech bicycling, hiking, skiing, and camping equipment—has compounded the effects of the enormous increase in the sheer number of us. Incalculable is the effect of cheap jet travel, which makes the entire country part of our backyard: there's hardly a place on the continent we can't reach in a single day by jet plane and the help of a rented car, no formerly unpeopled place we can't at least be on the edge of with our backpack, skis, or mountain bike. Swift and affordable access has converted the land, including what we still call "wilderness," into a sort of consumable—one that is accessible at any given moment to whatever fraction of a quarter billion people who have the wealth, the means, and the desire to consume it. That fraction, along with our technological capabilities, increases every day.

All this, of course, involves enormous consumption of energy, electrical power, gasoline, diesel, and jet fuel. The proliferation of roads and all the roadside baggage of our transportation system is matched by the spread of power plants, which with their smog and tentacles of powerlines now spread over what even recently were empty, clear landscapes. These manifestations of our need for power are now hard to avoid in what were, even a few decades ago, landscapes largely devoid of man-made artifacts, in the American Southwest as elsewhere. Thoreau's observation makes more sense now than in his own time: we don't ride the railroad, it rides us. Except that our "railroads" stretch not only over the entire land, but six or seven miles into the sky as well.

These are material facts. What are their consequences? Why did all this so matter to Abbey? Why does it matter to us?

To answer, let's start with a more or less typically polemical Abbey passage, an example of style and substance both, one that is characteristic late Abbey.

The worst sleaze is on the American side of the border in downtown Brownsville, among the bars, go-go joints, and block after block of little clothing stores. Here I see one of the saddest things I've ever seen, anywhere. Inside a shop labeled Ropas Usadas (Used Clothes), a dozen weary little Mexican women, all pregnant, sit among mountains of old clothing, each woman patiently sorting through these trash piles in search of children's garments and stacking her selections in a small heap at her feet. Both temperature and humidity are in the nineties. The air in the place is stifling, swarming with flies, and dense with the unmistakable, unforgettable smell of poverty. The manager of this pen, a swarthy, greasy-haired, crossbred, snake-eyed bandito, the only male in view, waits in the corner for the women to finish their sorting and hand over their faded paper pesos. Hordes of children play outside on the slime and broken glass in the street.

Watching this intolerable, unacceptable scene, which nevertheless we tolerate and accept, I think again of Stony Pass in the San Juans, the clear, cold mountain air, the peaks covered with fresh snow, and the bright virgin waters of the Rio Grande trickling from their multitude of secret beginnings under the rocks and the tundra and the alpine flowers. The elk were on the move, through the pines and aspen; in the evenings we'd hear the bull elk bugle forth his challenge to the world. That is another world, a sort of paradise compared to this, a world that these women and most of their children will never see. (1988, 152–53)

Although published in 1988, the year before Abbey died, this passage is representative of him early and late. Abbey was highly consistent— in his thinking, in the subjects (and juxtapositions of subjects) that inform his work, in his unchanging direct address to his central themes. Even more important, he was consistent in adhering to essential convictions: that the world is real, that we know it through our senses, and that we are compelled by an absolute moral imperative to respond to the world in a responsible way. A moral way.

Abbey was all through his life a student of philosophy, and he received a bachelor's and a master's degree in philosophy from the University of New Mexico. Friends have said that until the end of his life he read philosophers for recreation. His own works, both his essays and (to a lesser extent) his novels, are replete with explicit or, not so commonly, veiled references to dozens of philosophers and historians. It is simply perverse not to recognize that Abbey spent a lifetime thinking and writing about ideas—ideas enabling and governing the way we engage with the real material world and the world of human action, the latter in some inescapable and frightening ways even more "real." For Abbey knew that identifiable forces, practices, and institutions in the social, political, economic, and technological realms are just as determinative of our experience as the "natural" world. He knew also that these social, political, economic, and technological realities have been created by us (even if, especially if, inadvertently) over stretches of time. These worlds, Abbey insisted, create us in their turn.

Abbey never deviated from his rock-bottom certainty that such humanly created worlds share with nature the shaping of human destiny, and that they too are knowable. A corollary proposition persisting throughout Abbey's writing is that this reality and knowledge demand that we accept responsibility for our own affairs, that we come to grips with this world we inherit and at least potentially, at least partly, have control over. It is in this most basic of senses that Abbey was both a moralist and a thorough-going materialist. He never deviated from those three propositions: *The world is real. We can know the world. We are responsible for it.*

Everyone who has ever read anything by Abbey knows what has

to be said next: that Abbey always, and emphatically, emplaced the human world within the natural one—where, he insisted, it belongs. From the appearance of his first published books, Abbey has been tabbed a "nature writer," one of those in a large, very mixed bag that for a couple centuries has been accumulating all sorts of things, from the most sentimental and romantic to the most grittily scientific. Maybe we're now just too far from Emerson and Thoreau for us to remember that American nature writing at its most forceful has been inextricably associated with, even rooted in, philosophical and ethical thought. But it is precisely from that Emersonian-Thoreauvian tradition of thinking and writing about nature that Abbey comes. As did his transcendental progenitors of a century and a half ago, Abbey emplaces his human world within a larger natural one. And the logical clarity and moral force in the way he effects that emplacement in terms for our time is why he matters as much as he does—and one of the reasons he is so profoundly American, speaking so truly to the American ear.

That and the fact that he wrote about his quintessentially American subject beautifully, in a style simple and clear, a style splendidly apt for the coherence of his thought and his vision. Abbey wrote with a manifest life-long love for the American language, and an extraordinarily keen ear for the rhythms, vigor, and pungency of contemporary spoken American English. No modern American writer has so well captured the vitality of this oral culture, and no modern American writer more powerfully conveys the degree of involvement common people have through their speech with the mental and imaginative lives they lead. Consider, for example, the light, deft manner with which Abbey depicts the interactions between Doc Sarvis, Hayduke, and Seldom Seen Smith at that pivotal moment early in *The Monkey Wrench Gang* when the three plotters first hatch their plan of eco-sabotage. The doctor has just realized the dangers and implications for their safety and freedom in what they contemplate: "Are you certain this canyon is not bugged?" he asks. "I have the feeling that others are listening in to every word we say."

> "I know that feeling," Hayduke said, "but that's not what I'm thinking about right now. I'm thinking—"
> "What are you thinking about?"
> "I'm thinking: Why the fuck should we trust each other? I never even met you two guys before today."

Silence. The three men stared into the fire. The oversize surgeon. The elongated riverman. The brute from the Green Berets. A sigh. They looked at one another. And one thought: What the hell. And one thought: They look honest to me. And one thought: Men are not the enemy. Nor women either. Nor little children. Not in sequence but in unison, as one, they smiled. At each other. The bottle made its penultimate round.

"What the hell," Smith said, "we're only talkin'." (1975, 68)

Abbey's mastery of language is no matter of superficial stylistics: in its diction, its rhythms, and its unmistakable sane *referentiality*, his prose is an authentic voice of his time, of the values and feelings inhering in the language expressed in everyday American life. That is another major reason Abbey has, and always has had, such a passionately committed "following." People have loved this voice and still recognize it immediately as genuine, authentically American, something real in the ersatz wilderness of media language.

Several times Abbey said that he thought of himself as an entertainer. Clearly one of the things he meant by that was that he intended to give expression to the powerful point of view that he knew is part of common knowledge, common experience. He knew that he could give his readers that special, genuine pleasure that comes from hearing an extraordinarily powerful, lucid voice expressing truths recognizable by most people but rarely said so independently, clearly, or memorably. The pleasure in hearing such a voice honors the sensibility that common sense and common knowledge give rise to—and rise out of.

That sort of sensibility is one of the things community ultimately depends on. Abbey expresses and revivifies that sensibility as few contemporary, media-homogenized writers seem able to. What Abbey most significantly addresses is a powerful sense of fact, an intuition for the reality of experience. Abbey has always honored that reality. "The proof of a poet is that his country absorbs him as affectionately as he has absorbed it," wrote Whitman in 1855 (1959, 24). The grounds for acceptance are similar for both writers. They tell truth we recognize, in a language we know is ours—ours in some special sense growing out of the direct intuition that we are as much our language as our language is us. Its strengths are our strengths, and it is its common sense that delivers our world to us.

Another element of our shared consciousness is that material well-being—or the lack of it—is an irreducible datum; it is fact, reality, commonly sensed and unrelieved, unobscured by institutionalized "higher" values that would deny it primary significance in this country of immigrants, in this democracy of mixed-up races, religions, ethnic backgrounds, and all the rest. The sense of that reality is coupled with knowledge of another great and inescapable American reality that has been determinative in our history: the fact of our immense collective wealth. Social mobility based on economic opportunity is, and has been, a reality for us, but not for most peoples, most places, through most of time. American common sense tells us that poverty and physical want are evil—and escapable. A major hope for those "huddled masses" who have come here (and are still coming) in their millions was, and is, to escape poverty, want, material deprivation. And basic to American common moral sense is the conviction that material well-being is fundamental to any reasonably entertainable vision of a good, decent life and, conversely, that poverty and physical degradation are intrinsic evils, unredeemed and unredeemable. Which takes us back to "Round River Rendezvous: The Rio Grande," and Brownsville, Texas.

In that essay, Abbey effects what is for him an archetypal juxtaposition, nothing less than another polar opposition, when he contrasts the human "worst sleaze" he encounters at the Rio Grande's mouth on the U.S.-Mexican border with the beauty of the unpeopled natural scene at the river's headwaters near Stony Pass in Colorado's San Juan Mountains. On the one hand, he sees human degradation and suffering, the product of entrenched poverty and injustice: the "intolerable, unacceptable scene, which nevertheless we tolerate and accept." On the other, he sees "another world, a sort of paradise compared to this, a world that these women and most of their children will never see" (152–53).

Abbey dedicated his 1977 collection of essays, *The Journey Home*, to his mother and father. His father, he said, "taught me to hate injustice, to defy the powerful, and to speak for the voiceless." Eleven years later, in "A Writer's Credo," Abbey wrote that "the writer worthy of his calling must be more than an entertainer: he must be a seer, a prophet, the defender of life, freedom, openness, and always—always—a critic of society" (1988, 174). The connection between the passion for social justice and for nature is manifest in all of Abbey's work: no other modern American writer so vividly saw that the un-spoiled nature we've been lucky enough to inherit powerfully enables a critique of our society.

Although he clearly demanded much out of his own writing, Abbey frequently assailed mystifications and religiously conventional pieties in his fellow writers. In one (of many) scathing passages from his journals, reproduced in *Confessions of a Barbarian* (1994), he describes his aversion to aspects of Annie Dillard's writing (toward which he continued to be ambivalent), saying that "Dillard is, I believe, the only contemporary 'nature writer' who deliberately attempts to imitate [Thoreau]: the transcendentalist style, the high-flown (fly-blown) rhetoric, the raving about God. People who rave about God make me nervous" (1994, 254).

Parts of Abbey's journals also make clear what other passages clarify even further, especially in his later writing: that his regard for nature had multiple and deep roots, and was tantalizingly deeper than aesthetic appreciation. In one representative passage from the journals, he says, "My concern for wilderness is not aesthetic but physical, sensual, empathetic, spiritual, political, but above all moral: all beings are created equal, all are endowed by their Creator (whatever—God or Evolution or Nature) with certain inalienable rights. Among these rights are the right to life, liberty and the pursuit of happiness. . . ." (1994, 299).

In the passage from "Round River Rendezvous" quoted above, Abbey refers to the Colorado headwaters of the Rio Grande as a sort of paradise. Of course, in our historic religious traditions, "Paradise" is the place of perfect innocence, purity, and freedom from sin, degradation, suffering, and loss. It is a place of perfect justice, where man and all creation existed in harmony with God—before, of course, man's notorious disobedience and fall from God's favor. But Abbey clearly intended his use of the time-encrusted word to carry more modern and material associations.

For Abbey, the social and economic depravity that gives rise to such scenes of sordidness, degradation, hopelessness, debasement, and suffering as he witnesses in Brownsville's seamy stores selling "ropas usadas" constitutes an unforgivable insult to his (and, he hoped, our communally shared) moral sense. It is an insult to his sense of justice and his conviction that poverty, squalor, and human want amidst plenty are evil simply in themselves. But there is something further here. Abbey's frame of reference goes beyond the societal, political, and economic in a highly significant way—a way, nevertheless, not at all new with him. His sense of insult obviously rests not just in an awareness of the comparative degrees of material well-being on human scales, but in some philosophically absolute scale, rooted in an intense consciousness of the cosmic rightness he contemplated at the Rio Grande's headwaters in the mountains of Colorado.

Abbey repeatedly juxtaposes scenes of human degradation and suffering, usually in the cities, with a countervailing reality. That reality is an acute awareness of the existence of another world altogether, a world fully as real and in a profound way more commanding to the intellect because we know it signifies something far more permanent than any manifestation of the human. That world, we know when we think about it, will return after all our cities have disappeared into the dust, taking all our seemingly substantial interlocking institutions with them. Abbey shared this vision of an inevitably transient civilization with his great twentieth-century predecessor Robinson Jeffers. Jeffers expressed the view in many poems, among them "Carmel Point," a poem Abbey partially reprints in "A San Francisco Journal" (qtd. in Abbey 1988, 72). After personifying the landscape of his California seaside home, Jeffers attributes to the land "The extraordinary patience of things" in the face of man's despoliation of Carmel Point's natural beauty:

> Now the spoiler has come: does it care?
> Not faintly. It has all time. It knows the people are a
>   tide
> That swells and in time will ebb, and all
> Their works dissolve. Meanwhile the image of the pristine
>   beauty
> Lives in the very grain of the granite,
> Safe as the endless ocean that climbs our cliff.—As for
>   us:
> We must uncenter our minds from ourselves;
> We must unhumanize our views a little, and become
>   confident
> As the rock and ocean that we are made from.
>   (1988–1991, 3:399)

In another poem, and a more temperate mood, Jeffers modifies the implications in his vision of mankind's future, a vision manifestly close to Abbey's own expectations and hopes for the future. In "November

Surf," he speaks of a change in which humanity is better able to fulfill some of its nobler potentialities:

> The earth, in her childlike prophetic sleep,
> Keeps dreaming of the bath of a storm that prepares up the
>   long coast
> Of the future to scour more than her sea-lines:
> The cities gone down, the people fewer and the hawks more
>   numerous,
> The rivers mouth to source pure; when the two-footed
> Mammal, being someways one of the nobler animals, regains
> The dignity of room, the value of rareness.
>
> (1988–1991, 2:159)

Such kinships of vision make it impossible not to recognize that Abbey belongs in a line of philosophical American seekers of meaning in nature who were critics of their societies, often mordantly satirical critics—a line stretching all the way from Emerson and which includes Jeffers. But to see that is to find ourselves in the challenging position of having to recognize that this same Abbey, who is a modern Enlightenment rationalist materialist, is also a powerful moralist. His vision is based in his affinity with the long, classic American search for a morality based in our intuitive sense of the grandness of American nature.

The writer's task, Abbey wrote, is essentially the matter of "getting straight the connections between the fate of the author's fictional characters and the nature of the society which largely determines that fate" (1988, 171). But throughout his writing career he affirmed more clearly, more meaningfully, and more consistently than any other writer of our time that all societies, real or imagined, exist within the larger world of nature. A proper valuation of that nature, he always argued explicitly or implicitly, enables a morality, and the morality is a social and political one, based on grounds of reason.

Which only brings us around again to the central questions with Abbey, the inescapable and supremely difficult questions: What is it about nature that makes it signify so much to Abbey? And why does the preservation of some significant measure of it constitute a moral crusade to conserve some essential element in our shared American culture, indeed our national identity?

It is tempting to conclude that what so exercises Abbey is simply the knowledge that the balance between human world and natural world which he and we have known is now rapidly disappearing forever. The central anxiety in Abbey is that what will replace it is quite simply symbolized by those stores selling "ropas usadas" in places like Brownsville, Texas. For him, and for many who read him, the ongoing, far-advanced destruction of the natural world leaves the other as the face of the future, the specter of our fate.

Abbey's reaction is moral horror rooted in what can only be called revulsion at the actual human degradation he witnesses—and fears as the impending condition for a human race severed from its spiritual rootedness in a proper valuation of unpeopled nature. It therefore has to be said that Abbey's sensibility is founded in something very like a religious sense of the sacrality of unspoiled nature itself. Abbey never "raved about God"—for very sound, very sophisticated reasons entrenched in the history of Western philosophy. (Abbey did not look east, as Eliot and others have.) His kinship in this is with such highly modern minds as that of Spinoza, who saw Nature as God, God as Nature. Abbey mentally dueled with Spinoza through much of his life, but to detail the nature of such philosophical kinships would require other essays—or books. Suffice it to say that Abbey regarded our material world as real: some of it holy, some of it diabolical. And he knew that we, unfortunately, have to play God with our world, the only one we have.

For such reasons, we have to concede that when Abbey wrote in his introduction to *Desert Solitaire* that "For my own part I am pleased enough with surfaces—in fact they alone seem to me to be of much importance. . . . What else is there? What else do we need?" (1991, xi), he was throwing down a gauntlet that challenges us as much now as then. The world is real. Like Whitman's affirmation that "every atom belonging to me as good belongs to you" (1959, 25), Abbey's democratic acceptance of life, the world, and the people in it constitutes in itself a compelling argument because it is so manifestly rooted in apodictic (to use one of his philosophical words) sanity. The world is real—there to be loved, revered—and the humanly created world in its imperfections is there to be corrected, truly humanized, brought into concord with the unsullied nature that is the ground of its being. In actuality as religiously passionate as Jeffers, Abbey presents a humane vision based in his own, more modern "Inhumanism"—a sense of the inescapable groundedness of all human experience and human works in a fragile, vulnerable material world deserving better of us than it is getting.

Like Whitman, Abbey was an optimist whose optimism was founded in a belief in the essential good sense and good will of ordinary people—not their institutions, not their governments, not their economic systems. Abbey tells us in his essay "A Writer's Credo," originally delivered as a lecture at Harvard in May 1985, that "I write to make a difference. 'It is always a writer's duty,' said Samuel Johnson, 'to make the world better' " (1988, 178). To honor Abbey's implicit hope, to take the first step toward honoring his sense of the writer's duty, the least we can do is to understand him as well as our critical tools for understanding will allow.

Works Cited

Abbey, Edward. 1975. *The Monkey Wrench Gang.* Philadelphia and New York: J. B. Lippincott.

———. 1977. *The Journey Home: Some Words in Defense of the American West.* New York: E. P. Dutton.

———. 1988. *One Life at a Time, Please.* New York: Henry Holt.

———. [1968] 1991. *Desert Solitaire: A Season in the Wilderness.* Reprint, New York: Ballantine.

———. 1994. *Confessions of a Barbarian: Selections from the Journals of Edward Abbey, 1951–1989.* Ed. David Petersen. Boston and New York: Little, Brown and Co.

Bowden, Charles. 1990. "Hey, Who Was That Ornery Guy?" Afterword to *Black Sun,* by Edward Abbey. Santa Barbara, Calif.: Capra.

Jeffers, Robinson. 1988–91. *The Collected Poetry of Robinson Jeffers.* Ed. Tim Hunt. Stanford, Calif.: Stanford University Press.

Whitman, Walt. 1959. *Walt Whitman's Leaves of Grass: His Original Edition.* Ed. Malcolm Cowley. New York: Viking.

Magpie

SUEELLEN

CAMPBELL

Magpies are striking birds, bright patches of white setting off an elegant black iridescence of bronzes, greens, blues, reds, purples. Inquisitive, curious, and talkative, they're skilled in discovering things that have been concealed. "Usually nonchalant and absurdly dignified," writes one observer, they "at times assume the utmost interest in their occupation, and dart with surprising speed here and there" (Bent 1946, 145).

They make their living as generalists. They forage, hunt, and gather; they're opportunists and scavengers, quick at snatching tasty morsels and stashing their treasure. By reputation (though apparently not in fact), they have a keen eye for bright objects like jewelry. They build amazing nests: huge, spherical, layered, intricately woven, incorporating hundreds of miscellaneous pieces. These nests are messy but strong; other birds and even small mammals such as foxes use them for years.

Though they prefer partly open country in temperate regions (scrub, forest edges, riparian woodlands), they inhabit a wide range of habitats. They may, in fact, have lived in close association with human settlements for thousands of years. In the western United States, they're as likely to be found in a city park as in a wild stretch of grassland or foothills; in England, where their populations have grown dramatically in recent years, they're at home in urban wastelands and parklands, suburbs and farms. They thrive in margins and borders, in the spaces that link human territories with wild spaces.[1]

Magpies, I think, make good role models for critics, teachers, and students—in the ways they embody the advantages of being inquisitive, of foraging, of building something new out of apparently unrelated scraps. They may make particularly good models for ecological writers and critics. Seeking to inhabit similarly marginal spaces between human and wild, in our explorations of new critical territory we too might well thrive on an eclectic and improvisatory appetite.

Magpies, we might say, ask lots of questions, and questions are a wonderful tool for thinking. I ask them of myself when I'm researching and writing, and I show my students how to do the same—how to construct huge nests of questions; how to question their premises, their main terms, their personal involvement, their own questions; how to juggle several competing lines; how to sort research from thinking questions, and fresh meat from rusty metal; how to ask about silences, impervious surfaces, and things that seem "simple" or "natural"; how to follow tangents and also keep close enough to the material, drawing connections and distinctions, then questioning both; how to be limber, creative, and rigorous; how to keep asking "so what?" and deferring answers; how to enjoy open ends, loose ends, unravelled threads, complicated tangles.

In my classes, we keep our questions focused on the material we've all read. Alone, I forage much further. I talk to friends; browse through junk mail, magazines, bookstores; poke around in subjects I don't know; read literary theory; go hiking and traveling. I try to keep my peripheral vision sharp, since it's usually the glint of what I'm not looking for that raises the best questions, and I guard my status as amateur and sampler. I collect shiny tidbits and bring them home to my study, where I weave them into my nest of feathers and books, seashells and snapshots, snippets of paper and sage.

I want to demonstrate all this with a magpie's nest of questions about Edward Abbey's *Desert Solitaire: A Season in the Wilderness* (1968), a book I like very much and teach often but have never focused on as a critic.[2] It's as close as we come in modern American nature and environmental literature to a classic, or, perhaps more accurately, an icon—a book so engaging, influential, and well written that it tends to collect admiration and deflect critical questioning. It also raises many of the most interesting and complex issues in this field, not least those having to do with the genre of wilderness narratives and the sometimes invisible cultural ideas about wilderness these narratives embody.

A quick summary for unfamiliar readers: Based mainly on a couple of summers Abbey spent working as a park ranger in the late 1950s, *Desert Solitaire* is centered in Arches National Monument (now a national park), just north of the small Mormon town of Moab, Utah, in the northeast corner of the arid Colorado Plateau. Then a uranium-mining boomtown, Moab is now booming again with tourism (especially mountain biking and rafting). The book's organization is chronological (April through September) but also digressive, with chapters on local plants and animals, moving cattle with a local rancher, the tourist industry, searching for a dead man, side trips into the Grand Canyon, Glen Canyon, and the nearby mountains, the allure and mystery of the desert, and more. Abbey's tonal range is equally broad, encompassing invective and lyricism with equal skill. It has been very widely read (both in and out of academia) and correspondingly influential. When I teach nature-writing classes to students who are not literature majors and often not really readers, this is one book most of them have already read and loved; many of them want to be Edward Abbey.

In his very quirky but intriguing book *America*, Jean Baudrillard writes that deserts "are outside the sphere and circumference of desire" (1988, 63). Yet every time I read *Desert Solitaire*, I'm swamped with desire for that landscape. Is this Abbey's doing? What kinds of desire does he mention or evoke, using what language, in what contexts? I find dozens of intriguing passages.

Most of them invoke sex. We hear about the bee and the "soft, lovely, sweet, desirable" cactus flower (25); the list of things "we need" that links "the embrace of a friend or lover, the silk of a girl's thigh, the sunlight on rock and leaves" (xiii); the dancing gopher snakes whose "passion" turns Abbey into "a shameless voyeur" (20). There's the amazing description of a day floating down the river in Glen Canyon with a male friend, in which, "enjoying a very intimate relation with the river: only a layer of fabric between our bodies and the water," he feels "a sense of cradlelike security, of achievement and a joy, a pleasure almost equivalent to that first entrance—from the outside—into the neck of the womb" and remembers Mark Twain and the "erotic dreams of adolescence" (154). Here I think first of Leslie Fiedler's elucidation of the implied homosexuality in much American literature, and then of Eve Sedgwick's more recent theory of male homosocial relations, in which the bonds between men are forged over the body of a woman. There's an almost laughably

Freudian description of the land as "lovely and wild, with a virginal sweetness . . . [where] all is exposed and naked, dominated by the monolithic formations of sandstone which stand above the surface of the ground" (10). And perhaps most memorably, there's Abbey's response to his first daylight view of Arches: "Standing there, gaping at this monstrous and inhuman spectacle of rock and cloud and sky and space, I feel a ridiculous greed and possessiveness come over me. I want to know it all, possess it all, embrace the entire scene intimately, deeply, totally, as a man desires a beautiful woman" (5). This last passage follows by just one page his often quoted naming of what he sees as his own: "I put on a coat and step outside. Into the center of the world, God's navel, Abbey's country, the red wasteland" (4).

Naturally, all this raises a lot of feminist questions, so familiar is this linking of desire, sex, women, and landscape. In a class I might start with some of the big ones: Just what is *Desert Solitaire*'s relationship to this patriarchal tradition? Or: Why is it that none of the book's human characters is female? Does something important depend on their absence? What really interests me these days, though, is how touchy this subject is. My female students are usually intensely annoyed by Abbey's comments about women ("same old wife every night" [155]). My male students, like many male critics, react defensively, explaining how each individual passage is normal and thus unproblematic. A joke, they might say, is just a joke. What's at stake here? Why not just admit that, yes, he had some sexist views, but nothing unusual for the time? At a conference a few years ago I heard someone ask a question about Abbey's literary treatment of women and be told, in answer, that he loved his mother. As one of my friends said, so did Norman Bates.

This, of course, brings us to Freud. Is Abbey's loving his mother after all not irrelevant, the mother always the true object of desire? Which mother? I think of Donna Haraway's discussion (1992) of the intricate symbolic and political implications of a T-shirt showing that familiar photo of the earth floating in space with the caption "Love Your Mother." And what about the Land Rover ad I came across in *The New Yorker* (1995) just before Mother's Day—set in Abbey's country, beginning, "It costs $29,950 to bring a child into the world," and ending, "So why not call 1-800-FINE4WD for the dealer nearest you? And get to know the most bountiful mother of all. Nature." If we were to explore these images, what connections to Abbey would we find?

Or—a further tangent, more sticks for my growing nest—why have car ads so often been set in this landscape? What connects desire, consumption, and deserts? Consider the car chase and conclusion of that great road movie *Thelma and Louise,* supposedly set at the Grand Canyon, but filmed around Arches. Is the desert the mother in that film? For Baudrillard, the desert and speed are kin, and the goal is to reach the "point of no return" (1988, 10). Thelma and Louise do this; does Abbey? What if Ranger Abbey, not the dope-smoking Rasta mountain biker, had happened by the policeman trapped in his car trunk? And what about those mountain bikes: are they so popular in the Utah desert because they consume more miles, more slickrock? How many Moab fat-tire fans are also Abbey fans?

What else could we ask about Abbey's desire to "possess" the landscape? He himself connects it to greed for money and uranium. Consider, in this tangle, the long (and clearly fictional) story in "Rocks" about the uranium speculator Graham and his murder of his hapless miner-partner Husk—and Graham's sexual affair with Husk's wife, who sits by a canyon spring "half undressed" (71). How different is Abbey's greedy desire from a speculator's or a miner's? What complications are added when, at the book's very end, Abbey calls the desert's inhabitants his "children" and says, as he leaves, that he "surrenders" the "sweet virginal primitive land," his "by right of possession, possession by right of love" (267)?

There are other forms of desire in this book as well—for a "true home," for the "womb" of wilderness (166). Could we look at all of them in loosely Lacanian terms, as versions of the same yearning for something we can never have, because its absence is central to our identity? As Abbey says, "Even after years of intimate contact and search this quality of strangeness in the desert remains undiminished. Transparent and intangible as sunlight, yet always and everywhere present, it lures a man on and on, from the red-walled canyons to the smoke-blue ranges beyond, in a futile but fascinating quest for the great, unimaginable treasure which the desert seems to promise. Once caught by this golden lure you become a prospector for life, condemned, doomed, exalted" (242). "Where is the heart of the desert?" he asks, and answers, "I am convinced now that the desert has no heart, that it presents a riddle which has no answer, and that the riddle itself is an illusion created by some limitation or exaggeration of the displaced human consciousness" (243).

Could we say that Abbey's desert is an image of pure desire? If so, is it tied to the construction of the self? Would the concept from film theory of suture be relevant? Am I somehow stitched into the book as a participant in Abbey's desire? And is this desire linked, as in Lacan, to language? This passage continues: "One whiff of juniper smoke, a few careless words, one reckless and foolish poem—"The Waste Land," for instance—and I become as restive, irritable, brooding and dangerous as a wolf in a cage" (243). On my first backpacking trip in Canyonlands, years before I read *Desert Solitaire,* I too found myself chanting lines from "The Wasteland" (though then it was as a litany of misery; it was August). Now both Eliot and Abbey make me want to return. How much of our desire is language?

And so—with language and a missing center—we arrive at deconstruction and poststructuralism. I often find myself reading and teaching Derrida and Abbey back to back, and so I've seen how saturated *Desert Solitaire* is with passages about the power of writing— matched with passages repudiating that power. His is "a world of words" (xii); "Through naming comes knowing; we grasp an object, mentally, by giving it a name . . . And thus through language create a whole world, corresponding to the other world out there. Or we trust that it corresponds" (257); yet books and words are "a sort of mental smog that keeps getting between a man and the world, obscuring vision" (184). Quotations and references to some hundred different writers, philosophers, musicians pepper the book (the poets alone include Eliot, Lawrence, Housman, Rilke, Jeffers, Baudelaire, Whitman, Burns, Nashe, Shakespeare, Keats, Blake, Marvell, Raleigh, and Donne), making it an intensely literary book, a very textual text; and yet he hopes that "Serious critics, serious librarians, serious associate professors of English" will hate it (xii). Just as he yearns for the desert's absent heart, Abbey desires a direct connection with the real. How are we to understand this pervasive pattern of self-contradiction?

Like a magpie, I'm drawn to a few glinting tangents.

One takes off through anthropology. If the desert has no heart, no center, then what serves Abbey as a functional center? Talking about the way ethnographers contain the cultures they're studying, James Clifford focuses on the "powerful localizing strategy" of the observer's tent—pitched next to the chief's home in the village—and the larger, "complementary localization" of "the field" (1992, 98). Does Abbey represent his dwelling place as the power-holding center of his field? Clifford wonders about the image of the tent—"its mobility, thin flaps, providing an 'inside' where notebooks, special foods, a typewriter, could be kept, a base of operations minimally separated from 'the action' "—and I wonder about Abbey's small metal trailer and juniper-branch ramada—where he, too, cooks and writes. (He hangs a red bandanna, his "private flag," from the ramada poles [96].) Could we also identify something like the ethnographer's "chief," "informants," or "culture"? What would we see if we read Abbey's book as an ethnography?

Or what about the postmodern possibilities? Abbey calls language "a mighty loose net" (xii); how is his book like the Internet, like the purely textual Abbey web? What happens to the desert's "reality" when it becomes "virtual"? "The desert," Baudrillard says, "is an ecstatic form of disappearance" (1988, 5). Foucault went to Death Valley's Zabriskie Point to take acid—to a place that had already been textualized by Antonioni's film—and was, apparently, rendered speechless by the beauty of the sky. Do any of Abbey's actions resemble Foucault's quests for limit experiences? What about his most physical moments: his misery herding cattle in the heat of June, his solitary brush with death when he strands himself in Havasu Canyon? Are these points of disappearance or intensity, ecstasy or abjection? Is this where we see the body being disciplined? If so, into what, and why? (I'd love to follow this tangent—wilderness travel as Foucauldian discipline. One fall when I made myself miserable portaging through cold rain largely for the sake of an essay, what was the discipline? Where was text, where body? What did my bruises mean?) Abbey tells his readers to "crawl . . . over the sandstone and through the thornbush and cactus. When traces of blood begin to mark your trail you'll see something, maybe. Probably not" (xiv). What links blood, land, writing, vision?

Baudrillard again: "The acceleration of molecules in the heat contributes to a barely perceptible evaporation of meaning" (1988, 9). What happens when Abbey is hottest? Here we could look at his obsessive but futile pursuit of Moon-Eye, a horse who cries out for interpretation. He's solitary and independent (he's lived alone in a distant canyon for years), but he's also branded (written on, owned, possessed), he's feral (not wild), and he's gelded (one of many details that makes me wonder about the book's construction—or deconstruction—of masculinity). Abbey wonders if perhaps only the tracks of the horse exist (142); says he looks "like the idea—without the substance—of a horse" (149); describes him in varying ways as hollow; and, at the end, throwing his hackamore at the horse in defeat, says, "to Moon-Eye it must have looked as if I were pulling out my intestines" (150). What if we put this image next to the earlier "center of the world, God's navel, Abbey's country, the red wasteland" (4)?

And what about this hackamore throwing? Is there any connection to the book's notorious rock-throwing scenes? There are three interesting ones. First Abbey calls his book a "tombstone," a "bloody rock," and commands the reader: "Don't drop it on your foot— throw it at something big and glassy" (xiv). Then he throws a rock at a rabbit and kills it, in what he interprets as an experiment turned initiation into the world of predator and prey (34). And then he proposes his version of Samuel Johnson's refutation of Bishop Berkeley: "To refute the solipsist or the metaphysical idealist all that you have to do is take him out and throw a rock at his head: if he ducks he's a liar" (97). We might also consider two chapters: "Rocks," the one about Graham, Husk, and the destructive allure of uranium; and "The Heat of Noon: Rock and Tree and Cloud," the book's midpoint, which closes with this disappearing passage: "Through halfclosed eyes, for the light would otherwise be overpowering, I consider the tree, the lonely cloud, the sandstone bedrock of this part of the world and pray—in my fashion—for a vision of truth. I listen for signals from the sun—but that distant music is too high and pure for the human ear. I gaze at the tree and receive no response. I scrape my bare feet against the sand and rock under the table and am comforted by their solidity and resistance. I look at the cloud" (136). So a rock here is a book full of words; a predator's weapon; a radioactive sign of greed and violence; a symbol of realism; and an image of solidity that dissolves, as we read it, into sand and then cloud.

Just how solid are these rocks? Remember where we are: in the country of erosion, sedimentation, more erosion, and of arches—rocks with no center, hollow rocks. Abbey knows this perfectly well: he says he strides away from his dead rabbit through "melting sandstone" and jokes about using hairspray or Elmer's glue as preservatives. And, sounding like Baudrillard again, who describes nearby Monument Valley as "blocks of language suddenly rising high, then subjected to a pitiless erosion" (1988, 4), Abbey says Delicate Arch (now probably the most-photographed part of Arches and the emblem on some Utah license plates) can be seen as "a symbol, a sign, a fact, a thing without meaning or a meaning which includes all things" (34–36).

Okay, so we've got a world of words, here, even when it's about rocks, and if his part of Utah is now in some real way "Abbey's country," it isn't because he possessed or loved it, but because he wrote about it. Still, if Abbey were to throw a rock at my head, I'd duck. So how else can we look at this intersection between text and real? Let's collect some sticks from culture and history.

What kind of landscape does Abbey represent? Clearly it's a "wilderness" and a disappearing Eden. Since I've been reading environmental history, I'll take it as given that "wilderness" is nearly as much a cultural expression of desire as "Eden." What's left out of these constructs? A quick list of traces remaining in this book would include mining, ranching, Mormon settlers, tourists, the feral Moon-Eye, and the U.S. government—the salaried Abbey (whose fantasy of the perfect winter depends on unemployment checks), the National Park Service, Atomic Energy Commission, Air Force, Bureau of Reclamation, Bureau of Public Roads, Wildlife Service, BIA, BLM, Forest Service, and no doubt others—a lot of signs this wilderness isn't pristine. What could we learn about how all these land users have shaped Abbey's landscape?

And then, to quote Abbey, "What about the Indians?" He says, "There are no Indians in the Arches country now; they all left seven hundred years ago and won't be back for a long time" (99). Now this is what I'd call a suspicious statement. One of the best books I've read recently is Rebecca Solnit's *Savage Dreams: A Journey into the Hidden Wars of the American West* (1994), part of which traces the construction of Yosemite as a wilderness Eden through the killing and driving out of its native people. Did anything like this happen in "Abbey's country"? All my recent reading tells me that it must have. Are there any traces of this in *Desert Solitaire?*

Let's start with the Anasazi, about whom Abbey talks quite a bit, though always in the context of their disappearance, which, of course, helps legitimate the concept of wilderness. They also seem to serve as images of desire: Abbey calls them "naked" and "indolent," the same things he calls himself at his most blissful moments. And how about the drawings of petroglyphs that open every chapter in my edition? (The copyright page says they're "based on the author's copies of prehistoric Indian petroglyphs and pictographs found in various parts of southern Utah and northern Arizona.") Are these drawings evidence that the Anasazi have been reduced to art? Do they represent a strategy of marginalization, leaving space only around the text's edges? Do they signal the return of the repressed?

What if we think about marginalization in physical terms? What's on the margins of Arches and Canyonlands? Well, among other things, several large Indian reservations. Abbey does devote seven pages to the Navajo people, whose land is to the south, admiring their "poorly developed acquisitive instinct" and their "successful exploitation" of timber, oil, gas, coal, and uranium, and then criticizing their "uncontrolled population growth" and consequent overgrazing, ecological degradation, poverty, drug and alcohol use, broken families, and so on—in a stunning oversimplification and falsification. For one thing, as Richard White points out in *The Roots of Dependency,* between 1860 and 1930, while the Navajo population quadrupled, Arizona's total population grew by a factor of 67, New Mexico's by a factor of 7—while nobody "argued that Anglos or Chicanos . . . had a problem of overpopulation" (1983, 311). Is there some explanation for Abbey's myopia other than laziness, carelessness, or casual racism? For his sense of his wilderness landscape, must the Navajos be seen as negligible or blameworthy?

Think about his story of the car crash just outside Arches that left two dead men and the debris of alcohol, Marlboro cigarettes, and cowboy shirts, but no eagle feathers, buffalo robes, bows, arrows, medicine pouches, or drums—a story that Abbey ends, "Some Indians" (109). Why doesn't he know or seem to care whether the young men were, as he puts it, "Navajos? Apaches? beardless Utes?" Without their eagle feathers and medicine pouches, are these men as comfortably anonymous, even invisible, as the Anasazi?

I was even more troubled to realize that there are only two places in this book where Abbey even mentions the Utes, here and when he admires their name for a mountain. Nowhere does he say that he's surrounded also by three Ute reservations, a large one immediately to his north, or that a lot of what he calls his country was not long ago Ute country. (Indeed, I've been told, during Abbey's years at Arches, many Utes and Navajos still lived all around the area, ranching and farming—something you'd never guess from reading the book.) What can we make of such a stunning omission? Could he not have thought about this? Did he think it didn't matter? Is this something else he found it necessary to repress? How many of Abbey's central premises are built upon this silence? How many of our culture's?

What other big silences are there here, and how might they matter? What else happened between Abbey's first summer in Arches and the writing and publication of the book some ten years later? The book says nothing about the civil rights movement; close to nothing about the war in Vietnam; almost nothing about the Cold War. There is only a tiny bit more about the atomic age, primarily concerned with the economics of Moab's uranium boom. He mentions the long-term hazards from radiation that the miners face but says they're happy, partly because they need not doubt their manhood (65); he compares his knowledge of the impending Glen Canyon Dam to "strontium in the marrow of our bones" (185) (this is a specific reference to the way fallout from nuclear tests polluted milk in the very late '50s and early '60s); and he offers this amazing conclusion: "Let men in their madness blast every city on earth into black rubble and envelope the entire planet in a cloud of lethal gas—the canyons and hills, the springs and rocks will still be here, the sunlight will filter through, water will form and warmth shall be upon the land and after sufficient time, no matter how long, somewhere, living things will emerge and join and stand once again. . . . I have seen the place called Trinity, in New Mexico . . . already the grass has returned, and the cactus and the mesquite" (267–68). (What bizarre implications of intertextuality might emerge if we also remember that the Trinity site was named after a poem by John Donne?) What values underlie this statement of faith, with its biblical echoes? The "Love Your Mother" T-shirt Haraway talks about was from a relatively recent Mother's Day protest at the Nevada Test Site; would those activists have agreed with Abbey's affirmation?

Again, it was Solnit's book that alerted me to these passages—or the loud silences surrounding them—with its talk of the atomic tests in Nevada, and my interest has been sharpened by Carole Gallagher's *American Ground Zero: The Secret Nuclear War*. One woman told Gallagher about camping in Arches at about Abbey's time: "We pitched our tent in a rather primitive area, and there were stakes all around us with little cans on them—they were uranium claims. They were all through the park . . . everywhere. . . . The next year all of those claims were denied . . . what they were picking up with their geiger counters, was fallout" (1993, 267–68). During his summers in Utah, Abbey was almost certainly downwind from more than a few aboveground nuclear test explosions. He had to have known this, and been aware of the dangers of fallout. (I asked my mother what she knew about all this at the time, when she was raising small children in

Denver; her answer boiled down to "A lot more than Abbey admits to knowing.") What reason—conscious or subconscious—would he have had to repress this knowledge in this book? (This might be the place to ask about the strange shift into fiction with the story about the uranium miners in "Rocks." Surely this is a distancing move. And the fate of Husk's son Billy-Joe: what anxieties about fallout are displaced into the hallucinatory effects of sunstroke, severe sunburn [one of the immediate symptoms of fallout exposure], and datura?) Are the atomic tests the desert's secret heart? What kind of wilderness Eden is blanketed in nuclear fallout? For how many of our wilderness places is some similar denial necessary?

It's increasingly clear to me that environmental literature in general, and Abbey's book as an example, works partly by shutting out social and cultural complexities—an omission that's probably one source of the desire they embody and evoke. Mary Louise Pratt writes about the ways ethnographers use their arrival scenes to define their stance: in her terms, Abbey portrays himself as a "castaway," a strategy for idealizing the role of participant-observer and obscuring all the ways both observer and observed are tied to the larger world (1986, 38). Echoing Thoreau's "I went to the woods because I wished to live deliberately, to front only the essential facts of life," Abbey says, "I am here not only to evade for a while the clamor and filth and confusion of the cultural apparatus but also to confront, immediately and directly if it's possible, the bare bones of existence, the elemental and fundamental" (6). I'm starting to wonder about this balance between what is confronted and what is evaded, and what assumptions lie beneath it. What notion of the elemental ignores nuclear fallout? Why think it's necessary to leave society to find reality? What's lost by opposing wilderness and culture?

I happened to be rereading this book when the bomb exploded in Oklahoma City, and several of Abbey's ideological statements leapt into the spotlight, especially his argument that "the wilderness should be preserved . . . as a refuge from authoritarian government." He explains how to impose "a dictatorial regime": raze the wilderness, concentrate everyone (especially independent types) in big cities, encourage population growth, and control guns (130–31). What I once heard as cranky Ed Abbey and a prototype for the radical eco-activist group Earth First! now also sounds to me like the ultra-right-wing Militia, the source of that bomb. What could explain these echoes? Could there be any connection to Abbey's evasion or repression of so many important social events and issues? Are we seeing here—in his anarchistic politics, his forgetting of the Utes and Navajos, his ignoring of the nuclear tests—a case of what Michael Rogin calls "political amnesia," which, he says, "points to a cultural structure of motivated disavowal" (1994, 235)?

I wonder about Abbey's constant emphasis on individualism—his title, his central solitude, his pervasive vision of the desert as a space of individuals: "each rock and shrub and tree, each flower, each stem of grass, diverse and separate, vividly isolate" (99). His sense of unity, in contrast, is tightly limited, either to the food chain or to something mystical. When he talks about confronting "the bare bones of existence," he continues, "I dream of a hard and brutal mysticism in which the naked self merges with a non-human world and yet somehow survives still intact, individual, separate" (6). Rogin points out that one characteristic of American political culture is that it "linked freedom to expansion in nature rather than to social solidarity, to violent conquest of the racial other rather than peaceful coexistence" (239). Is there any room in Abbey's country for community, for ecological and human networks, for people living together, not always busy defending private space, perhaps even held together by government, taxes, laws? Is there room for a vision not of separation, but of connection?

With the magpie's tricks of foraging and inquisitiveness, it's easy to build big nests—messy but sturdy enough that if one branch falls out, others will hold the shape. One ornithologist deconstructed a very large magpie nest and found 1,573 sticks (Birkhead 1991, 140). I won't count the pieces in mine. Instead, I'll end with a few snippets about magpies, and leave the analogies and the questions to you. First, their name. One theory (which Abbey might have liked for reasons different from mine) says it refers to talkative women. Another is that it comes from the birds' habit of picking maggots out of the wounds of animals, especially those wounds caused by human mistreatment. Second: Many American ranchers and English sport hunters and gamekeepers have no use for them. In 1989, one member of the House of Lords advocated " 'capital punishment for the thieving and murderous magpie' " (Birkhead 1991, 221). Third: When a female is feeding her nestlings, she calls to them; if they don't respond, she taps their heads and pries open their bills. Given this emphatic coaching, the young soon become "a set of inquisitive chattering marauders" (Johns 1862, 261). And last: Abbey speaks of the

magpies' "handsome academic dress" (31)—but then we know what
he thought about academics.

Notes

1. On magpies, I consulted Bent (1946), Birkhead (1991), Goodwin
(1976), Johns (1862), Kerridge (1995), and Pyle (1993).
2. As I'll quote so often from this edition of *Desert Solitaire,* I'll simply
note page numbers parenthetically.

Works Cited

Abbey, Edward. 1968. *Desert Solitaire: A Season in the Wilderness.* New York:
Simon and Schuster.

Baudrillard, Jean. 1988. *America.* Trans. Chris Turner. London and New York:
Verso.

Bent, Arthur Cleveland. [1946] 1964. *Life Histories of North American Jays,
Crows and Titmice.* Vol. 1. Reprint, Washington: *Smithsonian Institution
Bulletin* 191.

Birkhead, Tim. 1991. *The Magpies.* London: T. and A. D. Poyser.

Clifford, James. 1992. "Traveling Cultures." In *Cultural Studies,* ed. Lawrence
Grossberg, Cary Nelson, and Paula A. Treichler. London and New York:
Routledge.

Gallagher, Carole. 1993. *American Ground Zero: The Secret Nuclear War.* New
York: Random House.

Goodwin, Derek. 1976. *Crows of the World.* Ithaca, N.Y.: Cornell University
Press.

Haraway, Donna. 1992. "The Promises of Monsters." In *Cultural Studies,* ed.
Lawrence Grossberg, Cary Nelson, and Paula A. Treichler. London and
New York: Routledge.

Johns, C. A. 1862. *British Birds in Their Haunts.* London: Society for Promoting Christian Knowledge.

Kerridge, Richard. August 31, 1995. Personal correspondence.

The New Yorker. May 1, 1995. Land Rover advertisement, p. 28.

Pratt, Mary Louise. 1986. "Fieldwork in Common Places." In *Writing Culture: The Poetics and Politics of Ethnography,* ed. James Clifford and George
E. Marcus. Berkeley: University of California Press.

Pyle, Robert Michael. 1993. *The Thunder Tree: Lessons from an Urban Wild-
land.* Boston and New York: Houghton Mifflin.

Rogin, Michael. 1994. " '*Make my day!*': Spectacle as Amnesia in Imperial Politics.* In *The New Historicism Reader,* ed. H. Aram Veeser. London and
New York: Routledge.

Solnit, Rebecca. 1994. *Savage Dreams: A Journey into the Hidden Wars of the
American West.* San Francisco: Sierra Club Books.

White, Richard. 1983. *The Roots of Dependency: Subsistence, Environment, and
Social Change Among the Choctaws, Pawnees, and Navajos.* Lincoln: University of Nebraska Press.

"I'm a humanist"

The Poetic Past in Desert Solitaire

DAVID J.

ROTHMAN

Edward Abbey aspired to be a great novelist yet is most likely to be remembered for his essays, especially *Desert Solitaire*. Abbey sensed this himself, and in a 1977 interview with James Hepworth, said, "I never wanted to be an environmental crusader, an environmental journalist. I wanted to be a fiction writer, a novelist. Then I dashed off that *Desert Solitaire* thing because it was easy to do. All I did was copy out of some journals that I'd kept" (qtd. in Hepworth and McNamee 1989, 40). Most critics have passed over such comments and underestimated Abbey's literary aspirations, preferring to see him primarily as an activist prophet of the environmental movement.[1]

This is understandable given Abbey's captivating fire and the fact that—continuing a great American tradition—he often disparages learning as opposed to a Romantic idealization of unmediated experience, particularly encounters with the natural world. In the "Author's Introduction" to *Desert Solitaire*, Abbey writes that "Serious critics, serious librarians, serious associate professors of English will if they read this work dislike it intensely; at least I hope so" (1990, xii). But Abbey's ambition betrays him repeatedly. As his friend Jack Loeffler has pointed out, Abbey's "intellect was enormous. He read incessantly and well and was able to quote major passages that had caught his fancy. . . . He had read all the major and many of the minor western philosophers" (1992, 45). Evidence for this, as well as for comparable literary training, runs throughout the book. After commenting at one point that the sound of distant thunder in the desert reminds him of 47

"The Wasteland" (*sic*),[2] Abbey pens an apparently anti-intellectual passage: "Here I am relaxing into memories of ancient books—a sure-fire sign of spiritual fatigue. That screen of words, that veil of ideas, issuing from the brain like a sort of mental smog that keeps getting between a man and the world, obscuring vision. Maya. Time to go back down to the river and reality, back to Newcomb and the boats, the smell of frying catfish—There's God for you! I descend" (1990, 184). Yet, as with other writers in the same tradition—such as Emerson, Whitman, D. H. Lawrence, and Allen Ginsberg (not to mention Rousseau)—Abbey purposefully leaves in the literary meditation that precedes his dismissal of it. Abbey is not merely denouncing "memories of ancient books," he is having a quarrel with himself about them. If anything, he seems to have taken Yeats's dictum as a challenge, and produced, if not poetry, then highly poetic rhetoric out of the quarrel with himself over such matters.[3]

The reason Abbey hoped "serious critics, serious librarians, serious associate professors of English" would dislike his book is not because of its anti-intellectualism, but because of the anarchic energy with which he reformulates the standard materials and institutional methods of literary writing. His cunning use of what we could call the imaginative past—a purposefully nonsystematic term that for me includes as much literature, philosophy, music, political theory, and other humanistic realms as possible—is in fact crucial to his mission as a writer. Perhaps we could characterize that mission as an extended meditation on what it means to be human in relation to the natural sublime, in particular the inhuman landscape of the American desert. As he writes of the desert near the end of *Desert Solitaire:* "What does it mean? It means nothing. It is as it is and has no need for meaning. The desert lies beneath and soars beyond any possible human qualifications. Therefore, sublime" (1990, 194). And yet, in many of his books, these "human qualifications" of the sublime desert are exactly what Abbey explores, albeit in unorthodox ways, such as the well-informed and gently self-parodic philosophical discourse of this passage itself, summed up in the word "therefore." His deep engagement with "human qualifications," all of which grow out of the imaginative past, guarantees that much of his book must remain obscure unless we, too, engage that past.

It is not hard to trace Abbey's intellectual background, but this still has not been done as carefully as it should be. Philosophically and politically, he was a self-proclaimed anarchist, and his reading in this area was wide and deep. He was also forthright about his debt to Thoreau and to Emerson, whom he characterized in his essay "Emerson" as "a scrivener of the imagination" (1988a, 207).

Abbey did not merely study Emerson—he took him as a model: "Emerson appeals not to experience, logic, sense or common sense, but to our innate idealism, our instinctive need for harmony and meaningfulness, a need which grows greater when the world grows more desperate" (1988a, 213). *Desert Solitaire* clearly speaks to the same needs Abbey identifies in "Emerson," beginning with the first sentence of the first chapter: "This is the most beautiful place on earth" (1990, 1). Further, the passage from "Emerson" suggests Abbey's own ambition, a literary ambition in the Bloomian sense. Abbey actually aims to go beyond Emerson, for he implies that in his own day the world is "more desperate" than it was in Emerson's, and therefore the Emersonian writer must address even greater needs for "harmony and meaningfulness" in the face of this greater desperation.

As a result, Abbey's self-conscious differences with Emerson are as profound as his imitations of him. While Abbey idealizes communion and correspondence with the beauty of the world, he does not explain away human destructiveness (as Emerson often did) but acknowledges it—dispassionately, angrily, ruefully, satirically, sadly. His ability to convey desire for Emersonian transcendence, coupled with full and often bitter acknowledgment of human foolishness and failure (including his own), produces a sense of reality so powerful that, to Abbey's credit, many of his readers seem to want to step over it into the desert that he imagines (see note 1). This is the case even though Abbey tells us that "This is not primarily a book about the desert" (1990, xii). As Abbey knows, whatever sense of reality emanates from the book does not depend primarily on description, but on "evocation" (1990, xii), which I take to mean intensely imagined relations with that which is described.

Abbey's emphasis on evocation explains his ability to convey an optimistic sense of activism in the face of environmental destruction. For imagination is always possible. As he writes in "Emerson" when defending his predecessor against hypothetical charges of being "a secluded dreamer," "When the occasion demanded, he could rise to action—at least to the action of public speech and open protest, which is really about all that we can expect from poets and philosophers" (1988a, 217). As this should make clear, Abbey emphasizes the imaginative connection between thinking and living rather than any systematic philosophy or activist program. This is the philosophical bedrock of his own program of speech as action and protest.

I am afraid that I am saying that Abbey was an intellectual, albeit one with a practical eye. His idea of a philosopher was not unlike Thoreau's in Walden: "To be a philosopher is not merely to have subtle thoughts, nor even to found a school, but so to love wisdom as to live according to its dictates, a life of simplicity, independence, magnanimity, and trust. It is to solve some of the problems of life, not only theoretically, but practically" (1950, 13).

Since this seems to be Abbey's primary concern, it shouldn't be too surprising that his essays are stronger than his novels (and his poetry, which is mostly awful), for the same reason that Emerson's and Thoreau's essays are stronger than their poetry. Abbey shares with them a discursive, analytical sensibility: he was actually at his creative best when envisioning the world, not when creating another. His gift was not for imagining plots and characters (though he did produce a few, notably Hayduke, who are highly compelling) but rather for thinking about relations, which he often accomplished through self-conscious, complex, and ironic reformulations of other artists' and philosophers' visions.

The foregoing may make it sound as if I think that *Desert Solitaire* is primarily a book of ideas. That would truly be murdering to dissect, and is not the case. Perhaps I should say that, in Abbey, we lost an intellectual; he does not expound on ideas, but rather uses and meditates upon his reading as he makes his way through the world. It also bears repeating that this is not the same as being an activist. Further, despite the importance of the pragmatic Thoreau, the Emerson of "public speech," and other, more systematic philosophers in Abbey's work, philosophy and essays are less important to him than another, less ideological source: poetry.

I want to state it as strongly as possible: Abbey's vision of nature and society is grounded in and refracted through poetry, particularly English and American poetry of the 19th and early 20th centuries. The background of his ideas may come from the various intellectual strains that I've touched on above, but his deepest involvement as a reader was with verse. In *Desert Solitaire,* poetry embodies the relatedness Abbey sought as a writer. It largely defines both thinking about and being in his relations with society and with nature.

Abbey's knowledge of poetry was not merely a function of study but of having been raised in a literate home. According to James Bishop, Jr., Abbey's father Paul "could recite every line of the works of Walt Whitman by heart" (1994, 63) and did so often for his family.[4] Abbey also developed a prodigious memory for poetry, and in his best work he inhabits it as much as he does the desert. He is so deeply and self-consciously indebted to poetry that he often weaves it into his work without citation, often without even indicating he is quoting (or echoing or parodying) verse, simply expecting the reader to recognize it.

Abbey quotes or refers to about thirty poets in *Desert Solitaire*: Neruda (who provides the epigraph), Keats, Dante, Thoreau, Whitman, Jeffers, Frost, D. H. Lawrence, Housman, Eliot, Sophocles, Ben Jonson (in verse drama), Philip Larkin, Shakespeare, Raleigh, Wordsworth, Hopkins, Blake, Marvell, Donne, William Henry Davies, Rilke, Burns, the Bible, Native American poetry, and various cowboy ballads. Because Abbey frequently quotes without giving any source, there are also passages I have been unable to identify.[5]

Far more important than any list are readings that show how Abbey engages the poets. He uses a wide range of techniques, from direct quotation with author citation (he rarely mentions a title), to quotation without citation, to parody with and without citation, to various modes of allusion that range from foregrounded quotation to obscure echo. His occasional mistakes (such as "The Wasteland" and others discussed below) suggest that he was indeed often working from memory, not even bothering to check the sources when reading proofs. Further, he generally expects his readers to pick up on his frequent parodies; otherwise, the passages in which they are embedded become at best hard to understand.

Even Abbey's direct citations are often complex. At one point in the chapter "Down The River," Abbey and his friend Ralph Newcomb see a man on the bank, and Abbey comments:

> We shall not see another of the tool-making breed for a long time and we could not care less.
> Misanthropy? Shakespeare could say
>> Man delights not me,
>> No, nor woman neither. . . .
> And Raleigh, too,
>> I wish I loved the human race,
>> I wish I loved its silly face.

And Jeffers:
> Be in nothing so moderate
> As in love of man.

(1990, 154–55)[6]

The passage is worth contemplation, for Abbey invokes the misanthropic verses only to dismiss them, going on to say, "But no, this is not at all what we feel at this moment, not at all what I mean" (1990, 155). In fact, he claims that the purpose of his sojourn on the river with Newcomb is "to renew our affection for ourselves and the human kind in general by a temporary, legal separation from the mass" (1990, 155). Why, then, go through the exercise of calling up the poetry only to deny it? The point is that a range of possible relations with other people, running the gamut from "misanthropy" to "affection," is refracted not only through the desert environment, but also through the imaginative past.

In general, Abbey is a good deal more obscure about his sources. In the chapter "Terra Incognita: Into the Maze," he produces a parody of the chorus to Burns's "Green Grow the Rashes, O," without in any way identifying his source. In this case, instead of dismissing the misanthropic lines of others, he takes a lighthearted poem and transforms it into obscene, misogynistic doggerel, displaying some misanthropy of his own. Burns's poem:

> Green grow the rashes, O;
> Green grow the rashes, O;
> The sweetest hours that e'er I spend,
> Are spent among the lasses, O.

(1990, 124)

In Abbey's parody, he and his friend Bob Waterman, who doesn't care much for poetry, have just rappelled down into the maze and are looking for water. Abbey digs down a few feet and finds some:

> There is a stand of wild cane nearby. I cut two stalks, a fat one and a thin one, and punch the pith out of the joints of the bigger one by using the smaller as a ramrod. Happy now, greatly relieved, I recall for Waterman's edification a few appropriate lines from Burns:
> > Green grow the rashes, O!
> > Green grow the rashes, O!

The lasses they have cozy bores,
The widows they have gashes, O!

(1990, 259)

The obscenity is a bit surprising, especially given Abbey's proclaimed
project in the book, "not only to evade for a while the clamor and filth
and confusion of the cultural apparatus but also to confront, immediately and directly if it's possible, the bare bones of existence, the elemental and fundamental, the bedrock which sustains us" (1990, 6).
Rather obviously, it is some of the "coarse, rude, bad-tempered, violently prejudiced, unconstructive . . . frankly antisocial" (1990, xii)
material Abbey promised in the "Author's Introduction." But why
choose to write in such a purposefully offensive way? What is the "way
of being wrong which is sometimes necessarily right" (1990, xii) that
justifies this language?

David Copland Morris cites the passage about evading cultural
"clamor and filth" as a preface to arguing that Abbey regularly treats
such high philosophical aspirations within himself to "a fortifying
bath of irony" (1993, 22), and I agree. In this case, having just solved
part of a dangerous physical predicament in the raw, natural world he
loves, Abbey reminds us just how human he is—literate, obscene,
rude, condescending, happy—in such a brutal landscape.

Those who disparage Abbey for his "incorrect" views in this and
so many other passages will simply meet him on the way back, as he is
perfectly aware that it is offensive. There is also a good deal more to it
than merely trying to shock. Part of the trick is that the obscenity occurs in the parody of a work whose original he does not provide. It is
cultivated and obscene at the same time. He knows that, far from undercutting the book, such a jumbling together of the literary, the parodic, and the obscene, all of it juxtaposed on the inhuman desert, is
what gives the book its vitality.

Abbey's use of the poetic past is often even more indirect. I think
that it extends into extraordinarily subtle echoes. The following paragraph occurs at the point where Abbey is first describing Arches, after
having arrived there to assume his duties as a park ranger: "Within this
vast perimeter, in the middle ground and foreground of the picture, a
rather personal demesne, are the 33,000 acres of Arches National
Monument of which I am now sole inhabitant, usufructuary, observer
and custodian" (1990, 5). There is some surprising diction in the paragraph. Legally, a "usufructuary" is someone who may enjoy and use

something that belongs to someone else, as long as it is returned undamaged. The word that should tip us off, however, is "demesne," whose most famous use in English poetry is surely in Keats's "On First Looking into Chapman's Homer." Both the way Abbey uses the word and the context in which he places it echo Keats's poem repeatedly:

> Much have I traveled in the realms of gold,
>   And many goodly states and kingdoms seen;
>   Round many western islands have I been
> Which bards in fealty to Apollo hold.
> Oft of one wide expanse had I been told
>   That deep-bowed Homer ruled as his demesne;
>   Yet did I never breathe its pure serene
> Till I heard Chapman speak out loud and bold;
> Then felt I like some watcher of the skies
>   When a new planet swims into his ken;
> Or like stout Cortez when with eagle eyes
>   He stared at the Pacific—and all his men
> Looked at each other with a wild surmise—
>   Silent, upon a peak in Darien.
>
>   (1977, 72)

Consider: Abbey is describing his first morning as a ranger in Arches, having arrived in darkness the night before. It is a moment of discovery, in which he watches the sun rise on "the center of the world, God's navel, Abbey's country, the red wasteland" (1990, 4).[7] And in the final words before the self-mocking paragraph quoted above, in which he will describe himself instead of the magnificent landscape around him, he compares it to the ocean: "To the east, under the spreading sunrise, are more mesas, more canyons, league on league of red cliff and arid tablelands, extending through purple haze over the bulging curve of the planet to the ranges of Colorado—a sea of desert" (1990, 5). Then, Abbey immediately characterizes the scene he has been taking in as a "vast perimeter," recalling Keats's "wide expanse." Cortés stares at the Pacific, and his men gaze wildly at each other; Abbey, a paragraph later, describes himself as "Standing there, gaping. . . . " (1990, 5).

Once we establish the context, the irony flows thickly, reinforcing the echoes. Cortés and his men gaze at each other; Abbey is solitary and likes it, in fact wishes he could remain in "solitaire" most of the time, even though he recognizes that it is neither desirable nor practical. In Keats's poem, Cortés and his men have literally accomplished the European discovery of the other half of the planet, a place which (for them) has no history, though they will now gladly provide one as they conquer, plunder, and colonize it.[8] Abbey recognizes that he has inherited that plunder. The way he uses Keats's poem to bring that historical fact to bear, in a context of wonder, on the view of a national monument—a place that is supposed to be protected from the destructive results of its own European discovery—is highly sarcastic, though it should be noted that Abbey aims the sarcasm mostly at himself. Arches is beautiful in part because of its idealized emptiness, which he is there to protect and perpetuate; he is hardly supposed to behave like Cortés. The wonder that the view evokes is real enough, but Abbey reminds himself that Arches is in fact not his demesne, that he does not, cannot really rule it.

Or can he? After all, Keats's poem is not about Cortés, but about Chapman's translation of Homer. It is a poem about reading, read-ing as a form of discovery. The "demesne" to which Keats refers is Homer's not because Homer owns it, but because we imagine it through Homer; Keats's travels in the poem are travels of his imagination as a reader. In Keats's poem, Homer's ownership of the Aegean's "wide expanse" is a metaphor for his imaginative power. Abbey is using "demesne" in exactly the same sense, even as he gently mocks himself. What emerges is an ambitious and serious project: to stake out an empty, lonely expanse as an imaginative demesne that has never been explored. Abbey audaciously aspires to make the Utah desert his imaginative demesne, just as Keats understood the Aegean to be Homer's. Abbey is writing himself into Keats's imagination. He describes himself—albeit ironically—not only as the "usufructuary" of Arches as a physical place, but also as the inheritor of a tradition of literary creativity (Homer) and discovery (Keats). He looks out on Arches not only through his own eyes, but also, with some irony, through Keats's poem, and by extension, Chapman's translation and Homer's epics.

There are hundreds of passages like this, and of even greater complexity, throughout *Desert Solitaire,* and they define Abbey's project as a writer. It is this use of the imaginative past that he acknowledges in the self-conscious comment quoted above, that in his book "the desert figures more as medium than as material" (1990, xii); much of the material is, in fact, imaginative. This helps to explain why he carefully revises Thoreau's famous dictum in "Walking"—that "in

Wildness is the preservation of the World" (1950, 613)—to "wilderness complements and completes civilization" (1990, 129), a sentiment he repeats in slightly different form throughout the book.

Abbey's revision of Thoreau intensifies and specifies it, substituting two transitive verbs for the copula, and making both nouns more particular: from "Wildness" to "wilderness," and from "World" to "civilization." Insofar as civilization must involve common, social aspirations, Abbey's version suggests, even more than Thoreau's, that wilderness is both real and imagined. For the only way to understand Abbey's verbs is to envision relations between the civic and the wild. Far more than Thoreau's "is," Abbey's "complements and completes" requires some notion of human agency even to make sense, just as Thoreau's "world" comprehends a good deal more than Abbey's "civilization," which is just the human part of it. Abbey's formulation emphasizes that the otherwise invisible connections between the human and a sublimely wild environment can thus literally give meaning to social life. Further, the fulfillment of civilization reveals itself most fully in highly interpretive abstraction, a relation between the civilized and the wild. The emphasis on relatedness is why Abbey draws so heavily on poetry, where relations are most powerfully imagined and embodied in words. He uses Keats's poem to forge his relation with the desert, history, and the literary past, thereby staking his own imaginative claim upon them in the first few pages of his book.

We can follow Abbey's curriculum quite a bit further and connect the idea of poetic relatedness to a passage in which Heidegger articulates a similar concept (a connection Abbey himself suggests, as I will show). As Heidegger puts it in "Poetically Man Dwells," a discussion of Holderlin: "Because man is, in his enduring the dimension [of what is meted out between earth and sky], his being must now and again be measured out. That requires a measure which involves at once the whole dimension in one. To discern this measure, to gauge it as the measure, and to accept it as the measure, means for the poet to make poetry. Poetry is this measure taking, its taking, indeed, for the dwelling of man" (1975, 223–24). Heidegger's abstraction nicely evokes the way Abbey uses poetry to think through complex relations, as a measuring of dwelling between earth and sky.

Where Abbey presumably disagrees with Heidegger's definition—as he suggests quite pointedly in a critical aside on Heidegger's work in general (1990, 248)—is that our poetry should not only create our own, human dwelling, but acknowledge the presence of the nonhuman, both animate and inanimate, upon the Earth. Abbey says, apropos of a vision of natural beauty in Arches, cleaning up garbage after the tourists have left, "Heidegger was wrong, as usual; man is *not* the only living thing that exists. He might well have taken a tip from a fellow countryman: *Wovon man nicht spreachen Kann, darueber muss man schweigen* (1990, 248; emphasis in original).[9] And yet, of course, while he suggests that Heidegger should have remained silent, Abbey is not silent.

Abbey's insistence on talking his way into a relation with the inarticulable desert brings us to the crucial relation he describes in *Desert Solitaire*, the one on which all the others depend, that between people and sublime, inhuman nature, animal, mineral, and vegetable. It also brings us to the greatest prophet of nature in American poetry, perhaps in all modern poetry: Robinson Jeffers. As Morris has written, "A case could be made that Jeffers is the strongest influence on *Desert Solitaire*, stronger even than Thoreau" (1993, 23), and I agree.[10] Abbey refers and alludes to Jeffers far more than any other poet in the book, easily a score of times, though the allusions are often sly and unannotated.

Abbey was deeply ambivalent about Jeffers. In "A San Francisco Journal" (written in 1986 for the *San Francisco Examiner* and republished in *One Life at a Time, Please* [1988a]), he describes a visit to Jeffers's home in Carmel, where the poet produced all of his mature work, characterizing it as "a literary pilgrimage to the shrine of one of America's best, most reclusive, least known and most unpopular poets" (1988a, 71). In the same passage, he writes:

. . . I admire Jeffers, but do not love him. He was not a wholly lovable man; not in his poetry: too grim, humorless, genuinely misanthropic, his entrails consumed by some secret bitterness. He told the truth in his work and nothing but the truth (a rare thing in poetry) but did not tell the whole truth. He could see joy in the lives of sea gulls and falcons, horses, hummingbirds, and dolphins, but not in the games and comedies of his fellow humans. There is grandeur in his verse, as in the roll of the sea against the Carmel rocks, but the music is a melancholy, dirgelike monotone. (1988a, 72–73)

Not long after, in 1988, *The Nation* printed a letter by Abbey in response to "Strong Counsel," an essay on Jeffers by Dana Gioia.[11]

Abbey wrote: "Jeffers is one of our great and basic American poets, right in there with Walt Whitman, Emily Dickinson, Robert Frost and William Carlos Williams. Jeffers in fact was more than a great poet; he was a great prophet. Everything he wrote about the corruption of empire, the death of democracy, the destruction of our planet and the absurd self-centered vanity of the human animal has come true tenfold since his time" (1988b, 4). The ambivalence exemplified by placing these two passages side by side was already part of Abbey's work twenty years before he wrote either one, in *Desert Solitaire*. In fact, it has much to do with the book's force.

Abbey was attracted and inspired by Jeffers's prophetic stance and apocalyptic vision of civilization, but repelled by the unrelieved misanthropy he saw in much of the work. When he evaluates Jeffers's performance on the stand in the *Examiner* article, it's unclear if it is as witness, victim, or accused, and Abbey isn't telling. At any rate, his interrogation of Jeffers is comic, for people are not called to testify about nature per se, only about crime, a human action. Perhaps this is Abbey's point—he will not abandon humanity for apocalyptic prophecy, as did Jeffers. He will, in fact, testify—despite his own Jeffersian temptations to misanthropy—about "joy . . . in the games and comedies of his fellow humans." Further, he will tell Jeffers's truth in a new place, the desert, and go beyond it, to tell the parts Jeffers left out or suppressed or could not see—the human parts. This is the curve of his creative quarrel with Jeffers throughout his own work.

With the publication of *Roan Stallion, Tamar, and Other Poems* in 1925, Jeffers rocketed to a fame shared by only a handful of contemporary writers in any genre. Jeffers's reputation declined rapidly beginning in the mid-1930s. The causes included his continuing emphasis on what was viewed as social detachment, in a time when more and more writers were calling for engaged art; his occasionally bitter philosophy of "Inhumanism," by which he meant a turning away from the corruption of human affairs to contemplate the immensity and sublimity of the natural world on its own terms; his advocacy of isolationism during World War II; the lurid violence of his narrative poems; and the harsh New Critical judgment that his poems lacked erudition, complexity, and craft, and were "hysterical."[12] Although Jeffers published more work of high quality, including a version of Euripides's *Medea* that enjoyed a successful run on Broadway in the late 1940s, by the time of his death in 1962 he had been all but forgotten by scholars and critics. Nonetheless, he has always retained a popular following, especially as a poet of the natural world.[13]

Writers in the environmental movement have sometimes looked to Jeffers as an apologist for, or precursor of, their views. This began some time ago with the Sierra Club's 1965 publication of *Not Man Apart: Photographs of the Big Sur Coast*, whose title and text come from Jeffers. The marriage is attractive but should ultimately be an uneasy one, as Jeffers is often apocalyptically pessimistic about humanity's ability to save itself, and he holds out virtually no hope of political solution to our self-destructive anthropocentrism, arguing that the only way to live sanely is for individuals to turn away from man to inhuman nature. As he wrote in "Roan Stallion," "Humanity is the start of the race; I say / Humanity is the mould to break away from, the crust to break through, the coal to break into fire, / The atom to be split" (1988, 1:189). While in his poetry Jeffers frequently referred to specific political developments that filled him with despair, he counseled himself, "Be angry at the sun for setting / If these things anger you" (1988, 3:24).[14]

Still, the environmentalist appropriation of Jeffers is understandable. In his best lyrical work, the inhuman (and often raw and terrifying) beauty of nature overwhelms all human concerns, and the reader is encouraged to look outward, into the natural world, to discover reality, truth, and the divine. Consider "The Place for No Story," a short lyric first published in *Thurso's Landing and Other Poems* (1931):

The coast hills at Sovranes Creek;
No trees, but dark scant pasture drawn thin
Over rock shaped like flame;
The old ocean at the land's foot, the vast
Gray extension beyond the long white violence;
A herd of cows and the bull
Far distant, hardly apparent up the dark slope;
And the gray air haunted with hawks:
This place is the noblest thing I have ever seen. No
    imaginable
Human presence here could do anything
But dilute the lonely self-watchful passion.

(1988, 2:157)

Jeffers insists on de-anthropomorphizing the world, and he shuns the pathetic fallacy with as much venom as Ruskin himself, if not more. He foregrounds nature as it is, in and of itself, independent of human concerns.[15]

Now consider the way that Abbey echoes the poem, typical of the way he weaves his ongoing discussion with Jeffers into *Desert Solitaire*. Near the end of the final chapter, "Bedrock and Paradox," Abbey is contemplating his departure from Arches: "In deep stillness, in a somber solemn light, these beings stand, these fins of sandstone hollowed out by time, the juniper trees so shaggy, tough and beautiful, the dead or dying pinyon pines, the little shrubs of rabbitbrush and blackbrush, the dried-up stalks of asters and sunflowers gone to seed, the black-rooted silver-blue sage. How difficult to imagine this place without a human presence; how necessary" (1990, 267). If the only connection to Jeffers's poem were the use of the words "human presence," that would not be enough. It is, of course, Abbey's use of the word "imagine" that shows just how deeply he is grappling with Jeffers, echoing Jeffers's poetic itinerary. We then see that Abbey's paragraph follows the rhetorical development of Jeffers's poem exactly: meditation on a beautiful landscape, followed by imagining what the absence of such a meditating mind might mean.

There are, however, significant differences between the two writers, which suggest not mere imitation on Abbey's part, but a conversation. Jeffers asserts that "human presence" can only "dilute the lonely self-watchful passion," lessening its "nobility" (an interesting anthropomorphism), beauty, and intensity. This is, of course, a paradox, as only human readers can imagine the absence of a human presence. It is a paradox that Jeffers acknowledges by ending the poem with the words "self-watchful passion," a supreme anthropomorphism, with powerful Christian overtones, to describe a supposedly inhuman nature.[16] After all, Christ underwent his passion to save mankind; Jeffers imagines a divine vitality independent of and indifferent to man. The force of the poetry comes from beautiful language juxtaposed against an imagination of its own triviality, or even its disfiguring effect on what it describes.

Abbey sees the paradox and breaks it apart only to reformulate it. Jeffers asserts the "Inhumanist" line, throwing it out as a paradoxical challenge and denigrating human consciousness in favor of inhuman nature. Abbey responds by saying this challenge not to view the world anthropomorphically is "difficult" yet "necessary." This is not simply restating Jeffers's view. Jeffers seems to assert that he, or some imagining part of him, is not really at Sovranes Creek, or only obliquely acknowledges his actual presence; Abbey is more honest and speaks to us less prophetically, less mystically, more conversationally, showing up that unlovable quality in Jeffers he later criticized, quoted above: "He could see joy in the lives of sea gulls and falcons, horses, hummingbirds, and dolphins, but not in the games and comedies of his fellow humans" (1988a, 72–73). Abbey, however inspired, refuses to be taken in by the prophetic stance, instead insisting on pointing out the human difficulty embedded in the paradox. He uses his conversation with the poet as a means to contemplate our relation to the natural world. He is concerned not only with that natural world, but also with the mind that contemplates it. That single word, "difficult"—an intellectual's word—changes everything, showing us how Abbey refuses to give up the "syphilization" (1990, 160) of which he is also so critical.

Indeed, what better place to try to come to terms with Jeffers and his prophecies than a place that is, by definition, "deserted?" In the rest of the passage, Abbey follows Jeffers in imagining the natural world surviving the worst that humanity can dish out, including its own nuclear destruction. At the same time, he refuses to leave the scene himself, acknowledging his individual humanity, refusing to give it over completely to inhumanist visions: "Feet on earth. Knock on wood. Touch stone. Good luck to all" (1990, 268).

Now the obscene parody of Burns that Abbey recites for Waterman in the Maze comes into sharper focus. As Abbey puts it in the first chapter, "The First Morning," after describing his Jeffersian project of completely de-anthropomorphizing the natural world, he still wishes to remain human:

I want to be able to look at and into a juniper tree, a piece of quartz, a vulture, a spider, and see it as it is in itself, devoid of all humanly ascribed qualities, anti-Kantian, even the categories of scientific description. To meet God or Medusa face to face, even if it means risking everything human in myself. I dream of a hard and brutal mysticism in which the naked self merges with a non-human world and yet somehow survives still intact, individual and separate. Paradox and bedrock. (1990, 6)

The words in the final sentence fragment, in reverse order, are, of course, the title of Abbey's final chapter, whose penultimate scene is the passage based on "The Place for No Story" explicated above. And the thoughtful, nasty, polemical, satirical, cantankerous, literate passages in between are evidence of that humanity in the wilderness, the humanity through which Abbey communicates with that which is outside himself—and wild. Abbey is critical of humanity but refuses to denounce it as violently as Jeffers: "... how ... could I be against humanity, without being against myself, whom I love—though not very much ... how could I be against civilization when all which I most willingly defend and venerate—including the love of wilderness—is comprehended by the term?" (1990, 244). Abbey is too critically aware, too ironic—too much of an intellectual—to swallow the inhumanist vision whole.

There are literally dozens of other passages in *Desert Solitaire* where those who know Jeffers's poetry well will see Abbey echoing or quoting him without acknowledgment, as in so many of the passages where he discusses his ambivalent feelings about anthropomorphism. In one passage Abbey encourages himself and the reader to imagine dying in the desert and being eaten by a buzzard: "Comfort yourself with the reflection that within a few hours, if all goes as planned, your human flesh will be working its way through the gizzard of a buzzard, your essence transfigured into the fierce greedy eyes and unimaginable consciousness of a turkey vulture. Whereupon you, too, will soar on motionless wings high over the ruck and rack of human suffering. For most of us a promotion in grade, for some the realization of an ideal" (1990, 117–18).

The "some" is, naturally, Jeffers, who wrote a lyric late in his life called "Vulture" in which he imagines exactly the same thing and which ends, after Jeffers has imagined telling the bird that he is old, but still very much alive,

> I tell you solemnly
> That I was sorry to have disappointed him. To be eaten
>   by that beak and become part of him, to share
>   those wings and those eyes—
> What a sublime end of one's body, what an enskyment;
>   what a life after death.
>
> (1988, 3:462)

As in other passages, Abbey pictures Jeffers as an admirable but harsh idealist.

Among the passages where Abbey refers to Jeffers explicitly is one in the chapter "Cliffrose and Bayonets," in which Abbey offers an ecstatic description of a blossoming cliffrose and then comments:

> If Housman were here he'd alter those lines to
>   Loveliest of shrubs the cliffrose now
>   Is hung with bloom along the bough. . . .
> The word "shrub" presents a challenge, at least to such verse as this; but poetry is nothing if not exact. The poets lie too much, said Jeffers. Exactly. We insist on precision around here, though it bend the poesy a little out of shape. (1990, 24)

Abbey has substituted "shrub" for "tree" and "cliffrose" for "cherry" in Housman's "Loveliest of Trees" (Abrams et al. 1974, 2:2274). And he is again quoting Jeffers from memory, for Jeffers attributes the phrase to Nietzsche, quoting it in the "Foreword" to his 1938 volume *The Selected Poetry of Robinson Jeffers:*

> Another formative principle came to me from a phrase of Nietzsche's: "The poets? The poets lie too much." I was nineteen when the phrase stuck in my mind; a dozen years passed before it worked effectively, and I decided not to tell lies in verse. Not to feign any emotion that I did not feel; not to pretend to believe in optimism or pessimism, or unreversible progress; not to say anything because it was popular, or generally accepted, or fashionable in intellectual circles, unless I myself believed it; and not to believe easily. (1959, xv)

Abbey is also once again arguing with Jeffers, using his Nietzschean words not to justify a critique of poetry that leads to a new vision for it, but only a burlesque, albeit one with a purpose, which is to open to the natural world in a new way. The passage leads directly to Abbey's later comment about Jeffers not telling "the whole truth." The sentiment he correctly ascribes to Jeffers (even if he gets the author wrong) would actually deform Housman's verse, as Abbey recognizes in his comments about the "challenge" of the word "shrub." Abbey's implication is that Housman's lies are actually fine with him—though at the same time, the shrub is indeed so beautiful that it provokes an ecstasy in him, and he insists on trying to find a way to speak to this ecstasy. The path he cunningly chooses is through the "world of words" (1990, xii) he has inherited, which he reweaves with wit and love. Jeffers speaks a truth which must be both accepted and expanded—even satirically bent when applied to nature, so as not to stomp the beauty out of all other art. How important is this to Abbey? He weaves it into the chapter's title, "Cliffrose and Bayonet."

Others of Abbey's explicit allusions are comparably complex, such as the close of his satirical eight-point plan on how "to impose a dictatorial regime upon the American people" (1990, 131), which includes the creation of gigantic cities, mechanization of agriculture, ongoing military conscription, razing the wilderness, and so on—all things, obviously, which he thinks are proceeding apace. This is Abbey at his ranting best, where the exaggeration drives home the foolishness of our behavior. Yet he closes, dispirited, by evoking Jeffers and Whitman: "Idle speculations, feeble and hopeless protest. It was all foreseen nearly half a century ago by the most cold-eyed and clear-eyed of our national poets, on California's shore, at the end of the open road. Shine, perishing republic" (1990, 132). The final sentence is the title of one of Jeffers's best-known lyrics, and Abbey's sigh of "feeble and hopeless protest" conjures not only with the poem's rhetoric and tone, but uses its actual diction:

> While this America settles in the mould of its
> vulgarity, heavily thickening to empire,
> And protest, only a bubble in the molten mass, pops and
> sighs out, and the mass hardens,
>
> I sadly smiling remember that the flower fades to make
> fruit, the fruit rots to make earth.
> (1988, 1:15)

Although Abbey is trading on Jeffers's contempt for the city, Abbey does not sign the "Author's Introduction" to his book as having been written in a beautiful place like Carmel in the 1920s, but at "Nelson's Marine Bar, Hoboken," a rather more urban and conspicuously social place than Jeffers's Hawk Tower in Carmel. Abbey, in fact, does not keep his distance from the city, "the thickening center," as Jeffers urges his sons to do at the end of his poem. He will not give up his humanity to love the inhuman world.[17]

I'd like to close with one more quotation from Jeffers that Abbey buries. The third chapter of *Desert Solitaire,* "The Serpents of Paradise," evokes Genesis and Milton even in its title. A few pages into the chapter, Abbey describes sitting on his doorstep one morning, drinking coffee, when he notices a lethargic rattlesnake curled up in the shade under the steps, practically under his feet. This leads him into a lengthy meditation about what to do: kill it? drive it away? allow it to stay? "Arches National Monument is meant to be among other things a sanctuary for wildlife—for all forms of wildlife. It is my duty as a park ranger to protect, preserve and defend all living things within the park boundaries, making no exceptions. Even if this were not the case I have personal convictions to uphold. Ideals, you might say. I prefer not to kill animals. I'm a humanist; I'd rather kill a *man* than a snake" (1990, 17; emphasis Abbey's).

In the end Abbey removes the now alert and angry snake (a small, but still dangerous rattler) on a long-handled spade and warns him that "if I catch you around the trailer again I'll chop your head off" (18). The snake does return (or "If not him, his twin brother" [18]), but Abbey captures a nonpoisonous gopher snake, a species that "has a reputation as the enemy of rattlesnakes, destroying or driving them away whenever encountered" (19). He keeps the gopher snake in his trailer for a few days and then releases it. It disappears, but so do the rattlers.

In this passage, as with the vulture, Abbey conjures with "ideals," and the final sentence once again relies on a complex allusion to Jeffers. In fact, it's impossible to understand what Abbey is doing without seeing the allusion. Consider the opening of part 2 of Jeffers's poem "Hurt Hawks." In the poem, the speaker nurses a redtail hawk with a broken wing for six weeks. The wing doesn't mend, and the speaker releases the hawk to die in the wilderness. The hawk returns at the end of the day, walking back,

> . . . asking for death,
> Not like a beggar, still eyed with the old
> Implacable arrogance. I gave him the lead gift in the
>   twilight. What fell was relaxed,
> Owl-downy, soft feminine feathers; but what
> Soared: the fierce rush: the night-herons by the
>   flooded river cried fear at its rising
> Before it was quite unsheathed from reality.
>   (1988, 1:377–78)

Abbey's quote comes from the opening of this second section of the poem, which reads "I'd sooner, except the penalties, kill a man than a hawk." There's the further joke, Abbey's saying that "I'm a humanist" to justify his own sentiment, an obvious inversion of Jeffers's "Inhumanism."[18]

Abbey's literary playfulness operates on several levels. He is obviously quite aware of the imagery of the snake in literature (including, I think, D. H. Lawrence's "Snake" [1977, 349–51], which resonates with some subsequent passages). Yet he takes a quotation from a poem about an injured hawk, not a healthy, poisonous snake. If anything, this intensifies the situation Jeffers describes, for the killing in "Hurt Hawks" is done out of a kind of mercy, whereas killing the rattler would be a form of self-defense. Jeffers is making a choice in a situation that involves no threat to himself; Abbey has at least this rationale as motivation. And yet, in the end, it is Abbey who finds a way to let nature solve its own problems rather than interfering directly.

Further, Abbey's joke about "humanism" is inspired. On the one hand, he affirms Jeffers's intense admiration of wild animals, and does so with a creature that has been far more maligned than the hawk in our mythology and literature, going even further in his "Inhumanism" than Jeffers by respecting an animal that could actually kill him. On the other hand, by using the term "humanism," undoing Jeffers's negation, Abbey suggests that his view of nature and wilderness is actually consonant with civilization, as he points out more explicitly elsewhere: " . . . wilderness is not a luxury but a necessity of the human spirit, and as vital to our lives as water and good bread. A civilization which destroys what little remains of the wild, the spare, the original, is cutting itself off from its origins and betraying the principle of civilization itself" (1990, 169).[19]

An anarchist and a humanist, Abbey's point is not that we should kill people to preserve wilderness or wild things (as Hamill thinks it is; see above, note 18). Rather, Abbey is suggesting that Jeffers was wrong to claim we must give up our humanism if we wish to preserve wilderness. For Abbey, unlike Jeffers, "wilderness is a necessary part of civilization" (1990, 47), not utterly opposed to it, and a truly humanistic philosophy is perfectly capable of articulating that idea.

After all, neither Abbey nor Jeffers faces an actual choice between wild animal and real person. Both are meditating on memory to make symbolic arguments about the relation between the human and the wild. Abbey's point is to affirm Jeffers's vision but at the same time return it to the humanist world of "you communal people," as Jeffers angrily denounces the anthropocentric cult of civilization in part 2 of "Hurt Hawks." Abbey refuses to choose between the communal world and Jeffers's "wild God of the world," the God of the hawk. Abbey accepts Jeffers's vision, but not the dichotomy between humanism and love of wilderness. It is as a "humanist" that Abbey sarcastically and satirically claims that he would rather kill a man than a snake, because civilization simply isn't measuring up to its wild counterpart.

The tone of many of the passages where Abbey calls upon poetry only serves to reemphasize that Abbey is not a poet. His gift is for conversation, not prophecy, and he knows it. As he puts it, at certain times during his stay in Arches,

> Alone-ness became loneliness and the sensation was strong enough to remind me (how could I have forgotten?) that the one thing better than solitude, the only thing better than solitude, is society.
>
> By society I do not mean the roar of city streets or the cultured and cultural talk of the schoolmen (reach for your revolver!)[20] or human life in general. I mean the society of a friend or friends or a good, friendly woman. (1990, 96–97)

Or, one might add, a reader—after all, who is he talking to, if not us? Abbey loves the wild, but he is also unashamed to be one of the communal people, at least at some level. His conversations with others, with the poets and philosophers, and thereby with himself, are what enable our conversation with him, in which he conveys a loving vision of the desert, that most inhuman, inhospitable, and least loved environment. Abbey called his book *Desert Solitaire*, but he is never really alone, even when he is by himself, for the cards that he turns up always contain the faces of other writers who have preceded him. His inhuman and inarticulably "sublime" desert (1990, 194) is also "a necessary part of civilization," (47) and his solitude is social.

Abbey was literate in the deepest sense, the point at which the written word becomes the medium of thinking, not just its tool. Through that deep literacy, he imagines our relations with each other, the past, and the natural world, the better to understand, inhabit, and transform those relations. "Through naming comes knowing," he writes, recalling a conversation with Waterman on the question of what—or whether—to name four stone formations one evening on the edge of The Maze (257). The question leads Abbey to call up Rilke, and to turn over in his mind the question of the relation between names and things in a stark, strange, beautiful place (and to put Waterman to sleep). Abbey was indeed a humanist, as he claimed, and it is through an informed humanism that he calls upon us to reimagine the world as best we can, the better to value and therefore preserve whatever wild beauty is left in it, both for its sake and for ours. His humanism does not take the form of the poetry or philosophy he loved to the point of parody, but rather the informal essay in the American vein, something very much like a conversation.

The reason *Desert Solitaire* will endure is because of the quality of this conversation to which Abbey invites us. It is a fully human conversation about our relations with wilderness. As a result, it is also a conversation about what is not wild in our relations with each other and the past, particularly the imaginative past. Of course, things will change no matter what kinds of conversations we have. If we want to change them for the better, however, we must imagine being able to do so. The fact that the American conception of the desert has in fact changed, albeit slowly and not enough, is testimony to the philosophical and, particularly, the poetic imagination that Abbey knew so well and made the paradoxical bedrock of his own work as a writer of the natural world.

It seems inevitable that critics transform strong writers into fodder for investigation, but if that's all I have done here, then I have failed. One of Abbey's great strengths, which he holds in common with many of the philosophers and poets he admired, is that he treats a very wide range of our relations with the world and with each other, and he treats them as if they matter. His faith in the web of relatedness is what gives his work its feeling of life itself, and however many anti-intellectual asides he may make, the way he places his own experience in the world of words is literary. The better we understand the powerful imaginative dimension of his writing, the more likely we are to reconceive our own relations to life and landscape, nature and society, wilderness and art.

Notes

1. Some of the most impassioned writing of this kind is to be found in the eulogies for Abbey quoted by James Bishop, Jr., in *Epitaph for a Desert Anarchist: The Life and Legacy of Edward Abbey* (1994). Speakers at the memorial service for Abbey two months after his death in 1989 included Wendell Berry (who also read a eulogy by Wallace Stegner), Dave Foreman, Terry Tempest Williams, Doug Peacock, Anne Zwinger, and Barry Lopez, among others. Bishop quotes Lopez as having said: "To read *Desert Solitaire* was to hear a clarion call like *Silent Spring*; to know this man was to know that integrity was not just admirable but humanly possible. And now his work courts the dimension of John Muir, not merely an iconoclastic hero but as a galvanizer" (205). However loving this remembrance, it casts a man who claimed to be, and was, primarily a writer as an activist. To depict Abbey's writing as primarily a "clarion call" to action is to simplify it considerably. This is not to suggest that Lopez is wrong in finding a moral imperative in Abbey's book, but rather that the guiding impulse behind it may have more to do with imagination than it does with activist "integrity." This is why the book survives, although the man is dead.

Works that do take up Abbey's literary ambitions include Richard Shelton's "Creeping up on *Desert Solitaire*" (Hepworth and McNamee 1989, 71–87), which traces the influence of John Charles Van Dyke's *The Desert* on Abbey's book; Diane Wakoski's "Joining the Visionary 'Inhumanists' " (1989, 117–30), which uses Jeffers's term (discussed at length below) to describe a tradition that also includes Whitman and Abbey; several articles by Paul T. Bryant, notably "Echoes, Allusions, and 'Reality' in *Hayduke Lives!*" (1991) and "The Structure and Unity of *Desert Solitaire*" (1993), in which he traces a wide range of allusions, argues for the book's aesthetic unity, and points out that Abbey "draws quite consciously upon a rich literary tradition" (17); and David Copland Morris's "Celebration and Irony: The Polyphonic Voice of Edward Abbey's *Desert Solitaire*" (1993), which shows how Abbey transforms a wide range of sources—including Thoreau, Jeffers, Heidegger, Wittgenstein, Rilke, and others—to his own ends.

2. The correct punctuation is "The Waste Land." See Abbey 1990, 243 for the same mistake.

3. In section 5 of his essay "Anima Hominis," which appears in *Essays,* Yeats writes, "We make out of the quarrel with others, rhetoric, but of the quarrel with ourselves, poetry" (1924, 492).

4. At another point Bishop writes that "[Abbey's] sensibilities, to a considerable extent, were shaped by his father, Paul Revere Abbey, a logger, trapper, and farmer, and an anarchist and agnostic of Swiss and German extraction. In the evening, after the work was done, he would read lines to the family from Walt Whitman such as "stand up for the stupid and the crazy" (1994, 55). Of course, as in many passages in the Bishop biography, there is some inconsistency here: having Paul Abbey "read" these lines contradicts the idea that the elder Abbey knew all of Whitman "by heart" (which is hard to believe). Still, it seems clear that poetry mattered in the family.

5. Following are two examples that I have not been able to identify (which I hope do not embarrass me). At one point, contemplating Venus and the emerging stars at dusk, Abbey quotes these verses:

Thou fair-haired angel of the evening,
Now, whilst the sun rests on the mountains, light
Thy bright torch of love; thy radiant crown
Put on, and smile upon our evening bed.
Smile on our loves.

(1990, 99)

On page 111, he quotes what may be a cowboy ballad I cannot identify:
Weep, all you little rains,
wail, winds, wail—
all along, along, along
the Colorado Trail.

(1990, 111)

6. The Shakespeare lines are from *Hamlet;* the Raleigh lines come from a poem of the later, much more obscure Sir Walter Raleigh (1861–1922), "Wishes of an Elderly Man; wished at a Garden Party"; the Jeffers lines come from "Shine, Perishing Republic." Abbey's mistakes in his quotations again suggest he is working from memory. He mislineates both the Shakespeare, which is prose, and the Jeffers, which is part of a single, longer sentence and line, "And boys, be in nothing so moderate as in love of man, a clever servant, insufferable master" (1988, 1:15). Further, Abbey may be misremembering the Shakespeare line, which is usually now represented as "Man delights not me— nor woman neither" (1981, 2.2.309). This is, of course, impossible to judge unless we know what edition Abbey read as a child.

7. Abbey may well have Eliot in mind again, considering this is the way he regularly spells the title of Eliot's poem, which also includes a famous passage about red rock.

8. Abbey presumably knew that Keats had it wrong, which complicates things even further. It was Balboa who was the first European to see the Pacific, in 1513.

9. See Morris (1993, 27–28) for an excellent discussion of this passage. The "countryman" to whom Abbey refers is Wittgenstein. Morris translates the quotation from the Tractatus as "Whereof one cannot speak, one must be silent."

10. Wakoski (1989) and Bryant (1993) also discuss Jeffers at some length.

11. Gioia's essay is a review of *Rock and Hawk: A Selection of Shorter Poems by Robinson Jeffers,* edited by Robert Hass (1987). Gioia's essay and Abbey's letter were both reprinted in the *Robinson Jeffers Newsletter* (Gioia 1988; Abbey 1988b), from which I take my texts. The Gioia essay originally appeared in *The Nation* on January 16, 1988, and the Abbey letter on March 19, 1988.

12. Yvor Winters used this term to characterize *The Women at Point Sur* in a review in *Poetry* (1930):
Mr. Jeffers . . . has never achieved . . . a close and masterly style. His writing is loose, turgid, and careless; like most anti-intellectualists, he relies on his feelings alone and has no standard of criticism for them outside of themselves. . . . Mr. Jeffers has no remaining method of sustaining his lyric . . . other than the employment of an accidental (i.e., non-narrative) chain

of anecdotes . . . his philosophical doctrine and his artistic dilemma alike
decree that these shall be anecdotes of hysteria. (Karman 1990, 85)
More than half a century later, Helen Vendler, although claiming to not
necessarily object to "hysteria" (1990, 14) in a poet, uses similar terms in a review of *Rock and Hawk* (Jeffers 1987), accusing Jeffers of being "a finally un-
satisfying poet—coarse, limited, and defective in self-knowledge" (13), whose
"unpurged . . . sadism" and "fascination with the socially deviant" are manifestations of "moral timidity" (15).

13. *The Woman at Point Sur and Other Poems* (1927), *Dear Judas and
Other Poems* (1929), and *The Double Axe and Other Poems* (1948) were all re-
issued in paperback by Liveright in 1977 and remain in print. In 1970 New Directions brought out a paperback edition of *Cawdor* and *Medea* in a single
volume which has gone through several printings and may still be in print. The
most recent anthology to appear is *Rock and Hawk: A Selection of Shorter Poems
by Robinson Jeffers* (1987), edited by Robert Hass. Alex A. Vardamis has written the most thorough essays on Jeffers's critical reception: "Robinson Jeffers,
Poet of Controversy" (1991) and *The Critical Reputation of Robinson Jeffers: A
Bibliographical Study* (1972). See also James Karman's introduction to *Critical
Essays on Robinson Jeffers* (1990), edited by Karman, and Jeanetta Boswell's
*Robinson Jeffers and the Critics, 1912–1983: A Bibliography of Secondary Sources
with Selective Annotations* (1986).

14. Jeffers scholars disagree to some extent about these issues, though
none dispute Jeffers's overall pessimism. Among others, Peter Quigley has argued that Jeffers uses his rhetoric about nature to provoke radically free political thinking along anarchist lines, thereby holding out the slim hope of change
once human consciousness has turned away from received epistemological categories. See his " 'Man-Devouring Stars': Jeffers' Decentering of American Political Rhetoric." Along these lines, it is worth noting that the title "Be Angry
at the Sun," which is the title poem of the volume in which it first appeared,
suggests Jeffers does not necessarily take his own advice in his own poem, or is
at least ambivalent about it. Without the final conditional clause of the sentence
in the poem, the title suggests that he in fact is angry at the sun, railing against
a political fate that, in the poem, he counsels himself to accept as natural and
inevitable.

15. For an extended discussion of Jeffers, Wordsworth, Ruskin, Pater, and
the pathetic fallacy, see my article " 'I have fallen in love outward': Robinson
Jeffers and the Pathetic Fallacy."

16. The root of "passion" is "pathos," or suffering, almost always understood in a human context.

17. Abbey also alludes to these lines from "Shine, Perishing Republic,"
without naming it, where he writes, "Civilization flows; culture thickens and
coagulates" (1990, 246).

18. The poet Sam Hamill, in his essay "Down the River Yin," completely
misses this allusion and naively takes Abbey to task for his "declarations of violent intent" (1989, 133).

19. Obviously, this and other similar passages have roots in Thoreau. But
note also, in this case, the clear allusion to Hopkins's "Pied Beauty," in which
the poet praises "All things counter, original, spare, strange" (1970, 70).

20. The phrase "When I hear anyone talk of culture, I reach for my revolver" is generally attributed to Goering.

Works Cited

Abbey, Edward. 1988a. *One Life at a Time, Please.* New York: Henry Holt.

———. 1988b. "Poetic Justice." *Robinson Jeffers Newsletter* 74:4. Originally published in *The Nation,* 19 Mar. 1988.

———. [1968] 1990. *Desert Solitaire: A Season in the Wilderness.* Reprint, New York: Simon and Schuster.

Abrams, M. H., et al., eds. 1974. *The Norton Anthology of English Literature.* 3d ed. Vol. 2. New York: W. W. Norton.

Alberts, S. S. 1933. *A Bibliography of the Works of Robinson Jeffers.* New York: Random House.

Bishop, James, Jr. 1994. *Epitaph for a Desert Anarchist: The Life and Legacy of Edward Abbey.* New York: Atheneum.

Boswell, Jeanetta. 1986. *Robinson Jeffers and the Critics, 1912–1983: A Bibliography of Secondary Sources with Selective Annotations.* Metuchen, N.J.: Scarecrow Press.

Burns, Robert. 1960. *Selected Poems of Robert Burns.* Ed. G. S. Fraser. London: Heinemann.

Bryant, Paul T. 1991. "Echoes, Allusions, and 'Reality' in *Hayduke Lives!*" *Western American Literature* 25 (4): 311–22.

———. 1993. "The Structure and Unity of *Desert Solitaire.*" *Western American Literature* 28 (1): 3–19.

Gioia, Dana. 1988. "Strong Counsel." *Robinson Jeffers Newsletter* 73:17–26. First published in *The Nation,* 16 Jan. 1988, 56–64.

Hamill, Sam. 1989. "Down the River Yin." In Hepworth and McNamee.

"Harrowed Marrow." 1932. *Time,* 4 Apr., 63–64.

Heidegger, Martin. 1975. *Poetry, Language, Thought.* Trans. Albert Hofstadter. New York: Harper and Row.

Hepworth, James, and Gregory McNamee, eds. 1989. *Resist Much, Obey Little: Some Notes on Edward Abbey.* Tucson, Ariz.: Harbinger House.

Hopkins, Gerard Manley. 1970. *The Poems of Gerard Manley Hopkins.* 4th ed., revised and enlarged. Ed. W. H. Gardner and N. H. MacKenzie. Oxford: Oxford University Press.

Jeffers, Robinson. 1925. *Roan Stallion, Tamar, and Other Poems.* New York: Boni and Liveright.

———. [1938] 1959. *The Selected Poetry of Robinson Jeffers.* Reprint, New York: Random House.

———. 1965. *Not Man Apart.* Ed. David Ross Brower. Foreword by Loren Eiseley. San Francisco: Sierra Club.

———. 1970. *Cawdor/Medea.* Introduction by William Everson. New York: New Directions.

———. [1929] 1977a. *Dear Judas and Other Poems.* Afterword by Robert J. Brophy. Reprint, New York: Liveright.

———. [1948] 1977b. *The Double Axe and Other Poems.* Foreword by William Everson. Afterword by Bill Hotchkiss. Reprint, New York: Liveright.

————. [1927] 1977c. *The Woman at Point Sur and Other Poems.* Afterword by Tim Hunt. Reprint, New York: Liveright.

————. 1987. *Rock and Hawk: A Selection of Shorter Poems by Robinson Jeffers.* Ed. Robert Hass. New York: Random House.

————. 1988–91. *The Collected Poetry of Robinson Jeffers.* 3 vols. Ed. Tim Hunt. Stanford, Calif.: Stanford University Press.

Karman, James. 1990. Introduction to *Critical Essays on Robinson Jeffers.* Ed. Karman. Boston: G. K. Hall and Co.

————, ed. 1990. *Critical Essays on Robinson Jeffers.* Boston: G. K. Hall.

Keats, John. 1977. *The Complete Poems.* Ed. John Barnard. New York: Penguin Books.

Lawrence, D. H. 1977. *The Complete Poems of D. H. Lawrence.* Ed. Vivian de Sola Pinto and F. Warren Roberts. New York: Penguin Books.

Loeffler, Jack. 1992. "Edward Abbey, Anarchism, and the Environment." *Western American Literature* 28 (1): 43–49.

Morris, David Copland. 1993. "Celebration and Irony: The Polyphonic Voice of Edward Abbey's *Desert Solitaire.*" *Western American Literature* 28 (1): 21–32.

Quigley, Peter. 1994 " 'Man-Devouring Stars': Jeffers' Decentering of American Political Rhetoric." In *History and English Studies,* ed. David Robertson, 125–48. Tampere, Finland: University of Tampere Press.

Rothman, David J. 1995. " 'I have fallen in love outward': Robinson Jeffers and the Pathetic Fallacy." *Hellas* 6 (1): 47–62.

Shakespeare, William. 1981. *Hamlet.* Ed. Harold Jenkins. The Arden Edition. London: Methuen.

Shelton, Richard. 1989. "Creeping up on *Desert Solitaire.*" In Hepworth and McNamee.

Thoreau, Henry David. 1950. *Walden and Other Writings.* Ed. Brooks Atkinson. New York: Random House.

Vardamis, Alex. 1972. *The Critical Reputation of Robinson Jeffers.* Hamden, Conn.: Archon Books.

————. 1991. "Robinson Jeffers, Poet of Controversy." In Zaller.

Vendler, Helen. 1990. "Huge Pits of Darkness, High Peaks of Light." *Robinson Jeffers Newsletter* 77:13–22. Originally published in *The New Yorker,* 26 Dec. 1988, 91–95.

Wakoski, Diane. 1989. "Joining the Visionary 'Inhumanists.' " In Hepworth and McNamee.

Winters, Yvor. 1990. Review of *The Women at Point Sur.* In Karman. Originally published in 1930 in *Poetry.*

Yeats, William Butler. 1924. *Essays.* New York: Macmillan.

Zaller, Robert, ed. 1991. *Centennial Essays for Robinson Jeffers.* Newark: University of Delaware Press.

Who Is the Lone Ranger?

Edward Abbey as Philosopher

DAVID

ROTHENBERG

Anyone who sets out to write some examining words about Edward Abbey is asking for trouble. It's like preparing to fight with an angry dog over a small table scrap, both of you trapped in a tiny pen. Except with Abbey the pen has no boundaries that you can see; it's not the desert spreading out in all directions, but the myriad canyons and ridges where literature and philosophy are ground against each other to form the mountains of our intellectual hope and possibility. For he has always asked the questions the best writers ask: How to unravel the greatest mysteries? How to attack the most important questions rigorously and still leave room for spontaneous beauty?

But he wants his dinner. I want mine. He doesn't want to be pushed out of the running. Abbey loathed critics, nature writers, anyone else who might encroach on his turf. Here's how he stared us down: "What a gutless pack of invertebrates you mostly are. What a fawning groveling writhing genteel array of . . . gutless fence-straddling castrated neutered craven equivocating vapid insipid timorous high-minded low-bellied spineless cool hip cowardly moral jellyfish! Banana slugs of literature!" (1994, 343). Who was he talking about? Everyone else but himself: critics, nature writers, even any other writers getting too much respect from the powers.

Sure, all real writers have a healthy animosity toward the critics who can make or break their reputation. Abbey lived out in the heart of the world, but he so craved attention from the heart of commerce. Why wouldn't the East Coast literary establishment ever welcome him? He wanted to be known as a novelist and fictioneer; they saw him as a regionalist: chronicler of a little-known and faraway core of America's presence. But Abbey needed the critics and baited them along. He also needed philosophy, and I believe he used it the way it should be used: outside the textbooks, far from the classroom, as a guide to transmute the experiences of a full and genuine life. For philosophy is not the same as literature, as we have all been told: it's supposed to make us angry, to perplex us, to leave us more questions than answers. What Abbey does with it is to make it literature in the end, so the results are also beautiful and, at their best, impossible to forget.

Abbey is an idol to many of us reluctant academics because he did it. He turned away from the institutions that spawned him. When they invited him to their inner sanctum, he walked. Not many remember that Abbey was a graduate student in philosophy at the University of New Mexico. Here is a thinly fictionalized scene from a meeting of his master's thesis committee, with the aged professors grilling Abbey's alter ego Henry Lightcap about the progress of his research.

> "And another question, Lightcap: Do you really want to be a professor of philosophy?"
> " . . . I certainly want to be a philosopher, sir, and live la vie philosophique goddamnit."
> Henry reflected. A fork in his road of life had most suddenly appeared dead ahead. To the right, the right way, a broad and shining highway led upward beyond the master of arts toward the PhD.—the tenured leisurely life of overpaid underworked professorhood. A respectable life. Anyone who is paid much for doing little is regraded with obligatory admiration. To the left a dingy path littered with beer cans and used toilet paper led downward in darkness to a life of shame, of part-time and seasonal work and unemployment compensation, of domestic strife, jug wine, uncertainty, shady deals, naive realism, stud poker, furtive philanderings, skeptical nominalism, pickup trucks, a gross and unalambicated nineteenth-century eight-ball materialism. He called his shot. I will not tell a lie. Looking at his three Inquisitors looking at him, he answered them collectively:
> "Not really," he said. (1990b, 196)

I have always wanted to tack this quote up on my office door. Sure, we can fight back. It can be hard to work honorably as a professor, teaching and talking, writing and reflecting. But I and many others have always felt the pull of the other way, the dangerous track of the loner, where you must go if you truly have the creative talents Abbey fought for and cultivated. There is so much more philosophy out beyond the bounds or the rules!

Yet Abbey was never without his regrets for the road not taken. He was not one to be easily satisfied with any one outcome, or another. I would say this is because he studied enough philosophy to get hooked on the idea that dilemma is worth more than solution, that the bird in the hand and the bird in the bush are worth more both being out there than choosing one over the other, if that makes any sense at all. Abbey was addicted to philosophical conundrums, and the love of uncertainty (which philosophy can breed into one) is probably what kept the man out of any club that would have someone like him for a member. Like Socrates, he said just those things that would make him unpopular, while teaching the rest of us a thing or two. Only he died long before his time, and our loss grows deeper with each thinking year.

I must confess that I speak from philosophy with more than a tinge of ambivalence. I never wanted to become a philosopher. I got into it through love of the Earth, through an apprenticeship with Norwegian coyote ecosopher Arne Naess, who told me I was too deep within it all to escape. But I tried, maybe am still trying, went through the same rite of passage Abbey ran from and still remain in the fold. For the moment. Why am I telling you this? Only to work it out for myself, to basically admit that philosophy and the wilderness are not so much strangers as they are necessary partners. Now, if I am honest and think all the way back, it was in *Desert Solitaire,* read when I was twelve, on a family trip into the desert, that I first heard of philosophy and tried to figure out what in hell the man was talking about. More than twenty years later, I realize the genius of a man who made real sense out of the timeless and impossible obsessions, brought them into a language that is deep yet accessible enough for all of us to understand.

And he lures us in by twisting our expectations, keeping his reflection always just a false peak beyond the familiar viewpoint. For right from the introduction, *Desert Solitaire* is expressly "not primarily a book about the desert. . . . I have tried to create a world of words in which the desert figures more as medium than as material. Not imitation but evocation has been the goal" (1971, x). The old extrapolator is using nature for his own purposes, just like every other human throughout history. He is making it into the stark landscape of his own dreams and doubts, constantly urging us not to follow him, insisting it can't be done, that the landscapes he has loved are no more. This guidebook instructs us to find our own roads, and to make sure they are ours and ours alone.

When Abbey announces on the first page that "this is the most beautiful place on earth," he immediately softens the pronouncement with the admission that "there are many such places." His litany includes places rural and urban, all localities that have mattered to him in his wanderings. My students in Newark are particularly intrigued by his being so enamored with Hoboken. I tell them that when I read this as a teenager, the word "Hoboken" became like a magic incantation, some kind of legendary place. I knew it was a seedy river town in Jersey, but if Abbey loved it, there must be something to the place. Later I learned he wrote most of *Solitaire* there, living with one of his early wives. And when I finally went to Hoboken, I learned what he was talking about: If we become sensitized to the inspiring qualities of place, any place, any home we deem serious enough to try out, then the immediacy of any view can lure us toward philosophy. Abbey looked across at Manhattan and saw the end. In the desert he could run from it, but so much for the beauties of death: "looking back at it from this desert perspective, you've got to admit that Wolf Hole, Arizona can never have so rich a death" (1977, 95). But he had to return to the desert, if only because there was so much more space to fill with the most stark kind of questions: "What do the coyotes mean when they yodel at the moon? What are the dolphins trying so patiently to tell us? Precisely what did those two enraptured gopher snakes have in mind when they came gliding toward my eyes over the naked sandstone? . . . They do not sweat and whine about their condition. They do not lie awake in the dark and weep for their sins. . . ." (1971, 24).

No remorse. No mercy. The strength of philosophy can be measured by one's confidence to stick with the questions and not rush on to answers. Abbey was in pursuit of raw experience, never attainable, always some place beyond where the mind might no longer wonder. He could not be satisfied and would never get enough of the trying or the groveling.

Those living in pure experience have nothing to say about it. The writer must step back and invent his persona. We will never come close to knowing who Abbey really is because he spent so much time trying to tell us, leaping between fiction and thinly disguised fact. But questioning can easily turn to defense. In the end a simple touch can win over an idea: "Do I seem to write only of the surfaces of things? Yet, it seems to me that only surfaces are of ultimate importance—the touch of a child's hand in yours, the taste of an apple, the embrace of friend or lover, sunlight on rock and leaf, music, the feel of a girl's skin on the inside of her thigh, the bark of a tree, the plunge of clear water, the face of the wind" (1994, 199).

When Abbey gets serious, it is over the emotion and memory of fleeting immediacy. This catalog of images we all know is the surest answer to the feeling of futility, as we know nothing beyond the human edges of a much deeper world. Phenomena, not noumena, like old Immanuel Kant said as he proceeded to write thousands of pages on why he had given up trying to know anything about the core of reality. Abbey is wise to refute it thus: and any commentary upon such clarity trudges down into the muck.

But I see Abbey smiling way up above me in the arc of the irreducible vultures above in the autumn sky. He remains a philosopher. He answers the question, but the questions still haunt him. Because they will never go away, he must go on asking, posing the big ones and returning with a joy in the mundane and the sudden. The bigger the question, the more he wants to laugh. I do not know whether or not this is an easy way out.

> "Newcomb," I explain, "we've got to go back."
> "But why?" he says. "Why? . . ."
> "Because," I explain. The role of the Explainer has become a well-established one in recent times. "Because they need us. Because civilization needs us."
> "What civilization?" he says.
> "You said it. That's why they need us."
> "But do we need them?" (1971, 205)

The dance of the philosophical dialogue is back, thousands of years after Plato. Philosophers always return to these dialogues for the back and forth, the living sense of the two sides of the best questions, hunting and pecking around the impervious answers. No explanation seems enough, but we should not be too fearful to try. Try as they might, philosophers have been unable to breathe much life into the dialogue form over the past two millennia. Literature, of course, has taken over: think of the philosophy debated in Dostoyevsky, even Shakespeare. But Abbey is the sparse talker, the cool breath of wind in the middle of the canyon heat. Who? Who? The end of the questions never matters as much as the need for the questions.

There is the love of questions, and then the need to make a difference in the struggling and bruised world. The impotence of philosophy seems inherent in its whole method: asking, twisting, playing around, never giving in. Abbey couldn't get enough of it, but as he watched his vision of the Great Southwest recede into the past, he knew it was time to take action. The action of a writer is of course to write, but a writer can concoct a fantasy of revenge against the way the world has become. That is the hook behind *The Monkey Wrench Gang,* his most popular novel, the invention of a band of rebels sworn to destroy the encroaching tools and artifacts of industrial civilization, the spirit of the megalopolis heading into the beautiful desert: billboards, bulldozers, powerlines, and dams. These are our enemies: not people, but the property and agents of blight on the landscape. It is time for the lovers of the desert to fight back. George Hayduke figured it out: "My job is to save the fucking wilderness. I don't know anything else worth saving" (1976, 211).

Wilderness matters most to Abbey, and that's not just because there are no people out there and he can finally be left alone in his perpetual curmudgeonhood. No, it is because this is where he feels enough openness to think, to fill the desert dryness with a culture of precision. He doesn't hear twanging guitars or lone plaintive flutes, but the harsh entwined string tonalities of Webern and Schoenberg, a music just right for a place that is "both agonized and deeply still" (1971, 286). Wilderness is home for the renegade survivalist of ideas, hiding remorsefully from the dying centers of culture, but at the same time endlessly craving attention from that culture. He could never really move away! Love of the word kept him in, craving approval from just those people most scared of his wildness, most content to keep it at bay in pretty words.

Enjoying this ambiguity rather than trying to break through it, I call Abbey more successful as philosopher than polemicist. He liked open questions, and he liked to twist the minds of those tribes who tried to claim him as one of their own. From wherever he stands, however alone he might seem, there is always someone a bit more lonely than he, an alter ego or a challenge, a dream at least of a more detached observer always one step farther from civilization than he would dare to step.

This starts with the old moon-eyed horse in *Desert Solitaire,* a formerly tame beast who had found the wild life by chance and lived alone up a dry canyon. "That," thinks Abbey, "is the kind of horse I would like." He endeavors to tame him, to lure him in. Walks up the canyon alone with a canteen. Old Moon-Eye appears, suspicious and at the edge of twilight view. Abbey sweet-talks him, lures him with the faint promise of the benefits of culture: "Moon-Eye, how long since you've stuck that ugly face of yours into a bucket of barley and bran? Remember what alfalfa tastes like, old pardner?" (1971, 165). Careful cajoling long after the sun sets. Abbey wants a horse as independent as he is. But Moon-Eye will have none of it. He turns alone back into his desert tracks, thus earning the author's respect. Not a wild horse, but an independent horse. Still out there, making his own way.

And Abbey, too, made sure no group can have him, although he did manage to achieve an inspirational effect that many writers dream of but few realize: he invented a fictional movement that then came to life: the Monkey Wrench Gang, whose final dream is taking out the great Glen Canyon Scam and restoring the fabulous canyon to its original sacred state. The novel is a rousing adventure of true believers fighting for the public good, long before having to answer to the scourge of being labeled "eco-terrorists" and the like. True enough, Abbey's fable of monkeywrenching vigilantes became reality in the mid-1980s with the emergence of the Earth First! movement, determined not to compromise in their defense of Mother Earth. Some welcomed their rousing brand of political theater into the now stodgy, mainstreaming eco-movement, while others feared it was all too silly, if not outright destructive in clearly malicious ways. For my part, I would say that Earth First! has been successful in the ways the Monkey Wrench Gang was successful: showing how fun it can be to fight back in the name of saving the wild, something that is so right to fight for, so important, and in so much danger. Also true to the fiction that begat it, real-life Earth First!ers were persecuted by the FBI and sent to jail for sentences upwards of ten years. Two activists were nearly blown up in a questionable bomb explosion: immediately following the accident the FBI accused the victims of planning a violent act, whereas all their previous demonstrations were nonviolent! The feds clearly became scared of Earth First!, not the least because they advocated the destruction of private property in the name of public good. And as good as we want the public to be, it is private property that the ideals of this nation hold the most sacred. In God we trust. All others have to pay for our attention, right?

For Abbey's part, he seemed to have a mixed relation with Earth First! I have seen films of him mumbling eloquent words at various gatherings of would-be miscreant defenders of nature, and I'm sure he was flattered by all the real-life effect his imagination wrought loose. Still, he never seemed all that comfortable out raising the crowd into a frenzy. Abbey remained foremost a writer: someone who sits safely behind a typewriter and lets his words take the risks for him, scaring off enemies and would-be friends, articulating with logic and emotion a convincing critique that is never easy to put down.

Abbey's final novel, rushed to completion as its author lay dying, brings the inevitable return of the Monkey Wrench Gang into the real Earth First!ed world of the late 1980s. Though I know I am in the minority here, I actually prefer it as a novel to the original, which seems to ramble on and on in an overly light vein. *Hayduke Lives!* is a series of character studies, working one by one through the members of the original gang as they contemplate how life's treated them in the years following the original ruckus. Abbey visits the Earth First! Round River Rendezvous, making it sound like a rousing gathering of wild country philosophers, angry redneck mountaineers, and pagan new paradigmists, all ready to save the world. The protagonist is the lovely Norwegian maiden Erika, "last name unknown, representing the song of Norway, the mind of Arne Naess, . . . the beauty of Greta Garbo" (1990a, 187), who speaks with a German accent throughout, mysteriously in love with a former Mormon missionary Oral Hatch now turned FBI mole. (When I showed these passages to Naess, he was honored that his name was known enough to articulate a character.)

The plot is questionable but hilarious, with the role of the original Gang in this gathering nonexistent. The goal is to stop the giant GOLIATH earth-moving machine that grinds along the desert creating an instant superhighway in its wake. The Earth First!ers, led by fearless Erika ("Ze Eart' she first!") aim to make a giant blockade across the plateau to stop the machine from paving over paradise as it lumbers maliciously along. But what can they do? Have a good time, put on a show, get TV and radio to pay attention, just as in real life, but ultimately they are dragged away by the cops and the machine still moves.

But wait! While Earth First! postures and talks and shouts and gathers, the Monkey Wrench Gang is getting the job done. No one knows where they are. No one remembers who they are. But they succeed in secret where the noisemakers are doomed to fail.

This is a powerful and typically cantankerous message for Abbey to cast forth to the activist group originally inspired by his fictional band of merry pranksters. They have become famous, in the newspapers and on television all across the land, and they have brought a wrenching humor to staid and confrontational environmentalism. But can they really stop the beast? The result is completely independent from the posturing. Leave no footprints. Leave no trace. Above all, never get caught. No one must know your name. That is a different strategy than that taken by Earth First!, which remains a protest theater group and lobbying faction in the eyes of the media. Stopping the encroachment of evil machinery is still best done in secret. The wild is preserved. No one hears about it. If anyone thanks you for your efforts, it will be nature—silent, unheralded, solemn, alive.

Philosophers have generally been uncomfortable with eco-sabotage and have offered careful arguments against it. Principles of nonviolence become of greater value than getting results. Your side always looks better if you take the moral high ground and do not resort to low and nasty tactics. But this all may be too cool for the real world, and Abbey may have been too real to stand on top of abstractions for all his days. He used philosophy to open up his vision, but when he took a stand, he went one step beyond frustration to an invisible pragmatism: get the job done, and make the action speak where the person behind it remains silent, someone of whom we can never speak. . . .

Still more remote than the Gang is the mysterious Lone Ranger, who appears sporadically in the *Monkey Wrench Gang* as the lonely savior about whom precious little can ever be told. There is always an outsider behind any of Abbey's revolutions, an extra spoke in the wheel of paradox, as strange and as necessary as the fact that Bonnie Abbzug will always remain the only Jewish gentile in southeast Utah. These observers at the edge of the action are illustrative of the realm of mystery pervasive in Abbey's works. The familiar but ghostly Lone Ranger, who helps out the Gang in key moments when you're not quite sure he's for real, is back in *Hayduke Lives!*, leaving the Reverend Bishop Love stranded with his soon-to-be second wife, pleasingly plump Ranger Dick. There is always someone watching from the sidelines, a character or plot line not quite visible to the reader or fellow journeyer with the old buzzard himself.

"Stop the car," cries the author at the end of *Solitaire*. "Let's go back" (1971, 303). They go on, and with sadness old Ed knows nothing will be the same when he returns. Nothing ever does stay the same, and that always saddens those who love the way things used to be. And lovers of wild places usually remember and rhapsodize those places as they were just one time and no other, before the stream of humanity descends upon them; first the writer, then those who read him and want to repeat the already impossible past.

This is what Jack Turner calls "Muir's Mistake," for how could the Sierra Club's founder not realize that such an organized society would prevent the lone and complete wonder he felt and described in the midst of the great and incontrovertible Sierra Nevada (1996, 36). Now that everyone goes there, they are not likely to be any more surprised than on a walk through a city park. Abbey knew this, and he specifically wanted no one to follow him. One early parable describes an overland journey through rutted Texas desert roads with one of his numerous wives, just after their wedding night. Far from the labeled highways, they pass a cryptic junction: "Hartung's Road. Take the Other." So adrift on the Other Path they go, until the brand new Ford is unable to continue. The woman storms off, and they never speak again. A few years later there's a book out: *Abbey's Road*. The implication is clear. It's up to us to take the other. Don't follow Cactus Ed. He's always made sure he's none too appealing as role model or source of wisdom, high or low. Nope. Too many unpleasantries of character and persuasion: dirty old man even at the age of twenty-five (if that is possible), racist, ranting bigot, sexist, perennial curmudgeon at best. But at least he can laugh at himself throughout. And, most importantly, he can inspire a kind of individualism that does allow us to join up with his spirit at the core, even though we are told to follow our own restless tracks when the crossroads come.

The totem image of "Abbey's Road—Take the Other" lingers as a mixture of Zen koan and fearsome backwoods retreatism. Would you follow the named path or go the anonymous way the words point to? Depends on your confidence, your trust in the directions. I admire Abbey, so would I want to do what he says? True enough, his road has already been taken. The unknown calls out. We ought to find our own way. Perhaps steer clear of the vulture by a thousand miles. If the country is still big enough for us to do so.

Here Abbey is not so dissimilar from a man he must have admired just a bit, Arne Naess, philosopher at the foundation of the deep ecology movement, inspirateur to the Earth First!ers, tacit supporter for the goals of the Monkey Wrench Gang, if not their methods. Well, Naess would probably prefer the Gang to Earth First!, because they are taciturn, secret, impossible to trace, though their results can be far-reaching. Polite and genteel, Naess wrote a careful philosophical analysis of Gandhism, showing it to be a consistent approach for conflict resolution (1974). Only after Rachel Carson's wake-up call to prevent a silent spring did Naess, a lifetime mountaineer, stop dumping garbage behind his mountain hideaway and realize that a thinker could do something serious to save the Earth. But all the while, as a teacher and policymaker around education, Naess had encouraged several generations of students to find their own roads, never founding a coherent school or singular way of seeing things.

With the recent popularity of deep ecology in the United States, there has been some tendency to idolize Naess and his ideas, taking his ideas of equal value for all living things and a putting of the Earth first, before human needs and aspirations, as a kind of gospel. But he never asked for that! He would rather we all articulate, experience, or at least live our own philosophies. No cloning of the master's words, please! He and Abbey would have gotten along fine, and it's a pity they never met. But at least we have him somewhat personified in the spirit of Erika ("Down wiss empire up wiss spring!" in a once again obtusely generic foreign accent).

Yes, as much as he savaged the academy, Abbey always respected philosophy, and he elevated its ability to inspire into something more: laughter, and a tool for making sense of the straining surge of remembering. The world is changing. And yet what we found there remains impossible to forget. Those who remember too much are often faulted for "romanticizing" the past. Charles Bowden told me recently that this is why he believes the public turned slightly against Abbey in the end: "He kept going on and on about the decline of the West, while the West went on and kept changing," into a corrupt, developers' paradise with levels of strange evil that made even the full range of Abbey's complaint seem tame. Could he have anticipated Charlie Keating (see Binstein and Bowden, 1994), a man more deeply sinister than any of the cartoon villains from Abbey's sketchbooks? The future will still grow darker before we can glimpse any light. Sure, we have lost things of inestimable beauty. And we must not repeat the grave errors of the past. But we will not be given back the past, no matter how crisply we remember it.

Abbey did not fare well with the future. His novel about the end of the world was entitled *Good News!* A more useful environmental philosophy will dare to imagine the future. And will, paradoxically, find it even more romantic than the past. Bowden, perhaps the Abbey of our present generation (with a dash of William Burroughs thrown into the sauce), offers us this to look forward to:

> This is how the future comes to me, how I stumble down un-mapped lanes and suddenly am in front of that cathouse where she waits unloved, the face of indeterminate colors, the lips smiling and the eyes knowing far too much. . . . There will be no first hundred days for this future, there will be no five year plans. There will be no program. Imagine the problem is that we cannot imagine a future where we possess less but are more. Imagine the problem is a future that terrifies us because we lose our machines but gain our feet and pounding hearts. (1996, 110)

Bowden is seduced by the future in a whorehouse of his own devising. She is alive and enveloping, and he's damn scared of her. And yet we strain for a chance at her and hope she will remember us when her time has come. There is an alluring irony here, but a chilling and powerful feminine spirit that is more serious than anything Abbey would ascribe to his women.

Abbey's women are part of the world of remorse, and usually part of his past. He rhapsodizes them as part of the good old long-gone days that puff themselves up into phantoms in his rickety memory. They leave him and do not return. Abbey's writing became increasingly a chronicle of times that are no more, of a life spent and continually reinvented as either fact or fiction, often little difference between. Abbey, Lightcap, the nameless, beak-nosed, worn journalist in Hayduke, scribbling down all the passion and belief around him.

Now tell me, what philosopher really wants to fit in? How can a speculator, a dreamer, an artist of concepts ever find a home? You always ostracize yourself when you take on the sacred myths: money, progress, personal space, happiness, self-realization. Can we get to any of these places while trashing the world? Can selfishness ever be safely stopped? By who? Who? Who.

The philosopher is safely unpopularized with his litany of questions. He takes down notes to transform the facts. But they never hold water. He wants the water to flow through them, he wants the sand to outlast his words. He has questioned the human situation long enough to know that the world will get on fine without us and not whip itself into irascible paradox and lazy impossibility.

Never afraid to be a hypocrite, at least Abbey is consistent: his fiction and his nonfiction, his private and public writings, all generally present the same unforgettable character amidst his friends, loves, and landscapes, only with slight variation. There is no question that this indefatigable questioner was a great writer, of quotable aphorisms, careful descriptions, and rambling novelizations. I believe it all will hold up over time, and we will still laugh and cry with Abbey many years down the line. From philosophy he learned that the most important questions can never be answered, yet one can go far by asking and posing them over and over again.

His life was one answer, but his inspiration should serve to set us adrift. Do not imitate, never join up. Take what you want, and make your life and ideas your own. Philosophy dries when it loses its original spirit of wonder, but the desert comes alive when one's attention is attuned. The philosopher is trained never to be satisfied with one response as opposed to another, and it's clear that forms of restlessness kept Abbey moving forward and around all through his life. The Lone Ranger can never stay any one place too long before his identity gets out. He's got to ride out of the picture and leave only clues as to who he was or why he was here. The words are the clues, the writings his legacy. May we never figure out too much about that grizzly buzzard, Edward Abbey. Worry not, we vultures will never pick him clean.

Works Cited

Abbey, Edward. [1968] 1971. *Desert Solitaire: A Season in the Wilderness.* Reprint, New York: Ballantine.

———. 1976. *The Monkey Wrench Gang.* New York: Avon.

———. 1977. "Manhattan Twilight, Hoboken Night." *The Journey Home.* New York: Dutton.

———. 1990a. *Hayduke Lives!* Boston: Little, Brown and Co.

———. 1990b. *The Fool's Progress.* New York: Avon.

———. 1994. *Confessions of a Barbarian*. Ed. David Petersen. Boston: Little, Brown and Co.

Binstein, Michael, and Charles Bowden. 1994. *Trust Me: Charles Keating and the Missing Billions*. New York: Random House.

Bowden, Charles. 1996. *Blood Orchid*. New York: Random House.

Naess, Arne. 1974. *Gandhi and Group Conflict*. Oslo: Universitetsforlaget.

Rothenberg, David. 1993. *Is It Painful to Think? Conversations With Arne Naess*. Minneapolis: University of Minnesota Press.

Turner, Jack. 1996. *The Abstract Wild*. Tucson: University of Arizona Press.

Nativity, Domesticity, and Exile in Edward Abbey's "One True Home"

TOM

LYNCH

Nature is not a place to visit—it is home. . . .
—Gary Snyder, "The Etiquette of Freedom"

BLOOMSBURY: You aren't worried about what academic people might do to your work?
ABBEY: No. I don't think about it. Let them do their work. I'll do mine.
—In *Resist Much, Obey Little: Some Notes on Edward Abbey*

Albuquerque, April 12, 1956: Today I became a father. Eight pounds twelve ounces and his name, it is called—Joshua Nathaneal Abbey.
—Abbey, *Confessions of a Barbarian*

On April first, 1956, only a few days prior to recording in his journal the birth of his son, Edward Abbey began the first of three seasons as a ranger in Arches National Monument. He immortalized this sojourn in the influential classic of nature writing *Desert Solitaire*, a work whose very title suggests that his experience of the desert was one essentially aloof from familial or other ties. As Abbey reveled in his desert solitude, his wife, Rita, and new son, Joshua, were summering in Hoboken. During subsequent years his wife and son visited periodically with him, but never for extended periods, and their presence at Arches is never portrayed in the book. What is intriguing about this chronology is not so much that Abbey would leave wife and newborn for the desert. Perhaps as a struggling writer he simply needed the work. Evading motives in the "Author's Introduction" to *Desert Solitaire,* he demurs that "Why I went there no longer matters" (Abbey 1971, ix); and the impulse for such a move was no doubt complex. But what strikes me as suggestive is that in this semi-autobiographical account of his time at Arches, Edward Abbey would make only passing and derisive mention of his wife, and none at all of the new son he so proudly announces in the privacy of his journal.

Such observations are not merely biographical trivia, for the absence of family from *Desert Solitaire* is, I think, essential to Abbey's conception of the value of his experience of "a season in the wilderness," as the book is subtitled. His job, he informs us, requires him to live and work at a "one-man station some twenty miles back in the interior, on my own. The way I wanted it" (1971, 2). His stance here seems well sanctioned by the tradition of literary natural history composition of which he is an heir (Thoreau's removal to Walden Pond, though often misconstrued as more antisocial than it was, serves as a paradigm), and in turn Abbey's solitary experience has influenced the way others conceptualize their relationship to the land.

Paradoxically, the opening of *Desert Solitaire* invokes the concept of "home." "This is the most beautiful place on earth," Abbey exults. "There are many such places. Every man, every woman, carries in heart and mind the image of the ideal place, the right place, the one true home, known or unknown, actual or visionary" (1971, 1). And he shortly proclaims the Arches region to be "Abbey's country" (1971, 4), so he accepts a considerable responsibility for distinguishing his in-placed vision from that of the tourists he tends to revile. "Home" is a significant term in eco-critical discourse. It implies a particularly intimate, enduring, and protective relationship with an area of the natural world. According to the school of deep ecology known as bioregionalism, the healing of the human relationship with nature will best be served if people learn to become true inhabitants of—at home in—their local environment rather than merely tourists or sojourners passing through it. Gary Snyder explains that the bioregional vision "prepares us to begin to be at home in this landscape. There are tens of millions of people in North America who were physically born here but who are not actually living here intellectually, imaginatively, or morally" (1990, 40).

In determining the degree to which a writer teaches us to be at home in a particular environment, a useful—though by no means foolproof—method would be to contrast his or her work with the work of writers who have inhabited the region for an extended period of time. In the American Southwest about which Edward Abbey writes, no one has lived longer than the Native Americans, whose tenure extends back at least 12,000 years according to archaeologists, and to the primordial time of Emergence according to native traditions.

It is not necessary, of course, that the vision of a newcomer to the Southwest, such as Abbey, conform in all ways to the vision of the region's native people, but still one may gain useful insights into his perspective by contrasting it with theirs. Gary Paul Nabhan has suggested the phrase "cultural parallax" to refer to "the difference in views between those who are actively participating in the dynamics of the habitats within their home range and those who view those habitats as 'landscapes' from the outside" (1995, 91). By bringing within the same scope of vision these different cultural perspectives on a natural region, we may gain a more multidimensional view. Hence a comparison of Edward Abbey's vision of the Southwest with the perspective of some Native American writers from the region, such as Leslie Marmon Silko (Laguna), Simon Ortiz (Acoma), and Luci Tapahonso (Navajo), will reveal to us aspects of Abbey's work that we might otherwise take for granted—especially if we share his cultural angle of vision—and might help us determine both the degree to which Abbey's perspective represents a new angle of observation of the western terrain and the degree to which he does or does not suggest a model for newcomers to become inhabitants of the desert Southwest. Our understanding of Abbey, and of the terrain he presents, can be enriched and challenged by contrasting him with Silko, Ortiz, and Tapahonso; unlike Abbey, they portray the natural world of the Colorado Plateau as a place imbued with the presence of family and ancestors, and their experience of those places is valuable precisely because of, rather than in spite of, that familial presence.

Culturally and personally, Abbey is a newcomer to the desert. He arrived first as a teenager in 1944, fell in love with the allure of the landscape, and returned after his war service, toting a suitcase stuffed with cultural predispositions that he was loath to jettison. In this light, Abbey's use of the term "home" is, I think, quite problematic, for though Abbey refers to the Arches country as his home, he continually exoticizes the desert Southwest, projecting it as a space antithetical to human comfort—especially by the standards of his Allegheny Mountain upbringing. Indeed, in his text to accompany Eliot Porter's photographs in *Appalachian Wilderness: The Great*

Smoky Mountains, published five years after *Desert Solitaire,* Abbey begins with "Going back to the Big Smokies always reminds me of coming home," and he goes on to describe his family's farm in rural Pennsylvania, consisting of a pleasant landscape where, "from the top of the hill you can look down into a long emerald valley where a slow stream meanders back and forth," and where one may take an "easy, pleasant sort of walk" down into that natal valley (1973, 9–10) . His portrayal of the Southwest is quite different. For example, in his essay "The Great American Desert" he emphasizes the harshness and danger of what he calls "God's forsaken country": "You will find the flora here as venomous, hooked, barbed, thorny, prickly, needled, sawtoothed, hairy, stickered, mean, bitter, sharp, wiry and fierce as the animals" (1977b, 14). Scott Slovic has commented on this feature of *Desert Solitaire,* a book, he says, that "contains many examples of the harshness and unfamiliarity of the desert landscape. Even features of the desert which most of us would consider predictable and commonplace, such as the general lack of water, and the occasional, sudden, deadly, and nourishing return of water in the form of deluges and flash floods are presented hyperbolically, sometimes nightmarishly, so that they become defamiliarized, alien" (1992, 93–94).

It is precisely this exotic, alien sense of the desert Abbey loves— and one's home, by definition, can never be exotic. Abbey's landscape is treacherous and hence alluring to the adventurous and macho spirit. Slovic proposes that

> unlike Wendell Berry who suggests that through careful "watchfulness" it is possible to "belong" to a particular piece of land, and unlike [Barry] Lopez who asserts that a receptive, "tolerant" approach even to a wholly exotic landscape makes "intimacy" possible, Abbey seems to discredit the very idea of anyone ever feeling calm and comfortable in the desert. . . . He realizes that prolonged habitation in such country is for spadefoot toads and coyotes, not for human beings. (Slovic 1992, 99)

Abbey values the desert for its ability to filter out the family matrix and liberate him as an individual. The more efficiently a natural place serves as such a filter, the more highly he values it, leading, perhaps, to his claim that "in the American Southwest only the wilderness is worth saving" (1977b, 17). To Abbey, the desert wilderness, the "one true home," is a defamiliarized landscape devoid of familial ties.

A particularly well known example of this occurs in *Desert Solitaire* when Abbey, along with friend Ralph Newcomb, embarks on a raft trip down the Colorado River through Glen Canyon shortly before the completion of Glen Canyon Dam. This trip was begun on June 25, 1959, less than a month after the birth of his second son, Aaron Paul Abbey (1994, 148), an event that, although never explicitly mentioned in the text, perhaps accounts for some of the images in the following passage. Disembarking from Hite's Ferry landing, Abbey celebrates his freedom: "Cutting the bloody cord, that's what we feel, the delirious exhilaration of independence, a rebirth backward in time and into primeval liberty, into freedom in the most simple, literal, primitive meaning of the word, . . . My God! I'm thinking, what incredible shit we put up with most of our lives—the domestic routine (same old wife every night), the stupid and useless and degrading jobs. . . " (1971, 177). Abbey portrays this journey into the natural world as an escape from domestic responsibility, a severing of the bloody cord binding him to home and wife.[1]

While I wish to make the case that such a relationship to the environment contrasts markedly to the sort of relationship espoused by Silko, Ortiz, and Tapahonso, I am wary of drawing too sharp a contrast between Abbey and these Native American authors; as Arnold Krupat (1992) warns, the Manichean approach to simplistic interethnic comparisons suffers from the terminal flaws of overgeneralization and essentialism. Abbey's perspective, though different, is not the polar opposite of that of his Native American neighbors. In particular, he, Silko, and Ortiz all express outrage at the destruction of the natural environment. In her apocalyptic novel *Almanac of the Dead,* Silko, no doubt influenced by Abbey's similar fantasy, even envisions the annihilation of Glen Canyon Dam at the hands of - ecosaboteurs. Ortiz consistently rages against the desecrations perpetrated by the uranium industry, most notably in his "Fight Back, For the Sake of the Land, For the Sake of the People." And certainly uranium mining and the development of the atomic bomb function as the epitome of evil in Silko's *Ceremony.* Like many Navajo families, Luci Tapahonso's was involved in and suffered health effects from uranium mining, though protest against the industry is not a prominent feature of her work. Curiously, Abbey's protests against the atomic industry and nuclear bomb testing are relatively slight, especially notable given that, as pointed out by SueEllen Campbell in this volume, fallout from the Nevada test site was settling on Arches National Monument throughout Abbey's stay there in the mid-1950s. But in terms of speaking against ecological outrages, Silko, Ortiz, and Abbey share a similar voice.[2]

Nevertheless—with these caveats noted—key distinctions do exist between the way Abbey and his Native American neighbors perceive their relationships to their common terrain. Throughout their work, Silko, Ortiz, and Tapahonso portray the natural world as a domestic place, a home full of family and friends. As generalized by Gregory Cajete, from Santa Clara Pueblo, "American Indians symbolically recognized their relationship to plants, animals, stones, trees, mountains, rivers, lakes, streams, and a host of other living entities. Through seeking, making, sharing, and celebrating these natural relationships, they came to perceive themselves as living in a sea of relationships" (1994, 74). This philosophical position linking humans to nature is underscored by the fact that among the Laguna, for example, "kinship terms are extended to express not only social relationships between people but also ritual relationships between individuals and groups and various aspects of nature" (Eggan 1950, 262). Such extension of kinship to the natural world extends the domestic sphere outward from hearth to cosmos, or rather, perhaps, incorporates humans as heirs of a cosmic lineage. Silko elaborates on this: "Human identity is linked with all the elements of Creation through the clan: you might belong to the Sun Clan or the Lizard Clan or the Corn Clan"; and she defines "clan" in a way to suggest that such a relationship is rooted in a family's origin: "Clan—A Social unit composed of families sharing common ancestors who trace their lineage back to the Emergence where their ancestors allied themselves with certain plants or animals or elements" (1987, 84–85). In other words, for Silko, humans connect to nature through, rather than severed from, the umbilicus of family.

This attitude of relationship pervades the work of Southwest native writers. For example, in his poem "We Have Been Told Many Things but We Know This to Be True," Simon Ortiz invokes the idea of family to express his connection to the land: "The land. The People. / They are in relation to each other. / We are in a family with each other" (1992, 324). This familial bond is not just an abstract, idealistic claim but informs much of Ortiz's work. Most of Ortiz's poems about his interaction with nature in the Four Corners area include the presence of his children, such as the following excerpt from

"Four Poems for a Child Son," subtitled, "It Was the Third Day, July 12, 1971":

> Hitchhiking on the way to Colorado,
> I heard your voice, "Look, Dad . . ."
>   A hawk
> sweeping its wings
>   clear
> through the whole sky
>   the blue
>   the slow wind
> fresh with the smell of summer alfalfa
> at the foot of the Jemez Mountains.
>
> (Ortiz 1992, 46)

In this poem it is his son, Raho, who directs Ortiz's attention to the natural world.

Similarly, when recounting the birth of his daughter, Rainy Dawn, in "To Insure Survival," he relates her both to the Earth and to his ancestors' emergence from it:

> You come forth
> the color of a stone cliff
> at dawn,
> changing colors,
> blue to red
> to all the colors of the earth.
>
> (Ortiz 1994, 48)

Experiencing the nativity of his daughter, Simon Ortiz reestablishes his own physical and mythological bond to his natal terrain. For Abbey, the birth of his children is unrelated to how he chooses to portray his connection to nature, but Ortiz illustrates how the birth of his daughter vitally renews his own sense of connection to the land.

Like Ortiz, Silko and Tapahonso portray the Southwest as a habitat imbued with their families' presence. In *Storyteller,* Silko explains how

> On Sundays Grandpa Hank liked to go driving.
> Usually we went to Los Lunas

because Grandma Lillie had relatives there.
We took the old winding road that follows
the San José river until it meets the Rio Puerco.
Not far from the junction of the rivers
is a high prominent mesa of dark volcanic rock.
On one of these Sunday drives long ago
Grandpa told us two of his grand-uncles had died there
killed by the Apaches who stole their sheep.
I remember looking very hard out the window of the car
at the great dark mesa and the rolling plains below it.

(Silko 1981, 246)

This concept of the terrain as a place suffused with family stories is shared by Tapahonso. In a context similar to Silko's, she recalls a family trip to Arizona. As the car passed the base of a mesa near Shiprock, her cousin interrupted the children's play with the remark, " 'See those rocks at the bottom?' " The children, Tapahonso continues, recognizing this reference to terrain as the opening of a story, "stopped playing and moved around her to listen." Her cousin then relates a tale about the death of an infant girl many years before. The infant's family, traveling through the area, buried her at the base of the mesa beneath those rocks. Tapahonso concludes her tale with the observation that "this land that may seem arid and forlorn to the newcomer is full of stories which hold the spirits of the people, those who live here today and those who lived centuries and other worlds ago. The nondescript rocks are not that at all, but rather a lasting and loving tribute to the death of a baby and the continuing memory of her family" (1993, 5–6).

While Tapahonso identifies with the land through the historical tales, Abbey, a relative newcomer, prefers unstoried landscapes. The culmination of *Desert Solitaire* is Abbey's descent with Bob Waterman into the Maze, a remote Utah canyonscape he refers to as "terra incognita." This designation suggests a direct connection to early European explorers and their discovery of allegedly unexplored and unnamed terrain. At the adventure's outset Abbey remarks, hoping to be the original intruders into that terrain, that he and Waterman will be "the first so far as we know," to enter the Maze, "since," he must caution, "the Indians left seven centuries before—if they were here at all" (1971, 289).

He soon discovers to his disappointment, however, that those pesky Indians had indeed preceded him: "We decide it best to climb out of The Maze before dark and save further exploration for tomorrow. We go back to the pool and the base of the ridge. On the way Waterman points out to me the petroglyph of a snake which I had missed. The Indians had been here. But nobody else, so far as we can tell" (1971, 293). The "but nobody else" here is telling; nobody else, it seems, who really counts. This dismissal of the Indian occupation is underscored when, upon departing, Waterman writes triumphantly in a BLM logbook, "First descent into The Maze." Reading the entry, Abbey reminds himself that they "cannot be absolutely certain of this" (1971, 295), but the petroglyph they have just seen should have made them certain. Waterman's inscription in the BLM log serves to obscure in historical consciousness the Indian inscription of the snake petroglyph.

For Abbey the Southwest may be a place with a history, but it is a history of a different people, and a history thus unnecessary to be taken wholly into account. In order to valorize their own experience as discoverers of virginal territory, Abbey and Waterman must, like their exploring forefathers, minimize the significance of the Indian presence. For, in such a worldview, it is much more thrilling to pursue new territory than to habitually reenter the same old habitat. Familiarity, or familiality, does indeed breed contempt. Rather than becoming cognizant of the stories expressed by his terra incognita— stories encrypted in the snake petroglyph—Abbey, complicit with Waterman, seeks to mute the voices in the land around him.

Silko responds quite differently to the petroglyphs she encounters. For example, after visiting Slim Man Canyon on the Navajo Reservation, she writes the following poem:

Slim Man Canyon
                    early summer Navajo Nation, 1972 for John
700 years ago

            people were living here
            water was running gently
            and the sun was warm
            on pumpkin flowers.
It was 700 years ago
deep in this canyon
            with sandstone rising high above

The rock   the silence   tall sky and flowing water
                    sunshine through cottonwood leaves
                  the willow smell in the wind
                                          700 years.
The rhythm
                the horses feet   moving strong through
                                                white deep sand.
Where I come from is like this
          the warmth, the fragrance, the silence.
Blue sky and rainclouds in the distance
              we ride together
                            past cliffs with stories and songs
                            painted on rock.
                                          700 years ago.
                                        (Silko 1979, 208)

Even away from Laguna, Silko hears the petroglyphs speak to her, creating a domestic serenity where people live among pumpkin gardens and compose stories and songs upon the rocks. Rather than annoy her with their reminder that she is not the first to enter this canyon, the petroglyphs comfort her with that message; they place her as a native rather than as a visitor to canyon country.

In explaining his preference for the desert over other environments, Abbey proposes that, unlike other landscapes, "the desert says nothing. Completely passive, acted upon but never acting, the desert lies there like the bare skeleton of Being, spare, sparse, austere, utterly worthless, inviting not love but contemplation." And, he continues, "there is something about the desert that the human sensibility cannot assimilate or has not so far been able to assimilate. Perhaps that is why it has scarcely been approached in poetry or fiction, music or painting. . . . Even after years of intimate contact and search this quality of strangeness in the desert remains undiminished" (1971, 270, 272). Tapahonso's poem "The Motion of Songs Rising," however, suggests a different understanding of the desert.

The October night is warm and clear.
We are standing on a small hill and in all directions,
        around us, the flat land listens to the songs rising.

The Holy ones are here dancing.
The Yeis are here.

In the west, Shiprock looms above the desert.
Tsé bit'a'í, old bird-shaped rock. She watches us.
Tsé bit'a'í, our mother who brought the people here on her
    back.
Our refuge from the floods long ago. It was worlds and
    centuries ago, yet she remains here. Nihimá, our mother.

(Tapahonso 1993, 67)

This poem portrays not a passive, exotic desert world of undiminished strangeness, unassimilated to human consciousness, but an active land fully, reciprocally, and harmoniously integrated with Tapahonso's culture. Tapahonso's terrain listens, watches, and cares for the people. The poem reveals the degree to which the Navajo have become at home in this desert:

The Yeis are dancing again, each step, our own strong
bodies. They are dancing the same dance, thousands of
years old. They are here for us now, grateful for
another harvest and our own good health.
The roasted corn I had this morning was fresh,
cooked all night and taken out of the ground this
morning. It was steamed and browned just right.

They are dancing and in the motion of songs rising,
our breathing becomes the morning moonlit air.
The fires are burning below as always.
We are restored.
We are restored.

(Tapahonso 1993, 68)

In Tapahonso's Southwest, the land gives forth corn for the health of the people, and the people breathe forth the dawn air; the people and their land seamlessly assimilate.

For Abbey, wilderness is the most desirable of natural environments, but not so much because it constitutes a more or less intact ecosystem where nature's other creatures can live autonomous lives, but because it is a place where the bloody cord that binds him to society is most easily broken. Though Abbey provides various justifications for the preservation of wilderness, the one he most passionately advocates is that wilderness is necessary for individualistic freedom. This linking of ecologically healthy wilderness and personal freedom contradicts the conclusions of environmental historian Donald Worster, who finds that groups that have managed to successfully live in a place for extended periods of time and to minimize their destruction of the biota around them have had one dominant characteristic:

> They have made rules, and many of them, rules based on intimate local experience, to govern their behavior. They have not tried to "live free" of nature or of the group; nor have they resented restraints on individual initiative or left it to each individual to decide completely how to behave. On the contrary, they have accepted many kinds of limits on themselves and enforced them on one another. . . . having these rules and enforcing them vigorously seems to be a requirement for long-term ecological survival. (1995, 80–81)

Abbey, however, sees things differently. His opposition to the construction of Glen Canyon Dam and the formation of Lake Powell is primarily based on the fact that the free-flowing canyon river represents liberation, whereas the placid, impounded lake constitutes an environment under social control. He mocks the rules for Lake Powell: "PLAY SAFE, read the official signboards; SKI ONLY IN CLOCKWISE DIRECTION; LET'S ALL HAVE FUN TOGETHER! With regulations enforced by water cops in government uniforms" (1971, 174). For Abbey the great evil of Glen Canyon Dam is not so much that it has submerged a canyon as that it has constrained his freedom.

Prior to the dam's completion, however, cut loose on the Colorado River with his friend Newcomb to drift calmly through Glen Canyon, Abbey celebrates his yet remaining freedom. It is a freedom "to commit murder and get away with it scot-free," he declares, uncharitably eyeing his innocent friend (1971, 177). Newcomb is in no real danger, we presume, but the fact that Abbey's mind so quickly turns from celebrating his wilderness freedom to pondering a violation of his last remaining social bond is telling. In an essay titled "Freedom and Wilderness, Wilderness and Freedom" he argues for wilderness by proclaiming that "even the maddest murderer of the sweetest wife should get a chance for a run to the sanctuary of the hills" (1977a, 229). This ideal of wilderness as a sanctuary for the desperado, for the murderer of domestic sweetness, is a recurring theme in his defense of wilderness because Abbey's wilderness ideology is firmly rooted in the mythology of the frontier—of an individualistic anarchy and contempt for what are perceived to be artificial rules and a disdain for the presumed civilizing influence of women. As Ann Ronald has pointed out, Abbey's persona in *Desert Solitaire* is a direct descendant of Shane and Lassiter. Like them, "Ed bears no apparent responsibilities other than the ones in the continuous present of *Desert Solitaire*. He frets more about wildlife and tourists than he does about wife and family" (1982, 68). Likewise Jack Burns's reincarnation as "the Lone Ranger" in *The Monkey Wrench Gang* reinforces the connection of his protagonists and his autobiographical persona to the traditional Western heroes who roam a mythic landscape dispensing extrajudicial justice against the wicked.

Such a vision is, in large degree, an adolescent fantasy. This is not surprising given the way Abbey first encountered the desert Southwest. In a story he has retold many times, Abbey first saw the desert standing on the California side of the Colorado River in Needles as a seventeen-year-old hitchhiking for a ride: "Across the river waited a land that filled me with strange excitement: crags and pinnacles of naked rock, the dark cores of ancient volcanoes, a vast and silent emptiness smoldering with heat, color, and indecipherable significance, above which floated a small number of pure, hard-edged clouds. For the first time I felt I was getting close to the West of my deepest imaginings—the place where the tangible and the mythical become the same" (1977c, 5). Several days later, from the open door of a boxcar, he watched the bright northern New Mexico landscape slide by, with its "queer foreign shapes of mesa and butte," and responded to it as a space "full of a powerful, mysterious promise" (10–11). Abbey's later attraction to wilderness can be seen as a nostalgia not just for a landscape in more pristine condition, but for the irresponsible and irrepressible life of a seventeen-year-old hitchhiker.

This suggestion that Abbey maintained essentially adolescent ideas about the desert may seem harsh, but it is unwittingly reinforced by the claim of Dave Petersen, editor of *Confessions of a Barbarian*, selections from Abbey's journals:

> When you read twenty-eight years of journals of a writer, you would expect . . . the gradual progression or development of a

weltanschauung, a worldview, plus a writing style. With Edward
Abbey, it was full blown from the first page of the first journal. He
was writing as eloquently then, he was thinking the things, saying
the things then, that he was saying in the last journal entry before
he died. . . . His worldview and in a large part his artistic talent
were completely developed by the time he was age twenty-five.
(Petersen 1993)

Unlike Abbey's sense of wilderness as concomitant with freedom,
Silko's connection to the land, reinforcing Worster's observations, is
full of rules governing reciprocal obligation and mature responsibility.
This sort of relationship is as exquisitely developed in *Ceremony* as in
any other work of American literature. In *Ceremony,* Tayo's healing
comes about through his acceptance of intertwined familial, communal, natural, and supernatural responsibilities. During his discussion
with the medicine man, Betonie, Tayo, resisting the prescribed cure,

> wanted to yell at the medicine man, to yell the things the white
> doctors had yelled at him—that he had to think only of himself,
> and not about the others, that he would never get well as long as
> he used words like "we" and "us." But he had known the answer
> all along . . . medicine didn't work that way, because the world
> didn't work that way. His sickness was only part of something
> larger, and his cure would be found only in something great and
> inclusive of everything. (Silko 1977, 125–126)

Tayo's cure includes, for example, fulfilling his promise to his Uncle
Josiah to care for the lost cattle. And it is fulfillment of this responsibility, rather than escape from it, that leads him on his quests into the
natural world.

Tayo's activities in nurturing the Earth with the myth-woman
Ts'eh Montaño, whom he encounters while pursuing and later tend-
ing Josiah's cattle, provide evidence that his cure is well underway.
For example, while with her he gathers pollen for ritual uses: "He
found flowers that had no bees, and gathered yellow pollen gently
with a small blue feather from Josiah's pouch; he imitated the gentle-
ness of the bees as they brushed their sticky-haired feet and bellies
softly against the flowers" (1977, 220). Shortly thereafter he encounters a snake: "He knelt over the arching tracks the snake left in the
sand and filled the delicate imprints with yellow pollen. As far as he

could see in all directions, the world was alive. He could feel the motion pushing out of the damp earth into the sunshine—the yellow spotted snake the first to emerge, carrying this message on his back to the people" (1977, 221). The snake brings to him a message of spring, and he reciprocates by honoring the snake with sacred pollen. Tayo gains healing by accepting ritualized adult responsibility in his engagement with nature.

While with Ts'eh, Tayo learns about his natural environment and his proper respectful attitude toward all of its beings: "He went with her to learn about the roots and plants she had gathered. When she found a place she got comfortable, spreading her blue shawl on the ground after she had cleared the area of pebbles and little sticks and made sure no ants were disturbed" (1977, 224). Silko's attention to Ts'eh's care for not disturbing the ants contrasts with Abbey's attitude in a similar context in *Desert Solitaire*. Like Tayo, Abbey is engaged in learning the plants that grow in his vicinity. Returning to his trailer from this botanical excursion around Arches, Abbey relates how "On the way I pass a large anthill, the domed city of the harvester ants. Omnivorous red devils with a vicious bite, they have denuded the ground surrounding their hill, destroying everything green and living within a radius of ten feet. I cannot resist the impulse to shove my walking stick into the bowels of their hive and rowel things up. Don't actually care for ants. Neurotic little pismires" (1971, 30). Abbey sees the ants as vicious devils not so much because of their bite, or because they eat the surrounding vegetation, but because they are social insects, residents of a "domed city." Anthills, he has complained, remind him "of New Jersey. Of California. Of Phoenix and Tucson" (1984, 46). Silko's vision of harmonic engagement with nature, however, would never sanction such gratuitous destruction of other beings. In her description in *Ceremony* of a witch, presumably Emo, trouncing melons in a field, Silko emphasizes his evil by citing that, "He looked back, down the long row. Tiny black ants were scurrying over shattered melons; . . . He trampled the ants with his boots" (1977, 62).

For Abbey, the lure of the desert Southwest lies in its condition of absence; in its emptiness is its appeal. Scanning juniper and pinyon and prickly-pear covered mesas stretching to the horizon across the Colorado Plateau, Abbey revels in the fact that "there was nothing out there. Nothing at all. Nothing but the desert. Nothing but the silent world" (1977b, 22). Silko, Ortiz, or Tapahonso, however, someone more at home in this terrain, would have seen an entirely different view: the plenitude of the pinyon nuts, a sacred hill or spring told about in old stories, the slope where a relative shot a particularly fat antelope. In short, a person at home would have seen not an empty landscape but a web of complex and historical intimacy, the sort of place that Silko recollects venturing forth into as a young girl: "I was never afraid. . . . I carried with me the feeling I'd acquired from listening to the old stories, that the land all around me was teeming with creatures that were related to human beings and to me. The stories had also left me with a feeling of familiarity and warmth for the mesas and hills and boulders where the incidents or actions in the stories had taken place" (in Turner 1989, 330–31). For Silko, stories evoke and are evoked by the terrain; tales and land are mutually arising and enriching, comforting in the familiarity their synergism generates. Such a perspective is apparent in *Ceremony,* as when Tayo is at Dripping Springs watching dragonflies and suddenly recognizes that "there were stories about the dragonflies too. He turned. Everywhere he looked, he saw a world made of stories, the long ago, time immemorial stories, as old Grandma called them" (1977, 95). An empty space becomes a domestic place through the intercession of stories. It is precisely in the storied-ness of this world that its hominess consists.

Abbey's emphasis on individualistic freedom pursued in an empty desert space might even be considered part of the witchery Tayo confronts in *Ceremony.* Tayo's cure comes from fulfilling his domestic responsibilities, attuning himself to the stories in the landscape, and establishing a nurturing relationship with the natural world. In spite of his frequent invocations of "home," however, Abbey persists in seeing nature in general, and wilderness in particular, as a place of exile, and the degree to which he does so suggests the degree to which he remains out of tune with the resonances of his terrain. Abbey's philosophy leads him to decry the destruction of his wilderness and the freedom it represents even as he unwittingly abets that destruction by espousing an anarchic individualism that makes him deaf to the stories and songs imbedded in the landscape and to the ecologically responsible communalism such stories celebrate.

Abbey's vision of the Southwest, in spite of an environmentalist inflection, remains firmly configured by the old paradigm of his ethnic Anglo-American experience: The West is, or at least should be, a place of escape—a place where a man can ride away, alone, into the sunset. But as Gregory Cajete suggests, "Indian people believed they had responsibilities to the land and all living things. These responsibilities were similar to those they had to each other" (1994, 83).

Abbey's journal for July 14, 1965—Moab, Utah: "Bolted. Left wife and kids and job for exile in the desert" (1994, 194).

Notes

1. This antidomestic attitude can also be fruitfully considered in light of what Barbara Ehrenreich has called "a male revolt . . . against the breadwinner ethic," which developed in the early 1950s (1983, 13). This revolt can most clearly be seen in the Beat movement, to which Abbey was attracted, but never a part: "In the Beat," according to Ehrenreich, "two strands of male protest— one directed against the white-collar work world and the other against the sub- urbanized family life that work was supposed to support—come together into the first all-out critique of American consumer culture" (52). In January 1958, while living in Half Moon Bay, California, Abbey praised Ginsberg's *Howl*—the anthem of the Beat movement— as "the best poem written in America by an American since—well, since Pearl Harbor. (So far as I know.) Yes, a beautifully shaggy little book. Wild and shaggy, and also highly accurate: 'Moloch whose heart is a cannibal dynamo,' etc. Very touching. My wife hates it, of course" (1994, 146).

2. And it is useful to remind ourselves that all *Homo sapiens,* regardless of our cultural differences, share many characteristics—though usually taken for granted—in our relationships with nature. Our common biology constrains the range of cultural variables. For example, we all see the world from a similar height through binocular vision and within the same narrow span of the elec- tromagnetic spectrum. Likewise, biology dictates nutritional needs and what foods we are capable of eating; culture then prescribes acceptable diets within that range of possibilities. Contrasting our species' relationship with nature with the relationship enacted by other species suggests that what we might see as major differences between cultures are relatively minor compared with our interspecies differences.

Works Cited

Abbey, Edward. [1968] 1971. *Desert Solitaire: A Season in the Wilderness.* Reprint, New York: Ballantine.
———. 1973. "Appalachian Pictures." In *Appalachian Wilderness: The Great Smoky Mountains.* Ed. Eliot Porter. New York: Ballantine.
———. 1977a. "Freedom and Wilderness, Wilderness and Freedom." In *The Journey Home.*
———. 1977b. "The Great American Desert." In *The Journey Home.*
———. 1977c. "Hallelujah on the Bum." In *The Journey Home.*
———. 1977d. *The Journey Home: Some Words in Defense of the American Desert.* New York: E. P. Dutton.
———. 1984. "A Walk in the Desert Hills." In *Beyond the Wall: Essays from the Outside.* New York: Holt, Rinehart and Winston.

———. 1994. *Confessions of a Barbarian: Selections from the Journals of Edward Abbey, 1951–1989.* Ed. David Petersen. Boston: Little, Brown and Co.

Cajete, Gregory. 1994. *Look to the Mountain: An Ecology of Indigenous Education.* Durango, Colo.: Kivakí Press.

Campbell, SueEllen. 1995. "Magpie." Keynote address presented at the first biennial conference of the Association for the Study of Literature and the Environment, Fort Collins, Colorado, 9–11 June. Also published as part of this volume.

Edward Abbey: A Voice in the Wilderness. 1993. Produced and directed by Eric Temple. Eric Temple Productions. Videocassette, 60 min.

Eggan, Fred. 1950. *Social Organization of the Western Pueblos.* Chicago: University of Chicago Press.

Ehrenreich, Barbara. 1983. *The Hearts of Men: American Dreams and the Flight from Commitment.* New York: Doubleday.

Krupat, Arnold. 1992. *Ethnocriticism: Ethnography, History, Literature.* Berkeley: University of California Press.

Nabhan, Gary Paul. 1995. "Cultural Parallax in Viewing North American Habitats." In *Reinventing Nature? Responses to Postmodern Deconstruction,* ed. Michael E. Soulé and Gary Lease. Washington, D.C.: Island Press.

Ortiz, Simon. 1992. *Woven Stone.* Tucson: University of Arizona Press.

Petersen, David. 1994. Introduction to *Confessions of a Barbarian,* by Edward Abbey. Boston: Little, Brown and Co.

Ronald, Ann. 1982. *The New West of Edward Abbey.* Albuquerque: University of New Mexico Press.

Silko, Leslie Marmon. 1977. *Ceremony.* New York: Viking Penguin.

———. 1979. "Slim Man Canyon." In *The Remembered Earth: An Anthology of Contemporary Native American Literature,* ed. Geary Hobson. Albuquerque: University of New Mexico Press.

———. 1981. *Storyteller.* New York: Seaver Books.

———. 1987. "Landscape, History, and the Pueblo Imagination." In *On Nature: Nature, Landscape, and Natural History,* ed. Daniel Halpern, 83–94. San Francisco: North Point Press.

Slovic, Scott. 1992. *Seeking Awareness in American Nature Writing: Henry Thoreau, Annie Dillard, Edward Abbey, Wendell Berry, Barry Lopez.* Salt Lake City: University of Utah Press.

Snyder, Gary. 1990. "The Place, the Region, and the Commons." In *The Practice of the Wild.* San Francisco: North Point Press.

Tapahonso, Luci. 1993. *Sáanii Dahataal: The Women are Singing.* Tucson: University of Arizona Press.

Turner, Frederick. 1989. *Spirit of Place: The Making of an American Literary Landscape.* San Francisco: Sierra Club Books.

Worster, Donald. 1995. "Nature and the Disorder of History." In *Reinventing Nature? Responses to Postmodern Deconstruction,* ed. Michael E. Soulé and Gary Lease. Washington, D.C.: Island Press.

Rage against the Machine

Edward Abbey and Neo-Luddite Thought

PAUL

LINDHOLDT

Thermite, dynamite, sugar in the gas tank. Falling billboards, falling in
flames. D.A.C.—direct action committee. What else can we do?
—Abbey, *Confessions of a Barbarian*

Abbey's selected journals, entitled *Confessions of a Barbarian*
and made available in 1994, furnish new fodder for readers
interested in studying the biographical bases for his fiction, his essays,
and his role as a leader of those outlaw activists known as members of
the radical environmental movement. It is a commonplace of Abbey
scholarship that *The Monkey Wrench Gang* generated and best articulated the goals of Earth First! The book appeared in 1975, Earth
First! began in 1980, and both express an uncompromising agenda
for public lands in the American West. From the book and its sequel,
Hayduke Lives! (1990), the editors of the *Earth First! Journal* borrowed names and slogans for use on bumper stickers and T-shirts;
Abbey spoke at Earth First! rallies, endorsed the group, and wore its
clothing in photos. Recent books, discussed below, explore the
movement and its debt to Abbey, but a more compelling set of connections between Abbey's writings and radical environmentalism remains unexplored: the connections to the philosophies of the
neo-Luddites. Adherents to the belief that technology has earned
and deserves our distrust and fear, neo-Luddites and their various
writings provide context for the biographical approach to Abbey's
fiction and essays.

A hermeneutics of suspicion has dominated Abbey criticism. Every political statement the author made seems subject to repudiation. Even though Abbey praised "the Socialist heritage bequeathed me by my father" (1994, 198), Edward S. Twining (1978) argued that he was a "radical conservative." Three years later, Jerry A. Herndon (1981) indulged in an oxymoron, "moderate extremism," to correct Abbey's self-conception. Despite Abbey's endorsing Earth First! and authoring the foreword to Dave Foreman's *Ecodefense* (1987), Ann Ronald (1982) and Scott Slovic (1992) have contended that Abbey is not promoting illegal action. And in the face of evidence that Abbey and his environmental followers have effectively shifted public opinion in favor of the environment, Daniel G. Payne has charged that "Abbey's impact was negligible—perhaps even, as some have suggested, counterproductive" (1995, 205).

For his part, Abbey took an exceedingly dim view of literary criticism. In 1953, before he got into print, he wrote, "Contemporary literary critics have donned the vestments of high priests and presume to instruct the writer not only in literary method but in what he shall and shall not write about, and in what he shall think about what he writes and does not write" (1994, 109). In this chapter, rather than regard Abbey and his politics with suspicion, I take him at his word, inconsistencies and all, and consider how the neo-Luddite scholarship provides a critical approach that may offer fresh perspectives on this key element of his work. In my unusual path of acquiescence, I join Wendell Berry, who wrote, "And so his defenders, it seems to me, are obliged to take him seriously, to assume that he generally means what he says, and, instead of apologizing for him, to acknowledge that he is not always right or always fair" (1985, 14).

The writing for which Abbey is most well known and admired outside academics is characterized by being stoutly opposed to technology. *The Monkey Wrench Gang* and *Hayduke Lives!* draw bull's-eyes upon the machine culture that is devastating the outdoors Abbey loved so much. Technology, not Bishop Love, is the antagonist of these books and others. The rollicking reprisals against Love—a buffoon whose ruinous machines get wrecked—comically relieve the mood and vary the pace in books whose characters are otherwise grave in opposition to the ruin of their beloved West. For precision's sake, I argue that technocracy, not technology, was the chief object of Abbey's distrust. No simple-minded vandal, he was concerned with *the moral imbalances created when society is managed chiefly by technical specialists.*[1] In the essay "A Writer's Credo," from *One Life at a Time, Please,* Abbey disclosed one of his chief purposes: "To oppose, resist, and sabotage the contemporary drift toward a global technocratic police state, whatever its ideological coloration" (1988b, 177–78), thus equating technocracy and totalitarianism. Nor was Abbey's antipathy to technocracy confined to his rhetoric and artifice. From his earliest journal entries until his last book, *Hayduke Lives!* (1990), he expressed a remarkably consistent desire to challenge and act against the powers of technical control. Writing books and essays, carping in print, is never enough, for "Sentiment without action is the ruin of the soul" (1984, xvi). Abbey believed that our convictions must be not only actively realized, by destructive force if necessary, but that attacking the tools of technocracy constitutes a viable middle ground between surrendering to its proponents on the one hand and practicing a violent anarchy on the other.

Skepticism regarding technology has come into its own in recent decades. Before Abbey began to write, only historian Lewis Mumford had published sustained critiques of technological processes ("technics," he called them), beginning in the 1930s and culminating with the monumental two-volume *The Myth of the Machine* (1967, 1970), the first sentence of whose prologue expresses misgivings about technology in the environment. Developing his unique theory of ecodefense, Abbey mated trepidation about technology and the environment with advanced knowledge of natural history and anarchy.[2] In his essays he invoked Mumford approvingly and called *The Monkey Wrench Gang* "Four little humans against the glittering Tower of the Power Complex, Mega-Machine. Should dedicate it to Lewis Mumford. He'd disown it. Not his type" (1994, 237). Forgoing a dedication to Mumford, then, Abbey dedicated his novel instead to the apocryphal leader of the Luddites, Ned Ludd. The actual quotation that comprises the dedication—from the earliest *Oxford English Dictionary* (OED) citation of "Luddite" (1847)—evidently was too lengthy and dated for Abbey's purposes, and so he supplanted it with an adapted or composite quote from a spurious dictionary. Not the OED but the *Oxford Universal Dictionary* is credited slyly with the definition of Ned Ludd: a "lunatic living about 1779, who in a fit of rage smashed up two frames belonging to a Leicestershire 'stockinger' " (1975, v).

Abbey's distrust of technocracy developed early in life. Most readers discover his distrust for themselves, but support from his journals can add biographical credibility to the pronouncements of the novels and the essays. Abbey's journals, spanning thirty-eight years, seem to have been written for his eyes only, and in them it seems he was less apt to indulge in the contrarian aesthetics that make his work a problem for some audiences. Biographer James Bishop, Jr., agrees with Wendell Berry that Abbey was ultimately an autobiographer, that his life and writing mesh intimately, and that he was most at home when "dismantling the instruments terrorizing nature through sabotage—whether allegorical, metaphorical, rhetorical, or real sabotage" (1994, 125). Earth First! cofounder Dave Foreman offers another angle of understanding. Like the Mudhead Kachinas of the Zunis, among whom Foreman once lived, Abbey relished irreverence: "While the most sacred rituals were being performed, the Mudheads were cutting up, making fun of everyone—as if a nun were mooning the faithful while the Pope gave his Easter blessing." Not only was Abbey accordingly "the Mudhead Kachina of the conservation movement," in Foreman's view (1991, 174), but so he was also as an artist. The hermeneutics of suspicion that color so much of Abbey scholarship are reactionary, for Abbey excoriated academic intellectualism as mercilessly as any other sacred cow.

The high seriousness of his counterparts in American environmental literature—Carson, Dillard, Lopez, Silko, for example—confirm him as Mudhead Kachina and make it hard to take him any other way. As Lawrence Buell understated it, Abbey preached against trashing the planet, "but with a raffish panache that unsolemnizes his jeremiads" (1995, 300). Abbey, we might say, interrupted his own extended lamentations and complaints with the verbal equivalent of belches, farts, and obscene jests. Not boorishness but self-effacement could have prompted his lapses away from polite taste, as corroborated by the many accounts of his shy and quiet personal demeanor. His contradictions and crankiness, political incorrectness, obscenities, and bad jokes grew out of his steady desire to "unsolemnize his jeremiads," to deconstruct and undercut his own moral thunder, the seriousness of his own environmental alarums. And for good reason. Cultural conventions are constantly conditioning Americans to expect nonstop economic growth, boundless technological expansion, and the degradation of the natural environment; sabotaging our literary expectations, as Abbey did, accordingly may force us, for a moment, to rethink the uses we make of the natural world.

Distrust of technology is rife in Abbey's essays and novels but perhaps most tellingly expressed in the journals. One can almost hear the sound of his teeth grinding between the lines when he wrote to himself in 1955, "Tolstoy's prophesy has been fulfilled: The advance of scientific technology has aided more the tyrant than the free man. Example: Every man can own and operate a rifle, but tanks and planes and atom bombs are and must be the property of the State" (1994, 126). Following Tolstoy, Abbey equated despotic rule with the ability to command technology, a fear that forms the thinking of neo-Luddites, who believe the widespread adoption of a technology facilitates the centralization of power.[3]

Almost certainly Abbey would have disagreed with Karl Marx, who foresaw technology as a viable means of liberating labor from the shackles of capital.[4] Marx accordingly discredited the Luddites of early industrial England for failing at first "to transfer their attacks from the material instruments of production to the form of society which utilizes those instruments" (1977, 554). As if responding to Marx, Abbey asserted in his journal in 1956, "Not socialism, not capitalism is the enemy but—industry and technology carried to excess, to and beyond the point of madness" (1994, 139). The passage suggests that technocracy can develop, madly and excessively, apart from all political persuasions. Seven years later, twelve years before its actual publication in 1975, he projected a book to be called "*The Wooden Shoe Gang* (or) *The Monkey Wrench Mob* (a novel about the 'Wilderness Avenger' and his desperate band; sabotage and laughter and wild wild fun)" (185). Abbey lived in the tension between capitulation to technocracy on the one hand, and anarchy on the other. If as a citizen he was helpless before the technological juggernaut, at least as an artist he could proffer some vicarious satisfaction.

Nor were Abbey's run-ins with technocracy exclusively vicarious. Most readers would agree that "If there was one transforming event in Abbey's life . . . it was the construction of Glen Canyon Dam" (Bishop 1994, 122). Much has been written about this debacle that drowned what many people believed to be the world's most beautiful canyon and created a lake 120 miles long. It has been the subject of books, films, and essays too numerous to name, and Abbey returned to it again and again in his work. But medical technology rankled him just as much. In a journal entry for 1957 he raved against "The Mad Scientist—once a baroque villain, now a dominant, honored and commonplace figure in modern life" (1994, 139). In ways he never shared publicly, this figure gained an upper hand when Abbey watched the father of his second wife, Rita, die slowly in a New Jersey hospital in 1962: "It's like some kind of nightmarish experiment: the mad scientist, once a creature of fiction, now lives everywhere, and dominates our lives" (175). Prosthetics, drugs, tubes, tents, and tools—the applied sciences run amok—robbed the father of dignity and compounded Abbey's recollection of the grueling knee surgery he himself underwent in 1960, a memory to which twelve published journal pages are devoted. When his third wife, Judy, died of leukemia in 1970, the drama was reenacted and his technophobic sentiments confirmed by "the repulsive degradations of the hospital routine" he witnessed again (225). Violent death in wilderness solitude, he admitted, he found preferable to "the ultimate horror: death in a hospital bed, surrounded by the engines of medical technology and technicians making notes" (217). A common element in these garish scenarios is the mute and dehumanized attendants dedicated to effecting technical ends. In his own death he would not capitulate, however. Instead he died at home, as he intended, and was buried in the desert by friends.

Abbey's journal likewise offers glimpses of the biographical bases for his most germane and famous novel, *The Monkey Wrench Gang* (1975). The influence of this book on the neo-Luddite subculture may be difficult to fully appreciate, but it can be expressed in part by noting the way the title has been commonized—as a verb, "to monkeywrench," and as a noun, "monkeywrenching"—in books by Foreman (1991), Manes (1990), and Scarce (1990). A telling journal entry from 1966 has Abbey resolving "to raze more billboards" (1994, 209), that activity associated most closely with Doc Sarvis of the novel, who is first seen with an "empty gas can banging on his insouciant shanks" as he torches those highway eyesores (1975, 17). Abbey's confessing to razing billboards suggests that he anticipated no scrutiny of his journal, no prying into his private life. This confession likewise strengthens the evidence that he acted out the capers of his characters before he committed them to print. Wendell Berry's assertion that Abbey was an autobiographer, not an environmentalist (1985, 12), gains support in the posthumous film *Edward Abbey: A Voice in the Wilderness* (1993), in which Abbey's friends Charles Bowden and Jack Loeffler testify to his euphemistic "field research" for the book, a point Loeffler (1993) has developed in print and that Abbey's friend William Eastlake also confirmed (1985, 20).

There is, finally, the journal entry that serves as this chapter's epigraph: "Thermite, dynamite, sugar in the gas tank. Falling billboards, falling in flames. D.A.C.—direct action committee. What else can we do?" (1994, 188). Out of context the passage has a lyric rhythm and tone and could serve as credo for his radical followers, but in context it is clouded by the darkest despair. Writing in 1964 from Hoboken, New Jersey, where he had gone to be with Rita to try to patch up their ailing marriage, he was homesick for the desert Southwest, doubtful that the domesticity would persist, drawn by "the sweet unbelievably lovely girls" around him, fretful about his lack of money. Outside of a year in Scotland on a Fulbright fellowship in 1951, that was the only time after 1947 that he would live away from the Southwest. A thrall to forces beyond his control—a bad marriage, love of a distant land, raging libido, economic straits—he was artistically thinking in imagery. The imagery of the passage suggests he wanted to sabotage those frustrating circumstances of his life to bring his despair to a decisive if irrational end. Eight months after writing this telling passage, he would flee New Jersey and return to the Southwest, to Utah, confessing in his journal, "Bolted. Left wife and kids and job for exile in the desert" (194). Similarly displacing his anxieties, Henry Lightcap opens the autobiographical novel *The Fool's Progress* (1988a) by taking his .357 Magnum pistol and shooting his refrigerator, domestic emblem of the failed relationship with his partner Elaine.

History has been unkind to the Luddites. Those who wrecked power looms in the English lace and textile industry between 1811 and 1816 are spoken of today as simpletons and reactionaries instead of as skilled laborers bent on protecting their trade, families, livelihoods, and communities. One reason may be the Marxist disposition to defend machinery as a way to liberate workers. "Luddite" itself, from the uprising's leader, Ned Ludd, is used mostly today as a term of derision or dismissal. And yet these revolutionaries of the English Midlands were effectual enough to necessitate the assembling of some 14,000 troops to quell them (Sale 1995). Efforts to resist technology today, even to "unplug" from it, are considered foolish, vain, futile. The alleged Unabomber, Ted Kaczynski, is a murderous Luddite in the media's eyes.

Such views ignore the strain of thoughtful skepticism, known generally as neo-Luddism, that has coalesced since psychologist Chellis Glendinning issued her "Notes toward a Neo-Luddite Manifesto" (1990a), an article that grew out of her book *When Technology Wounds,* a study of "the increasing threat modern technologies pose to our health and to the survival of the earth" (1990b, iv). Com-

puters, TVs, microwaves; pesticides, fertilizers, preservatives; nuclear
power, internal combustion, electromagnetic radiation—such technical innovations and the imbalances that accompany them inspire neo-
Luddite thought. Abbey himself eschewed television and computers;
he wrote jeremiads against overreliance on chemical agriculture and
cars; his antipathy to the progress of technocracy is readily documented. The neo-Luddites who follow in Abbey's wake deserve to be
heard out, taken seriously, and assumed to mean what they say, not
only for the light that their ideas shed upon his literary works and
days. All the elements of a cultural and literary criticism are inherent
in their writings, which need only to be sifted and distilled.

A foundational belief, best expressed by Glendinning in her manifesto, is that "All technologies are political" (1990a, 51). They are
never neutral tools. Recognizing this fact, Abbey invented in *Hayduke
Lives!* the outsized and outlandish walking excavator GOLIATH, which
is all political. Weighing 27 million pounds, wearing "130-foot
shoes" (1990, 62), the machine is not built on anything approaching
human scale. Parodically, however, it is personified. It levels desert
terrain, devastates life, doing the will of boosters like Bishop Love
who promote the mining industry and tourist trade. This political
agenda is most evident in the chapter "Seldom's Nightmare," in
which the machine pursues Seldom Seen Smith and plays promo-
tional voice tapes that praise how manufacturer "Bucyrus-Erie keeps
pace with our world's most urgent requirements" (64). The machine
has been consciously structured—like all technologies, in the views of
neo-Luddites—to offer its makers "a surefire method of expanding
their markets and controlling social and political thought," as Glendinning observed in her manifesto (1990a, 51). In a glaring satire of
multinational corporations and their neocolonial patterns of trade
that technology facilitates, the machine mistakenly mixes up its voice
tapes and begins to play an in-store ad for a K-Mart "patio dinette
set" that has been built, presumably, from the raw materials dragged
out of Earth by the machine itself (Abbey 1990, 63). In another book
and context, Abbey wrote, "Such is the nature and structure of the industrial megamachine (in Lewis Mumford's term), which is now attacking the American wilderness" (1988, 30).

This leads to a second major tenet of neo-Luddism. In the words
of critic Herbert Read in 1955, "Only a person serving an apprenticeship to nature can be trusted with machines" (qtd. in Sale 1995,
265). While the influence of technology on industrialized people may

be an open question, the effects of technoindustrial processes on nature are staggering, as Abbey so well knew. "We live in a time," he wrote, "when technology and technologists seem determined to make the earth unfit to live upon" (1979, 123). In the technocratic worldview, by and large, nature is at best a "resource" and at worst inferior, lifeless, inert. Not to Abbey, however. In an overlooked dimension of his environmental advocacy, he asserts repeatedly that all of nature is conscious, aware of sense impressions. Aspen trees are "*beings,* alive, sentient, transpiring" (1977, 208). He grieves junipers bulldozed for a new roadway in *The Monkey Wrench Gang* and mounts a brief sermon: "No one knows precisely how sentient is a pinyon pine, for example, or to what degree such woody organisms can feel pain or fear, and in any case the road builders had more important things to worry about, but this much is clearly established as a scientific fact: a living tree, once uprooted, takes many days to wholly die" (1975, 76).

Another overlooked element of Abbey's neo-Luddism is his support of animal rights. In a passage that should be quoted at length to be appreciated, he pleads for laboratory animals and against their "deliberate torture," which he finds "Not merely comparable but analogous," causally connected, to political despotism and tyranny. Like the eco-feminists, he concludes resolutely, "Contempt for animal life leads to contempt for human life" (1988, 170–71). Not only does technology empower us to vanquish nature, but it physically removes us from our own industrial consequences. Seated atop a Cat D8, a dragline, or a corporate skyscraper, the technocrat never witnesses what he has wrought. On the ground, however, the impacts are hard to overlook. "I have seen what men and heavy equipment can do to even the most angular and singular of earthly landscapes," Abbey wrote (1984, 55). He had served his apprenticeship to nature while serving as ranger for the National Park Service and the Forest Service.

A third major principle of neo-Luddite thought concerns the effects of corporate technology on third-world people. Borrowing from Mumford, Mander discusses "the corporation as a kind of machine, more persevering than the human actors within it, that operates by its own rules" (1991, 287). By the rules of that machine, a human being is little more impediment than an animal, stone, or tree. As Mander illustrates, the management of native villages by unsolicited technocratic powers has thoroughly unraveled many traditional cultures throughout the Americas. Abbey similarly lamented the economic determinism impacting Pueblo Indians whose agrarian economy has served them so well for so long. "When the children and grand-children of corn farmers, deer hunters, and pastoralists study auto mechanics and computer programming, it seems unlikely that the roots and essence of an earth-based culture can survive" (1988, 155). Mander details how introductions of technology-for-profit have prescribed social engineering, harmed dietary intake, altered community relations, implemented cash economies, and despoiled or stolen the farmlands of indigenous people. In his account of a trip to Alaska, among natives who used to clean infants with their tongues and fingers, Abbey wryly noted the sudden proliferation of disposable plastic diapers: "Old ways die easily—they tumble over themselves in a rush to die—when confronted by the frills of high-tech civilization" (1984, 180). Resistance seems futile.

A fourth element of neo-Luddite philosophy spells out the necessity of "resistance." This element, according to Kirkpatrick Sale, must be "based on some grasp of moral principles and rooted in some sense of moral revulsion" (1995, 269)—which is to say, violence against life cannot be tolerated. Abbey's entire canon and his personal philosophy corroborate this view; nonviolent resistance is at the center of all he advocated. He made a distinction clearly between sabotage (damage to machines) and violence (harm to living things). "Terrorism" is defined as an act that puts life in jeopardy, a violation of the Monkey Wrench Gang's first rule: no one gets hurt. The English Luddites violated this principle when they assassinated manufacturer William Horsfall (Sale 1995, 145–47), an act that brought the full force of the law upon their heads.

Some Abbey critics allege that the shooting death of the security guard at the conclusion of *Hayduke Lives!* (1990) represents a violation of the gang's code of ethics, too. But several extenuating circumstances moderate that harsh judgment. First, the character who pulled the trigger, Jack Burns, is not a member of the gang and had not learned about or committed to its rules; he is a throwback to Abbey's earlier novels and to the Wild West code that licensed bloodshed. Second, the stakes had changed greatly between the publication of the first book in 1975 and its sequel fifteen years later; forces of technocracy, devastating the West at rapid pace, had reached fantastic proportions, as exemplified by the futuristic GOLIATH dragline, thus mandating the tactics of full-blown revolutionary violence. The gang's enemies at the conclusion of the first novel, remember, were willing to blow Hayduke to bits. By neo-Luddite lights, however, *Hayduke Lives!* falls outside the pale of acceptability, just as the terrorist acts of the Unabomber do.

A fifth and resounding parallel between neo-Luddite philosophy and Abbey's work includes, again in Sale's words, a belief that "the edifice of industrial civilization . . . seems certain to crumble of its own accumulated excesses and instabilities" (1995, 278). The attentive reader need not look far to find, either in Abbey's fiction or nonfiction, cataclysmic prognostications. The premise of the entire novel *Good News* (1980) is that the system has crashed; displaced urbanites are waging war upon rural people and economies. In Sale's elaboration, civilization's "sustained assault on its environment" always has resulted historically "in rebellion, warfare, and dissolution" (1995, 278). In the words of Dave Foreman, Abbey's radical environmentalist disciple, "Modern society is a driverless hot rod without brakes, going ninety miles an hour down a dead-end street with a brick wall at the end" (1991, 45). In the words of Abbey himself, "I predict that the military-industrial state will disappear from the surface of the earth within a century" (1988b, 28).

These writers all envision a new society emerging from the collapse of technocracy. For Abbey, this new society will take the pastoral shape of "scattered human populations modest in number that live by fishing, hunting, food-gathering, small-scale ranching and farming" (1988b, 28). For Foreman, "Bioregionalism is what is on the other side of that wall" (1991, 45). Sale, who like Abbey and Berry eschews computers, sees one of the neo-Luddites' tasks today as imagining the shape of "alternative societies" (1995, 278) that will resolve, unlike their ancestors, "to fashion their technologies with the restraints and obligations of nature intertwined" (279). The cataclysmic scenarios of the neo-Luddites share a vision of the future, arising dialectically from technocratic excesses and the ensuing cataclysm, that necessitates learning new ways to love nature and incorporate it meaningfully into society.

Although Abbey was a neo-Luddite in thought and deed and artifice, he was also opposed to categorizations and almost certainly would have resisted such comparisons as these. He was an individual. To pigeonhole him is to take away that individuality. Surely his militancy would alienate some of the growing tribe of neo-Luddites, which includes Amish and Quakers, antiwar activists, New Age visionaries, and more. His views on guns and immigration and feminism would alienate others among their kindred. Still, it remains worth considering how much Abbey contributed—artistically, polemically—to the growing philosophy of neo-Luddism. One great contribution of his writing certainly is to have given tongue to notions that otherwise would have remained unarticulated—often thought but rarely expressed in public—like the writing on the wall of the cafe toilet stall that Henry Lightcap visits in the autobiographical novel *The Fool's Progress,* a wall scrawled with the sentiments of the discontented "*vox populi clamantis in deserto*" (1988a, 136).

Notes

1. My working definition of technocracy. Offering an example of "how wolf technocracy can run amok," author Rick Bass, in *The Ninemile Wolves,* criticizes radio collars attached to endangered species in the wild, which can taint the experiences of those animals. "Just behind the collar are trappers, helicopters, computers—*knowledge,* instead of mystery" (1992, 92).

2. Abbey's 1959 M.A. thesis in philosophy at the University of New Mexico, entitled "Anarchism and the Morality of Violence," focused on the anarchists Proudhon, Sorel, Godwin, Bakunin, and Kropotkin (Loeffler 1993).

3. Compare Jerry Mander, "Computer technology has already produced an unprecedented degree of military centralization" (1991, 69).

4. Abbey had some basis for judging production. He was employed both as a county welfare office caseworker and as a technical writer for General Electric, the latter job the subject of humorously ironic digressions in essays in *The Journey Home* (1977, 99–100) and *Beyond the Wall* (1984, 182–83). In the latter the employer's name gets changed unaccountably to "Western Electric."

Works Cited

Abbey, Edward. 1975. *The Monkey Wrench Gang.* New York: Lippincott.

———. 1977. *The Journey Home: Some Words in Defense of the American West.* New York: Dutton.

———. 1980. *Good News.* New York: Dutton.

———. 1984. *Beyond the Wall: Essays from the Outside.* New York: Holt, Rinehart and Winston.

———. 1988a. *The Fool's Progress.* New York: Henry Holt.

———. 1988b. *One Life at a Time, Please.* New York: Henry Holt.

———. 1990. *Hayduke Lives!* Boston: Little, Brown and Co.

———. [1979] 1991. *Abbey's Road.* Reprint, New York: Plume.

———. 1994. *Confessions of a Barbarian: Selections from the Journals of Edward Abbey, 1951–1989.* Ed. David Petersen. Boston: Little, Brown and Co.

Bass, Rick. 1992. *The Ninemile Wolves.* New York: Ballantine.

Berry, Wendell. 1985. "A Few Words in Favor of Edward Abbey." In Hepworth and McNamee.

Bishop, James, Jr. 1994. *Epitaph for a Desert Anarchist: The Life and Legacy of Edward Abbey.* New York: Atheneum.

Buell, Lawrence. 1995. *The Environmental Imagination: Thoreau, Nature Writing, and the Formation of American Culture.* Cambridge, Mass.: Harvard University Press.

Eastlake, William. 1985. "A Note on Ed Abbey." In Hepworth and McNamee.

Edward Abbey: A Voice in the Wilderness. 1993. Dir. Eric Temple. Temple Productions. Videocassette, 60 min.

Foreman, Dave. 1991. *Confessions of an Eco-Warrior.* New York: Crown.

Foreman, Dave, and Bill Haywood. 1987. 2d ed. *Ecodefense: A Field Guide to Monkeywrenching.* Tucson, Ariz.: Ned Ludd.

Glendinning, Chellis. 1990a. "Notes toward a Neo-Luddite Manifesto." *Utne Reader* (Mar./Apr.): 50–51.

———. 1990b. *When Technology Wounds: The Human Consequences of Progress.* New York: William Morrow.

Hepworth, James, and Gregory McNamee, eds. 1985. *Resist Much, Obey Little: Some Notes on Edward Abbey.* Salt Lake City: Dream Garden.

Herndon, Jerry A. 1981. " 'Moderate Extremism': Edward Abbey and 'The Moon-Eyed Horse.' " *Western American Literature* 16 (2): 97–103.

Loeffler, Jack. 1993. "Edward Abbey, Anarchism, and the Environment." *Western American Literature* 28 (2): 43–49.

Mander, Jerry. 1991. *In the Absence of the Sacred: The Failure of Technology and the Survival of the Indian Nations.* San Francisco: Sierra Club Books.

Manes, Christopher. 1990. *Green Rage: Radical Environmentalism and the Unmaking of Civilization.* Boston: Little, Brown and Co.

Marx, Karl. 1977. *Capital: A Critique of Political Economy.* Vol. 1. Trans. Ben Fowkes. New York: Vintage.

Mumford, Lewis. 1967. *Technics and Human Development.* Vol. 1 of *The Myth of the Machine.* New York: Harcourt, Brace and World.

———. 1970. *The Pentagon of Power.* Vol. 2 of *The Myth of the Machine.* New York: Harcourt, Brace Jovanovich.

Payne, Daniel G. 1995. "Monkey Wrenching, Environmental Extremism, and the Problematical Edward Abbey." *Southwestern American Literature* 21 (1): 195–208.

Ronald, Ann. 1982. *The New West of Edward Abbey.* Albuquerque: University of New Mexico Press.

Sale, Kirkpatrick. 1995. *Rebels Against the Future: The Luddites and Their War on the Industrial Revolution—Lessons for the Computer Age.* Reading, Mass.: Addison-Wesley.

Scarce, Rik. 1990. *Eco-Warriors: Understanding the Radical Environmental Movement.* Chicago: Noble.

Slovic, Scott. 1992. *Seeking Awareness in American Nature Writing.* Salt Lake City: University of Utah Press.

Twining, Edward S. 1978. "Edward Abbey, American: Another Radical Conservative." *Denver Quarterly* 12 (4): 3–15.

Edward Abbey's Inadvertent Postmodernism

Theory, Autobiography, and Politics

WILLIAM

CHALOUPKA

Even nature, postmodernism might point out, doesn't grow on trees.
—Linda Hutcheon, *The Politics of Postmodernism*

The scene is the early 1980s. About 150 Tucson notables gather around a swimming pool in the desert-landscaped backyard of a comfortable home.[1] The occasion is the publication of *Saving Water in a Desert City*, a book that reported findings on water conservation and management (Martin et al. 1984). The book had emerged from a heavily funded project that involved scholars from several University of Arizona departments. There were top-level city bureaucrats there, scholars, and the cream of the liberal green crowd in Tucson. It was an event.

The social festivities were interrupted for a few brief speeches honoring the book and its authors. The water department director praised the book, calling it a sound and farsighted prescription of a policy direction in the growing desert Southwest. Other speakers followed that theme. The mayor's office weighed in with similar approval, as did other dignitaries. To conclude the evening's program, coauthor Helen Ingram introduced Edward Abbey, who approached the front with Coors in hand. "Saving water in a desert city? That's crap," Abbey began. He went on to suggest an alternative water politics for the region's cities: "Let the water roar." In brief remarks, he managed to express unmistakable and wholesale contempt for the research project being honored that evening. He made it clear that he thought that the fate of humans (certainly in that region) had already been decided. We might as well move the squandering along, rather than pretending that our meager, belated efforts would "save" anything. Indeed, Abbey suggested, the sooner the water was used up, the better the result likely would be for the desert, which is what mattered most to him. Water conservation simply allows more people to live in a place where they shouldn't be. Abbey advocated quite a different personal politics of Southwest water; he suggested taking six showers a day, the better to make the water situation as dire as possible.

As soon as Abbey started on this line, a few graduate-student troublemakers at the back of the crowd started giggling. Then a few other guests also joined in the laughter, if a bit nervously. By the time he finished, perhaps half the crowd was laughing. For her part, Ingram smiled; she knew Abbey and must have expected some mischief when she asked him to speak. Attendees wondered whether she got more trouble than she had expected.

Environmentalists are often disarmingly open about their aspiration to found a new ideology, even at a time when one might well doubt whether anyone, anywhere is interested in finding a "new ideology." In this respect, at least, environmental thought resembles some instances of feminism, multiculturalism, or neoconservatism; each strives, at times, to provide the type of fundamental map of politics usually associated with ideology. The 1992 campaign made this point even more explicitly with the nomination of Albert Gore for vice president. Gore called for environmental protection to be a foundational principle for the post–Cold War period, both in his acceptance speech to the Democratic Convention and in a best-selling book (Gore 1992). As a founding principle, environmentalism could properly be expected to effectively explain or criticize almost any event in terms of a rational set of presumptions and preferences.

These ambitions, in themselves, imply a sense of importance. But greens also display a restiveness with contemporary ideology and, in Michel Foucault's terms, a sense of specificity about the ideological project in general.[2] At times, ecology has even been portrayed as a "subversive science," a sort of anti-science in its capacity for critique and intervention into the various hegemonies of power. In the influential 1969 anthology *The Subversive Science: Essays Toward An Ecology of Man,* coeditor Paul Shepard announced that "the ideological status of ecology is that of a resistance movement" (1969, 9). One important theme within environmental thought, bioregionalism, emphasizes specificity, location, and relativism—and thus is at least at some tension with the greater claims of ideology.

As compelling as that positioning (as resistance movement or bioregionalism) was, it did not necessarily end the environmental movement's uncertainty about ideology and the relationship of ideology to movement and politics. Sometimes presenting itself as an ideology, environmentalism has also had to defend itself from attacks— often attacks that took as their first article the ideological character of green claims. The political right—once allied with both conservationists and a more marginal movement concerned with pure food, water, and air—now attacks environmentalism as being, somehow, both a dogmatic outbreak of political correctness and, at the same time, a bastion of liberal middle- and upper-middle-class privilege.[3] The left sometimes even attacks environmentalism as an excuse for apolitical diversions insufficiently attuned to issues of social justice and corporate power (Luke 1993; Lucas Jennings and Jennings 1993).

While environmentalists have engaged both sets of critics, some internal critics argue that the movement has taken to sidestepping its ideology problem (Dowie 1995). Its radicals often simply appeal to an earlier mode of life, perhaps a premodern or even pre-Christian way of organizing life. They try to get over by arrogantly proclaiming their "depth," a patently ideological claim. At the same time, the movement's pragmatists translate environmental terms into the language of liberalism, proposing that trees or grizzly bears should have rights, too.

Some of this has been merely nostalgic or opportunistic, and thus deserves little serious attention. But a larger problem exists with environmental thought, a problem that may help explain the character of the attacks it has absorbed, as well as its inability to adequately respond to those attacks. At the same time that every other ideology is now confronted with assaults (both political and theoretical) on its basic authority structure, environmentalists have continued to dodge the question. For Marxists, monarchists, and statist liberals, that challenge pertained to their claims of inevitability, timelessness, or judgments that assumed their realistic permanence. For feminists and multiculturalists, the challenge has been framed in terms of their "nature" claims.

To a greater or lesser extent, each of these political movements has responded, theoretically or politically, to its challengers. But for environmentalists, more than for any other movement or ideology that wishes to challenge mainstream beliefs and power, "nature" has been beyond reproach. As troublesome as environmentalism's nature problem has been, however, it is not beyond theoretical solution.[4] Feminism, especially, has understood that a lively theoretical discussion of nature, essentialisms, and politics has been forming for some time under the rubrics of literary criticism, postmodernism, and deconstruction.[5] To cite one sample of the theoretical purchase gained by feminist theory in this move, consider Jane Flax's critique of Freud as a writer who "displaces conflicts within culture onto conflicts between 'nature' and culture; hence he renders their social sources, especially in gender relations . . . opaque and inaccessible" (1990, 235).[6]

Ed Abbey, in his intensely personal mix of philosophy, autobiography, and politics, effectively proposed another way out of the ideological (or religious) trap environmentalism had fallen into. Showing how a green could compose himself—a desiring, political, questioning self—Abbey modeled an alternative. This model, like most such constructs, was not without its own catastrophes. Taken too literally and fed by an insufficiently theorized righteousness, Abbey provided an almost disastrous model to Earth First! and others (arguably including himself). But at its best, the Abbey project showed how even the cranky, ambivalent, and dialectical elements of contingent politics could inform a life. The contemporary concern with the self need not flatten into lives of arrogant faux modesty—the personal displacement of politics into the pursuit of narrow accomplishments limited to recycling, bicycling, and pinched conservation. Instead, green could be expressive.

Oddly enough, an intellectual tradition Abbey himself would surely have ridiculed provides a good place to start. Contemporary literary criticism has long understood the role that *rhetorics of* nature play in *constructions of* modern authority. Paul de Man's famous reading of Rousseau, for example, challenges the familiar romantic reading. De Man denies that Rousseau uses nature to represent "a homogeneous mode of being" (1979, 249), instead finding a deconstructive process. As political theorist Shane Phelan summarizes the argument, "nature does not 'refer' to a time/place/mode so much as it constitutes a conceptual opposition between nature/culture, private/

public, female/male, particular/general. . . . There is no point at which nature is reached, and no time when denaturation is complete" (1993, 50).

More often, of course, postmodernists have addressed the question as it pertains to the human nature basis for modernist social theory. This is most obviously the case for Foucault, whose many studies often turned on a display of the construction process by which some seemingly elemental category in fact emerged from a specific historical, professional, or cultural context. Given the considerable role that nature questions have played in language approaches, it is not surprising that some of those authors have theorized environmental politics, as well as the social sciences, public policy, and other concerns.

Slavoj Zizek summarized the problem of environmentalism in the context of the other areas of contemporary intellectual activism. The Enlightenment "contaminates all preceding organic unity and changes it retroactively into an affected pose" (Zizek 1992, 185–86). Those who investigate, say, oriental religious wisdom see that as a way to reject the West. The cheap, trashy, commercialized versions of such quests (Zizek cites newspaper adds for TM, transcendental meditation) turn out to reveal the problem shared with more serious investigations; both are already in service of an existing economic and "social machine, facilitating the untroubled run of its nuts and bolts." The "oriental wisdom" was already betrayed "the moment we uprooted it from its pretechnological life world and transfunctionalized it into individual therapeutic means" (Zizek 1992, 185).

No way remains to recontextualize belief and life; protests get absorbed. Every attempt to reduce complex political and social circumstance to simple religious or ideological code falls into a trap. The world rigorously proceeds along multiple paths, with the economic confounding the theological, the psychological confounding the ideological, and so on. The need for simple remedy is at odds with the simultaneous need for multidimensional understanding. The trap is constant—and constantly shifting. Although Zizek does not quite say it, he writes as if the only way to respond is with a cranky set of displacements: juxtaposition of low culture and high theory, for example, or serious topics and frivolous postures.

Zizek frames a challenge to any late-modernist movement that tries to shed its skin as a way to solve the problems it identifies, still, in thoroughly modernist ways; "Those who preach . . . 'openness toward non-European cultures,' etc., thereby unknowingly affirm their 'Eurocentrism,' since what they demand is imaginable only within the 'European' horizon" (Zizek 1992, 185). This idea—the inextricability of modernist adversaries from one another—could be derived from any number of theoretical approaches, but it is something that contemporary literary theories are particularly well suited to identify. Likewise, the thoroughly cultural origins of even the most naturalistic claims is something literary approaches would notice and incorporate into their arguments. Even the very idea of cultural pluralism is itself a cultural artifact, Zizek explains, rooted in the Cartesian presumption that the individual (the self, the subject) is empty and without prior predilections (from historical and cultural context or, ironically, from the nature of the organism itself).

The path back to some imagined pre-Cartesian unity is no easy road; intentional forgetfulness could be an ironic stance, or could merely signal obliviousness. Taken too seriously, it cannot confront modernity, which has so well equipped itself to fend off all challenges to its hegemony. Zizek formulates his own point, then, in an odd way. He leaps from "the idea of cultural pluralism" to (in his very next sentence) "undoubtedly . . . the problem of our time: the ecological crisis" (1992, 185), combining with that jarring juxtaposition an obvious sympathy for that crisis with an insight about the structures of environmental theory and politics.

Zizek's analysis shows how obvious the American environmentalists' problem is; an Eastern European intellectual with very little experience with contemporary American politics has the movement's quandary pegged immediately, if in terms that might never occur to environmentalists themselves. Zizek first notes that greens have flocked to the idea that the most obvious (as he puts it, the most "natural") reaction to ecological crisis is an "ideological gesture," a self-conscious "shift from the Protestant-Cartesian (mechanistic, anthropocentric) to a new post-Cartesian (holistic, organic) paradigm." This approach argues that the crisis is rooted in modern selves and the identities we form as technological dominators; "so, to get out of the crisis, one has to commit oneself to a new attitude of assent, of complying with things instead of exerting control over them, to an attitude which conceives nature as a living organism (the earth as Gaia, a living body, etc.) and man as its subordinated part" (185). But this break, as obvious as it is to most greens, contains a trap. It relies on precisely what it denounces, the modern habit of seeing the natural world as an artifact of human interest.

What we have here is a desperate endeavor to return to the pre-Enlightenment, to a world in which the split between facts and meaning has not yet taken place, to a world where a deep sense inheres to nature itself, to a world animated by an invisible soul, to a world of a preestablished harmony between man, society, and cosmos, guaranteed by a set of metaphorical equivalencies (society as a corporate body, for example)—an endeavor problematic not because of its utopian nature but due to the fact that, once the bacillus of Enlightenment has infected us, its very success corroborates subjectivism. That is to say, the more we emphasize the break with anthropocentrism, man's subordination to the totality of nature, *the more this totality of nature is perceived, in an implicit way, from the standpoint of the human interest* (Zizek 1992, 186).

The search for "some self-posited ground authorizing us to exert power, be it nation or Earth as an organism . . . remains thoroughly within the confines of the 'modern age subjectivity'—the very remedy against ecological catastrophe regenerates its alleged cause" (186). Zizek's response to all this is typically cryptic in the extreme, but we know he wants us to acknowledge and study the crisis of the self (in this terminology, "the subject"); "subjectivization is a way to elude the void which 'is' the subject, it is ultimately a defense mechanism against the subject. Paradoxically, therefore, the only true step out of 'modern-age subjectivism' is to acknowledge [its crisis]" (186).

Environmentalists bring a tension along with them as well. There is a contention, a subversion, a resistance built into the environmentalist position, even if there is also a prospectively hegemonic ideology. This tension shows in the way greens deal with political strategy, when they ask basic questions of efficacy and agency. Some activists head off to Washington, lobbying and fund-raising as successfully as anyone. Others head for the woods or the trash pile, relying more or less uncritically on the intentionally modest personal habits of recycling, for example, or backcountry living, or alternative modes of transportation. The extreme range of actions greens regard as valid is a clue to their arrogance or, more charitably, to a problem of theory that is not yet resolved. And, as I have argued elsewhere, the connection between one's own daily practices, on the one hand, and the larger (and more expressive and symbolic) political world, on the other hand, are not obvious (Chaloupka 1992, chap. 5). The green habit of hoping to extrapolate political change from personal change is not their only odd connection to modernity. While greens have become more careful about how they use science, they still seem not to have understood the role of culture—specifically, rhetoric—in the seemingly natural object from which they wish to derive political direction.

Zizek's admonition is to embrace the problematics of subjectivity rather than try to refuse it through commitment to a simpler pre- or extra-modern code. Zizek deploys Lacan to theorize the traps and contradictions inherent in contemporary constructions of the self. His approach is compelling, but hardly necessary. My argument is that Ed Abbey, in his own cantankerous way, was challenging contemporary notions of the self—the dominant modernist version that privileges consumerism, avoidance of politics, and deference to economic arrangements, but also the trapped green sensibility that promotes dreamy wholeness, denial, and science (if its own brand of that science) as a response to social and ecological ills.

Abbey's work is sometimes derided as autobiography rather than political theory or politics itself. Even a friendly reviewer, Wendell Berry, made that distinction, arguing that Abbey was an autobiographer *rather than* an environmentalist. "This is important, for if he is writing as an autobiographer, he cannot be writing as an environmentalist, or as a specialist of any other kind. As an autobiographer, his work is self-defense" (1995, 32). This is an odd distinction, one that makes sense only if one understands the trap Zizek has explained. If environmentalism has placed all its bets on the possibility of a perspective removed from human affairs, then it makes sense to call an autobiographer.

Berry meant that as a compliment; he thought Abbey had focused the issue of survival. Other reviewers issued the compliment with a decidedly backhanded flair, meaning to imply that Abbey's politics did not make enough sense to be taken seriously.[7] On the face of it, either claim makes too fine a distinction. Most all political (and even scientific) writing can be read as autobiographical. This is especially true for Americans who, as the authors of an important recent study on the autobiographical literary form suggest, "are habitual authenticators of our own lives" (Smith and Watson 1996, 2).

Abbey's autobiographical position worked to answer both of the problems I have been raising thus far. While Berry praised Abbey's concern for survival in terms that made it clear he saw Abbey's project as quite close to his own, Abbey actually played out political positions in his work that Berry would never have imagined. You will never see Berry advocating for six showers a day in a dialectical protest against

Tucson's growth. Abbey responded to the problem Zizek posed by making subjectivity the central issue. He also responded to the archetypal green concern with modesty and caution by challenging greens to think politically.

The classic deconstructive strategy in the face of seemingly solid cultural perceptions and "realities" is to show how these social "facts" were in fact constructed by a traceable process. In the case of environmental thought, this strategy has sought to show that the idyllic perfection greens attribute to nature or wilderness was itself a construction that displaced other ways of seeing the natural world.

Donna Haraway provides a useful example of this approach in the first chapter of *Primate Visions* (1989)—tellingly titled "Teddy Bear Patriarchy: Taxidermy in the Garden of Eden." The "garden" she invokes is New York's Museum of Natural History. Rather than announce that it is a text, susceptible to interpretation according to the narratives it contains, Haraway just does it. Whereas the museum announces, in so many overt and covert ways, that it is about nature—an Edenic garden—Haraway intervenes with the obvious; it surely is about taxidermy, too. All those stuffed animals!

There is a powerful rhetoric of truth at work in the museum, a "sense of telling a true story," as Haraway puts it (40). That rhetoric is based on an identifiable set of practices, including "the selection of individual animals, the formation of groups of 'typical' specimens" (40). But finding typical specimens raises issues that have long been "fundamental in the history of biology" (40). The solution here involves perfection, and not only physical perfection: "Cowardice would disqualify the most lovely and properly proportioned beast" (41). And the perfection rhetoric is supported by a commitment to hierarchy; "there was a hierarchy of game according to species: lions, elephants, and giraffes far outranked wild asses or antelope. The gorilla was the supreme achievement, almost a definition of perfection in the heart of the garden at the moment of origin" (41).

At one level, these commitments to perfection of physicality, moral character, and hierarchy are simply preferences that underscore similar choices made elsewhere in the culture. But Haraway understands how these preferences bespeak other, more important cultural events. After all, this perfection is in the service of memory, an ineffable but crucial cultural event and procedure. "Taxidermy was the craft of remembering this perfect experience. Realism was a supreme achievement of the artifactual art of memory, a rhetorical achievement crucial to the foundations of Western science. Memory was an art of reproduction" (41).

Haraway's eventual target is the construction of identities, especially identities of gender. And, after her impressive reading of authoritative constructions, Haraway's judgment is compelling; "Gender is a concept developed to contest the naturalization of sexual difference in multiple arenas of struggle" (290). Using the concept of gender, feminists seek to contest historical arrangements that constitute "men" and "women," thus creating antagonisms and hierarchies for individuals to live out. Feminists are thus well situated to understand that something similar (and related) happens in the natural sciences, which are engaged in "constructions and reconstructions," too. As Haraway summarizes, "These discourses are central to western social technologies for mapping the distinction between nature and society, history, or culture. These fields of knowledge and power map the scope for dreams and projects of social action. . . . Biology is an historical discourse, not the body itself" (290).[8]

In precisely the same way, environmentalism is also historical discourse, not nature itself. In his own way, Abbey practiced a similar strategy. Like other greens, he often chose to reify "nature" as a tactical way to challenge powers that threatened the stability of beloved sites (in his case, the desert Southwest). But Abbey broke the presumed linkage between those sites and the politics that greens had assembled to protect them. The water example with which I began this essay provides a clear glimpse of Abbey's alter-strategy.

In that story, the "love of place" is severed from ideologically informed, modest practices of conservation. In typically loud and petulant fashion, Abbey denied that personal practice is the only imaginable way to engage the political arena. After this severance, one is left to identify other, better political tactics and strategies. And Abbey's cantankerousness behavior that evening in Tucson also teaches a lesson about that search for new approaches. The political calculus can be cruel, especially once one understands that personal modesty does not necessarily constitute the most effective way to produce a modest and sensible state. There are risks to thinking politically. The more public the exercise, the more perilous the risks.

To be more precise, Abbey was engaged, throughout his work, in the project of showing himself in the process of constructing special cultural sites—locales that were identified with "nature," but which were thoroughly social in their force and consequence. Foucault explained how the construction of such sites, which he called "heterotopias" in contrast to "utopias," is a thoroughly human activity rather than an interface with "nature":

> There are . . . real places—places that do exist and that are formed in the very founding of society—which are something like counter-sites, a kind of effectively enacted utopia in which the real sites, all the other real sites that can be found within the culture, are simultaneously represented, contested, and inverted. Places of this kind are outside of all places, even though it may be possible to indicate their location in reality. Because these places are absolutely different from all the sites that they reflect and speak about, I shall call them, by way of contrast to utopias, heterotopias. (1986, 24)

Of the various types of heterotopias Foucault identified, the one that relates to Abbey's project is the "crisis heterotopia," which constructs "privileged or sacred or forbidden places, reserved for individuals who are, in relation to society . . . in a state of crisis" (24). Such places are constructed and identified in order to put participants at some external relationship with the ordinary context that brings them into crisis. This description completely reorganizes the way we think about "wilderness theory," for example—and does it fully in congruence with Zizek's critique.[9] The attempt at nostalgia that Zizek criticizes is by no means necessary; there are entirely different ways to conceptualize a defense of wilderness.

Abbey's project fits this reconceptualization perfectly. When singing the praises of his beloved Southwest, Abbey would simultaneously denigrate its badlands for their inhospitability. The point of his desert excursions was what they meant for life in the city; the desert formed an exception, a contrast, perhaps even (the point that caused Abbey no end of trouble) a place of retreat for those who would seriously disrupt the city. In this conceptualization, the visitor to the desert is putting his or her own subjectivity on the line. The desert is dangerous, threatening, and above all, different. The traveler learns what attitudes and moods seemed "natural" because of his or her setting, rather than because of nature. One prepares for return, honing responses in a context of space, not another debate over what ideology should pertain between modernist society and "nature." This is precisely Zizek's point.

Green naturalism opens the doors to backlash and resentment by fostering an arrogant posture—visible, for example, when greens call themselves the defenders of wildlife, or rivers, or nature itself. The same arrogance has kept environmentalists from making serious coalitions with the timber workers who are as much victim of corporate practices as the owls the greens seek to protect. Prospective allies have been driven away by a flurry of self-certain and adamant globalist pronouncements. Social theorist Andrew Ross, for example, argues that environmentalists share more with the corporate types than they can recognize within their social-theory context: "Like global models of corporate planetary management, which take the planet as an economic unit, Gaian philosophy demonstrates the danger of taking the planet as a zoological unit" (1991, 17). Whether it is done by corporate suits or greens, the consequence is globalism, not the localism greens say they prefer. As Ross explains, "In either case, humanity appears as a mythical species, stripped of all the rich specificity that differentiates human societies and communities, and oblivious to all of the differences in race, gender, class, and nationality that serve to justify and police the structures of human domination within and between these societies" (17).

It is not at all obvious that this globalization is necessary. Even in terms of such a scientific issue as global warming, this generalizing impulse can be problematized. While Ross concedes that scientific climatology, for example, will play the role of "primary authority in defining the exact shape of the global crisis," he finds other players that the scientists (and their most opportunistic green followers) risk missing; "There are a host of questions related to the climate debates that touch upon local and cultural, rather than global and scientific, interpretations of the weather. Here, we come across the vast spectrum of cultural differences in living with and interpreting the physical world that have little to do with the 'universal' claims of global climate modeling." Different cultures experience weather differently, have vastly different ideas about the practicality of solutions, and even diverge when trying to theorize "the whole world." As Ross details, even the language and moral lessons we draw from weather (e.g., weather proverbs) differ from place to place, even within the same bioregion. Thus, even at environmentalism's most scientific moments, there is a rather easily discovered role for culture, language, and the specificities these patterns produce and then operate through (19–20).

At first glance, the difference between heterotopia and utopia might seem the kind of distinction without difference that marks some arguments as "purely academic." But, as Zizek's argument explains, there are problems with an environmentalism that hangs on too tightly to a metaphysics of nature. When the green metaphysic attaches good values to the Earth itself (at a very abstract level), it risks missing the contentiousness that makes politics political. In Ross's argument, this issue comes up when he assesses green globalism: ". . . we cannot expect all the changes to be progressive. Globalism will generate new power relations as the old national allegiances lose their sway. Just as the social costs to capitalism of environmental regulation are likely to be internally absorbed and handed on to consumers, so too, there are cultural costs to be borne in transforming people into global citizens" (24). A political perspective, more comfortable with the ambiguous projects of negotiation and contention, does not necessarily see this in the simple terms of profound catastrophe, but as a predictable part of such a global project as environmentalism—one that must be considered as events unfold.

As Ross concludes, environmentalist discourse often avoids such ambiguities, instead circling in self-reinforcing and self-defeating ways, making political issues more difficult to address. Global warming holds out the promise that more of us will adopt identities as global citizens, but globalism has a downside that current green thought has trouble engaging. This is not simply a problem with green globalism; Ross's argument contains a broader issue. An overly ideological claim risks missing politics, believing that its ideological clarity will, by force of its own argument, produce sufficient clarity to motivate mass (or elite) political action. Given how contingent the political world now is, successful resistance movements find ways to deal with the ambiguity of contemporary public life.[10]

What is more, ambiguity is not simply a matter of accurate perceptions; how a political movement handles ambiguity can alter the movement's prospects. Ross cites the left's clear and compelling stories about how new computer technologies, applied in offices and to personal files, constitute a threat to freedom. The "critical left position—or what is sometimes referred to as the 'paranoid' position—on information technology . . . imagines or constructs a totalizing, monolithic picture of systematic domination" (1991, 26). While he acknowledges the efficacy of "this story [as] an indispensable form of 'consciousness-raising,' " Ross still suggests that this might not be the "best story to tell," if one takes the strategic moment of politics seriously (26). "Such narratives do little to discourage paranoia. The critical habit of finding unrelieved domination everywhere has certain consequences, one of which is to create a siege mentality, reinforcing the inertia, helplessness, and despair that such critiques set out to oppose in the first place. What follows is a politics that can speak only from a victim's position" (28).

Ross's arguments and case studies demonstrate the possibility of an environmentalism more attuned to its political age. In this chapter, I have argued that Ed Abbey's work functions against the grain of green ideology, moderating debilitating aspects of the metaphysical stance, politicizing situations that otherwise would have been plowed under in the rush to general, theological pronouncement. Rather than playing the victim, Abbey proposed another response. Abbey is not the only corrective force already present within the environmental scene. Many environmentalists are attentive to specificity in a way that their ideological globalism contradicts. Wilderness preservation involves particular sites, usually embracing cultural as well as physical features. The same goes for land-use planning issues, which are often addressed as environmental issues. It is not that a localized green discourse is impossible or unimaginable, but that the possibility has been foreclosed by purposefully globalized theoretical commitments.

To put this in slightly different terms, the problem is that modern environmentalism is under-theorized, especially when it comes to the web of issues surrounding nature, language, and politics. This does not pose itself as a problem for environmentalism in any short run. The sometimes awkward combination of communitarianism, scientism, and critique has served greens well—in part, no doubt, because it places them within the boundaries of contemporary modernist discourse. But the tensions show up throughout the green camp, evidenced by its diffident and often inarticulate sense of politics. It is no easy thing for a religion to articulate itself politically or to make actual, strategic political decisions. "Nature" serves as a trope of reconciliation, but it is, in many ways, an impossible promise. Such unlikely utopianisms can frustrate, baffle, or invite successful counterattack.

And when environmentalists encounter an active and powerful politi- cal opposition, their sense of realism (of the universal, of globalism) becomes increasingly hard to hold.

After almost two decades of bitterly contested environmental politics, it is worth reminding ourselves how hegemonic this position once was. Even Richard Nixon was capable of strong environmentalist claims, as suggested by this comment in his 1970 State of the Union Address: "Restoring Nature to its natural state is a cause beyond party and beyond factions. It has become a common cause of all the people of this country." Still, although nobody seemed to notice it in 1970, the environmentalists had already been set up for the next two decades of attack. Having accomplished extraordinary legislative suc- cess—accompanied by strongly favorable public opinion—it would have seemed odd, in the early 1970s, to admonish greens about their globalisms and their unacknowledged debt to modernism.

Nonetheless, Abbey clearly understood this problem, even before the green heyday of the early 1970s. One possible explanation lies in Abbey's philosophical training. Most reviewers emphasize his obvious enthrallment with anarchism (his diaries show him wondering what an anarchist would look like, and several of his books identify protag- onists as anarchists). Fair enough, but Abbey's anarchism was sup- ported not only by classical liberal and romantic theory, but also by the more ambivalent precedent of classical cynicism. Abbey studied Diogenes, the original cynic (Bishop 1995, 84). And he seems famil- iar with contemporary takes on cynicism, as when he has his arch- villain fascist leader in *Good Times* say, "Cynicism is the cutting edge of truth" (Abbey 1980, 227) an echo of well-known literary apho- risms on the topic. Oscar Wilde said, "I am not at all cynical, I am only experienced—that's pretty much the same thing," and Anton Chekov wrote that "no cynicism can outdo life" (Sloterdijk 1987, xxxii).

Clearly, Abbey himself would have found this analysis bad hog- wash, or worse. As a popularizer, Abbey was bringing a certain philo- sophical bent to an audience broad enough to alter the political situation, a goal that was, arguably, accomplished during his lifetime. In that sense, my reading is revisionist—a "theft" of Abbey, hopefully in the spirit of his own rugged appropriations. While Abbey pursued the broader stage, there remains work for some of us to do, examin- ing the theoretical underpinnings of environmentalism. When we un- dertake that project, Abbey will be a useful exception to the green project of his time. Understanding how that project was exceptional will help us to untangle the difficulties facing green thought and politics in our era.

Notes

1. This account was assembled from personal interviews (Aug. 1996) with two persons who were in attendance.

2. Foucault never dealt with environmentalism in a systematic way, but interview comments support this characterization (Foucault 1988, 15).

3. The conservative opposition to environmentalism coalesced around an *Atlantic* article, published in the mid-1970s, then published in a book (Tucker 1982).

4. Some of these efforts have been less than encouraging. See, for example, an exchange that at least tried to approach these issues, in a prominent journal of green theory. Cheney (1989a, 1989b) attempted to bring environmentalism's concern with place and specificity to the fore, while also making its totalizing tendency an issue. But Cheney also idealized a premodern origin in general terms—a theoretical strategy fraught with its own difficulties. The rather overbearing response generated by these articles is even more interesting. Mick Smith (1993) criticized Cheney on his intent to theorize modernity, surely an odd criticism from the environmental position. For an example of a more serious take on the nature issue, see Cronon (1995).

5. For one strong example of such theorizing, see Judith Butler (1990). On occasion, feminists, including Carolyn Merchant (1990), have addressed both essentialism as it relates to feminism, and nature as it relates to environmentalism. This would be a promising area for further study. Shane Phelan (1993) suggests that Merchant is less attentive to the constitution of nature than to that of gender. "She [treats] nature unproblematically as that which is not human, not social, not conventional. Never does she question what nature 'is' " (Phelan 1993, 58).

6. This argument is cited and expanded upon by Shane Phelan (1993, 45–46).

7. Bishop (1995, 174) quotes one unnamed writer friend of Abbey derogating Abbey's fiction as "little more than comic books."

8. There is, now, an active theoretical camp, eco-feminism, that takes this insight seriously. But, politically, the eco-feminists do not seem to have been able, yet, to convince greens in general that they must take seriously the contingent, constructed aspect of their beloved "nature" if their politics is going to work.

9. This argument is made at length in Cawley and Chaloupka (1993).

10. "Studies of youth subcultures . . . have taught us that the political meaning of certain forms of cultural 'resistance' is notoriously difficult to read. These meanings are either highly coded or expressed indirectly through media—private peer languages, customized consumer styles, unorthodox leisure patterns, categories of insider knowledge and behavior—that have no fixed or inherent political significance" (Ross 1991, 122).

Works Cited

Abbey, Edward. 1980. *Good News*. New York: Penguin.

Bennett, Jane, and William Chaloupka, eds. 1993. *In the Nature of Things: Language, Politics, and the Environment*. Minneapolis: University of Minnesota Press.

Bishop, James, Jr. 1995. *Epitaph for a Desert Anarchist: The Life and Legacy of Edward Abbey*. New York: Simon and Schuster.

Butler, Judith. 1990. *Gender Trouble: Feminism and the Subversion of Identity*. New York: Routledge.

Cawley, R. McGreggor, and William Chaloupka. 1993. "The Great Wild Hope: Nature, Environmentalism, and the Open Secret." In Bennett and Chaloupka, 3–23.

Chaloupka, William. 1992. *Knowing Nukes: The Politics and Culture of the Atom*. Minneapolis: University of Minnesota Press.

Cheney, Jim. 1989a. "The Neo-Stoicism of Radical Environmentalism." *Environmental Ethics* 11 (4) (autumn): 293–325.

———. 1989b. "Postmodern Environmental Ethics: Ethics as Bioregional Narrative." *Environmental Ethics* 11 (2) (spring): 117–34.

Cronon, William, ed. 1995. *Uncommon Ground: Toward Reinventing Nature*. New York: Norton.

de Man, Paul. 1979. *Allegories of Reading: Figural Language in Rousseau, Nietzsche, Rilke, and Proust*. New Haven: Yale University Press.

Dowie, Mark. 1995. *Losing Ground: American Environmentalism at the Close of the Twentieth Century*. Cambridge, Mass.: MIT Press.

Flax, Jane. 1990. *Thinking Fragments: Psychoanalysis, Feminism, and Postmodernism in the Contemporary West*. Berkeley: University of California Press.

Foucault, Michel. 1986. "Of Other Spaces." *Diacritics* 16 (1) (spring): 22–28.

———. 1988. "The Ethic of Care for the Self as a Practice of Freedom: An Interview." In *The Final Foucault*, ed. James Bernauer and David Rasmussen, trans. J. D. Gauthier, 1–20. Cambridge, Mass.: MIT Press.

Gore, Albert. 1992. *Earth in the Balance: Ecology and the Human Spirit*. New York: Houghton Mifflin.

Haraway, Donna. 1989. *Primate Visions*. New York: Routledge.

Hutcheon, Linda. 1989. *The Politics of Postmodernism*. New York: Routledge.

Lucas Jennings, Cheri, and Bruce H. Jennings. 1993. "Green Fields/Brown Skin: Posting as a Sign of Recognition." In Bennett and Chaloupka, 173–96.

Luke, Timothy W. 1993. "Green Consumerism: Ecology and the Ruse of Recycling." In Bennett and Chaloupka, 154–72.

Martin, William E., Helen M. Ingram, Nancy K. Laney, and Adrian H. Griffin. 1984. *Saving Water In a Desert City*. Washington, D.C.: Resources for the Future.

Merchant, Carolyn. 1990. *The Death of Nature: Women, Ecology, and the Scientific Revolution*. New York: HarperCollins.

Nixon, Richard. 1970. "State of the Union Address." In *Public Papers of the Presidents of the United States*. Washington, D.C.: U.S. Government Printing Office.

Phelan, Shane. 1993. "Intimate Distance: The Dislocation of Nature in Modernity." In Bennett and Chaloupka, 44–62.

Ross, Andrew. 1991. "Is Global Culture Warming Up?" *Social Text* 9 (3) (autumn): 3–30.

Shepard, Paul. 1969. Introduction to *The Subversive Science: Essays Toward an Ecology of Man,* ed. Paul Shepard and Daniel McKinley. Boston: Houghton Mifflin.

Sloterdijk, Peter. 1987. *Critique of Cynical Reason.* Trans. Michael Eldred. Minneapolis: University of Minnesota Press.

Smith, Mick. 1993. "Cheney and the Myth of Postmodernism." *Environmental Ethics* 15 (10) (winter): 3–15.

Smith, Sidonie, and Julia Watson. Introduction to *Getting a Life: Everyday Uses of Autobiography,* ed. Smith and Watson. Minneapolis: University of Minnesota Press.

Tucker, William. 1982. *Progress and Privilege.* Garden City, N.Y.: Anchor/Doubleday.

Zizek, Slavoj. 1992. *Enjoy Your Symptom! Jacques Lacan in Hollywood and Out.* New York: Routledge.

Abbey as Anarchist

HAROLD

ALDERMAN

Edward Abbey was, of course, primarily a writer and not a philosopher. This is true despite his short career at Yale and despite his M.A. in philosophy from the University of New Mexico, where he wrote his thesis on anarchism. The advantages of Abbey's literary career for us all (as readers) and for the early environmental movement in particular do not need elaboration here.

But when it is time to try to tease out the philosophical implications of a writer's work, it is important to remember what he once studied and what he once aspired to do. These things, then, are taken as warranted assumptions: Abbey did have serious philosophical interests, interests that never got fully and explicitly expressed, except in the ways available to a great novelist. That is, Abbey used several of his characters to represent what, at different points in his life, he himself thought and felt about some important environmental and political matters. But none of these characters expresses the whole restless, probing, independent thought of Edward Abbey.

Was Abbey, then, an anarchist? My first answer can be fairly directly stated: "Damn straight!" But, alas, I am a "professional" philosopher–at least one who makes his living teaching philosophy– and this unambiguous answer will have to be heavily qualified along the way. My final answer to the question of Abbey's anarchism will be constructed from a comparison of philosophical anarchism and Abbey's published works–mainly *The Brave Cowboy, The Monkey Wrench Gang, Desert Solitaire,* and *Confessions of a Barbarian.* The truth is that Abbey's philosophical commitments were mostly a 137 matter of deeply held feelings and attitudes about things for which he cared very greatly: the Western environment, a preoccupation with the essence of beauty, and his own personal liberty. As corollaries of these preoccupations, Abbey also greatly distrusted governments, mass movements, and the tyranny of charismatic leaders, of which he himself was clearly one. Might we not on Abbeyan grounds then distrust Edward Abbey?

So, let me once again ask the question, "Was Edward Abbey an anarchist?" And this time–first qualification–the answer is, "Yes and no." Abbey was an instinctive anarchist, a man with a deeply held skepticism about social movements and an equally deeply held belief that human beings are not made better by involvement in governments.

In thinking about anarchism, it is important to keep in mind that there is no such thing as an anarchist movement in the sense that there was once a Marxism or a Catholic Christianity. In principle, there could never be such a movement. Throughout the eighteenth and nineteenth centuries, a fundamental debate between anarchists was over the question of cooperation between them, and there was very little of that.

The theory of anarchism quickly resolves into two different poles: a social anarchism and a political anarchism. Both of these movements accept the notion of a natural man whose life was better before involvement in government. In the state of nature, as John Locke—most definitely not an anarchist—argued, there are certain natural rights, which generally no state can violate (1924). In general, Locke's minimalist descriptions of a state of nature, a condition that existed before governments and which is the proper residence of natural man, generally underlies anarchist thinking about state legitimacy. In Locke's view, under certain conditions—for example, public order—these natural rights may be violated. In the views of both political and social anarchism, the violation of individual rights is the point of all states. And, as also in Locke, the whole question of natural rights and state legitimacy turns on the question of property. For Locke, property rights are acquired in nature by a sort of first acquisition or by a reworking of natural materials. Thus one either has land or one reworks what is produced on the land. Someone has oil; someone turns the oil into gasoline. In either case, one acquires property rights. It is these property rights that are the cornerstone of Locke's theory of justice. For Locke, a sort of natural tension evolves between individual rights and property rights.

The solution of the social anarchists to the conflict between states and individuals is withdrawal from politics in an effort to discover the natural state and thus liberate natural man. This version of anarchism generally holds that the only thing that matters in human life is freedom. The inevitable enemy of freedom is government. Therefore, like Nietzsche, social anarchists believe that the genuine human being begins "only where the state ends." Such an anarchism generally insists that there can be no legitimate state, no government, that could ever have as its only concern the autonomy of individuals. In this view a justified and morally warranted state is impossible. Given this, the only choice is withdrawal from the state. One opts out to save oneself; or one becomes, as does Joseph Conrad's Professor, a walking bomb, ever armed to resist the state (1953). In the conflict between state legitimacy and personal autonomy, the social anarchist always says "No!" to the state. He simply walks away. Is this Edward Abbey? Certainly sounds familiar. When did he ever remain freely constrained by anything?

Political anarchism, in contrast, tentatively "allied" itself with early communist movements in search of a form of government that could reverse this history of state oppression, generally arguing, on other grounds than the Marxists, for the very same political solution. What was needed, then, to make this historic reversal of state oppression? Most generally, the answer was: eliminate private property, Locke's most fundamental natural right. Yet the arguments for this elimination are greatly different in the anarchist and communist views. On the one hand there were the economic determinists, the Marxists, whose putative knowledge of the laws of history gave them—in their own view—an inside edge on social change. Thus the Communist Party would use its revolutionary advantage to change the laws of production, eliminate private property, and establish something like a proletarian justice. So it went—at least in theory.

The left-wing political anarchists generally resisted economic determinism as a form of justification. Where there is a call to abolish private property, the justifications generally proceed as follows: (1) Pierre-Joseph Proudhon says that positive law must be an expression not of will but of fact; (2) Michael Bakunin argues that we must overthrow the "permanent conspiracy" of all governments against the people; (3) Peter Kropotkin argues that we must restore the natural solidarity of the masses and live closer to something like the state of nature (see Horowitz 1980).

Each of these attempts to justify the elimination of private property itself contains enormous difficulties, which cannot be addressed here. But it is important to note that none of them involves economic determinism. In each of these three anarchistic positions a new, more perfect form of justice will emerge following the elimination of private property. In each of the four positions—including the Marxist—there is also a generally unexamined commitment to the belief that there is something morally virtuous in the masses. I do not find this last anarchistic element represented in Abbey's work. There is little or no populist yearning on his part for oppression of the masses. Nor does Abbey's work express a strong call to eliminate private property. There are, of course, many passages where Abbey rails against "industrial tourism," large corporations, and industrial farming. But these railings are against things that threaten to destroy wilderness, and it is wilderness that always remains the deepest and most fundamental of Abbey's commitments (1980, 189). If Abbey is an anarchist, in some sense, it is clear that his style of argument is not that of the classical anarchists (Proudhon, Bakunin, or Kropotkin). Nor is he an anarchist in the sense that a key element in his work is a call for the elimination of private property.

There is, however, another form of nineteenth-century anarchism that I have, so far, not mentioned. Max Stirner represents this alternative version. Basically Stirner argues for an extreme form of egoism as the natural state of man, basing his argument on one of the most consistent forms of psychological egoism since its original version in Thomas Hobbes. In Stirner's view, life is a history of discovering one's "ownness," of appropriating everything to one's self. In this view, life is essentially an unavoidable history of combat and self-assertiveness in which one struggles against the anti-egoistic abstractions of God, state, and the notion of man as an abstract class (1982). Stirner's psychological egoism clearly marks him as a right-wing anarchist, one whose idea of justice is inimical to that of the left-wing anarchists who speak of sympathy and solidarity. Stirner, then, quite clearly rejects all states and mass movements as the enemy of egoism. There is much of this anarchism in Abbey's work and life.

In general, anarchism as a philosophical movement begins in several eighteenth- and nineteenth-century thinkers, all of whom share a healthy distrust of governments and authority. Bakunin, Proudhon, Kropotkin, and Stirner best represent the extremes of anarchistic thought, the full range of possible anarchistic philosophy. All of them, of course, oppose government as the enemy of autonomy. Indeed, the word "anarchism" in Greek is privative, signifying a refusal to be ruled by another. Abbey clearly is an anarchist in the root sense of the word, his refusals to be "ruled by another" clearly marked in his writing and in his life. Long periods as a fire lookout or ranger emphasize Abbey's preference for his own company and for solitude—a social anarchist's instinct. Abbey undoubtedly enjoyed the irony of being a government employee arguing for the overthrow of all governments. But the preference for solitude is also an instinct of mystics and deranged people. Was Abbey deranged? Clearly not. Was he, then, perhaps a mystic?

If mysticism is the yearning to experience some sort of unity with all things, then Edward Abbey was a mystic. But he was a nontheological mystic whose religious temperament could find no doctrinal expression. In this regard, Abbey—like Nietzsche before him—was a deeply religious man, someone who wanted to experience the wholeness of nature in each of its parts, a man who believed not that God (Christian sense) was expressed in nature, but that nature was a god (Greek sense). So why single out Abbey's anarchism when dealing with this preference for solitude? Why not the mystical element of his thought? Or perhaps the aesthetic element? For it is only when one is alone that one can experience the beauty of wilderness, experience the "wild beautiful utterly useless truth" (Abbey 1980, 106). In this Abbey clearly learns from John Muir, the original wanderer in the wilderness.

To understand why it is that the anarchistic elements of his thought may provide the best access to what Abbey is after, let us consider the first incarnation of John W. Burns: riding his horse, Whiskey, across the plains, cutting fences, deliberately picking a fight to get into jail in order to help a friend escape. If Burns is an Abbey mouthpiece, then Abbey is clearly in some sense or other an anarchist. John Burns, however, is a natural anarchist, someone who does not have to learn it. In that sense Burns is, in William James's sense, one of the once born, someone who does not need to struggle for his insight, someone who may, in fact, not be able to express that insight.

The quarrel between Burns and Paul Bondi, an East Coast intellectual, is instructive. Bondi's refusal to escape from jail is based on some Socratic commitment he feels to the society in which he lives. Burns simply does not understand, making the argument that the two of them should go back to the mountains. There is, then, a quarrel between them over whether one has any obligations to governments. Bondi says yes and opts to stay in jail, do his time. He is clearly a passive resister, quite willing to pay his dues (go to jail) in order to meet his sense of social obligation. But Jack Burns is an outlaw and simply cannot understand Paul's arguments. Paul is married, has a family, is committed. But Jack, the "outlaw," chooses to remain in his outlawry. He insists on living beyond the reaches of fences and governments. He prefers to be somewhere on his horse—out in the mountains, out in the desert, down in Mexico. Each of these things is symbolic of autonomy. Jack may not be able to save Paul, but he can—and does—save himself. This is true whether or not Burns dies at the end of *The Brave Cowboy*. If he dies, he dies preserving his principles, the scent of freedom still in his nostrils.

Is John W. Burns an anarchist? Yes—of a kind, an instinctive kind. He thinks he knows what is original nature in all of us—a longing for unrestricted freedom. Jack Burns has this freedom. Yet Edward Abbey was himself an Easterner, someone who had to learn to love the West. He is, in some important senses, then, not Burns at all. Rather, at this stage of his career Abbey is much more like Paul, caught perhaps by a society from which he is trying to flee, yet which always draws him back. Paul's argument for his social responsibility is really Abbey's.

The central role played by Hayduke in *The Monkey Wrench Gang* can shed further light on a later incarnation of Abbey as anarchist. Hayduke is a character larger than life and captive of nothing but his appetites and passions—for Bonnie, against the rape of the wilderness. Hayduke, a Vietnam War veteran and Green Beret, is one of Abbey's most successful comic characters but not the subject of a joke and clearly not the butt of someone's wit—except maybe Bonnie's. What makes Hayduke a comic hero is his largeness in relation to everything around him—everything, that is, except the desert. Everything he does is so out of proportion that he reminds one of a Rabelaisian character, striding across the environment, singing and indifferently leaving behind body wastes. He is Pantagruel hiking across the countryside, leaving footprints in stone. Or perhaps he is Don Quixote tilting with windmills, arguing with Sancho Panza over the reality of exactly what he is doing. Whether it is drinking, fighting, or grunting at Bonnie, Hayduke is too large to be contained by any role other than that of a sort of comic Superman—a strictly imaginary character.

But Hayduke is not just imaginary; he can *only* be imaginary. Like Paul Bunyan and his ox Babe, Hayduke is too large for the world.

At this later stage of his career, is Abbey, in the character of Hayduke, an anarchist? Yes. Clearly so. But again his anarchism is a sort of instinctive, gut-level anarchism. Hayduke makes no theories, states no claims, agrees to nothing. He is the eternal resister, living in the forests of our dreams, the eternal resister who in the words of Walt Whitman must always, "Resist much. Obey little." He is the anarchist as actor, defined by what he does rather than by what he says. He subscribes to no doctrines, makes no commitments, subscribes to no creeds, joins no parties—except the one on the raft with Bonnie, Doc, and Seldom Seen. Thus Hayduke, like his improbable father, John W. Burns, is a sort of instinctive anarchist, more of the throw-a-wooden-shoe-and-stop-the-machine variety. One cannot make a theoretician out of Hayduke. One either sees the point of what he does or one doesn't. One acts to share and preserve Hayduke's own vision of wilderness, or one gets out of his way. Or perhaps one calls the cops.

From neither John W. Burns nor George W. Hayduke can one derive a political theory of anarchism. There is in what they do no theory of the state and its destruction, no theory of justice, no theory about class structure, and certainly no theory about the economic organization of the good society. One learns from these two instinctive anarchists the way one learns from the great teachers of both the Eastern and Western traditions: by emulating what they do. Buddha shows us the way beyond illusion. Socrates writes nothing. Christ says, "Follow me," not "Listen to me." But in the actions of the great moral exemplars, there is much· to be learned. What doctrinal elements might be elicited from what Hayduke and Burns do?

Before answering this question, let me review once again the teachings of the classical nineteenth-century anarchists Bakunin, Kropotkin, and Proudhon on the one hand and Stirner on the other. The first three define the teachings of left-wing anarchism, while Stirner defines a right-wing anarchism, a sort of radical libertarianism that eschews all governmental restriction. It shall, I think, come not altogether as a surprise that Abbey is as much of a right-wing as a left-wing anarchist. On the right wing is his fierce, libertarian individualism, and on the left is his emphasis on mutual aid. How could Abbey—a man who could not tolerate too much company, a man who, like Nietzsche, sought the solitude of mountains—be simply either one of these two? Perhaps there is in Abbey's works as much of Nietzsche's social anarchism as there is classical anarchist theory. Perhaps, indeed, there is more. We move, then, from instinctive anarchism—in which there is always the need to break boundaries, to explore otherness, to resist much—to the question of Abbey's philosophical anarchism. How could Edward Abbey, the quintessential marginal and reluctant dweller on the edge of the human world, the man who was always dreaming of Australia, have anything so naive as a philosophical theory? Let us attend to this question.

In a remarkable essay titled "The Dilemma in Philosophy," William James proposes that everyone's philosophy can be understood as a function of his temperament. He further proposes that the most important thing we can know about someone is his philosophy. The philosophy James means in this passage, he says, is not technical and not gotten from books. Rather, it is "our more or less dumb sense of what life deeply and honestly means" (James 1949, 4). In this sense, John W. Burns and George W. Hayduke both had philosophies, and in the same sense, what they say and do expresses (or, better, exaggerates) Edward Abbey's philosophy.

In order to better understand anyone's philosophy, James proposes that philosophies are of two basically different kinds: the tender-minded and the tough-minded, distinguishing these two types into eight different subcategories. The tender-minded philosopher is a tender-footed Bostonian, and the tough-minded is a "rocky mountain tough" (James 1949, 13). Perhaps it is the case that Edward Abbey started his life somewhat more like the first of these and ended it a great deal more like the second. In any case, it is fairly clear that both Burns and Hayduke were "rocky mountain toughs," philosophical exemplars that Abbey—as an Easterner—wanted to have imitated. It may be that Edward Abbey, the author, was seduced by two of his own creations. Thus Abbey himself may stop and admire a cliffrose, the juniper's static pose, or the sunflowers and scarlet penstemon, or he may admire the line of the mountains south of Moab, Utah; or he may say that the slickrock desert and the canyon lands around Moab are the most beautiful places in the world (Abbey 1980, chap. 1). But these are the judgments of a tender-minded Bostonian, not a Rocky Mountain tough. Burns does not stop to admire; he rides on talking to his horse. Hayduke finishes his beer, crumples the can, and throws it into the canyon. Then he opens another beer. Perhaps on this count, Burns and Hayduke are Abbey's tough-minded alter ego. They are more—in some senses—than their author; they have transcended their singular parent, Edward Abbey.

In order to better understand the complexity of Abbey's philosophy (James's sense), let us consider the two Jamesian categories a little further. The tender-minded philosopher is "rationalistic, intellectualistic, idealistic, optimistic, religious, free-willist, monistic, and dogmatical." The tough-minded philosopher is, in contrast, "empiricist, sensationalistic, materialist, pessimistic, irreligious, fatalistic, pluralistic, and skeptical" (James 1949, 12). In neither of these two major philosophical categories does James claim a kind of perfect consistency. It is quite possible to combine traits from the two different lists. One can be, at least in part, both a Bostonian and a Rocky Mountain tough. Nonetheless, each individual pair of traits is something like a genuine pair of contradictories in which one of the pairs must be false and one must be true. At least this is how the pairings are often viewed, and how they are so viewed by James. Thus, for example, one might not be both "intellectualistic" (going by theories) and "sensationalistic" (committed to observation). But one can clearly be both rationalistic and fatalistic. So also for the other subcategories.

What, then, is the point of this apparent detour into Jamesian philosophy? Let me make it all clear by briefly analyzing Abbey in terms of James's two categories, the tender- and the tough-minded. One of the things that distinguishes Abbey's work is his remarkable attention to details of the Southwestern desert. So he must be empiricist (going by facts) and sensationalistic (committed to details of observation). To this extent Abbey is tough-minded. So also, it seems to me, must he be materialistic, meaning his fundamental metaphysical assumptions are naturalistic rather than idealistic in the Berkeleyian sense. On the next pair, Abbey seems to me to be clearly optimistic rather than pessimistic, despite the many ruminations on death throughout his journals. I have earlier argued that Abbey was religious rather than irreligious in that he was concerned to get a sense of the wholeness of nature in each of its parts (Abbey 1980, 200-201).

On the issue of free will, Abbey seems clearly "free-willist," in James's sense, rather than "fatalistic" (the belief that the universe is a complex machine that grinds us all down). Just look at what the free will of Hayduke accomplishes in *The Monkey Wrench Gang.* In terms of his views about the "oneness" of the world, Abbey seems fairly clearly to be exploring the world in its wholeness (he believes there is some underlying deep explanatory principle, even if he doesn't know what it is); but he makes his explorations in a way that often makes him sound like a pluralist (we at least know a number of different explanatory principles of which we can be reasonably sure and are willing to try almost anything). Except for his commitment to saving wilderness, there is nothing dogmatic in Abbey's work; and the dogmatism here means not that Abbey doesn't argue for this commitment to the principle of saving wilderness, but that he believes there is no evidence that could count against it. Yet the probing, exploratory character of his work suggests at least a methodological skepticism and a deeply ironic mind.

So although I originally argued that, in contrast to Burns and Hayduke, Abbey was tender-minded, when we attend to the details of the contrast between James's tender- and tough-minded types, the situation begins to look a little more cloudy. Thus Abbey is: empiricist, sensationalistic, materialistic, optimistic, religious (special sense), free-willist, both pluralistic (epistemology) and monistic (his nature mysticism); and finally, he seems both skeptical and dogmatic. Looking at the classical anarchists, as a group they seem to be more rationalistic (arguing from first principles), intellectualistic (their styles of argument are a prioristic and logical rather than empirical), and mostly materialistic, thus reversing the first two categories in James's typology. On the next three categories the situation is reversed twice: the anarchists seem to be dubiously pessimistic, clearly irreligious, and frequently unclear on the fatalistic/free-willist pairing. And on the last two pairings, the classical anarchists most often seem both monistic (a single principle of explanation) and dogmatic (their first principles are held categorically).

Whether in terms of James's neutral system of classification or in terms of specific comparisons to the anarchists on other grounds, the work of Edward Abbey often seems less like that of a classical anarchist than is reported, or less even than Abbey himself apparently wanted it to be. He is anarchistic in the original Greek sense of "refusing to be ruled by another." Anarchistic also in the Nietzschean social sense that "the genuine individual begins only where the state ends." In both these senses, Burns and Hayduke reflect Abbey's anarchism. But, for the kind of reasons I have shown, we must be very guarded in putting Abbey in any ideological camp. For it seems a practical certainty that Abbey would have revolted against any ideology as soon as it came to power—including the environmental movement, where the environmentalist becomes a bureaucrat. Where would Edward Abbey have stood with such a transformed and bureaucratized environmental movement? I am not sure of the answer to that question. But the question is not what would he have done, but what should he have done, given his own professed claims to be an anarchist.

Where are we left, then, with Abbey and the question of his anarchism? He himself tries to answer this question in his journal where he writes, "I am a Communist myself. . . . Insofar as Communism does not conflict with my more basic Jeffersonian anarchism" (1994, 59). But what, in heaven's name, is a communist–Jeffersonian anarchist? And, of course, the three positions are in conflict—most thoroughly and utterly. And, in any event, what is a Jeffersonian anarchist in Abbey's sense, if not a libertarian, someone who—unlike Jefferson—refuses all government restraint? Abbey, in this passage, clearly announces that the oxymoronic position of "Jeffersonian anarchism" is his "more basic position." Nor does it help much when Abbey writes, "Anarchism is the secret yearning toward brotherhood" (1994, 39). So also are Christianity, Judaism, and Buddhism, and Abbey explicitly denounces all theological versions of this yearning. Somewhat more to the point, Abbey writes, "What is Anarchism? Nothing as remote and melodramatic as most people imagine, thinking of Bakunin and the Russian nihilists; [rather it] means simply the widest possible decentralization . . . of power, political and economic" (127). But if we take this as Abbey's statement on the nature of anarchy, it is reasonably clear that he was not an anarchist at all in any strict sense of that word. Perhaps we must conclude that he used the term "anarchism" as a sort of mask, a mask he used principally to taunt the bourgeoisie.

It would be helpful if we could turn to Abbey's 1959 M.A. thesis, "Anarchism and the Morality of Violence," to see where he stands as an anarchist. But, alas, that is not the case. The thesis first succinctly describes anarchism as "alone among contemporary political doctrines in opposing the institution of the state . . . while denying the necessity of centralized authority" (1959, 1). There is no doubt that Abbey has great sympathy with this description. Yet the thesis does not elaborate this point, nor does it explain the necessity of opposition to "the gigantic and fantastically-complex social machine" that modern nations have become (2). Abbey understands that the history of anarchism involves a complex theoretical preoccupation with the necessity of violence, coupled with opposition to authority. Yet in his concluding remarks he argues that since the anarchists have not justified their appeals to the "critical situation" of choice between resistance and surrender to social evil, they have also "failed to justify violence" (75). Anarchism, he argues in the opening of his thesis, remains "embarrassed by its traditional association with illegality and violence" (2). These remarks are clearly and unequivocally stated by a young man on the way to becoming a significant writer.

Let me then ask the question once again: Where are we left with Abbey and the issue of his putative anarchism? We are left with a man whose work is preoccupied with the sense of beauty, with his mystical and personal sense of oneness with nature, with his own autonomy, with his belief in the intrinsic value of things natural, and with a probing, Socratic, and ironic wit. That is, we are left with a man whose work seems to elude classification. It was Abbey himself who said it is of "The free man I sing, the antiauthoritarian, the libertine" (1994, 8). And it was Abbey who advised a friend to "avoid ideology" (285) and who said, "I speak only for myself" (338). He was the man who wrote, "The wilderness is our only true and native home" (339). A man with such a deep and abiding love of the desert, the realm of solitude, could never be contained within the boundaries of a political ideology. Abbey understood that above and beyond all ideology, he was sure only of this: "THIS IS WHAT YOU SHALL DO: Love the earth and sun and the animals. Stand up for the stupid and the crazy. Take off your hat to no man" (356). It is the sentiment expressed in this quotation that yields what can be learned from the actions of J. W. Burns and G. W. Hayduke. It is this same adversarial spirit that Abbey most admires in what, I think, he mistakenly calls his anarchism.

So, then, is Abbey an anarchist? The answer this time must be "no." The truth is that Abbey had no developed political theory. And classical anarchy is, above all things, a political philosophy, a theory about justice, about how the goods and the chastisements in a society are to be distributed. Is Abbey, then, anarchistic? Does the adjective work where the noun fails to describe the restless spirit of a genius? The answer, it seems, is a clear and resounding "Yes!" And here, I think, we are as close to understanding Abbey as we can get. He was a man in perpetual rebellion—against himself, against the status quo, and against the mediocrity of the past that crushed the human spirit. The great rebels, like Edward Paul Abbey, are not contained by the names of ideology.

Works Cited

Abbey, Edward. 1956. *The Brave Cowboy*. New York: Dodd, Mead and Company.

———. 1959. "Anarchism and the Morality of Violence." M.A. thesis, University of New Mexico.

———. 1975. *The Monkey Wrench Gang*. New York: Avon.

———. 1980. *Desert Solitaire*. New York: Ballantine.

———. 1994. *Confessions of a Barbarian*. New York: Little, Brown and Co.

Conrad, Joseph. 1953. *The Secret Agent*. New York: Doubleday.

Horowitz, Irving L. 1964. *The Anarchists*. New York: Dell.

James, William. 1949. *Pragmatism*. New York: Longmans, Green and Company.

Locke, John. 1924. *On Civil Government*. London: Everyman's Library.

Stirner, Max. 1982. *The Ego and His Own*. New York: Western World Press.

"Getting the Desert into a Book"

Nature Writing and the Problem of Representation in a Postmodern World

CLAIRE

LAWRENCE

Ecological critics and poststructuralists often believe that their fields have nothing in common; poststructuralists see eco-critics as simple and essentializing, and eco-critics see poststructuralists as amoral, nihilistic, and incapable of action. Although framed in global terms, this disagreement is not necessarily about worldview, but each group's view of the way the world is represented in a text. The perceived point of irreconcilability between poststructuralism and nature writing is the idea of the real and therefore the designation of what is meaningful. The argument may be paraphrased as follows: poststructuralists posit that reality cannot be apprehended because we are unable to move outside of systems of representation; however, this is often read as a denial of the existence of a reality outside of language. Eco-critics study texts that emphasize place, the physical world, and the threat to the many fragile ecosystems on the planet and thus feel they have much at stake in some concept of a real, extratextual world.

In his article "Revaluing Nature: Toward an Ecological Criticism," Glen Love implies that what he sees as the poststructuralist bent of many English departments is the reason for the generic denigration of nature writing: "Perversely enough, it is just this sort of literature rooted in a real world which is ignored or devalued by such modish surveys as the recently published *Columbia Literary History of the United States*" (1990, 207). Later in the article he foresees a revaluation of nature writing, "with realist and other discourse which values unity rising over poststructuralist nihilism," and "voices assert-

150

ing the significance of a value-laden landscape and a meaningful earth" getting the recognition they deserve (212). Arran Gare's *Postmodernism and the Environmental Crisis* presents this characterization of the poststructuralists: "the existence of people who take linguistic idealism seriously is an important social phenomenon, suggesting a class of people who are so politically impotent and lead such impoverished lives that they have lost all sense of what action in the world is" (1995, 109).

On the other hand, there is a noticeable lack of discussion on the subject of the natural world by the poststructuralists. This is in part because, as James Applewhite explains in his article "Postmodernist Allegory and the Denial of Nature," the term "nature" holds little value for the poststructuralist critics due to its association with a romantic and essentializing view of the world: "The reputation of *nature* and *the natural* as theoretical and critical terms is undermined most deeply by the continuing modernist prejudice against romantic associations. Part of the liability of postmodernism is its inheritance, from modernism, of a failure to evaluate romanticism properly" (1989, 14). According to Applewhite, "Postmodernist theory appears to tell us . . . that there *is* no natural" (7). He quotes as his proponent of postmodernism Craig Owens: "nature in postmodernist art 'is treated as wholly domesticated by culture; the "natural" can be approached only through its cultural representation' " (3). Jean Baudrillard's vision of the desert in America seems to vividly illustrate this conception. He looks out and sees only human construction: "Here in the transversality of the desert and the irony of geology, the transpolitical finds its generic, mental space. The inhumanity of our ulterior, asocial, superficial world immediately finds its aesthetic form here, its ecstatic form. For the desert is simply that: an ecstatic critique of culture, an ecstatic form of disappearance" (1988, 5).

Though a few important bridges have been built between poststructuralism and eco-criticism,[1] the debate goes on. This article attempts to find another such bridge in the work of Edward Abbey; it argues that the two critical systems are not really as much at odds as it seems when it comes to the issues of language and textuality he discusses. Examination of Abbey's writing reveals important connections between postmodernism and eco-criticism. In fact, most nature writers, because they must somehow translate land and ocean and animals and birds into words, are forced to confront the problem of representation in a way that is much more complicated than most proponents of poststructuralist theory give them credit for. In other words, nature writing, precisely because its project is to describe the real, which cannot be approached, let alone be contained in description, brings its writer to a point of crisis with language that any postmodernist would envy.[2] This predestined and continual failure of language leads to understanding. A poststructuralist recognition of the nature of representation—the rupture in the relationship between word and object—is often part of the process of writing about the natural world.

In order to understand this debate over the status of the real, it is necessary to explain certain poststructuralist theories that inform the postmodern aesthetic. Poststructuralism is based partially on semiotics, a branch of the study of linguistics pioneered by Charles Sanders Peirce and Ferdinand de Saussure at the beginning of the twentieth century.[3] Saussure identifies the basic structure of language as the relationship between signifier (the name of an object) and signified (the idea of an object).[4] Peirce adds to the equation the referent (the object itself). The signifier and the signified together make up the sign; the referent exists outside of the signifying system. According to Kaja Silverman, "Peirce argues that we have direct experience, but indirect knowledge of reality. The former teaches us that there is a world of things, but gives us no intellectual access to them, while the latter supplies the only means of knowing those things, but no way of verifying our knowledge. Reality bumps up against us, impinges upon us, yet until we have found a way of representing that reality, it remains impervious to thought" (1983, 16). Thus experience is always mediated by language; it is impossible to apprehend an object *except through a system of representation.*

Silverman thinks Peirce maintained a belief that reality could be truly represented, but he had to admit that the means for determining the truth of that representation were inaccessible. She characterizes much of his work as contradictory; Peirce believed in the referent in spite of the fact that in his writings about the signifying transaction, it was in effect excluded as much as in Saussure's. For Peirce, "the sign or signifier represents in some capacity or other the object or referent, which is itself available only as an interpretant or signified, and in so doing elicits within the mind of an individual another interpretant or signified. That interpretant or signified will in all likelihood generate additional ones, in a kind of relay of signification" (Silverman 1983, 17).

Silverman sees Saussure's and Peirce's work as prefiguring the view of signification advanced by Derrida, perhaps the most widely influential of the poststructuralists. For Derrida, we exist in a vast web of signifying chains, much like Peirce's "relay" described above. For Derrida as well, there is no way of getting at the object behind the word because we have access to nothing behind the word except another representation: "writing is exemplary . . . because it makes manifest the principle of deferral upon which all forms of signification rely. Its syntagms dramatize the fact that signification occurs along a chain in which one term displaces another before being itself displaced: '. . . the signified always already functions as [another] signifier' " (Silverman 1983, 34–35). Thus what lies at the end of a signifying chain is not reality but another signifying chain. As in Peirce's model, the object is inaccessible. Derrida, however, unlike Peirce, does not make a concerted effort to claim the referent. In "Structure, Sign, and Play in the Discourse of the Human Sciences," Derrida makes it clear that there is no point of origin or end to the series:

> The substitute does not substitute itself for anything which has somehow existed before it. Henceforth, it was necessary to begin thinking that there was no center, that the center could not be thought in the form of a present-being, that the center had no natural site, that it was not a fixed locus but a function, a sort of nonlocus in which an infinite number of sign-substitutions came into play. This was the moment when language invaded the universal problematic, the moment when, in the absence of a center or origin, everything became discourse . . . that is to say, a system in which the central signified, the original or transcendental signified, is never absolutely present outside a system of differences. The absence of the transcendental signified extends the domain and the play of signification infinitely. (1978, 280)

In Derrida's philosophy, the "transcendental signified" is a term that Western metaphysics has used as a guarantor of meaning in a system (for example, God in Christianity or consciousness in romanticism), and it is supposed to exist independently of that system. By showing that these transcendental signifieds do not reside outside their systems but rather derive all their value from being within a structure, Derrida foregrounds the idea that meaning does not exist except within a signifying system, in relationships that exist between signifiers, signifieds, and other signs.

In contrast to the poststructuralist view of representation are the realistic, nonfictional elements assumed to be a component of most nature writing, fictional or not. Thomas J. Lyon's brief essay "A Taxonomy of Nature Writing" attempts a systematic categorization of nature writing in order to present it as a coherent genre. His choices about the definitive elements of that genre are telling. In his characterization, nature writing retains a stress on observation inherited from the travel narratives, field guides, and natural histories out of which he believes it originated. He speaks often of "the facts" of nature. Thus the literature of nature has as one of its basic assumptions that there is something out there, beyond or before the human, to be observed and quantified. Indeed, he says, "the fundamental goal of the genre is to turn our attention outward to the activity of nature" (1989, 7).

While Lyon's description of the genre may not be agreed upon by all eco-critics, it is undeniable that nature writing owes a debt to scientific observation. This leads to certain expectations: one of the conventions of scientific writing is that there is no ironic distance between the writing subject and the object being described. There is also no reflection on the nature of language. In this tradition, the real would be seen as something that exists behind the transparent word; scientific writing is based on the idea that language is a sort of clear window on the world, through which one can see an object or a scene. There is always a reality behind language, always an observable, accessible referent to which the text refers. Therefore, most writers of scientific observation would say a page of description reproduces a desert or a forest, whereas a poststructuralist would say the text represents it.[5]

It is now possible to see why the debate is phrased in the terms it is. As genre, nature writing brings to the reader certain expectations of a scientific stance where observation leads to truth. In the poststructuralist model, meaning is arbitrary, something that occurs within a system of signs, not something monolithic, unified, or stable. However, the realization that meaning is contingent—or "context bound," as Derrida would have it—is often read as a statement that meaning is nonexistent,[6] hence the assumption that a postmodernist would not desire to write about a meaningful earth or a value-laden landscape. In *Postmodernism and the Environmental Crisis,* Gare claims that the logic that leads to this conclusion is evident: "That it is even possible to talk about the nature of being is questioned by some postmodernists on the grounds that it is impossible to get beyond language to know reality itself. There is no 'extra-text' " (1995, 109). At first, Gare seems much in keeping with poststructuralist theory, but he jumps from pointing out an inability *to know* reality to its nonexistence. The fear this move seems to reveal is that if in the poststructuralist model the real is *not* something that can be pointed to, touched, tasted, or owned, then it is also not something that can be saved from overpopulation, pollution, and degradation. However, and this is a crucial point that many miss, Derrida (as well as other poststructuralists) does not necessarily deny the existence of the referent or the real.

In *Dissemination,* Derrida discusses textual positionings and their consequences on/to the reader: "The text is remarkable in that the reader (here in exemplary fashion) can never choose his own place in it, nor can the spectator. There is . . . no tenable place for him opposite the text, outside the text . . . no spot, in other words, where he would stand before an already *written* text" (1981, 290). Derrida cannot claim or disclaim the referent since for him the space outside the text is inaccessible. The reader has "no *tenable* place outside the text"; what is not tenable cannot be retained or spoken. But, once again, he does not necessarily deny this space ontological status. Instead, he calls into question the structures by which we think we know it, and reveals their connection to ideology. His concern is that we have constructed this ideology as natural, the Truth, when it is actually something that is a product of representation.

Baudrillard's explanation of his relationship to the desert is helpful here. It is an almost textbook-perfect postmodern encounter with nature:

> It is useless to seek to strip the desert of its cinematic aspects in order to restore its original essence; those features are thoroughly superimposed upon it and will not go away. The cinema has absorbed everything–Indians, *mesas,* canyons, skies. And yet it is the most striking spectacle in the world. Should we prefer "authentic" deserts and deep oases? For us . . . the only natural spectacle

that is really gripping is the one which offers both the most moving profundity *and at the same time the total simulacrum of that
profundity.* (1988, 69–70)

Baudrillard's stance is one of acceptance of the many layers of culture
(and ideology) interposed between us and nature. But he does not
deny the existence of nature in its original: "Cinema is not alone in
having given us a cinematic vision of the desert. Nature itself pulled
off the finest of its special effects here, long before men came on the
scene" (69). He just realizes and, like a good postmodernist, revels in
the fact that any encounter we might have with the desert is culturally
overdetermined. The innocent, pure response to the world many nature writers (including Abbey) crave is not an option.

It is now easy to see why realistic nature writing is often set up as
distinctly not postmodern; we expect of it a "truthful" description of
place in which language disappears to reveal the world behind it, not
a Baudrillardian discourse on the implications of meaning. It becomes
clear that most of the disagreement between poststructuralists and
eco-critics stems from generic expectations. But in actuality, much
environmental literature addresses the problem of signification in
what might be considered quite postmodern ways, often calling into
question the mimetic illusion and the connection between language
and the objects it represents. I intend to illustrate this by looking at
the relationship to realistic writing exhibited by Edward Abbey in
Desert Solitaire (1968). I believe the nature of Abbey's project, the attempt to fit or to contain the natural world in words, compels him to
address the problem of representation in an arguably postmodern
manner. Abbey is very interested in troubling the connection between
sign and referent, word and object, and like Derrida he sees this as a
political act, a way to disrupt recalcitrant ideologies that are embedded in discourse.

The introduction to Abbey's *Desert Solitaire* posits language as a
stumbling block to any kind of realistic writing about the natural
world. Written after the book was completed, it reveals that he recognizes the real as something that exceeds representation. This "ending" is very different from the place where he started. The project he
sets out for himself in the first chapter is an attempt to get at the
essence of reality through living in the desert and, by implication,
through writing about it.

> I am here not only to evade for a while the clamor and filth and confusion of the cultural apparatus but also to confront, immediately and directly if it's possible, the possible, the bare bones of existence, the elemental and fundamental, the bedrock which sustains us. I want to be able to look at and into a juniper tree, a piece of quartz, a vulture, a spider, and see it as it is in itself, devoid of all humanly ascribed qualities, anti-Kantian, even the categories of scientific description. (1991, 6)

This is a very different stance from Baudrillard's. Abbey wants the cultural taken out of his vision of the desert; he longs for some kind of pure, innocent experience of nature. Lyon cites this idea that culture is somehow tainted as part of a tradition of nature writing: "Essays of solitude or escape from the city, as might be expected, work much with the contrast between conventional existence and the more intense, more wakeful life in contact with nature. This subtype . . . tends to be much more critical and radical . . . [like] Thoreau at Walden, anathematizing the false economy of society" (1989, 6). Abbey also desires some kind of prelapsarian unity with nature, an incorporation into the world of things: "I dream of a hard and brutal mysticism in which the naked self merges with a non-human world and yet somehow survives still intact, individual, separate" (1991, 6).

A poststructuralist would, of course, say this project is doomed. And this is what Abbey comes to realize. In that same first chapter, Abbey himself is unable to describe the natural world without reference to some sort of cultural overwriting. The hoodoos he sees on his drive into his campsite are "weird humps of pale rock on either side, like petrified elephants, dinosaurs, stone-age hobgoblins" (2); the Arches are "windows in stone," "jug handles," or "flying buttresses" (5). Abbey's only access to the object is through culturally determined metaphor. As Baudrillard says, perception itself is structured by culture. Furthermore, Abbey is unable to incorporate himself perfectly into the natural scene. Near the end of the book he realizes the failure of his original project. Instead of getting at the metaphysical center of the desert, he is even more alienated than when he began: "Where is the heart of the desert? I used to think it was somewhere in the American Southwest. . . . Not so. I am convinced now that the desert has no heart, that it presents a riddle which has no answer, and that the riddle itself is an illusion created by some limitation or exaggeration of the displaced human consciousness" (273). *Desert Solitaire* therefore charts Abbey's growing recognition that his perceptual apparatus, and thus his writing, can never contain the metaphysical essence he seeks. It is thus telling that he chooses this observation as the reader's first contact with *Desert Solitaire;* the book becomes the story of the failure of language to apprehend the real.

In this context the introduction becomes a sort of cautionary manifesto for anyone who would attempt to write a book about nature. The structure of desire for, and disappointment in, language's ability to contain nature is played out again and again. Abbey places his work in the tradition of scientific observation. "In recording my impressions of the natural scene I have striven above all for accuracy, since I believe that there is a kind of poetry, even a kind of truth, in simple fact" (x). However, he quickly undercuts that statement by his focus on the failure of that kind of description: "Language makes a mighty loose net with which to go fishing for simple facts, when facts are infinite" (x). Abbey sets up *Desert Solitaire* as a book that runs contrary to expectations of the genre of nature writing: "This is not primarily a book about the desert. . . . since you cannot get the desert into a book any more than a fisherman can haul up the sea with his nets, I have tried to create a world of words in which the desert figures more as medium than as material. . . . Not imitation but evocation has been the goal" (x). In pointing out the difficulty of "getting the desert into a book," Abbey makes a statement about the inadequacy of signifying systems when it comes to reproducing the real; he realizes from the start that "evocation" is all that can be striven for. Writer, reader, and word are all alienated from the referent.

Abbey's problem is that the object is always out of reach; we can only represent it, not apprehend or contain it: "you cannot get the desert into a book any more than a fisherman can haul up the sea with his nets." One might say that the desert is irreproduceable because it is so vast, but Abbey anticipates that question: "If a man knew enough he could write a whole book about the juniper tree. Not juniper trees in general but that one particular juniper tree which grows from a ledge of naked sandstone near the old entrance to Arches National Monument" (x). Abbey makes it clear that the nature of signification itself is the source of trouble.

Therefore, *Desert Solitaire* "is not a book about the desert" because such a book would be impossible to write. This realization of the unrepresentable character of the natural world is something that J. Hillis Miller sees as a common literary event. In his essay "Nature and the Linguistic Moment," Miller describes this momentary breakdown in the mimetic illusion occasioned by the pressure on language that sometimes occurs in the attempt to represent nature. Though this breakdown seems to have an affiliation with new critical theories, it is also a postmodern moment in its recognition that language's irreducible figurativeness distances us from the referent. Miller's idea of the "linguistic moment" is:

> the moment when language as such, the means of representation in literature, becomes problematic, something to be interrogated, explored, or thematized in itself . . . [if] this linguistic moment becomes explicit enough and prolonged enough so that it can displace Nature or human nature as the primary focus of imaginative activity. The linguistic moment tends to involve a recognition of the irreducibly figurative nature of language, a seeing of language not as a mere instrument for expressing something that could exist without it–a state of mind or an element of nature–but as in one way or another creative, inaugurating, constitutive. . . . in the linguistic moment is a more or less explicit rejection of unitary origin. (Miller 1977, 450)

The problem of "getting the desert into a book" is a prime example of the linguistic moment as Miller defines it. Abbey's recognition that the desert cannot be reproduced leads to a questioning of signification itself. If language is irreducibly figurative, there is no literal way to speak about nature in its essence—again, no way to get at the real object. Abbey has to "create a world of words in which the desert figures more as medium than as material" (x).

This process of representation frustrates Abbey. Later in the introduction he continues to question it. He makes it clear that the idea of the real or, more accurately, our stake in looking for something we can call reality is also something to be interrogated:

> It will be objected that the book deals too much with mere appearances, with the surface of things, and fails to engage and reveal the patterns of unifying relationships which form the true underlying reality of existence. Here I must confess that I know

nothing whatever about true underlying reality, having never met any. . . .

For my own part I am pleased enough with surfaces. . . . (xi)

By saying he has never "met" a true underlying reality, Abbey critiques the ideas of essence and truth by throwing them into the realm of the ridiculous. In a similar move, he questions the structure of representation by inverting ideas we might consider to be "deep" and calling them "surface." What this does is foreground the fact that what we consider "deep" and "surface" are constructed within the representative relationship and do not exist as independent values. Again, it seems like Abbey's project, or at least his relationship to representation, is much in keeping with the postmodern aesthetic. He takes things that we have come to accept unquestioningly (truth, the realistic illusion), shows that they are constructs, and empties them of their ideological content by reversing their positions.

The most subversive part of the introduction, its last few lines, is understandable not only in terms of Abbey's recognition of the distance between word and object, but also as a deconstructive statement. Abbey craves the referent but sees that his attempt to fix it in words is doomed. The world of which he writes is not static; it is already disappearing: ". . . most of what I write about in this book is already gone or going under fast. This is not a travel guide but an elegy. A memorial. You're holding a tombstone in your hands. A bloody rock. Don't drop it on your foot—throw it at something big and glassy. What do you have to lose?" (xii). Here Abbey is really playing with the idea of a referent; the world disappears, the book becomes object (tombstone, rock). And he is angry with this state of things. *Desert Solitaire* is a very poor substitute for the desert, the world "out there." This is the comparison that is being made. He also creates a paradoxical reading position with his calling attention to the book *as book*, hateful object to be thrown at a window or wall. The realistic illusion only works if the reader forgets about language, forgets about the fact that he/she is experiencing reality through a medium. This is the whole idea of transparency; to call this into question by foregrounding textuality is to erase the reader's idea of a real unfolding before him/her and to focus him/her back on language.

Abbey's goal is political. Like Thoreau, he wants to "wake up his neighbors." Abbey does not want his reader to be too comfortable with unexamined language. He associates reading the book with the passivity of "industrial tourism." He fears that a book could substitute for the desert in a society used to the passive consumption of images. He tells his reader, "Do not jump into your automobile next June and rush out to the Canyon country hoping to see some of that which I have attempted to evoke in these pages" (xii). This kind of second-hand experience will not lead anywhere: "you've got to get out of the goddamned [car] and walk. . . . When traces of blood begin to mark your trail you'll see something, maybe. Probably not" (xii). Again, Abbey seems caught between a desire for the real and the recognition that he can never have access to it.

Near the end of *Desert Solitaire* is a passage that attempts to answer the questions about representation that Abbey asks in the introduction. It occurs after Abbey and a friend, Bob Waterman, have climbed into an unmapped area in southern Utah known as the Maze and are wondering what to name a rock formation they have found. Abbey votes for something poetic, majestic, like "Altars of the Moon." But Waterman asks, why name it at all? Abbey worries that naming is somehow necessary: "But at once another disturbing thought comes to mind: if we don't name them someone else surely will. Then, says Waterman in effect, let the shame be on their heads. True, I agree, and yet–and yet Rilke said that things don't truly exist until the poet gives them names" (288).

Again there is the idea that discourse is unavoidable and yet necessary: an object is unapproachable until we give it a word that corresponds to it. But more importantly, Abbey here recognizes the hegemony inherent in the act of naming. Naming is associated with shame, domination, and ownership. In a sense, Abbey parallels Michel Foucault's analyses of medicine, the asylum, and prison reform:[7] it is through the construction of a knowledge, a language, that we can know and thus control. Abbey's passage continues:

> Through naming comes knowing; we grasp an object, mentally, by giving it a name—hension, prehension, apprehension. And thus through language create a whole world, corresponding to the other world out there. Or we trust that it corresponds. Or perhaps, like a German poet, we cease to care, becoming more concerned with the naming than with the things named; the former becomes more real than the latter. And so in the end the world is lost again. No, the world remains–those unique, particular, incorrigibly individual junipers and sandstone monoliths–and

it is we who are lost. Again. Round and round, through the endless labyrinth of thought–the maze. (288–89)

Language is implicated in the disappearance of the world or, more accurately, in our dissociation from the world, which is lost for us because we have no relationship to it that is not distanced by naming.

The scene in the Maze not only connects with the introduction
but with another chapter of *Desert Solitaire* that is about naming,
"Cliffrose and Bayonets," in which Abbey goes out and, Adam-like,
names everything in his kingdom, the desert around him. He calls it
"inspect[ing] the garden," taking inventory (26). What goes on in
most of this chapter meets our expectations of traditional nature writing: the natural world is described, named, and explained in scientific
detail.

> Still within sight of the housetrailer, I can see the princess plume
> with its tall golden racemes. . . .
>
> Not quite within eyeshot but close by, in a shady dampish se-
> cret place, the sacred datura—moonflower, moonlily, thorn-
> apple—blooms in the night, soft white trumpet-shaped flowers
> that open only in darkness and close with the coming of the
> heat. . . .
>
> Most of the plants I have named so far belong to what ecolo-
> gists call the pinyon pine–juniper community, typical of the high,
> dry, sandy soils of the tablelands. Descend to the alkali flats of Salt
> Valley and you find an entirely different grouping: shadscale,
> fourwinged saltbrush, greasewood, spiny horsebrush, asters, milk
> vetch, budsage, galletagrass. (32–33)

Abbey describes and thus reproduces a place for the reader. His descriptions are lyrical, his lists of plants and rock formations exhaustive.

As an environmentalist, a natural historian, Abbey participates in
a tradition that invests the text with a semblance of the natural and lo-
cates the reader in that space. However, Foucault describes the conventions of natural history as being based upon imposed differential
relationships between organisms as well as arbitrary relationships in
language:

> Thus arranged and understood, natural history has as a condition
> of its possibility the common affinity of things and language with

representation; but it exists as a task only in so far as things and language happen to be separate. It must therefore reduce the distance between them so as to bring language as close as possible to the observing gaze, and the things observed as close as possible to words. Natural history is nothing more than the nomination of the visible. Hence its air of simplicity and the apparent naïveté it has from a distance, so simple does it appear and so obviously imposed by things themselves. (1973, 132)

Foucault believes natural history is completely inaccurate because a real correspondence between word and thing can never be set up (143).

It is just this innocence that Abbey, too, is interested in disrupting. In the midst of a natural history, a catalog of beauties, the most disruptive event described in the book occurs: Abbey gratuitously kills a rabbit; he "throw[s] the stone with all [he's] got straight at his furry head" (38). The death of the rabbit is a complete shock to the reader. It ruptures the nice natural description that has preceded it and remains a part of *Desert Solitaire* that most readers are unable to incorporate even after they have finished reading. Again, a questioning of representation is part of the disruption. When Abbey is pondering whether or not to give the rabbit a head start or to "brain the little bastard where it is," he asks the reader to "notice the terminology": "A sportsman is one who gives his quarry a chance to escape with its life. This is known as fair play, or sportsmanship. Animals have no sense of sportsmanship. Some, like the mountain lion, are vicious–if attacked they defend themselves. Others, like the rabbit, run away, which is cowardly." He continues, "I'm a scientist not a sportsman and we've got an important experiment under way here, for which the rabbit has been volunteered." Abbey seems to be saying here that he is able to kill the rabbit because he has defined his relationship to it precisely; he has given it a name. He is a scientist. The rabbit is cowardly. Indeed, once he has killed it, he says, "The wicked rabbit is dead" (38).

Language is implicated here in a misreading of the world; the reader recognizes that the rabbit is not "wicked" and that Abbey has just executed ultimate power over it only because he was able to call it "wicked." Again, naming is dangerous. After the event Abbey says that killing the rabbit makes him more a part of the natural world: "No longer do I feel so isolated from the sparse and furtive life around me, a stranger from another world. I have entered into this one" (38). He says this makes him "rejoice" in his "innocence and power" (39). I do not believe that the attempt to turn the scene into something about vitality and connectedness is completely successful. Something about the disruption is not contained and leaves a bad taste in the reader's mouth. Language—Abbey's attempt to structure the event (and insert himself into the natural world by partaking of its perceived violence)—fails. The reader can no longer see Abbey (the scientist) or what he says as innocent. He has transgressed a boundary; he is no longer a reliable narrator.

At the end of this chapter about naming is a passage about the different ways it is possible to see Delicate Arch, an arresting, unusual rock formation in Arches National Park. The passage is a sort of deconstruction of perception, again foregrounding the idea that what we see as the nature of an object is dependent on its role in a system of representation:

> There are several ways of looking at Delicate Arch. Depending on your preconceptions you may see the eroded remnant of a sandstone fin, a giant engagement ring cemented in rock, a bowlegged pair of petrified cowboy chaps. . . . There are the inevitable pious Midwesterners who climb a mile and a half under the desert sun to view Delicate Arch and find only God . . . and the equally inevitable students of geology who look at the arch and see only Lyell. . . . You may see a symbol, a sign, a fact, a thing without meaning or a meaning which includes all things. (41)

At the end of a chapter—which has been about naming, about putting the word and the object together—Abbey undermines the whole relationship, making sure that his readers know that there is no natural correspondence between the object, Delicate Arch, and the language that represents it.[8] Again, it seems Abbey is deconstructing writing and the idea of accurate description and thus the representative illusion. This connects back to his original goal: to get at the essence of things. He cannot.

Abbey's location of the metaphysical in the natural world is an inheritance from Emerson, who wrote in his essay "Nature" that language is a reflection of spirit and that nature's function is to provide spirit with words through which it can be apprehended. "But this origin of all words that convey a spiritual import–so conspicuous a fact in the history of language–is our least debt to nature. It is not words only that are emblematic; it is things which are emblematic. Every natural fact is the symbol of some spiritual fact" (1882, 29). Emerson believed that humans speak in metaphors taken from the natural world: "1. Words are signs of natural facts. 2. Particular natural facts are symbols of particular spiritual facts. 3. Nature is the symbol of spirit" (28). It seems by implication that language is sacred. This is something that every writer, including Abbey, wants to believe. The realization that this is not the case is the Fall, a fall from an idea of language as innocent of ideology to a recognition of complicity.

So what is the point of detailing the poststructural aspects of Abbey's writing, of charting his struggle with the representative illusion? If Edward Abbey can be considered a postmodern writer, what does that do to the argument over the nature of representation, and over the representation of nature? Postmodernism does not privilege language; it merely phrases its questions in terms of language. Ecocriticism, by assuming a sign-object equality, privileges language far more because it elevates the sign to the level of object. The word pair "Delicate Arch" is not the formation itself. The formation, Delicate Arch, is only significant because humans have selected it from the many other arches, and have selected arches from the many other geological formations, as aesthetically valuable and meaningful. As environmental critics, whether we are postmodernists as well or not, we should be aware of the politics of representation and should be wary of any ideology that foregrounds itself as natural, including the representative illusion. The designation of the natural and the reading of the natural is always cultural. When one enters an environment, one sees it through the filters of cultural knowledge and language. *Desert Solitaire* has a lesson: if we unquestioningly adhere to the realistic conventions of traditional nature writing, we run a risk of reproducing oppressive power structures. As Peter Quigley warns, "environmental movements and literary expression have tended to posit pre-ideological essences, thereby replicating patterns of power and authority. . . . Because traditional and contemporary postures of ecological resistance share too many features with the power structure they wish to oppose, they could benefit from a thorough reconsideration in light of poststructural philosophy" (1992, 291).

Language's relationship to ideology must be constantly interrogated. Edward Abbey was ahead of his time in realizing that environmental literature's unique relationship to representation often leads to that important moment of disruption, when one comes to believe that essence and truth are nothing but a function of discourse.

Notes

1. See Peter Quigley's discussion of resistance that accepts textuality, "Rethinking Resistance: Environmentalism, Literature, and Poststructural Theory," and to some extent Jim Cheney's "Postmodern Environmental Ethics: Ethics as Bioregional Narrative," both in *Environmental Ethics*.

2. Roland Barthes devotes an entire book, *The Pleasure of the Text,* to praising the "text of bliss" that "unsettles the reader's historical, cultural, psychological assumptions . . . [and] brings to a crisis his relation with language" (1975, 14). He assumes that disrupting representation also disrupts ideology, perhaps part of the reason that so many are uncomfortable with postmodernism.

3. The following discussion of semiotics and poststructuralist theory is based on Kaja Silverman's *The Subject of Semiotics.*

4. Saussure's idea of the signifier is not a "word" per se but what he calls a "sound-image," which is "the image of one of those sounds which we shape within our minds when we think, whereas the signified would be the meaning which that sound-image generates" (see Silverman 1983, 6).

5. The distinction between reproduction and representation can be explained in terms of a photographic metaphor. A writer of scientific texts, while not assuming that a photograph is the same as the desert, would say that it is more or less a pure, unbiased reproduction of an observable fact. A poststructuralist would say that the photograph is replete with ideology, that what the photographer chose to shoot was completely structured by ideology and by the continuous flow of images (Westerns, tourist brochures)—in other words, that the photograph was an image much distanced from the original object.

6. In the long quotation cited above, "everything became discourse" is often taken out of context. The qualification that follows: "that is to say, a system in which the central signified, the original or transcendental signified, is never absolutely present outside of a system of differences" is ignored and the "never absolutely present" is taken as complete absence.

7. See Michel Foucault's *The Birth of the Clinic: An Archaeology of Medical Perception, Madness and Civilization: A History of Insanity in the Age of Reason,* and *Discipline and Punish: The Birth of the Prison.*

8. It is interesting to note that Delicate Arch has been turned into an icon, a signifier for "Utah-ness" and a sort of state pride, culminating in its appearance on Utah's centennial license plates.

Works Cited

Abbey, Edward. [1968] 1991. *Desert Solitaire: A Season in the Wilderness.* New York: Ballantine. Page references are to reprint edition.

Applewhite, James. 1989. "Postmodernist Allegory and the Denial of Nature." *The Kenyon Review* 11 (winter): 1–17.

Barthes, Roland. 1975. *The Pleasure of the Text.* Trans. Richard Miller. New York: Hill and Wang.

Baudrillard, Jean. 1988. *America.* Trans. Chris Turner. London: Verso.

Cheney, Jim. 1989. "Postmodern Environmental Ethics: Ethics as Bioregional Narrative." *Environmental Ethics* 11 (summer): 117–34.

Derrida, Jacques. 1978. "Structure, Sign, and Play in the Discourse of the Human Sciences." In *Writing and Difference,* 278–93. Trans. Alan Bass. Chicago: University of Chicago Press.

———. 1981. *Dissemination.* Trans. Barbara Johnson. Chicago: University of Chicago Press.

Emerson, Ralph Waldo. 1882. "Nature." In *Miscellanies: Embracing Nature, Addresses, Lectures,* vol. 5 of *Works of Ralph Waldo Emerson,* 15–67. Boston: Houghton, Mifflin and Co.

Foucault, Michel. 1965a. *The Birth of the Clinic: An Archaeology of Medical Perception.* Trans. A. M. Sheridan Smith. New York: Vintage.

———. 1965b. *Madness and Civilization: A History of Insanity in the Age of Reason.* Trans. Richard Howard. New York: Vintage.

———. 1973. *The Order of Things: An Archaeology of the Human Sciences.* New York: Vintage.

———. 1979. *Discipline and Punish: The Birth of the Prison.* Trans. Alan Sheridan. New York: Vintage.

Gare, Arran E. 1995. *Postmodernism and the Environmental Crisis.* New York: Routledge.

Love, Glen. 1990. "Revaluing Nature: Toward an Ecological Criticism." *Western American Literature* 25 (Nov.): 201–15.

Lyon, Thomas J. 1989. "A Taxonomy of Nature Writing." In *This Incomperable Lande: A Book of American Nature Writing,* ed. Thomas J. Lyon, 3–7. New York: Houghton Mifflin and Co.

Miller, J. Hillis. 1977. "Nature and the Linguistic Moment." In *Nature and the Victorian Imagination,* ed. U. C. Knoepflmacher and G. B. Tennyson, 440–51. Berkeley: University of California Press.

Quigley, Peter. 1992. "Rethinking Resistance: Environmentalism, Literature, and Poststructural Theory." *Environmental Ethics* 14 (4): 291–306.

Silverman, Kaja. 1983. *The Subject of Semiotics.* New York: Oxford University Press.

Surviving Doom and Gloom

Edward Abbey's Desert Comedies

REBECCA

RAGLON

"**O**ne of the penalties of an ecological education is that one lives alone in a world of wounds," Aldo Leopold wrote in *A Sand County Almanac* (1949, 145). Because of the enormous destruction of natural habitat and the exploitation of resources during and following the Second World War, the sense of living in a world of "wounds" has continued to intensify. Nature writing, the literary genre that has traditionally celebrated the natural world, began to change as well. In addition to expressing an aesthetic appreciation of a particular landscape, writers now found themselves more and more often struggling to record the habits of some animal on the verge of extinction, or writing about a last bit of wild ground before it was "developed." While a desire to preserve a loved landscape has been an aspect of the genre since its conception, the elegiac tone threatening to engulf contemporary nature writing is something new. The titles alone, ranging from Rachel Carson's *Silent Spring* to Farley Mowat's *Sea of Slaughter*, tell a suggestive story about the changing character of nature writing in the second half of the twentieth century.

Among the pages of ecological apocalypse and gloom, however, Edward Abbey's work stands out. Not only does Abbey offer a significant variation to the anguished tone of much environmental writing, but in addition his work challenges the pieties and moralizing tendency of some nature writers. According to the novelist Joyce Carol Oates, nature elicits a "painfully limited set of responses in 'nature writers'—REVERENCE, AWE, PIETY, MYSTICAL ONENESS" (1987, 236). According to Oates, however, this is because nature itself "has no sense of humor: in its beauty, as in its ugliness, or its neutrality, there is no laughter" (236). Although Oates's shrewd comments offer a telling critique of some aspects of the genre, they also reveal a lack of acquaintance with the work of Edward Abbey and the very different qualities of his brand of nature writing.

What distinguishes Abbey from the majority of twentieth-century nature writers is his use of comedy. In a mournful time of extinction and loss, Abbey's work is humorous. In a time of despair over seemingly inevitable "development," Abbey's satire deflates powerful social forces and offers hope. Furthermore, his comedy is full-bodied: as an accomplished and very funny writer, he employs a full range of comedic effects, from the effervescence of romantic comedy to parody, and from irony to the harsher, angrier strains of satire. These are all elements of Abbey's literary style, and all are used in service of a larger and more pressing need to defend the wild spaces of the American Southwest. In books like *The Monkey Wrench Gang* (1975), Abbey's comic style is thus not only used to entertain but, on another level, is employed because comedy can dismantle the beliefs that underlie the status quo. In Abbey's work, then, comedy has a dual function, serving both literary needs and political concerns. In addition, nature itself is viewed not as a place where "the sea is a cup of death and the land is a stained altar stone" (Dillard 1974, 178) but as a source of our greatest human joys. For Abbey, the world is neither grim nor tragic, and the natural order is actually a rather humorous affair. Even that most solemn of solemn mysteries—death—has underpinnings of comedy in Abbey's view. Style and theme are thus continually intertwined in Abbey's work, each one nourishing the other. Nature is a joyful place—and laughter can diffuse encroaching dangers.

While Abbey is one of the most satiric of American writers, able to expose human folly (including his own) with a shrewd jeer, his work also provides a striking example of the effectiveness of comedy in undercutting those broader cultural preoccupations that some theorists believe have proven lethal for the natural world. Joseph Meeker, for example, in one of the first attempts to write about the relationship of ecology to literature, discusses how our cultural attachment to a tragic view of life has proven detrimental to a wiser sense of our place in the natural world. According to Meeker, the very basis of tragedy is human self-aggrandizement coupled with the belief that "some truth exists in the universe which is more valuable than life itself" (1972, 37). In contrast to this tragic worldview, comedy values the continuation of life above all else: "Comedy, like evolution, like life itself, is careless of morality, goodness, truth, beauty, heroism, and all such abstract values men say they live by. Its only concern is to affirm man's capacity for survival and to celebrate the continuity of life itself, despite all moralities. Comedy is a celebration, a ritual renewal of biological welfare as it persists in spite of any reasons there may be for feeling metaphysical despair" (24).

In outlining his arguments for an ecological literature, Meeker writes that we may well expect "earth art" to be comic, for "comedy illustrates that survival depends upon man's ability to change himself rather than his environment, and upon his ability to accept limitations rather than to curse fate for limiting him" (39). Much of Abbey's work seems to echo these sentiments: not only is he impatient with people who do not realize that humans possess a paradise here on earth, but over and over again, throughout his many works, he exults not only in his own but in other creatures' survival in the desert. Because the world is neither grim nor tragic, there is no need to escape it or bemoan our harsh fate. What there is a need for, however, is a strategy for changing ourselves in order to ensure not only our survival but also the survival of other creatures. How better to achieve this than by shifting our focus away from an inflated sense of "tragedy" onto a more flexible and life-affirming "comedy of survival"? Survival, in other words, *requires* comedy, for it is comedy that tears away the veil from a tragic conception of life. This becomes particularly clear in works like *The Monkey Wrench Gang*, which employs comedy both thematically and stylistically in order to diffuse a growing sense of helplessness over the outrages being perpetuated in the Southwest. If life is not tragic, then there is indeed something worth preserving "out there."

Abbey does not subscribe to the inevitably tragic idea that we are the only "self-conscious" creatures in a terrifyingly "empty" universe. This kind of thinking is self-aggrandizement at its worse, and self-aggrandizement is a common human gesture. As a way of commenting on this mistaken notion, Abbey fills the desert spaces of *Desert Solitaire* and other books with a rich and satisfying cast of nonhuman characters who nevertheless behave with egoistic self-regard. Far from encountering a vast "indifference" in nature, Abbey finds a world filled with love-struck snakes, self-pitying cows, vicious gnats; even nonliving things appear to share characteristics of the living, as when

Abbey notices the flames in his fireplace "eating" the wood. Everything, in fact, in this spare, arid desert region is alive—as alive as a human being. "Heidegger was wrong, as usual: man is *not* the only living thing that exists," Abbey muses in a philosophical mood (1991, 279). While frankly anthropomorphic, it is Abbey's comic vision that saves his work from being labeled maudlin or from the charges of sentimentality often leveled against writers of animal stories such as Ernest Thompson Seton or Charles G. D. Roberts.

Literary critics, perhaps also wary of appearing "sentimental," have tended to place Abbey's work rather firmly within the "Darwinian universe"—the nineteenth-century version, which in Tennyson's words is "red in tooth and claw" (Ronald 1982, 62). It is perhaps more accurate to say that Abbey's universe is one composed of struggle, but struggle mitigated by joy, which Abbey suggests has survival value for all species: "I suspect that the morose and fearful are doomed to quick extinction" (1991, 143). When he hears the sound of spadefoot toads after a desert rain, he wonders if "these small beings are singing not only to claim their stake in the pond, not only to attract a mate, but also out of spontaneous love and joy, a contrapuntal choral celebration of coolness and wetness after weeks of desert fire, for love of their own existence, however brief it may be" (143).

Edward Abbey first saw the silent spaces of the American Southwest in 1944. He was seventeen and had left his home in Pennsylvania to hitchhike around the country before being sent off to war. Abbey goes back to that first moment in the American desert again and again in his writings. As he stood at the doors of a swaying box car, watching the Arizona landscape flash by, he felt that this was the West of his "deepest imaginings—the place where the tangible and the mythical become the same" (1977, 184). Over the next two years as an infantryman in Italy, Abbey kept the memory of that place alive, above all, "the radiance of that high desert sunlight, which first stirs, then exhilarates your senses, your mind, your soul" (184). It was a place that was to haunt him throughout his life. It would take years, however, before he would discover that place as his subject: as something he not only would try to evoke in both his fiction and "personal histories," but also something he would be called upon to defend.

It would also take him a while to find the comic voice that would provide a match for his subject matter. Although best known for his nonfiction nature writing, Abbey began by writing fiction. His first novel, *Jonathan Troy,* had an Eastern setting and was followed in 1956 by *The Brave Cowboy,* subtitled "An Old Tale in a New Time." It is an interesting work that examines the cowboy heritage of the West in terms of present-day realities, but it lacks the satirical edge that characterizes the best of his later works and which is first glimpsed in the 1962 novel *Fire on the Mountain* (1962). Abbey liked to characterize this work as a trifle, "written with one hand, one dusty desert March" while he was working as a park ranger (qtd. in Standiford 1970, 397). Critics generally have concurred with Abbey's flippant assessment, finding that *Fire on the Mountain* lacks the richness of his other novels. Garth McCann calls it Abbey's "least effective novel" (1977, 17), while Ann Ronald finds the book "lacking in complexity" (1982, 47).

Seen solely as a failed tragedy, the book does, indeed, seem flawed: within a comic context, however, the book reveals the beginnings of Abbey's flamboyant satirical style. For the first time, Abbey begins to take chances by making the outspoken and outrageous statements that have found favor among environmentalists if not among literary critics. As Peter Wild observes, Abbey is a hero of environmentalists, "a hero whose panache, because at times zany and laughable, though in essence serious, gave them heart in what they saw as a grim life-and-death struggle over the earth's future" (1979, 195). In fact, *Fire on the Mountain* can be read as a type of early environmental "handbook" for activists, containing instructions similar to the "instructions" to be found in the pages of Abbey's later and better-known novel *The Monkey Wrench Gang.* Essentially the story of the U.S. government's repossession of a cattle rancher's land, the narrative is told from the viewpoint of Billy Vogelin Starr. Billy is a twelve-year-old boy from the East who goes to New Mexico every summer to stay at his grandfather's ranch. At the ranch, Billy discovers a child's paradise, though if the ranch were his, he would have "sold the cattle and stocked the place with wild horses and buffalo, coyotes and wolves, and let the beef industry go to ruin" (1962, 14).

Early in the book, Billy, the grandfather (John Vogelin), and a friend are out on a ride with a visitor from the Range Management Bureau. As the group passes a yucca, the bureaucrat asks Vogelin what yuccas are good for. In answering the question, Vogelin begins by using the standard conservationist argument for pleading their cases: a defense of nature based on human self-interest. In trying to humor the bureaucrat by trying to convince him that the yucca is, indeed, good "for" something, Vogelin falls into what John Livingston calls the "fallacy" of wildlife conservation. According to Livingston, the idea that the "right" for any form of life to exist can be based on its utility to humans has never been an effective way to argue. Hidden within such utilitarian arguments is the message that "*if we can't be good, at least we can be prudent*" (Livingston 1981, 42). Unfortunately, being prudent can take on a life of its own, as Vogelin soon learns.

Speaking to the bureaucrat, Vogelin notes that Indians make baskets out of the yuccas, use the stalks for fences, make medicine out of the flowers. But the bureaucrat easily defeats the utility argument when he asks who needs baskets when you have paper, cellophane, and cardboard; who needs shade when you can turn the air conditioner on; and as for medicine, it's available in Juarez for five dollars a gallon. The yucca, then, as Vogelin is forced to admit, is not really good "for" anything; it doesn't hold the soil down and hardly casts enough shade to shelter a rabbit. In admitting this, the bureaucrat sees a way to finally defeat Vogelin.

> The yucca is not good for anything, he says. It drinks your water, and it eats the minerals in your ground but it doesn't do you one—one nickel's worth of good. What should I do about it? I asked him. Kill them, he said. Kill every horny one of the ugly things. And don't stop there, he said; look at those cottonwood trees along the wash, sucking your river dry. What can I do about that? I asked. Ring them, he said. They're bleeding you like vampires—cut them down. Think of the awful waste. Don't you believe in conservation? (Abbey 1962, 37)

In satirizing the bureaucrat's logic, Abbey also takes the opportunity to critique the conservationist ethic still prevalent in the 1950s and early 1960s. Conservation was a plank in nineteenth-century political thought that attempted to introduce "science, rationality, and expertise" into the management of public and corporate affairs. The justification for rationally managing "nature" for the benefit of humans was part of the same program. Conservation, generally seen as a positive force for the preservation of wilderness, was actually a new technique used to serve industrialization (Worster 1973). Far from being wilderness preservationists, these efficiency conservationists saw the environment as something that needed to be harnessed and made more "productive" (Koppes 1988, 234). Abbey, in taking a preservationist's stance, strips away the protective covering on this "gospel of efficiency" with satiric brilliance.

Another target of Abbey's satire is the idea of the "wild West." When Billy first arrives in Baker, New Mexico, he goes to the Wagon Wheel Bar with his grandfather. It is a good bar according to Billy, gloomy and quiet and cool, wrapped in an aura of Western romance, for "men had died in this place." Hanging over the bar is a mural,

> A great primitive picture twenty feet long and ten feet high showing Thieves Mountain against an immaculate blue sky and three ragged black buzzards circling above a horseman in the heart of the White Sands. The horse trudged over the dunes with hanging head and closed eyes. The rider sat slumped in the saddle, a dark stain of blood on his shirt, the shaft of an arrow sticking out of his back, and a rifle hanging loosely from his limp left arm. The artist had given the painting a title: "Desert Doom, or Forty Miles From Hope." (1962, 12)

The picture contains every visual cliché associated with the West and is immensely appealing to Billy. Consequently, on his way out to the ranch, he sees a "landscape" similar to the one pictured in the Wagon Wheel Bar. This is an amusing introduction to the problem of how things are viewed, of how we learn to frame things in our mind's eye and transpose that onto a living landscape. The very concept of "landscape" is fixed and static: but it suggests only one way of experiencing nature. It is interesting to see how Abbey first presents the cliché and then modifies the "picture" by gradually infusing it with movement, and process, and the sense that the drama of nature continues independent of the human drama. For example, Billy is keenly aware that the cottonwood trees along the river are "alive," whispering, and "enjoying the best hour of the day" (35).

The most significant aspect of the book, however, is found less in stylistic comic elements and more in its wider comedic theme. Northrop Frye contends that the thematic underpinning of the comic mode lies in the "integration of society, which usually takes the form of incorporating a central character into it" (1957, 43). In other words, the disorder that reigns in the center of *A Midsummer Night's Dream* will, by the play's end, be resolved, with the human characters returned to society and each lover once again with their "true" partner. In Abbey's case—as it would be for most environmentally minded writers—"society" is, however, considerably enlarged to include any number of nonhuman lives. One of Abbey's themes thus becomes the integration of Billy into the wider "society" of his grandfather's ranch. There's a sense of freedom and adventure that contact with the land gives to Billy, and life on the ranch nourishes him both physically and spiritually. On the ranch, the fragrance of simmering pinto beans, chili, and fresh baked bread is the scent of homecoming; here there is none of the "soft sweet rotten food" that feeds the civilized world (1962, 124). The air in the desert is clear, filled with nothing but "light, oxygen, and the promise of lightning. Good for breathing and seeing" (41).

For Billy, a boy from the city, living on the ranch also means living his dreams. He rides horses, pretends to be an officer of the U.S. Cavalry, and is keenly aware of a mystery that lies beyond the hard edges of reality, mysteries that tempt his waking mind. Billy asks what is on the summit of Thieves Mountain, convinced that there is "something" besides rock, flowers, and an eagle's nest. One night on the mountain, when Billy goes to the stream for water, he happens to see on a crag above him "a pair of yellow eyes gleaming in a sleek head . . . a dark powerful shape of unforeseeable hugeness crouched as if to leap" (67). The encounter with the mountain lion is an encounter with the wild heart of the land: Billy's deepest "integration" with the mountain is found in his imagining that he alone can hear the lion scream.

Desert Solitaire was a departure for Abbey because it was his first work of nonfiction; nevertheless, as in *Fire on the Mountain,* the purpose of *Desert Solitaire* is also broadly comedic. Once again the action tells of the *integration* of a "hero" (Abbey) into society. Once again, "society" is very broadly defined and is seen to include a wide range of other creatures. The act of integration begins when Abbey's narrator steps out of the small trailer which is his home in the desert. The trailer symbolizes the last outpost of technology and is described by Abbey as being "cold as a tomb, a jail, a cave" (1991, 4). The trailer is equipped with all the "indispensable" conveniences: a gas cookstove and refrigerator, a sink with hot running water, and a small electric generator to provide light. With the generator running and lights on, however, he is "shut off from the natural world and sealed up, encapsulated, in a box of artificial light and tyrannical noise" (15). It is necessary to open his doors and move out into the natural world, a move that exchanges a "great and unbounded world for a small, comparatively meager one" (15). When he leaves his "outpost of technology" (4) and turns the generator off, he finds the night flows back to him. He is no longer shut off and isolated, for the "night stillness embraces and includes me; I can see the stars again and the world of starlight" (15).

In *Desert Solitaire* Abbey employs every comic device, from a parody of A. E. Houseman—"Loveliest of shrubs the cliffrose now / Is hung with bloom along the bough"—to ridicule: "Operatives from the Chamber of Commerce look into red canyons and see only green, stand among flowers snorting out money, and hear, while thunderstorms rumble over mountains, the fall of a dollar bill on motel carpeting" (57). The cult of the cowboy, in particular, needs to be put to rest if a more truthful version of the West is ever to emerge. While working cowboys disappear, make-believe cowboys "multiply like flies on a pecan pie" (126). Everywhere west of the Mississippi, Abbey sees "Mr. and Mrs. Cattleman couple in authentic matching Western costume—the husband with sunburnt nose and belly bulging over a steer horn buckle heavy enough to kill a horse with, and his wife, a tall tough broad in gabardines and boots with a look on her face that would make a Comanche blanch" (126).

Abbey also takes on the tone of the narrator of "A Modest Proposal" (mild and eminently reasonable) to make outrageous statements about an abiding national tragedy, that is, the disinheritance of the American Indian.

> Among these people a liberal hospitality is taken for granted and selfishness regarded with horror. Shackled by such primitive attitudes, is it any wonder that the Navajos have not yet been able to get in step with the rest of us? . . .
> . . . They must learn that courtesy and hospitality are not simply the customs of any decent society but are rather a special kind of commodity which can be peddled for money. (122–23)

Abbey consistently employs pathetic fallacy in his descriptions of the natural world, but no crocuses shiver in his prose. Abbey's metaphors are more robust: the spectacle of a flash flood, made comic in Abbey's world, is described as having a sort of "forelip about a foot high streaming in front making hissing sucking noises like a giant amoeba, nosing to the right and nosing to the left as if on the spoor of something good to eat" (138). In one obsessive hunt for water, the author crouches by a small spring: "No other water within miles, the local gnat population fought me for every drop. To keep them out of the canteen, I had to place a handkerchief over the opening as I filled it. Then they attacked my eyes, drawn irresistibly by the liquid shine of the human eyeball. Embittered little bastards. Never have I tasted better water" (133).

Or we see Abbey, the modern-day cowboy, tormented by heat, hunger, and flies, attacking a cow, who is tormented by the same things, and who quite naturally prefers the shade of a tamarisk to any thought of moving on. In frustration the narrator beats her, kicks her, and yanks at her tail. "At last, groaning and farting with exaggerated self-pity, she hoisted her rear end, then her front end, and plodded off to join the gang" (103). Abbey is kinder to a gopher snake who lives in his trailer and occasionally wraps himself around the narrator's body for warmth. "We are compatible," Abbey writes. "From my point of view, friends" (22).

Abbey can risk talking about "his friend" the snake because he does not sidestep the harsher aspects of the natural order. But as would be expected in Abbey's universe, even death itself does not resonate with tragic overtones. Death, too, it seems, has its place in a world that is essentially joyful and comic. Early in *Desert Solitaire*, as Abbey is surveying "his" realm, he decides to conduct an experiment. Imagining himself starving, and with no weapons but his bare hands, he asks himself what would he do, what could he do about the rabbit that crossed his path. Abbey picks up a rock, throws it at the rabbit, and to his surprise, kills it: "But shock is succeeded by a mild elation. . . . No longer do I feel so isolated from the sparse and furtive life around me, a stranger from another world. I have entered into this one. We are kindred all of us, killer and victim, predator and prey, me and the sly coyote, the soaring buzzard, the elegant gopher snake, the trembling cottontail, the foul worms that feed on our entrails, all of them, all of us. Long live diversity, long live the earth!" (38–39).

Death is a constant part of life, a fact that reverberates with graphic intensity in the desert. Death is also the ultimate form of limitation imposed upon human aspiration, but is this a tragic fact, or one that can be, must be, accommodated? Roy Scobie, one of the last "real cowboys," confesses that he's afraid of having a heart attack while out on his horse: "The manner of death he fears does not sound bad to me; to me it seems like a decent, clean way of taking off, surely better than the slow rot in a hospital oxygen tent" (94). Yet Abbey is also honest enough to admit that at his age death is "little more than a fascinating abstraction."

Life in the desert contains a constant reminder of the nearness of death, however. To go for a walk in the heat without adequate water, for example, could be fatal. "The desert is a land of surprises, some of them terrible surprises" (132). To die in the desert has little comfort other than the reflection that "if all goes as planned, your human flesh will be working its way through the gizzard of a buzzard, your essence transfigured into the fierce greedy eyes and unimaginable consciousness of a turkey vulture" (135). When Abbey finds the body of a lost tourist, his first impulse is to congratulate the dead man on his choice of a place to die: on the edge of a point, in the shade of a juniper. Then, for relief, the rescue party "meditates" on the tourist's death by joking about his fate. If they had known him, perhaps they would have been able to mourn by dancing, drinking, and making love. But they didn't know him, and they feel a certain abstract "satisfaction" with the man's death, for "his departure makes room for the living" (242).

This is cold comfort, and Abbey knows it. There is something in us, he goes on to admit, that rebels against this harsh brand of nature's "economy," a rebellion that complicates our existence on Earth. How can anyone not be satisfied with this world, Abbey asks again and again throughout his work. "If a man's imagination were not so weak, so easily tired, if his capacity for wonder not so limited, he would abandon forever such fantasies of the supernal" (200). Oddly enough, however, fear of death fuels both "supernal" fantasies and our love of life. For example, in one of Abbey's desert walks, he finds himself trapped in a side canyon. He knows his fate is "Fatal. Death by starvation, slow and tedious" (227). What disturbs him most at that moment, what makes him shed tears ("All alone, I didn't have to be brave"), is the sight of a cloud passing the narrow opening of the canyon (229). It is delicate and inaccessible, and Abbey thinks he has never seen anything quite so beautiful. The author, of course, does survive and at the top of the "treacherous" canyons finds himself crying again, "the hot delicious tears of victory" (230). Before he can get back to his camp, however, he gets caught in a downpour and takes shelter in a small cave, littered with bird, rat, rabbit, and coyote droppings. Although he suffered through the night "wet, cold, aching, hungry, wretched" it was nevertheless "one of the happiest nights of [his] life" (231). Survival—just being alive—is a kind of victory. If we love life, Abbey seems to say, it is because we can—at any moment—lose it.

Along with the literary projects he completed during the 1950s, Abbey also wrote a master's thesis in philosophy in 1959 at the University of New Mexico. The thesis was entitled "Anarchism and the Morality of Violence." Abbey was attracted to this topic because he believed anarchism to be "alone among contemporary political doctrines in opposing the institution of the state" (1959, 1). Even this scholarly interest, however, would be stood on its head and given a humorous treatment in his fifth and most popular book of fiction, *The Monkey Wrench Gang* (1975). In this novel Abbey can and does indulge in the sense of loss common to so many twentieth-century nature writers, but he also demands from himself and his readers a new response, some way to evade the attitude of defeat lurking within doom-and-gloom environmentalism. Once again, comedy serves him well, suggesting that a manic response is the only appropriate one in a world gone mad.

Even Abbey's considerable verbal inventiveness seems to falter, however, in the face of the new devastation wreacked upon the Western landscape by machines. As his four main characters (the Monkey Wrench Gang) stare into an Arizona strip mine, the view is one that would be "difficult to describe in any known terrestrial language" (1976, 159). Nevertheless, Abbey is willing to try: the scene is compared to the war of the worlds, or to Vietnam, a devastation which is the product of a "conglomerated cartel spread out upon half the planet Earth like a global kraken, pan-tentacled, wall-eyed and parrot beaked, its brain a bank of computer data centers, its blood the flow of money, its heart a radioactive dynamo, its language the technotronic monologue of numbers imprinted on magnetic tape" (159).

The four characters opposing the destruction are diverse anarchists, ranging from George Hayduke—Vietnam veteran and "good healthy psychopath" who has a taste for destruction—to Bonnie Abbzug, a refugee from the Bronx who finds in the companionship of her fellow gang members a "community of soldiers" that brings a moral purpose to her life. The other two members are Doc Sarvis, conducting his own personal campaign to beautify America by burning billboards, and Seldom Seen Smith, a man made desperate enough by the changes he sees happening to pray for a little "precision earthquake" (32) to jar loose Glen Canyon Dam.

This odd assortment of characters gathers for a river-rafting trip down the Colorado, and one night, around a campfire, a "crafty intimacy" overtakes them. One by one, they confess certain deep-rooted secrets, such as Doc's desire to blow the Glen Canyon Dam to "shitaree." It is Doc who tells the others about Ned Ludd and *les sabots:* those clear-sighted individuals who "saw what was coming and acted directly." Without any further discussion, a decision of sorts is made, and Abbey takes a moment to mock the theorists who were the subject of his own early academic work:

"Do we know what we're doing and why?"
"No."
"Do we care?"
"We'll work it all out as we go along. Let our practice form our doctrine, thus assuring precise theoretical coherence." (65)

In *The Monkey Wrench Gang* Abbey develops his ideas of the need for "constructive vandalism" (104) to save the planet. Abbey gives the vandalism of the gang a manic, wild humor, and by directing their creative violence solely against machines, he is able to expose the real violence of his society. Even if violence is as American as pizza pie, as Hayduke points out (163), Abbey is careful to redefine the parameters of this violence. This is not to go as far as Ann Ronald, who characterizes the gang's activities as "nonviolent assault" (1982, 182). On the contrary, Abbey frequently reminds his readers that this "playful romp" has a deadly serious mission. While the gang members never intend to kill anyone, they are inadvertently involved in numerous incidents where people could get killed—and almost do. Although Abbey does not eliminate this aspect of violence (to do so would eliminate a great deal of the dramatic tension in the book), there is never any question of deliberately directing violent tactics against humans. The only targets are the machines that perpetuate the dominance of "man" over "nature."

This targeting of machines is a crucial element in Abbey's portrayal of violence, upon which the whole comedy of the book depends. The machine, which in one scene has its "life blood drained out with pulsing throbs" (86), is not really alive in spite of Abbey's amusing and persistent attempts to so personify it. The double irony here, of course, hinges on the recognition that the little pinyon pine the tractor's blade pushes over with "nonchalant ease" really *is* alive and takes many days to die. Yet life is continually and casually sacrificed to the machine, and in *The Monkey Wrench Gang* Abbey raises a fundamental question when he obliquely asks which act is then truly the most violent. The awful realization for readers of the novel is that technological societies place the greatest value on the "life" of their machines. Even the gang members are infected with this pervasive reverence. For example, after dismantling a twenty-seven-ton "compactor" (80), they stand "awed by the enormity of their crime. By the sacrilege of it" (81).

In order to dismantle this feeling of "sacrilege," Abbey embeds his imagined violent acts in an array of comic situations, again using a full array of comic devices. As in his other work, he uses exaggeration, parody, irony, ridicule, and satire. He takes aim at an incredibly diverse number of targets, including Marshall McLuhan, B. F. Skinner, and Chairman Mao, and he doesn't pause when it comes time to mock himself as the author of *Desert Solipsism* or as the park ranger Edwin P. Abbott, "tall, slim, able, not too bright" (189). In *The Monkey Wrench Gang* Abbey also introduces a new comedic element (for him) in his use of a traditional "happy ending." Hayduke, despite all evidence to the contrary, survives, while Seldom Seen Smith, Doc Sarvis, and Bonnie Abbzug are given light jail sentences and probation. Doc and Bonnie are married and move from Albuquerque to Green River, Utah (pop. 1,200), where they can live a life of balanced environmentalism (Bonnie no longer has to chauffeur Doc around the ugly streets of Albuquerque because they ride their bikes to work). Even their old implacable enemies—the ironically named Love brothers—have a change of heart and quit the search-and-rescue team that had so relentlessly pursued the eco-raiders. In this case, at least two heroes and a heroine are reintegrated into human society, and the implication is that some fundamental readjustment has occurred, both within themselves and within society at large, that allows them to coexist. Finally, the "epilogue" ("The New Beginning") links up to the prologue (the "Aftermath") when Hayduke learns that the old gang members were not the ones responsible for the destruction of the Glen Canyon Bridge, implying that another, unidentified movement has begun in the Southwest and will carry on the work of change.

In employing comedy and in refining his concept of violence by directing it solely against nonhuman targets, Abbey is able to challenge our notions of what is sacred and expose the real violence in society. Although Abbey wanted his book to entertain, he also held out the hope that it would be read as "something more." Abbey always enjoyed poking fun at sacred cows, wherever he found them: it was his credo that a writer "must be a critic of the society in which he lives," whose works should "oppose, resist, and sabotage the contemporary drift toward a global technocratic police state" (1988, 161, 177). According to Abbey's own romantic notions, then, *The Monkey Wrench Gang* should be read in the spirit of resistance, and its comic tone should not be viewed as masking his more serious intent. Violence in *The Monkey Wrench Gang* is more than just "wish fulfillment."

As the gang watches the GEM (Giant Earth Mover) of Arizona at work—"waddling forward, ducklike" an "enormous structure of powerhouse, control cabin, chassis, superstructure, crane, cables and ore bucket"—they think to themselves, "we are so small, they are so huge" (1976, 160). This, too, becomes a refrain and is a challenge to their creative vandalism. Their job is to "keep it like it was" (77). Unlike the bad man in a classic Western showdown, however, the forces of good and evil are no longer conceived as equals. The real enemy is the machine, but the machine is backed by a technological juggernaut, the state, the army, the police. However, a "them and us" scenario develops only when one or more of the main characters feels the strain of being an "outlaw." When Smith argues that the military personnel are "people, too, like us," Hayduke, the only real outlaw of the group, spits back, "They're not like us. . . . They're different. They come from the moon. They'll spend a million dollars to burn one gook to death" (90).

Generally, however, evil is pictured as more diffuse, found everywhere, even in the most banal settings. Hayduke walks into a café and sees "Two silver-gray cowboy hats and two wide important rumps in gabardine. He spotted them instantly as the kind of men who wear bolo ties and shoot doves and eat Vienna sausages out of a can on fishing jaunts. The kind of folks that made American what it is today" (261–62). In scenes like this, Abbey makes us laugh at the powerful, and in the act of laughing, the process of demystifying society's sacred cows begins.

Works Cited
Abbey, Edward. 1959. "Anarchism and the Morality of Violence." M.A. thesis, University of New Mexico.

————. 1962. *Fire on the Mountain*. New York: Dial Press.

————. [1975] 1976. *The Monkey Wrench Gang*. Reprint, New York: Avon.

————. 1977. *The Journey Home*. New York: E. P. Dutton.

————. 1988. *One Life at a Time, Please*. New York: Henry Holt.

————. [1968] 1991. *Desert Solitaire*. Reprint, New York: Ballantine.

Dillard, Annie. 1974. *Pilgrim at Tinker Creek*. New York: Harper Perennial.

Frye, Northrop. 1957. *Anatomy of Criticism*. Princeton, N.J.: Princeton University Press.

Halpern, Daniel, ed. 1987. *On Nature*. San Francisco: North Point Press.

Koppes, Clayton. 1988. "Efficiency, Equity, Esthetics." In *The Ends of the Earth*, ed. Donald Worster. Cambridge: Cambridge University Press.

Leopold, Aldo. 1949. *A Sand County Almanac*. Oxford: Oxford University Press.

Livingston, John A. 1981. *The Fallacy of Wildlife Conservation*. Toronto: McClelland and Stewart.

McCann, Garth. 1977. *Edward Abbey*. Boise State Western Writers Series, no. 29. Boise, Idaho: Boise State University.

Meeker, Joseph. 1972. *The Comedy of Survival*. New York: Charles Scribner's Sons.

Oates, Joyce Carol. 1987. "Against Nature." In Halpern.

Ronald, Ann. 1982. *The New West of Edward Abbey*. Albuquerque: University of New Mexico Press.

Standiford, Les. 1970. "Desert Places: An Exchange with Edward Abbey." *Western Humanities Review* 24.

Wild, Peter. 1979. *Pioneer Conservationists of Western America*. Missoula, Mont.: Mountain Press.

Worster, Donald. 1973. *American Environmentalism*. New York: John Wiley and Sons.

Nietzschean Themes in the Works of Edward Abbey

STEVE

NORWICK

Most readers find many of Edward Abbey's images and state-ments interesting but puzzling, troubling, challenging, and even nonsensical. I believe that most of these confusing, and bold, passages are Nietzschean. The influence is pervasive, evidenced by nu-merous quotes and several Nietzschean themes in his novels and essays. The purpose of this chapter is: (1) to shed light on the Nietz-schean quality of Abbey's thought, and (2) to give a few examples of how understanding his brand of Nietzscheanism sheds light on his artistic and political motives.

There is no doubt that Abbey was familiar with Nietzsche, whom he had certainly read as a philosophy student. There are direct quota-tions from Nietzsche in many of Abbey's books, including ironic references to professional outdoorsmen and -women as "Uber-menchen" (1984, 170), though Abbey did not actually use the con-cept. Several times he repeated Nietzsche's call to be "True to the earth" (Nietzsche 1964 11:7). At the Grand Canyon, Abbey quoted Nietzsche's admonition, "Gaze not too long into the abyss, Lest the abyss gaze into thee" (Abbey 1984, 118). In *A Fool's Progress* Henry Lightcap contemplates suicide, saying, "The thought of suicide, as Nietzsche says, has got me through many a bad night" (Abbey 1990, 6) and "The married philosopher is a figure out of a stage farce" (37). Abbey's posthumously published poem "Due Notice" is a paraphrase of several of Nietzsche's aphorisms (1994b, 66). The title itself is clearly a reference to the famous dream in which Nietzsche ate the green Earth like an apple.

Most major turn-of-the-century English-language authors were moved by the bold originality of Nietzsche's writing style, which was often aphoristic, but few wrote like him (Bridgwater 1972). Even though his writing often seems bombastic and hysterical in English translations, he was extremely antisentimental. This antisentimentalism contrasts sharply with the rhythmic poetic prose that Abbey read in the Oscar Levy translations, much of whose diction is quasi-King James biblical. Abbey's style in his novels and nature essays was not noticeably influenced by Nietzsche except in the most important passages. In short, passionate paragraphs, Abbey delivers his message using powerful, rhythmic, long lines. Consider, for example, the following description from *Desert Solitaire:* "Despite its clarity and simplicity, however, the desert wears at the same time, paradoxically, a veil of mystery. Motionless and silent it evokes in us an elusive hint of something unknown, unknowable, about to be revealed. Since the desert does not act it seems to be waiting—but waiting for what?" (1971b, 270–71).

Abbey was aware of his tendency to rely on rhythm, and he feared it was not appropriate for his audience. In his journal he recorded his efforts to remove rhythm from his prose (1994a, 82, 130, 156), but in other selections from his journals (*Confessions of a Barbarian* [1994a]) and in his aphorisms (*A Voice Crying in the Wilderness: Vox Clamantis in Deserto* [1994c]) we can see that Abbey was secretly using a style very much like the Oscar Levy translations, just for his own amusement and as inspiration for his other writing.

Nietzsche used startling phrases, often oxymorons that seem to be nonsense. He did not use the rhetorical forms that accompany most supposedly "rational" arguments, and he did not generally write syllogistically. Instead he advanced ideas through metaphors and parables and even contradictions. He was often paradoxical and believed that "In order to interest clever persons in a theory, it is sometimes only necessary to put it before them in the form of a prodigious paradox" (1964, 6:270). Abbey followed this tradition by emphasizing the unity of dissimilar objects. According to him, World War II brought "Hitler, war and general prosperity" (1971b, 4). He described smog as "tender, velvety smog" (1971, 1). He loved the beautiful flowers of the dangerously barbed desert plants (28), a visual contradiction of danger and beauty. He ironically described the "Friendship Dance" at which the Havasupai and Haulapai Indians dance, get drunk, and brawl (224).

A striking example of one of his many oxymorons is Abbey's description of the desert wilderness as "remote and at the same time intimate " (190). In a naive sense this is simply physically impossible. In a visual sense, the desert is strangely remote because, unlike most landscapes, one can see for miles. Yet unlike a forest or city, the desert is intimately exposed to the casual viewer. In a poetic sense, the desert remains remote even to a hiker and naturalist like Abbey because it is so strange to European culture. And yet, at moments, it seems like a surrealistic dream, which is an intimate, interior, personal process. Abbey repeatedly called attention to the desert's dreamlike character. A dream—in which things happen that are physically impossible and socially and personally unacceptable—is remote from our waking experience, and yet our dreams express our most intimate feelings.

Although Nietzsche wrote often of the "Joyful Wisdom" (1964, vol. 10) and a need to laugh heartily, the Levy translations do not carry a convincing merriment to most English readers (e.g., 1964, 11:187, 193). In fact, Nietzsche and his famous literary followers—including H. G. Wells, Eugene O'Neill, Theodore Dreiser, James Joyce, and D. H. Lawrence—were not generally a cheery lot. Barring his disciples Oscar Wilde, George Bernard Shaw, and H. L. Mencken, there was not a belly laugh in the bunch. In contrast, Edward Abbey was a clown, and a very funny one at that. Most readers laugh at Abbey or with Abbey in many places. Of all his books, only two lack a relaxed, pleasant sense of sarcasm and self-irony: *Cactus Country,* a natural history text, heavily edited by the Time-Life staff, and *Black Sun,* the powerful tragedy dedicated to his young wife who died of leukemia. In general, however, Abbey tackled important topics with humor and a well-developed sense of fun. Given Nietzsche's recognition of joyfulness as a sign of authenticity, he likely would have approved.

Everything in Nietzsche seems both strongly physical and deeply symbolic. He used concrete images and gave them a sense of symbolic importance, although the underlying meaning of the symbol is often obscure. Similarly, Abbey is famous for his stark and striking descriptions of strange desert landscapes. He often hinted that these places are haunted or have symbolic meaning. For example, his favorite juniper tree "stands half-alive, half dead, the silvery wind-rubbed claw of wood projected stiffly at the sun. A single cloud floats in the sky to the northeast, motionless, a magical coalescence of vapor where a few minutes before there was nothing visible but the hot, deep, black-grained blueness of infinity" (1971b, 155).

The literary persona of Abbey and his conscious act of masking are also strikingly similar to Nietzsche. Masking was a major theme in Nietzsche's work (see Alderman 1977, 1–17), and he and Freud are considered the founders of the modern belief that each personality has many different parts, which are created not only by the physical and social environment of the individual but also by the person. Nietzsche called this process of self-creation "masking," and he equated having original thoughts with creating one's own mask. Nietzsche, who was a very complex person with many masks, wrote that "Every profound spirit needs a mask; nay, more, around every profound spirit there continually grows a mask" (1964, 12:56). Edward Abbey also presented himself that way, "I'm so complicated a person I don't know *what* role to effect, and I'm not clever enough to pass myself off as what I truly am, a complicated person" (1994a, 116). Abbey also admitted that some of his protagonists were personal portraits and masks (311).

Like Nietzsche, Abbey was complexly aware of himself making his own mask. In his journal entry of November 29, 1976, Abbey wrote, "The Edward Abbey of my books is largely a fictional creation, the true adventures of an imaginary person. The real Edward Abbey? I think I hardly know him. A shy, retiring, very timid fellow, obviously. Somewhat of a recluse, emerging rarely from his fictional den only when lured by money, vice, the prospect of applause" (1994, 246–47). The "I" here is the literary persona speaking as if he did not know the real personality who writes the books. What are we to make of a person who writes as his literary persona in a very personal journal that he nearly destroyed before he died (Clarke Abbey, pers. comm.). The complex, introverted self-consciousness with which Abbey's self creates selves is truly Nietzschean. Perhaps Abbey had absorbed so much of Nietzsche's antitranscendentalism that he really believed that only the surface of nature and the mask of people are real, that perhaps even "man is a dream, thought an illusion" (Abbey 1971b, 144).

Nietzsche portrayed himself and his other persona, Zarathustra, as "honest fools" (1964, 5:41; 11:5, 73). He vowed "To cling to life, blindly and madly, with no other aim . . . with all of the perverted desire of a fool" (5:149). He insisted that "looking down on ourselves . . . we must discover the hero and likewise the fool that is hidden in our passion for knowledge . . . in order not to lose the free dominion over things" (10:146). Abbey also presented himself as a fool. He mocked his foolish nature exploits, as when describing how he faced the cataracts of the Grand Canyon in an undersized dingy after forgetting his life jacket (1971b, 173–220), or when he walked alone across a waterless 115 miles of Sonoran Desert for the sheer pleasure of experiencing his strength and the otherness of the desert (1984, 1–49). Abbey's fictional autobiography, *The Fool's Progress,* is subtitled "an honest novel," an oxymoron echoing Nietzsche's wish to be "an honest fool." In *Desert Solitaire,* a visitor asks, "Any dangerous animals out here, ranger?" to which Abbey replies, "Just tourists." The tourists laugh, but Abbey thinks to himself, "Tell the truth, they never believe you" (1971b, 263).

In *The Fool's Progress,* Abbey not only has his protagonist do foolish things, but he also points out that the truth is funny to ordinary people, whom he considers to be less wise than the protagonist, who seems foolish to them. The ancient concept of the truth-telling wise fool is common in many pagan religions and in Native North American, Greek, and Nordic mythology. Saint Joseph was portrayed as a holy fool in the Middle Ages. Saint Francis (Armstrong 1973; Sorrell 1988) and Henry David Thoreau (as noted by Emerson in February 1838 in his journal) deliberately presented themselves as fools. Erasmus (*In Praise of Folly*) and John Bunyan (*Pilgrim's Progress*), both devout Christians, wrote that Jesus and true Christians are fools from the worldly point of view. The most famous wise fool in English literature is the court jester in King Lear. Nietzsche's Zarathustra is also a fool (e.g., 1964, 11:186), and so are Abbey's fictional protagonists.

Most modern literary nature writers present a pleasant, friendly, mild, and placid persona, even those who are, or were, not so in real life. Consider the voices of mainstream canonical nature writers such as Gilbert White, John Burroughs, John Muir, Enos Mills, Mary Austin, Henry Beston, Joseph Wood Krutch, Aldo Leopold, Sigrud Olson, and John Hay. Rachel Carson, who was called "shrill" by the chemical pesticide producers, also had a sweet, poetic, lyric style in most of her work. Nietzsche suggested, however, that the true nature lover "might be disagreeable, stingy, and conceited" (1964, 7:35), and Abbey seems to have set out to prove the point. He was the first modern English-speaking nature writer to present himself as a humorous but somewhat unpleasant, self-mocking curmudgeon. In this he was followed by Edward Hoagland, Charles Bowden, Colin Fletcher, and others, including a new brand of tough, world-wise women nature writers such as Gretel Ehrlich, Ann La Bastille, and Terry Tempest Williams.

Nietzsche's prose is complexly ironic. Although he accused Socrates of being doubly ironic—that is, of mocking his own ironic statements—Nietzsche was also capable of being ironic about his own irony without canceling the first by the second. This complexity is a deep sign of circular self-consciousness and the awareness of masking that is central to all Nietzschean enterprises (Alderman 1977, 1–17). It is also one of the profoundly Nietzschean aspects of Abbey's work. This complex irony sets Abbey apart from all other environmental writers, who are often ironic about others but rarely about themselves, and never doubly ironic. For example, most nature writers have at least a few ironic passages in which they mock commercial enterprises, especially land developers who would destroy important habitat. Calvin Rustram would be one well-known but not very literary example. Only a few nature writers make ironic self-references, although Muir did mock himself when admitting his fear of falling from Mount Ritter in chapter 4 of *The Mountains of California* (1894).

Abbey, in contrast, was often ironic about his own irony. Writing about his parents' home in Appalachia, he described it as "shotgun country, redneck territory, hillbilly heaven. A lounging sullen homicidal primitive in every doorway. My people" (1990, 460). This passage begins with a comic ironic comment on the stereotype of the Appalachian residents. Then the irony becomes so exaggerated that it is clear that Abbey's protagonist is mocking himself for acting superior to his peasant roots. To my knowledge, no other nature writers in English use this double irony, though it is well developed in some popular general writers, including the Midwestern radio humorist Garrison Keillor and the playwright and screenwriter Wallace Shawn.

The admiration of natural dangers expressed by Nietzsche and Abbey goes back to the notion of the sublime in seventeenth-century landscape painting. The great Italian and Dutch landscape painters accepted the danger of the ocean or mountains or storm as a manifestation of God (Nicholson 1959). Danger was popularized in nature writing by John Muir, but it continued to be described in a sentimental and Christian tone. Nietzsche accepted and affirmed the aesthetic of violence but challenged the religious and sentimental part of the tradition. He asked, "Is there a pessimism of strength? An intellectual predilection for what is hard, awful, evil, problematical in existence, owing to well-being, to exuberant health, to fullness of existence?"

(1964, 1:2). Abbey can also be considered Nietzschean in this way. He admired the violence of nature and even the ugly sides of his human characters because his own exuberant persona was so strong that he was not spiritually endangered by evil or physical hazard, even if he was physically in danger. For Nietzsche and Abbey, one of the things that makes life worth living is the joy of surviving violence.

Nineteenth- and early-twentieth-century natural history essayists presented a rather puritanical persona. For example, Thoreau ("Former Inhabitants; and Winter Visitors," *Walden*), John Muir (*My First Summer in the Sierra*), and Mary Austin (*Earth Horizon*) were all teetotalers and happy to say so. Most twentieth-century nature writers appear clearly descended from the New England tradition, adopting personas that are almost universally modest. Until recently, there was neither sex nor strong drink in American nature writing. Then we were introduced to the persona of Abbey's essays: a swaggering, macho, physically strong, healthy, lusty, often drunken, nature-loving, and, on a few occasions, mildly evil satyr. This was unique in American literary natural history writing. Nietzsche, however, identified the satyr as the "archetype of man" and "the true man" (1964, 1:63). In the late nineteenth century, numerous British Nietzscheans adopted this playful, anarchic, Pan-like stance (Bridgman 1972), but only Abbey has gone so far as to call himself a "satyr-maniac" (1994a, 216).

The following is a rather long list of themes. Because Nietzsche was an early advocate of many ideas that became commonplace in American nature writing and environmental-activist circles, no one of them proves that Abbey was a Nietzschean. For example, Nietzsche wrote that "The earth hath a skin; and this skin hath diseases. One of these diseases, for example, is called man" (1964, 11:157). Abbey also used the notion of urban humanity as a disease (usually cancer) in essays and especially in the novels *The Monkey Wrench Gang*, *Hayduke Lives!*, and *Good News*. This by itself proves nothing, but the large number of similar themes is very strongly suggestive, though clearly not positive proof, that Abbey was reading from Nietzsche as he wrote.

Both Abbey and Nietzsche opposed the common conceit that nature is a book written by God. Nietzsche insisted that nature is "no text" (1964, 6:19, 12:32). Abbey turned the metaphor completely around when he described his own book, *Desert Solitaire*, his attack on the urbanization of the national parks: "This is not a travel guide but an elegy. A memorial. You're holding a tombstone in your hands. A bloody rock. Don't drop it on your foot—throw it at something big and glassy. What do you have to lose?" (1971, xii). Not only is the earth not a book, but this political book about a very rocky part of the earth is itself not to be read but to be used as a rock.

Nietzsche repeatedly advised, "Flee into thy solitude," and he also wrote, "I love the forest. It is bad to live in cities" (1964, 11:61, 144). At times, however, Zarathustra had to leave the wilderness for the city, as did Abbey at the end of *Desert Solitaire*. Most American environmental writers express a distaste for cities at all times. Abbey hated cities and mocked the life of city dwellers at every opportunity, but he had Nietzsche's ambivalence. There were times when he wrote with humor and irony about wanting to go to the city: "Space-age sleaze. High-tech slums. Nothing new. But the streets and sidewalks are full of people, during business hours, and that too, like the pool-rooms and cigar shops, is a pleasing sight" (1990, 212).

Most English-speaking nature writers are sentimental "nature lovers." Nietzsche hated "The insipid and cowardly notion 'Nature' invented by Nature enthusiasts" who desired to "live according to Nature" (1964, 14:274). Nietzsche mocked them and pointed out that nature is "boundlessly extravagant, boundlessly indifferent, without purpose or consideration, without pity or justice, at once fruitful and barren and uncertain" (12:13). He insisted that "To be natural means, to dare to be as immoral as Nature is" (14:98). Abbey was also very antisentimental. His desert is "cruel, clear, inhuman . . . motionless and emotionless at the same time" (1971b, 286) with utter "indifference manifest to our presence, our absence, our coming, our staying or our going" (301). This view of the natural world is still repugnant to most "nature lovers."

Nietzsche and Abbey both disliked domestic animals, especially herd animals, and they liked most wild animals. Nietzsche called modern urban man "the domestic animal, the gregarious animal, the sick animal—the Christian" (1964, 16:129). Abbey hated cows and sheep (1971b, 66), and he loved all wildlife except perhaps ants and gnats. He hated ants because he associated them with urban life and fascism. He wanted a flash flood to drown the "great ant-civilizations" (139), and he enjoyed destroying "their evil nests" (152).

Nietzsche was an early advocate of visualizing the feelings of animals from their perspective (1964, 10:200). He was far ahead of his time in opposing the anthropomorphism and personification of nature (152). Modern nature writers try to see the world from the animals' point of view without anthropomorphism. Abbey is a master of this. For example, in *Desert Solitaire,* he explores a snake's view of the world (1971b, 22), the feelings of a frog (143), and a vulture's perspective (154). Abbey's usually successful avoidance of anthropomorphism did not come without a struggle. He wrote, "The personification of the natural is exactly the tendency I wish to suppress in myself" (6).

Nietzsche was interested in the "doppelganger," the mysterious other person who is oneself. He wanted "to see one's self transformed before one's self, and then to act as if one had really entered into another body, into another character" (1964, 1:67). In nineteenth-century German romantic poetry and fiction, and also in the fiction of Edgar Allan Poe ("The Man in the Crowd") and Joseph Conrad ("The Secret Sharer"), the double is a mysterious person. To Nietzsche the double was also sometimes a totemic animal, and he likened himself to a lion, a camel, and an eagle (1964, 11:120–21, 234). Abbey's most memorable animal characterizations are of the buzzard (a recurrent figure in his work) and the moon-eyed horse (1971b, 157–71). Abbey uses the horse to expose all of the human virtues and quirks that he admired and abhorred in himself. Both Abbey and the horse are independent, spoiled, antisocial, crazy, desert loving, rigid as stone, like a statue of Don Quixote by Giacometti. These likenesses allow Abbey to analyze and lampoon himself just as Nietzsche proposed.

Both Nietzsche and Abbey were lovers of solitude and wilderness. Nietzsche's persona is a "lonely wanderer" (1964, 6:405). Sometimes he saw himself as Icarus escaping from the Labyrinth, flying toward the light, falling into the sea, and somehow returning. "I see thee follow thy path . . . with unfathomable eyes, wet and sad as a plummet which has returned to the light . . . out of every depth" (12:251). He wandered mostly in wild places. These places offered solitude, something unavailable for a "pious" man because God is always reading his mind or talking to him (10:328). But an atheist is a wilderness traveler who can hear "the voice of nature . . . in the mild sunshine of a constant mental joyfulness" (6:265). Nietzsche associated freedom of mind and wilderness and silence (11:122), and he bragged about his mental wilderness exploits. "Where silence is required—If we speak of freethinking as of a highly dangerous journey over glaciers and frozen seas, we find that those who do not care to travel on this track are offended, as if they had been reproached with cowardice and weak knees" (7:20).

Nietzsche's persona Zarathustra said that he admired "him who goeth into God-forsaken wildernesses, and hath broken his venerating heart. In the yellow sands and burnt by the sun, he doubtless peereth thirstily at the isles rich fountains, where life reposeth under shady trees. But his thirst doth not persuade him to become like those comfortable ones: for where there are oases, there are also idols" (11:121). This one passage involves the recurrent themes of wilderness, loneliness, renunciation of false comforts of traditional religion, and the seductive dangers of city life that also appear in the essays and novels of Edward Abbey.

Nietzsche called his persona Zarathustra "The Solitary" (7:295) and "The Recluse" (313). Abbey (quoting Robinson Crusoe) called himself "a solitaire." Nietzsche believed that in nature's solitude "we enjoy those short spans of deep communion with ourselves and with Nature. He who fortifies himself completely against boredom fortifies himself against himself too. He will never drink the most powerful elixir from his own innermost spring" (295). Nietzsche's Recluse was not avoiding the needs of society; he was saving "forces which will some day be urgently needed by culture" (314). Nietzsche was never really alone because "We are only in our own society always," and he felt that "all that is akin to me in nature . . . speaks to me, praises me, urges me forward and comforts me" (10:188). Zarathustra's apotheosis is his "stillest hour; that is the name of my terrible mistress" (11:175). At the stillest hour, "the dream beginneth," and this sensation makes him ask, "Did the ground give way?" (176).

Abbey's essays all come to their climaxes in the stillness of the desert, where he also experienced his own inner struggle to quiet his mind in the presence of wilderness. He often mocked himself because, alone in areas of great natural beauty, he usually became lonely for female companionship when he should have been overcome by the glories of the wilderness. And yet he was able to create powerful literary climaxes recounting moments of great peril and self-discovery in utter solitude. For example, in "Havasu" (1971b) he describes being stuck alone on a ledge while descending a dry watercourse miles from any other human being. Alternating between resignation to his fate, a resolution to try anything, and calling uselessly for help, he comes to understand the beauty and indifference of the wilderness. In a remarkable admission for a usually macho character, he tells us that he cried twice: first when he realized that he was doomed, and then when, almost beyond belief, he was able to climb up and over the overhanging face without equipment.

Nietzsche's description of true artists, wanderers, and poets reads like a description of Abbey's desert wanderings: "the spirit and the power of the dream come over us and we ascend, with open eyes and indifferent to all danger, the most dangerous paths, to the roofs and towers of fantasy, and without any giddiness, as persons born to climbing—we the night walkers by day! We artists! . . . We moon-struck and God-struck ones! We death-silent, untiring wanderers on heights which we do not see as heights, but as our plains, as our places of safety!" (1964 10:98). Abbey repeatedly wrote that one major pur-pose of wilderness areas was to serve as the refuge for free people and even as the base for revolutionary armies. Nietzsche stated that "in mountains, forests and solitudes [are] all the free spirits . . . who like himself, alternately merry and thoughtful, are wanderers and philoso-phers" (6:406, 11:122). He also associated wild country and radical ideas. "A true believer must be to us an object of veneration, but the same holds good of a true, sincere, convinced unbeliever. With men of the latter stamp we are near the high mountains where mighty rivers have their source" (7:49).

A number of Nietzschean social themes reappear in Abbey's work. Nietzsche advocated a simple but not ascetic life (12:66). He opposed and mocked both ostentatious consumption and asceticism: "We . . . want to be the poets of our lives, and first of all in the small-est and most commonplace matters" (10:233); "Verily, he who pos-sesseth little is so much the less possessed: blessed be moderate poverty" (11:57). Abbey expressed similar opinions, especially in his later books, such as *Fool's Progress,* where his protagonist mocks his two closest college friends, a self-indulgent, wealthy drunk and a hip-pie, eco-freak ascetic (1990, 181–244).

Nietzsche often attacked materialism and the gospel of progress (1964, 14:72–73). He hated unnecessary commercial activity. "One is now ashamed of repose. . . . Thinking is done with a stop watch as dining is done with the eyes fixed on the financial newspaper" (10:254). He warned that "in the face of the monstrous machine, the individual despairs and surrenders" (14:29). This is the underlying political theme of all of Abbey's political nonfiction, especially *Desert Solitaire,* and his novels *The Brave Cowboy, Fire on the Mountain, The*

Monkey Wrench Gang, and *Hayduke Lives!.* Abbey especially attacked roads, dams, cities, and commerce, which all cause destruction of nature. His novels have become "the texts" of the Luddite elements in the United States today, especially the Earth First! movement.

Nietzsche was an advocate of social anarchy. He wrote that before civilization there was a "natural war of all against all," but the wars that created the modern nation-states were worse than that. To him, the state used violence to preserve itself: "The State [is] for the majority of men a continually flowing source of hardship" (1964, 2:10–11). He felt that we all live in "the state, where the slow suicide of all—is called life" (11:55). He literally demonized the government: "A state is called the coldest of all cold monsters. Coldly lieth it also; and this lie creepeth from its mouth: I, the state, am the people." He denied that the state should hold property, saying, "what ever [the state] hath it hath stolen" (54). Nietzsche attacked some of the German idealists who had provided philosophical support for the German national government, writing, "the doctrine . . . that the state is the highest end of man and there is no higher duty than to serve it: I regard this not as a relapse into paganism, but into stupidity" (4:135). He also attacked the government's use of religion. He said that the state uses priests to subvert freedom and to make the state "something wholly sacred" (6:338). He felt that this collusion between church and state had created "the new idol!" which is served by the "preachers of death" (11:54–55).

Nietzsche believed that "There where the state ceaseth—there only commenceth the man who is not superfluous . . . there where the state ceaseth . . . Do ye not see it, the rainbow and the bridges of the Superman?" (57). The image of the rainbow bridge is taken from Norse myth—the bridge connecting the pagans' heaven-on-Earth of the gods. At the end of the world, the giants will storm the bridge and set it afire (MacCulloch 1964, 23). Nietzsche was strongly opposed to the belief in gods or God. Perhaps this passage represents the end of the reign of ordinary humans by the evolution of Supermen, whom Nietzsche expected to symbolically destroy the bridge between the gods and humanity.

Even though he was an anarchist, Nietzsche did not offer specific plans to demolish the state, and he did not picture a utopia. He did not approve of nineteenth-century working-class anarchists because they acted out of envy of the rich, not out of their own creative power:

"The Christian and the Anarchist—both are decadents" (1964, 16:87). "The Anarchist and the Christian are offspring of the same womb" (220).

Edward Abbey considered himself an anarchist (1994a, 59, 257) and at the University of New Mexico he titled his master's thesis "Anarchism and the Morality of Violence." Abbey, like Nietzsche, thought of anarchism as a social movement. He wanted to ignore the state and the demands of polite society. Neither Nietzsche nor Abbey was the type of political anarchist who personally wanted to blow up state buildings or assassinate political leaders. Abbey wrote that "Anarchism is a secret yearning toward brotherhood. Anarchism is the demand for community" (1994a, 139). When he was near death, Abbey asked his friends to "Wrap my body in my anarch's flag" (276). Like Nietzsche, Abbey was not an advocate of any of the political forms of anarchism, even environmental anarchism such as Murray Bookchin's. Abbey did not have any specific plan to reach anarchy and did not design or advocate any particular utopian scheme. Abbey's and Nietzsche's anarchism is instead characterized by advocating extreme individualism. And for both writers, social anarchism was perhaps their most important issue.

To some readers who do not appreciate his irony, Nietzsche sounds like an anti-Semite, racist, and social Darwinist, but not to the late-nineteenth-century Nietzscheans who were liberals and who opposed overt racism. Here, too, Abbey resembles Nietzsche. Whereas most modern literary natural history writers in English also are liberals, antiracists, and opponents of anti-Semitism (Bridgman 1972), the persona of Abbey's essays is a mild, self-mocking racist (although he clearly disapproved of racism) (1971b, 97–98; 1994a, 220, 285, 305–7, 316, 333, 336, 352).

Nietzsche was an early advocate of population control, believing that overpopulation would lead to tyranny: "Many too many are born: for the superfluous ones was the state devised!" (1964, 11:55). Abbey believed that overpopulation leads not only to political tyranny but also to environmental damage. His mocking proposals for several politically unacceptable forms of birth control as well as U.S. immigration enforcement appeared in *Mother Jones* and several newspapers in 1983 (1994a, 307).

Abbey and Nietzsche also seem to have similar attitudes about women. Nietzsche, who seems to be a misogynist in some passages

(1964, 11:75, 16:198), but many important modern feminists have found inspiration in his works (see Patton 1993). Abbey also seems sexist to some readers, and he actually mocked himself for it. His review of Susan Brownmiller's *Femininity* and Gloria Steinem's *Outrageous Acts* is a self-mocking, sexist essay in which he goes out of his way to insult both authors as well as Margaret Thatcher and Indira Gandhi, and to outrage feminists by quoting Doris Lessing, Joan Didion, and Margaret Mead out of context so that they appear to agree with his ironic, self-deprecating, comic sexism (1988, 199–205). *Black Sun* and *The Fool's Progress* both explore the problems that sexism created for Abbey and the women in his life.

Most of the English-speaking Nietzscheans were socialists or other leftists. Most American environmental or nature writers also tend to be anticapitalists, often dwelling on the ravages of industry on the natural environment. Nietzsche himself was very antisocialist. Abbey was not pro-industry, but he was primarily concerned with the destruction of the natural environment by federal agencies and other socialized segments of the American economy. "Industrial Tourism and the National Parks" (1971b) is primarily an attack on the U.S. Park Service for building too many roads and not promoting walking in the wilderness. *Fire on the Mountain* (1962) is an attack on the U.S. military. *The Monkey Wrench Gang* (1975) and *The Journey Home* (1977) are directed at federal agencies, the Bureau of Reclamation, the Corps of Engineers, the Forest Service, the Bureau of Land Management, and federally funded highway projects.

Nietzsche and Abbey both revered the descriptive field sciences, though they deplored the effects of science and engineering on the culture of their times. The simplest facts of natural history had special value to them both. Nietzsche wrote that "natural History . . . should be expounded that every reader or listener may be continually aroused to strive after mental and physical health and soundness, after the feeling of joy" (1964, 7:99). Abbey believed "that there is a kind of poetry, even a kind of truth in simple fact" (1971, x; see also p. 69).

Much of Nietzsche's work is an attack on professional academics, including philosophy teachers and writers (1964, 11:31, 12:257, 16:106). Abbey criticized English professors and literary critics (1971, x; 1990, 192–96) and also philosophers: "Heidegger was wrong, as usual, man is not the only living thing that exists" (1971b, 279). This is perhaps an unfair caricature of Heidegger, but it is typical of both Abbey and Nietzsche. Like Nietzsche, Abbey changed his mind about people he knew and writers he read. Later in life he praised Heidegger and likened him to Nietzsche and Zarathustra (1994a, 259). The most important issue in Nietzsche's work is the belief in free will. He admired the ancient prophet Zarathustra because the latter believed strongly and fundamentally in human free will. Nietzsche was not convinced that it really existed, but he demanded that we believe it possible. Sometimes he feared that free will was an illusion (1964, 5:41, 106; 10:153) and that all actions in the world are predetermined (15:140). In other places he seems to believe that there truly is free will. Abbey epitomized the same ambivalence in one sentence: "I am free, I am compelled, to contemplate . . . the human labyrinth of hope and despair" (1971b, 155).

One of Nietzsche's greatest contributions to Western thought is the idea that value and meaning are given by people to the world. Nietzsche wrote that "it is absurd to praise and blame nature" (1964, 6:107). Abbey emphasized the different meanings of the desert. For tourists who look at Delicate Arch, the most famous attraction in Arches National Monument, he says, "Suit yourself. You may see a symbol, a sign, a fact, a thing without meaning or a meaning which includes all things" (1971b, 41). Later he explains his feeling that "the desert reveals itself nakedly and cruelly with no meaning but its own existence" (155). And again, at the end of *Desert Solitaire,* he repeats the idea forcefully: "What does it mean? It means nothing. It is as it is and has no need for meaning. The desert lies beneath and soars beyond any possible human qualifications" (219).

Both Nietzsche and Abbey denied that morality comes from God. Nietzsche's anti-Christian position is still notorious, even among people who know nothing else about him. Abbey was not just an atheist but an active anti-Christian, and he made mocking references to Christianity. He wanted to sacrifice lambs to a coyote (1971b, 35); he claimed that a "Higher Power" helped him ruthlessly and needlessly kill a rabbit with a stone (38); tourists were "pilgrims" (40) who should be seeing the beauty of the countryside but who "find only God" (41). When a fisherman makes an obscene gesture at him, Abbey asks, "Invoking the Deity?" (198). And Abbey never wrote "the Bible"; he instead had to write, ironically, "the Holy Bible" (e.g., 256). Glorious sunsets were "God's own celestial pizza pies" (298). He stated flatly that Protestantism is a form of mental illness (118), and he claimed that he was "Beyond atheism, nontheism. I am not an atheist but an earthiest. Be true to the earth" (208). The last sentence is a direct quote from Nietzsche (1964, 11:7).

Unlike any other nature writer today or in the past, Abbey doubted the possibility of unmediated contact with the world, yet he also avoided being an idealist. He was able to do this because his attitudes toward the nature of reality and the act of knowing are the same as those of Nietzsche. The latter wrote that "semblance" is truth (1964, 12:50–51); "The real world . . . was always the world of appearance over again" (15:70; 84 sec. B); "consciousness remains on the surface" (15: sec. 676). Abbey emphasized appearance and surface. In the preface of *Desert Solitaire*, Abbey wrote, "It will be objected that the book deals too much with mere appearances, with the surface of things, and fails to engage and reveal the patterns of unifying relationships which form the true underlying reality of existence. Here I must confess that I know nothing whatever about true underlying reality, having never met any" (1971b, xi).

The attitude that there is only appearance is exemplified even by Abbey's favorite tree, a twisted, half-dead juniper. "The essence of the juniper continues to elude me unless, as I presently suspect, its surface is also the essence" (30). Unlike most nature writers from Emerson to the present, Abbey did not fool himself into thinking that he was mystically in touch with the spirit of nature. He wrote of his favorite tree, "Intuition, sympathy, empathy, all fail to guide me into the heart of this being—if it has a heart." (30–31). He often expressed his belief that the land is indifferent "to our presence" (301). This is perhaps Abbey's most important contribution to nature writing, to break openly and totally with the transcendental tradition from which American nature writing descends.

Nietzsche felt that the personal apprehension of beauty in nature or art was only the beginning of a long process by which we became ennobled by thinking and even dreaming of the experience. "The noblest kind of beauty is that which . . . slowly filters into our minds, which we take away with us almost unnoticed, and which we encounter again in our dreams; but which, however, after having long lain modestly on our hearts, takes entire possession of us" (1964, 6:156). This is an excellent description of the developing love for the desert that Abbey fosters in readers, especially those from temperate climates.

Nietzsche wrote that the dreaming imagination creates the illusion of being (6:26, 14:14, 15:177). "There are no eternally enduring substances; matter is just another such error as God" (10:153). Nietzsche wrote that "there are no things"; they are fictions invented by us (15:117). This is probably the root of Abbey's interest in the dream state. He is unique among English-language nature writers in his playful suggestion that nature is a bad dream. He wrote about troubling dreams of nature, a very unusual topic for a nature writer, though it is becoming more common. He loved the desert, but he usually described it with words that emphasize its surreal aspect, such as "weird" (1971b, 2, 41, 102, 151, 193, 272), "fantastic" (3, 41, 205, 282), "monstrous" (6), "strange" (11, 13, 28, 29, 43, 137, 225), "grotesque" (11, 271), "bizarre" (29), "haunted" (40), "queer" (40), "illogical" (41), "unholy" (137), "malevolent" (204), and "unearthly" (218, 245). In Abbey's books the desert has hobgoblins (2, 133), ogres (6), skulls (37), voodoo (43), gargoyles (133, 165), ghosts (171, 204, 222, 233), phantom deer (248), and banshees (235). It is "a hoodoo land" (218, 245).

The Nietzschean interpretation that I have proposed above explains many odd passages in the writings of Edward Abbey. For example, there are many references to a flowing, returning, and becoming in nature that are treated very differently from the usual nutrient cycling in nature writing. This is because Abbey, like Nietzsche, sees the biogeochemical cycle as a Viconian returning (Vico 1948, bk. 5). This view is reflected in Abbey's essays, in which everything is moving and flowing; it could be his central theme. This is common enough in nature writing, but with Abbey it was an obsession. *Desert Solitaire* is constructed by the intertwining of a series of mythic images of flow, birth, thread, river, the maze, death, and return that unify and direct the landscape descriptions, travel notes, and political propaganda into a powerful symphonic whole. It is not unusual for nature writers to dwell on a theme of flow when describing rivers and nutrient cycles, but Abbey's flux and return images have an odd Nietzschean twist. For example, his hero Hayduke returned from the almost-dead once, and Jack Burns from *The Brave Cowboy* was brought back to life five times to be a character in *Fire on the Mountain, Good News, The Monkey Wrench Gang,* and *Hayduke Lives!*.

The theme of the Viconian flux and the eternal return are central to Nietzsche's thought. The central test of each human being is the question, Do you love life so much that you can bear to live it over and over again? It is not clear if Abbey completely accepted the challenge because many of his references to the eternal return are humorous. But it is clear that the returning hero makes sense and fits into the natural flux that is the source of such important imagery in his work. If Abbey is not a Nietzschean, then his eternally returning hero Jack Burns is just peculiar.

Edward Abbey's treatment of the food chain is another example of a theme that seems very odd unless one employs a Nietzschean interpretation. For the past twenty-five years I have taught a course in which about twenty students read *Desert Solitaire*. I have only had two or three students who were not disgusted by the passage describing how Abbey needlessly killed a harmless cottontail rabbit with a rock (1971b, 38). I find that young readers, in particular, many of whom idealized Abbey up to this point, are put off and hurt by this passage. It is one of the most puzzling and troubling aspects of Abbey's works for most of my students. Worst of all, he does not even skin and eat the remains but leaves the body there to feed the vultures. However, this section of the book is much more understandable, perhaps even more acceptable, if one considers that Abbey is challenging us to accept that we are part of the food chain. This challenge was first raised by Nietzsche, who wrote, "Every moment devours the preceding one, every birth is the death of innumerable beings; begetting, living, murdering, all is one" (1964, 2:8). Of course, Nietzsche was partly being ironic because the nature enthusiasts he was mocking all said that they longed to merge with nature, but they did not mean they wanted to be eaten by a bear.

Nietzsche's alter ego, Zarathustra, returned from hunting in the wilderness, "but even yet a wild beast gazeth out of his seriousness—an unconquered wild beast!" (11:139). For Nietzsche and Abbey, the hunter and hunted become one at the moment of death and consumption. The back cover of *The Journey Home* is a self-portrait of Abbey as a buzzard. Abbey wrote often of his wish to die in the desert and to be eaten by buzzards, "transfigured into the fierce greedy eyes and unimaginable consciousness of a turkey vulture. Whereupon you, too, will soar on motionless wings high over the ruck and rack of human suffering. For most of us a promotion in grade, for some the realization of an ideal" (1971b, 135). Did Abbey remember the following passage from *Zarathustra* and imagine himself as the human buzzard that he later drew? "Awake and hearken, ye lonesome ones! From the future come winds with stealthy pinions, and to fine ears good tidings are proclaimed" (1964, 11:89). Nietzsche may have had angels or eagles in mind, but he also knew that the real Zoroastrians who followed Zarathustra did not bury their dead but left them on towers to be eaten by vultures.

Nietzsche wrote, "The weaker vessel is driven to the stronger . . . if possible to become one with it" (15:130). Abbey dramatized this in numerous passages, most of which involve predation. Abbey mused,

> One can imagine easily the fondness, the sympathy, the genuine affection with which the owl regards the rabbit before rending it into edible portions.
>
> Is the affection reciprocated? In that moment of truce, of utter surrender, when the rabbit still alive offers no resistance but only waits, is it possible that the rabbit also loves the owl? (1971b, 112)

He noted ironically that young American Indians dress and act like drug store cowboys; is this another case of the loser loving and becoming one with the winner, as with the rabbit and owl?

I have not yet had a student who agreed with the fancy that the rabbit loves the owl, but Nietzsche and Abbey demanded that the "nature lover" accept the true personal meaning of the food chain as a test of honesty to the Earth. Abbey killed a rabbit and left it for the vultures. He wrote, "We are kindred all of us, killer and victim, predator and prey, me and the sly coyote, the soaring buzzard, the elegant gopher snake, the trembling cottontail, the foul worms that feed on our entrails, all of them, all of us. Long live diversity, long live the earth" (38). This last passage is fully Nietzschean, and if you accept the Nietzschean interpretation of the love of the rabbit and the Indian for their destroyers, these passages make sense. If Abbey is not a Nietzschean, these passages are not only disturbing and puzzling but also repugnant and out of place in these books about nature.

In conclusion, it is obvious that Edward Abbey read and valued the works of Nietzsche. Abbey's poetry in *Earth Apples* (1994b) and his book of aphorisms, *A Voice Crying in the Wilderness* (1994c), are unmistakably Nietzschean in feeling and subject matter. He used many themes in his works that had been used earlier by Nietzsche, and he used them so often and as such a profound part of his writing, I believe that he should be called a Nietzschean. Many readers often find Abbey's images and statements contradictory, challenging, and even nonsensical, but as I have argued, some of these confusing and bold passages are understandable from a Nietzschean perspective.

When critics explain that Shelly was a Platonist, it is illuminating because Platonism is commonly included in a college education. Even though deconstructionism, which began with Nietzsche, is now popular in some literary circles, few English scholars or literary critics have read, much less digested, the philosophy of Nietzsche. Nevertheless, I hope that other readers of nature writing will be tempted to carry out more intensive Nietzschean analyses of Abbey's work. For example, examining the act of masking in Abbey would require careful study; and closer looks at the influence of Nietzschean social anarchism and its relationship to political anarchism in Abbey's work would certainly have positive results. The influence of Nietzschean epistemology on Abbey's perception of the desert might also give valuable insights into the author's way of presenting landscape. Another interesting project would be to develop a chronology of Abbey's taste in philosophers and his writing subjects and styles.

I hope that other readers will find that a Nietzschean perspective is helpful in interpreting some of the puzzling and even troubling ideas and images that make Abbey's writing so interesting to the general public, environmentalists, and to academic readers. He is only one of a set of important nature writers whose works can be illuminated by some background in Nietzsche. Jack London considered himself a Nietzschean, and it is likely that the influence extended, directly or indirectly to his literary circle, including George Sterling and perhaps Mary Austin. It has been suspected for many years that Nietzsche was a major influence on Robinson Jeffers—also a friend of London, Austin, and Sterling—and it seems likely that William Everson and Richard Shelton are Nietzschean. Abbey quoted both Jeffers and Shelton more than once.

It is time for the readers and writers of literary natural history essays to realize that Nietzsche, as much or perhaps more than Emerson, was a philosopher of nature and that he influenced many of the most important writers in Europe and America in his day. Through them, many of his positive feelings for nature have been transmitted to people who have never read his books. Most of all, we must recognize, even celebrate, the rebirth of his philosophy in the works of Edward Abbey, who has inspired so many young people to care for the natural world. Nietzsche and Abbey were prickly and problematic people—and demanding writers—but they have captured the imagination of a generation that cannot be reached by sentimental nature writing, but who have taken up the challenge Nietzsche presented over a century ago: "Be true to the earth."

Notes

I received significant assistance in understanding Nietzsche by reading *Nietzsche's Gift* (1977) by Dr. Harold Alderman of the philosophy department at Sonoma State University, and he was kind enough to read this essay in an early form and when nearly completed, in the process correcting several errors. Clarke Abbey graciously took the time to answer my questions andy clarify several matters of importance. Dr. Ann Ronald of the University of Nevada, Reno, generously read an early version of the paper. The editor of this volume, Dr. Peter Quigley, made numerous suggestions concerning both style and substance that greatly improved this contribution.

Works Cited

Abbey, Edward. 1956. *The Brave Cowboy.* Albuquerque: University of New Mexico Press.

———. 1959. "Anarchism and the Morality of Violence." M.A. thesis, University of New Mexico.

———. 1962. *Fire on the Mountain.* Albuquerque: University of New Mexico Press.

———. 1971a. *Black Sun.* Santa Barbara, Calif.: Capra.

———. [1968] 1971b. *Desert Solitaire.* Reprint, New York: Ballantine.

———. 1973. *Cactus Country.* New York: Time-Life.

———. 1975. *The Monkey Wrench Gang.* Philadelphia: Lippincott.

———. 1977. *The Journey Home.* New York: Dutton.

———. 1979. *Abbey's Road.* New York: Dutton.

———. 1980. *Good News.* New York: Elsevier-Dutton.

———. 1981. *Down the River.* New York: Dutton.

———. 1984. *Beyond the Wall.* New York: Holt, Rinehart and Winston.

———. 1988. *One Life at a Time, Please.* New York: Henry Holt.

———. 1989. *Hayduke Lives!* Boston: Little, Brown and Co.

———. 1990. *The Fool's Progress.* New York: Henry Holt.

———. 1994a. *Confessions of a Barbarian: Selections from the Journals of Edward Abbey.* Ed. David Petersen. Boston: Little, Brown and Co.

———. 1994b. *Earth Apples: The Complete Poetry of Edward Abbey.* Ed. David Petersen. New York: St. Martin's Press.

———. 1994c. *A Voice Crying in the Wilderness: Vox Clamantis in Deserto.* New York: St. Martin's Press.

Picture Books:

———. 1970. *Appalachian Wilderness: The Great Smoky Mountains.* Photos by Eliot Porter. New York: Dutton.

———. 1971. *Slickrock.* Photos by Philip Hyde. New York: Scribner's.

———. 1977. *The Hidden Canyon*. Photos by John Blaustein. New York: Penguin.

———. 1979. *Desert Images*. Photos by David Muench. New York: Chanticleer Press.

Alderman, Harold. 1977. *Nietzsche's Gift*. Athens: Ohio University Press.

Armstrong, Edward A. 1973. *Saint Francis: Nature Mystic*. Berkeley: University of California Press.

Bridgman, Patrick. 1972. *Nietzsche in Anglosaxony: A Study of Nietzsche's Impact on English and American Literature*. Leicester, England: University Press.

Emerson, Ralph Waldo. 1911. *Journals of Ralph Waldo Emerson: 1820–1872*. Boston: Houghton, Mifflin.

Hepworth, James, and Gregory McNamee, eds. 1985. *Resist Much, Obey Little: Some Notes on Edward Abbey*. Salt Lake City: Dream Garden Press.

Kauffmann, LeRoy C. 1963. "The Influence of Friedrich Nietzsche on American Literature." Ph.D. diss., University of Pennsylvania.

Lutts, Ralph H. 1990. *The Nature Fakers: Wildlife, Science, and Sentiment*. Golden, Colo.: Fulcrum Press.

MacCulloch, Canon John A. 1964. "Eddic Mythology." In *Mythology of All Races*, vol. 2. New York: Cooper Square.

McCann, Garth. 1977. *Edward Abbey*. Boise State University Western Writers Series, no. 29. Boise, Idaho: Boise State University Press.

Morland, M. A. 1958. "Nietzsche and the Nineties." *Contemporary Review* (Apr.).

Muir, John. 1894. *The Mountains of California*. New York: Century.

Nietzsche, Friedrich. [1909] 1964. *The Complete Works of Friedrich Nietzsche*. 16 vols. Ed. Oscar Levy. Reprint, New York: Russell and Russell.

Nicholson, Marjorie Hope. 1959. *Mountain Gloom and Mountain Glory*. Ithaca, N.Y.: Cornell University Press.

Patton, Paul, ed. 1993. *Nietzsche, Feminism, and Political Theory*. London: Routledge.

Ronald, Ann. 1982. *The New West of Edward Abbey*. Albuquerque: University of New Mexico Press.

Sorrell, Roger D. 1988. *St. Francis of Assisi and Nature*. Oxford: Oxford University Press.

Vico, Giambattista. 1948. *The New Science of Giambattista Vico*. 3d ed. Trans. Thomas G. Bergin and Max H. Fisch. Ithaca, N.Y.: Cornell University Press.

Edward Abbey's Cow

BARBARA

BARNEY

NELSON

the line dividing I and Not-I, us and them, or him and her is not (cannot)
always (be) as clear as we would like it to be. Despite our desperate,
eternal attempt to separate, contain and mend, categories always leak.
—Trinh T. Minh-ha, *Woman Native Other*

Several years ago I sat in a cattleman's meeting and listened to
the president encourage members to call for a ban on Edward
Abbey's books. I wondered if we were thinking about the same author. Surely the cattleman president didn't want to ban *The Brave
Cowboy* (1992a), the story of a horseman's last stand against civilization, or *Fire on the Mountain* (1992b), the story of an old rancher's
last stand against federal forced taking of his land, or *Good News*
(1980), the story of a future war between urban bad guys and rural
good guys?

The cattleman president seemed to object mostly to Abbey's
Monkey Wrench Gang (1976), a book now credited with inspiring the
dismantling of windmills and destruction of water troughs. But that
was never Abbey's intention. Some of his characters were actually trying to preserve "prime grazing land for sheep and cattle" (154). His
book is about people who were trying to stop encroaching civilization; it's not a tirade against ranching. But Abbey is not totally innocent as charged. He did stand before a packed house in Bozeman,
Montana, in 1985 and deliver a blistering address, later published as

206

the essay "Free Speech: The Cowboy and His Cow," in which he attacked public land grazing (1988).

Defending him, Kentucky farmer and author Wendell Berry explained how Abbey constantly drew fire from special-interest groups, would not stay in bounds, would not support the ideology they thought he should represent. According to Berry, Abbey fans often say, "Well, he did *say* that. But . . . ," before trying to defend his latest stunt. As a cattlewoman, I find myself in exactly that position when I read that published Montana speech. Well, Abbey did say that "Western cattlemen are nothing more than welfare parasites. They've been getting a free ride on the public lands for over a century, and I think it's time we phased it out. I'm in favor of putting the public lands livestock grazers out of business" (12).

But Abbey's kindest words regarding cows appear in a book called *Slickrock* (1987), which he wrote as a Sierra Club publication. Why would he attack cows in front of a ranching audience and defend them to a Sierra Club audience?

On the surface, his writing sometimes appears to be simple political journalism, but Edward Abbey wrote literature, not didactic eco-rant speeches. As he searched the Southwest for signs and symbols to work into his prose, he found the cowboy and his horse the stuff of orientalized[1] myth: too heroic, too tragic, too remote, too exotic, and too romantic. He found Sonoran Desert plants and animals too regional. The Gila Monster, barrel cactus, wild burro, scorpion, tarantula, even the stately saguaro signified little more than fear, adaptability, Spartan independence, or tenacity outside desert borders. Surprisingly, he did find one complex and overlooked world-class symbol in the Southwest: the humble cow.

Richard Shelton quotes Abbey as saying *Desert Solitaire* (1990) is "not primarily about the desert." So, Shelton asks, "If *Desert Solitaire* is not primarily about the desert, what is it about?" (1985, 72). Maybe cows?

Cows are everywhere in Abbey's writing: hiding in every slickrock canyon, grazing and drowning along every free-flowing river, tracking up and defecating in every desert, and ruining the imaginations of those who follow them around. Throughout his entire work, it seems Edward Abbey was periodically obsessed with cow images and metaphors. He calls himself a "sick calf" (1981, 184), dreams of giving up the writing life to carve "the image, say, of a cow" into redwood logs with a hatchet, but luckily sells a manuscript for enough money "to choke a cow" instead (1988, 54–57). He writes about the cowbird and the cowtongue prickly pear (1984, 112, 119), cowflies, and bullbats—"birds with a bovine bellow" (1990, 35, 208). During Wallace Stegner's river trip through Glen Canyon, he found drowned sheep and deer (1969, 120); in Abbey's version of the same canyon trip, it was always a drowned cow. Stegner could certainly never classify Abbey's books as "big hat, no cows" (1993, 136).

The history of cows in the West goes back to 1610, when the Virginia colonies imported cattle from the West Indies. Native Americans wiped them out again in 1622. Next, a colony of Dutch settlers brought cattle to New York in 1619, and four years after the Mayflower landed, the first British cattle arrived in Massachusetts. However, a hundred years before this more famous Eastern assault, the cow had already migrated into the desert Southwest with the Hispanic explorer Hernando Cortés (1485–1547). Four hundred years later, by the time white settlers finally arrived, the cow had become almost ubiquitous in the Southwest. Anglo ranchers actually enjoyed only a very brief historical moment. A few years after Arizona became a state, government agencies ousted all residents (or so seemed the intention), including the cow, and replaced them with state parks, national monuments, military reservations, national parks, proving grounds, and national recreation areas. When Abbey takes "A Walk in the Desert Hills" across this same southern Arizona desert where the cow first touched hoof, he seems happy the place is free of cow dung, saying, "I give thanks again for the United States Air Force" (1984, 19). I can't quite take him seriously, however. Perhaps no one better than Abbey knew that the entire U.S./Mexico border area was once someone's home, some cow's pasture, but now belonged mostly to the government, against which he thought true patriots should be willing to defend their country (1989, 19).

As Abbey walks along, irony builds: "Only one animal remains conspicuous in this region, by its absence—the cow" (1984, 19), and "nothing human" lives here or ever did (27). A few pages later, as his need for water becomes critical, he says, "There has got to be water at Gray's Well—a rancher named Henry Gray once lived there—and if there isn't I'll die, and what of it?" (39). And what of the fact that Abbey probably once looked after that very windmill when he worked for Henry Gray (1973, 67)? Even Anglo ranchers had been "dispossessed," writes cultural geographer Paul Starrs, "by a government opposed to grazing partly because it was a Hispanic practice" (1994, 4). In one of Abbey's last books, *One Life at a Time, Please,* he says, "Here on this international boundary, in this neutral zone, one's actual citizenship makes little difference" (1988, 151). Government agencies had displaced Native Americans, Hispanics, Anglos, and cows equally. I believe Edward Abbey, the hiker, would trust cattlemen of any race to maintain windmills in the desert, but would have no such faith in government employees to perform the same critical task.

As a writer, hiker, and river rat who passionately loved the desert, and who also politically championed anarchy and personal freedom, Abbey often found himself sympathizing with conflicting perspectives. Theorist Trinh T. Minh-ha,[2] a nonwhite/female/writer, describes her own similar complicated position as a "triple bind." This triple bind comes from the dilemma of trying to decide whether her loyalties lie with her race, her gender, or a bigger picture. Although Abbey would definitely be labeled as "other" to a woman of color, I think he found himself in much the same dilemma and solved it much as Trinh does: with a plural voice. Trinh describes her own writing voice as a combination between a capitalized "I" representing the all-knowing "Author" and a lower-case "i" representing herself situated in a specific community. Trinh's "I/i" voice carefully tries to speak for multiple positions (1989, 9). In "The Poetry Center Interview," Abbey also admits he created a voice in his nonfiction, gave that character his own name, and that "some people mistake the creation for the author" (Hepworth 1985, 42).

Abbey as cocksure white male author is often ready to shoot even God. Ann Ronald calls this "Cactus Ed" narrator his "dramatic persona" (1982, 66–67). Like the traditional desert storyteller Coyote, Cactus Ed is obsessed with sex, ribald humor, and irreverence. Using Trinh's system, this voice can be represented with capital letters as "ED." Behind the bluster is a quieter, more serious voice, represented as "ed" with small letters. This voice is sympathetic, other directed, unsure, and groping. Abbey, like Trinh, types his way between his blustering narrator and his groping human self as ED/ed. He is not ashamed of his own personality and heritage, yet he is not willing to assume a didactic dictatorship, nor the responsibility to become a model for society. His thoughts are as good as the next person's, and he has a right to voice them, but he does not consider them superior, only equal. This ED/ed perspective gives him a very modern complex voice with ancient desert storyteller roots.

Abbey's political views toward the cow are not quite so clearly negative if the reader begins to listen to the combined ED/ed voice, cussing cows in one breath and respectfully calling them wild desert animals in the next. When he "shouts his message," Ronald has noted, "it is least likely to be taken seriously" (199). Trinh explains this as an author's disorienting tactic: "Never does one open the discussion by coming right to the heart of the matter. For the heart of the matter is always somewhere else" (1989, 1). When ED shouts his message, as in the cow essay, the reader can be fairly certain he is after something other than agreement; "the heart of the matter" is somewhere else. When ED shouts, he is often lying, trying to cause trouble, trying to make people think or fight back.

Quite often Abbey's ED voice is confrontational. Ronald observes that his *Slickrock* essays are "openly propagandistic" and editorially were "reinforced by the Sierra Club's urgency to trumpet a battle call" (1982, 114, 121). This is an accurate observation regarding his desire to protect the southern Utah canyon country from development. Abbey may not have agreed, however, that the national park service would do a better job of protecting those canyons than local people. As already mentioned, some of Abbey's kindest words toward cows strangely appear in the same work. In a book intentionally aimed at a Sierra Club audience, he describes pastoral Native American cattle raisers, remembers he "got hungry and saw God in the form of a beef pie," and he and backpacker/river rat friends waste an evening rescuing a heifer from quicksand. ED/ed even bestows a closing benediction: "I hope *our* heifer got out of there in time" (1987, 19, 21, 49–50; emphasis added). Since *Slickrock*'s Sierra Club audience was actively involved in antigrazing issues, perhaps Abbey—as a beef eater, and perhaps wondering if his beloved desert may have evolved due to the long history of cattle grazing in the Southwest—may have felt this particular audience needed to hear some kind words toward cows and, without being too obvious and losing that audience, hoped to soften their political stance toward grazing.

According to Ronald (1982, 114–15), Abbey's political views, in contrast to the way he expressed them in *Slickrock*, were "reined in" by the Time-Life editors of *Cactus Country* (1973). But here ED rants that cows were "once a major problem at Organ Pipe," were guilty of "overgrazing," "trampling the seedling cacti, stripping the soil of its natural cover," and that cattle caused mesquite invasion. He warns that when the grass is gone, goats, and then archaeologists, will follow the cattle (70, 94–95). Abbey wrote *Cactus Country* for a general audience and perhaps intended to prod them into environmental awareness. I would argue further than Abbey's "Free Speech: The Cowboy and His Cow" essay was a desperate final attempt to prod rural Western people into action. He laments sadly in "Telluride Blues—A Hatchet Job" that cowboys "don't seem to like to fight so much anymore" but tended instead to passively allow developers to "tear up good deer- and cattle-country," ruin little towns like Telluride, or turn their "hayfields, ranches, homes, [and] small towns" into coal (1977, 108, 123, 171, 175).[3]

In 1984, Abbey included two *Cactus Country* chapters ("Down to the Sea of Cortez" and "The Ancient Dust") and three *Slickrock* chapters ("How It Was," "Days and Nights in Old Pariah," and "The Damnation of a Canyon") in *Beyond the Wall*. In this collection, Abbey seems to be further softening his earlier statements toward grazing and cows. For one thing, he did not select the cow-bashing chapters from *Cactus Country*, but in addition, he made two intriguing editorial changes in the original text. In *Cactus Country*, he observes that water trails indicated "visitation of *not only* the usual starving scrub cattle *but also* many of the more common desert mammals" (1973, 149; emphasis added). In *Beyond the Wall*, this was changed to "visitation of the usual scrub cattle and other desert mammals" (1984, 145). Cattle are no longer singled out from "other desert mammals" by the use of "not only . . . but also." In the revised sentence, cows are just another desert mammal, and just as "common." A few pages later in *Cactus Country*, Abbey says the area is "inhabited only by a few starving scrub cattle and wild animals" (1973, 154), which he rewrites as "inhabited by starving cattle and *other* wild animals" (1984, 152; emphasis added). Adding the heavy word "other" draws a new circle that is obviously meant to include cattle as wild animals. Although *Slickrock* also contains a few negative cow statements, Abbey chose not to republish them. The one negative sentence about cows that did appear in a selected chapter—"At that time I did not realize that what looked so open and free was, even then, tied up in cattle grazing permits, defacto property of the local ranchers" (1987, 22)—was edited out.

One of Abbey's greatest frustrations throughout his life was the fact that people seldom reacted to his books as planned (1989, xi). When he insulted them, they sometimes loved it. His negative words about cows, intended to prod people into environmental awareness, had been taken up as weapons to use against rural people. That was never Abbey's intention. Although Abbey's books are filled with critical comments about "agribusiness" and "overgrazing," he carefully attempts to define the difference between agribusiness and the family farm/ranch and staunchly defends the latter.[4] For example, in *Desert Solitaire* he lists ways to impose a "dictatorial regime" upon the American people. The first step, he says, is to concentrate people into cities. Second, he says, is "Mechanize agriculture to the highest degree of refinement, thus forcing most of the scattered farm and ranching population into the cities. Such a policy is desirable because farmers, woodsmen, cowboys, Indians, fishermen and other relatively self-sufficient types are difficult to manage unless displaced from their natural environment" (1990, 131). Juxtaposing "Thus I Reply to Rene Dubos" in *Down the River* (1981), "The Second Rape of the West" in *Journey Home* (1977), and David Remley's recap (1985) of the true story behind *Fire on the Mountain* more accurately reveals Abbey's complex views on farming and ranching, views which support sustainable communities, rural people, and rural work.

Debating another volatile subject, ED/ed investigates the cow's position in the tangled food chain. Historically, he notes, even noble Native Americans ate some animals into extinction (1982, 56; 1984, 156; 1977, 148–49). He wonders whether today's human could or should give up agribusiness's wheat and return to eating chuckwallas (1984, 156), or whether we could eat piñon nuts "fast enough to keep from starving to death" (1990, 253). He realizes returning to slash-and-burn agriculture or a hunter-gatherer society may not be a utopian solution: "[U]ntil the coming of the white man the natives spent half their lives on the edge of starvation. Famine was common" (1984, 190). My own well-fed personal friends—Crow, Northern Cheyenne, Sioux, Paiute, and Apache cattle ranchers—laugh when I ask if they would like to return to the good old days.

On another track, ED/ed questions whether eating plants is wiser or more moral than eating meat. In the booming voice of ED (woman defiler and beer-can tosser), of course, he says he prefers beef—big bloody slabs. Gluttonously, he considers "Worst of all" a boss who "skimps on food" (1990, 89). But ED/ed considering Abbey's own precious food chain periodically thinks about eating grass (252), but decides that the "sere, brown, short, tough native grasses that are the best cattle feed in the world" do not make good human food, and that land "too arid for conventional farming . . . will still support a beef-growing industry" (1977, 170).

With some tongue in cheek, ED says plants probably feel pain and scream (207), have "hearts" (1984, 46), and could be considered "friends" (144). ED enjoys taunting his readers with the fact that vegetarians, like the cow and the chuckwalla, can be "big, fat, ugly, [and] remarkably stupid" (1991a, 74, 84), just like beef eaters. Again while writing for the Sierra Club, ED humorously stresses the idea that he perceives "no moral superiority in the position of the ethical vegetarian who . . . uproots harmless carrots, mutilates innocent turnips, violates cabbages and plunders fruit trees to keep body and soul conjoined" (1973, 115). However, in *Beyond the Wall*, ED/ed's dichotomy-blurring and hierarchy-rejecting voice takes the subject more seriously, as indeed world hunger deserves.

Ronald notes that in "Turning an idea from side to side, [Abbey] balances one alternative against another. He poses an idea, then abandons it, suggests its opposite, then rejects them both" (1982, 97). The more serious voice of ED/ed looks at the food chain from several perspectives. In Alaska, where plant life is very scarce, his humorous argument with a vegetarian has a serious undertone: "Every time we eat a cow, I remind him, we save the life of a moose, two caribou, four mule deer, or eight char squared. . . . Whose side are you on, Jensen?" (1984, 174–75). The ED/ed voice also subtly notes that humans who eat huckleberries steal food from grizzlies, eating mushrooms competes with deer (1977, 39, 49), and meat production "sacrifices" (1991b, 116) can be juxtaposed against vegetable-production sacrifices:

> Like many rivers these days the San Juan is bound for practical ends, condemned by industrial agriculture to expire in a thousand irrigation ditches, transmogrified from living river into iceberg lettuce, square tomatoes, celery, onions, Swiss chard, and radishes. . . . Like fish, chickens, cows, pigs, and lambs, the rivers too are penned and domesticated and diverted. . . . Don't think about it. Nobody else does. Except animal liberationists. And vegetarians— those murderers of zucchini! those bean sprout killers! (127)

Although ED jokes about murdering plants, the ED/ed voice seriously challenges the prejudice: "To speak of 'harvesting' other living creatures . . . as if they were *no more than a crop*, exposes the meanest, cruelest, most narrow and homocentric of possible human attitudes toward the life that surrounds us" (1988, 39; emphasis added). Abbey believes that interdependent food sources are ecosystems and webs, not pyramids and chains. Eating lower on a food chain is simply one more form of elitist human classification.[5] ED/ed argues that a spider chewing on a mosquito full of human blood (1977, 35) or bacteria feasting on human flesh (1991a, 134) indicate a complicated and unsympathetic web instead of a hierarchy with humans both at the top and bottom.

As his intense food-chain investigation becomes more complex, Abbey suggests that all animals are potential "overgrazers." Porcupines gnaw bark from piñon pines, and deer eat "themselves out of house and home." Ants have "denuded the ground surrounding their hill," bees are "gluttonous," a juniper clutches "at the rock on which it feeds," and even the wind eats rocks (1990, 25–30). A dust to ancient dust cycle is completed as Abbey describes rocks with lips and teeth.[6] He concludes, as deep ecologists preach, that "even a rock is a being" and philosophically returns to the cow: "Only a fool, milking his cow, denies the cow's reality. Be true to the earth, said Nietzsche" (1991a, 128). Abbey's world is entirely animistic, so his precariously perched ED/ed voice offers no easy solutions: "There seems to be no alternative to eating, much as one might prefer a more ascetic manner of life" (1988, 116).

To set a thought-provoking and symbolic example, ED claims that he wants to be reincarnated as a croaking, obnoxious, carrion-eating buzzard. Perhaps the first words Abbey read in praise of the buzzard were in "The Scavengers," written by Mary Austin.[7] In her stories, buzzards, vultures, and condors often help find lost people. She observes that buzzards are despised for their imagined lack of cleanliness, and that our European-inspired morals and distaste for certain jobs or foods reappear as a distaste for certain animals and animal behaviors. Therefore, housekeepers, garbage collectors, and undertakers are despised. Stealing or scavenging, she argues, can be forms of sharing or keeping the desert clean. She says, "The vulture merits respect for his bigness and for his bandit airs, but he is a somber bird, with none of the buzzard's frank satisfaction in his offensiveness" (1988, 19). She describes scavengers providing an unappreciated but important service by taking out the trash and keeping the desert clean—except for tin cans, which she scorns as the worst "disfigurement" found in the desert (22). So, Abbey, with frank satisfaction in his offensiveness, tosses his beer cans all over Austin's nice clean desert—just like a man.

Taking his reincarnation somewhat more seriously, Abbey does not want buzzards to go hungry, so he must also consider what a buzzard eats. Again, he was quite familiar with Austin's observation that "In mid-desert where there are no cattle, there are no birds of carrion" (5). Tramping around the desert Southwest, he noticed that while a lone buzzard might be found pecking at a road-kill rabbit, the gathering and feasting of the clan mainly occurred around dead cows: "Arizona is where the vultures swarm like flies about the starving cattle on the cow-burnt range" (1977, 147). In Mexico he finds even more scavengers: "Above the cattle the vultures swarm like flies, attracted by the sight and smell of dying meat" (1991b, 149), and with a positive slant, "The inevitable vultures soaring overhead reminded us, though, that somewhere in this brushy wilderness was life, sentient creating, living meat" (1984, 139). Again, with frank satisfaction in his offensiveness, he brags about gluttonous river trip meals where he and friends "stuff faces and stomachs" (1988, 118), and about gorging on huge bloody slabs of dead cow meat, derisively referring to vegetarian meals as "pussy food" (1991b, 33, 45).

Austin was also careful to point out that cattle did not come into the Southwest via the European's east-to-west frontier thrust, reminding the reader that cattle herding was first introduced by the "free riding vaqueros who need no trails and can find cattle where to the layman no cattle exist" (1988, 58). In the essay "Down to the Sea of Cortez," Abbey also gives credit to the Spanish vaquero and the ancient arrival of desert cattle. He calls overgrazing "the old story" and describes Mexican scrub cattle as desert wildlife with Abbey-like affection:

Scrub cattle ranging through the bush galloped off like gnus and wildebeests at our approach. I never saw such weird, scrawny, pied, mottled, humped, long-horned and camel-necked brutes trying to pass as domestic livestock. Most looked like a genetic hash of Hereford, Charolais, Brahman, Angus, moose, ibex, tapir and nightmare. Weaned on cactus, snakeweed and thistle, they showed the gleam of the sun through the translucent barrel of their rib cages. But they could run, they were alive—not only alive but vigorous. I was tempted to think, watching their angular hind ends jouncing away through the dust, that the meat on those critters, if you could find any, might just taste better than the aerated, water-injected, hormone-inflated beef we Americans get from today's semiautomated feedlots in the States. (1984, 138–39)

Abbey's description contains subtle admiration both for the hardy Mexican cattle and the hardy people who survive on so much less than the overstuffed, industrialized, north-of-the-border variety. The cattle breeds listed in this passage also represent a genetic hash of world countries: England, France, India, Scotland, North America, South America, Asia, and Africa. The hides of the breeds listed come in red, white, yellow, black, and brown, but do not correspond to skin colors of humans found in the same area.

Although often under fire as a racist for comments like, "Stop every *campesino* at our southern border, give him a handgun, a good rifle, and a case of ammunition, and send him home" (1988, 44), Abbey actually demonstrates great respect for third world cultures. For example, he dismisses the Peace Corps as "a typical piece of American cultural insolence" (187). Refusing to subscribe to the condescending idea that Mexican people need our "help," Abbey uses the cow to symbolically reveal his genuine respect for those who can live, adapt, and thrive in his beloved desert—a place where the white male author was only tough enough to visit with a backpack full of imported food and water.

Symbolically, perhaps baiting feminist readers, the cow is also very gender specific throughout Abbey's writing: female. The toilet truck driver in *The Brave Cowboy* describes middle-aged women as "domesticated cows" (1992, 93). In *Black Sun*, Ballentine asks why he should buy a cow (referring to women) when he can get all the milk he needs (referring to sex) through the fence (1982, 50). A very drunk ED, evidently preferring women with hips, observes that cowgirls, accompanying their men into an Arizona bar, are "heifers" who "couldn't calve a salamander" (1991a, 165). Cows are dumb enough to drown (1984, 100, 102) or bog down in quicksand (1977, 190–93) and need to be rescued (1990, 92). ED and a friend will eat cows but don't want to drink after them (163). True to his "dramatic persona," ED shows affectionate concern only for a young (and we can safely presume pretty) heifer who has gotten her helpless little self stuck (1984, 72–75). Trinh contends that both "Lady and whore were bred to please" (1989, 97). We might easily add the domestic cow. Abbey might add men. Today the cow crosses genders. On one hand, she conjures a domestic female image as an overweight, middle-aged, bawling, slow, slothful, not too intelligent stomper of stream banks, dropper of dung, drawer of flies, and slinger of sagging udders. On the other hand, she represents the shameful, over-gassed, shit-encrusted symbol of manifest destiny, overgrazing, overproduction, overconsumption, overeating, and the overbearing booted and spurred white males of the American West—strangely similar to Abbey's persona.

In *Beyond the Wall,* Abbey quotes his friend Doug Peacock as saying, "It ain't wilderness . . . unless there's a critter out there that can kill and eat you." Peacock refers, of course, to the grizzly bear, against whom they are armed with modern weapons (therefore wilderness for GRIZ but not humans). ED, who claims never to have seen a grizzly, argues that the great bear is a "myth" (1984, 165–67). Abbey was intimately acquainted with one dangerous animal he knew was not a myth: the cow. William Eastlake reveals that he taught Abbey how to ride and "punch" cattle, but "when the cattle started to punch back, Ed decided to become a writer" (1985, 20). In truth, the female cow has hurt, crippled, and killed more humans than the dreaded female grizzly. Hunting wild, sharp-horned bulls along the Rio Grande is today considered one of North America's most dangerous "sports." The female grizzly may be a myth, but Abbey knows the female cow is not. ED's booming voice recommends opening a hunting season on cows (1988, 17).

Again analyzing the more complicated voice of ED/ed, the gender-specific cow takes on even more symbolic baggage with the addition of scientific fact. Scientists classify bison and cattle into separate genera (*Bos* and *Bison*), although they can readily mate, as only related species can. The difference between them? One rib: bison have fourteen, and cows, of course, have only thirteen! A bison conjures in the American imagination a very male image: a patriarchal harem ruler. Perhaps, because the cow is one rib short, like Eve, she is somehow "less of a man" than the noble bison. Like Eve, she also carries the blame for all our sins on her innocent shoulders. When ED/ed writes about "Cow Heaven" in the essay "Big Bend" (1988, 135), or the Garden of Eden in *Beyond the Wall,* cows have been banished: "not a house in sight, not even a cow or horse. Eden at the dawn of creation" (1984, 57). Deer, which he calls "a giant rodent—a rat with antlers" (1988, 17), were allowed in the Garden, but not cows:

"Everywhere deer sign, nowhere the faintest trace of man. We have stumbled into a miniature Eden" (1977, 199).

In fact, Abbey's writing often deals with humans who for one reason or another have been kicked out of Eden, banned from their wilderness homes. He also reminds us that "The American Indians had no word for what we call 'wilderness.' For them the wilderness was home" (1991b, 237). In *Slickrock,* ED/ed pointedly asks his Sierra Club audience, "What would it be like to *live* in this place?" (1987, 62; emphasis Abbey's). "The Carson Productions Interview," in which Edward Abbey speaks as an interviewee, is straight talk and not literature. During this interview Abbey said, "[T]he newly-approved Tellico Dam . . . has destroyed the habitat not only of the famous little fish known as snail darter but also forced 341 farm families off their land" (Balian 1985, 59). National parks, wildlife refuges, gunnery ranges, dams, and wilderness areas are still throwing the less powerful out of Eden: Native Americans, Hispanic settlers, ranchers, farmers, women, children, and cows. Edward Abbey did not approve. Instead, he had hoped that someday we would be able to accept humans in Paradise where "wilderness is not a playground but their natural native home" (1988, 28), that cities will be smaller, more scattered, and that across the desert, "blue-eyed Navajo bedouins will herd their sheep and horses" (1990, 127).

Seldom studied as a serious symbol in the sophisticated '90s, the cow is no stranger to the nature-writing canon. In *Teaching a Stone to Talk,* Annie Dillard fondly recalls her own cowperson days:

> I liked . . . the way the animals always broke loose. . . . two people and a clever cow can kill a morning. . . . You laugh for a while, exhausted, and silence is restored; the beasts are back in their pastures, the fences are not fixed but disguised as if they were fixed, ensuring the animals' temporary resignation; and a great calm descends, a lack of urgency, a sense of having to invent something to do until the next time you must run and chase cattle. (1992, 131)

She also contemplated cattle throughout her Pulitzer-winning pilgrimage at Tinker Creek. In the opening pages she crosses "the bridge that is really the steers' fence" (1974, 13). She remembers the "old Hebrew ordinance" to sacrifice an unblemished red heifer "which has never known the yoke." The priest must "burn her wholly, without looking away" (267). Looping through fecundity, food chains, and the horns of the altar, she concludes that the pasture she has been walking through is "the steers' pasture" (263). With even the simplest interpretation, the above cattle-chasing example gives humans a purpose, and sacrificing steers or heifers puts food on the table, satisfying two basic survival needs. This seems to call for a new attitude toward cattle. Native Americans worshipped their food source; we cuss ours.

When Henry David Thoreau explained his wildness idea in "Walking," he also did so through the cow: "I love to see the domestic animals reassert their native rights—any evidence that they have not wholly lost their original wild habits and vigor; as when my neighbor's cow breaks out of her pasture early in the spring and boldly swims the river, a cold gray tide, twenty-five or thirty rods wide, swollen by the melted snow. It is the buffalo crossing the Mississippi" (1982, 618). Wildness, Thoreau says, remains preserved under the "thick hides of cattle and horses." Occasionally we see "evidence that they have not wholly lost their original wild habits and vigor," and he rejoices that "horses and steers have to be broken before they can be made the slaves of men" (218–19). This semidormant wildness in cattle gives Thoreau hope that humans also retain the seeds of instinct. No matter how oppressed, reasons Thoreau, the human spirit can never be truly broken.[8] In "Wild Apples" (1980), Thoreau also argues that the cow helps apple trees return to a wild state.

Like Thoreau, Abbey also spends considerable time thinking about boundaries between domesticity and wildness, nature's profane and sacred dualities. He says the call of the loon is "that wild, lorn, romantic cry, one of the most thrilling sounds in all North America. Sound of the ancient wilderness, lakes, forest, moonlight, birchbark canoes" (1977, 41). Ronald calls it the "Sound of sacrality" (1982, 130). Yet both Abbey and Thoreau say almost the same thing about the domestic rooster. Abbey's version: "The call of the male chicken, if not so familiar, would seem to us like the wildest, most thrilling cry in all of nature" (1991a, 97). Thoreau's version: "The note of this once wild Indian pheasant is certainly the most remarkable of any bird's, and if they could be naturalized without being domesticated, it would soon become the most famous sound in our woods. . . . No wonder that man added this bird to his tame stock" (1982, 378).

While hiking Glacier National Park's "Peaceable Kingdom," ED/ed passes six mountain goats, "grazing not fifty feet from the trail;

indifferent to my presence," and five bighorn rams bedded down on the trail. He says he "approached to within twenty feet, waved my arms and whistled; grudgingly they got up and let me through" (1977, 50). In contrast, when he waves his arms and a stick at "half-wild" cattle who have forgotten who they belong to (1990, 84), "they bolt suddenly for the trees, like deer" (230). The cow's heritage is in fact wild, noble, and savage. Worldwide, the cow was once the proud symbol of wildness and danger, hunted in protected walled forests by only the richest lords. The modern cow descended from extinct wild ungulates like the African, Asian, and European aurochs (*Bos taurus primigenius*). Scotland's legendary, long extinct, wild white cattle were also ancestors, as were India's endangered beautiful red Gaur (*Bos gaurus*). The cow's family tree includes Caesar's urus, Indonesia's Banteng, and the hairy wild yak (*Bos grunniens*). Even the European and Asian wisent (*Bison bonasus*), a small, light-colored buffalo, contributed to the wild gene pool. Shakespeare, alluding to the wildness in cows, said they were bothered more by the breeze than by the tiger (*Troilus and Cressida*, I.iii.48).

Like all wild animals and Abbey's ideal humans, cows risk their lives for their territories, often freely choosing the most awful brush and prickly-pear choked canyon (1990, 84–85), an island available only by swimming (1977, 192), or canyons subject to flash floods and carpeted with quicksand (1984, 75). His ED/ed voice further blurs boundaries between wild and domestic when he concludes that wildness is a state of mind, not genetically imposed. One of the few major sources of protein that the desert has proven able to produce sustainably is beef, and Abbey's books consistently portray cattle as indigenous wild animals whose almost five-hundred-year presence has produced a mutually beneficial dialectic with the desert Southwest. Abbey did not want to see cows kicked out of paradise because of some imaginary dichotomy between wild and domestic. As Wallace Stegner said, "I have known enough range cattle to recognize them as wild animals; . . . they belong on the frontier, moreover, and have a look of rightness" (1969, 151).

The cow, quietly marbling in streaks of literary fat from Greek myth through the Bible, from India to South America, from Aesop to Darwin, has paradoxically represented god, monster, disguise, sacrifice, laborer, wealth, and poverty. Io, one of the mortal women Zeus loved, was changed into a white cow by his jealous wife. Animals are often described as "graven images," such as the golden calf, or as unclean and forbidden meat. Nomads, whose herds of cattle "munch[ed] their way across the Sahara, Persia, Arabia, Morocco, Ethiopia" were feared, hated, and thought of as expanding "traditions, arrogance, and destructiveness" (Shepard 1973, 17). Jeremy Rifkin declares, "It might come as a surprise to many, then, that much of the religious experience of the West, from before recorded history until well into the Christian era, was dominated by bull gods and goddesses, the cult of the bovine" (1992, 19). Cow worship was and is a worldwide phenomena. Yi-Fu Tuan recounts how in ancient Upper Egypt, "the cow goddess of the sky (Hathor) was believed to have given birth to the sun" (1984, 71). In New Guinea, Peter Mark found that "cattle stand at the summit of the hierarchy of animals." Young men wear masks decorated with cattle horns during coming of age ceremonies, and cattle are sacrificed to ensure rain (1992, 50).

Edward Abbey had a larger audience in mind than members of Earth First!. He did say he wanted sacred cows kept out of his elk pastures (1988, 19), but what better way to explain noncapitalist democracy to a Hindu reader than ED/ed's desire to be reincarnated not into the rich man's caste, but as an untouchable, one who must patiently wait until a sacred cow dies of its own volition and becomes carrion before his/her children can eat—just one of the many reasons why the cow is sacred in both the poverty-stricken American Southwest and India. When ED calls public-land cattlemen "sacred cows," I believe ED/ed wants the reader to find out just why India's strict vegetarians hold the cow sacred. Although suffering constant ridicule from modern agribusinessmen, India's cow is an ecological miracle, responsible for keeping the soil fertile and providing nonpolluting cooking fuel, as well as milk and meat, to the lowest and poorest castes. In a country where farmers can't afford and, perhaps wisely, have chosen not to become dependent on gasoline and tractors, the cow provides natural muscle to plow the fields, haul produce to market, and furnish transportation. From plaster for the walls to leather businesses, the cow actually makes India's teeming vegetarian population possible.[9]

In "Down the River with Henry Thoreau," Abbey notes, "*Walden* has been published abroad in every country where English can be read, as in India—God knows they need it there—or can be translated, as in Russia, where they need it even more. The Kremlin's commissars of literature have classified Thoreau as a nineteenth-century social reformer, proving once again that censors can read but seldom understand" (1991b, 73). Obviously, Abbey's thinking and writing ranged beyond simple rhetorical jousting between environmentalists and ranchers in the American Southwest.

In one of the last chapters of the last books Abbey ever wrote, he discusses another "nature" writer, Ralph Waldo Emerson, and in so doing tries to point his readers toward this deeper consideration of his own work:

> Emerson tried to discover for himself an original and meaningful relationship to the world, a personal viewpoint that would salvage his deeply religious sensibility and lend aid to his pressing emotional needs. Since Christianity could no longer serve these needs, he attempted to find a new synthesis through Germanic idealism, Hindu theosophy, Confucian ethics, poetic romanticism, and his inescapable background of rugged Yankee individualism. His version of philosophic idealism, which he called Transcendentalism—borrowing the term from Kant—was an effort to override or transcend these dualisms through the identification of Mind (always capitalized) with Spirit (likewise), and the equation of both with Absolute Spirit which in turn becomes another term for—the World, the Universe, the All-in-One. (1988, 211)

Applied to Abbey's own books, this interpretation can help readers plunge beyond a surface analysis of his Cactus Ed dramatic persona to his complicated and worldly ED/ed voice.

So. What is Abbey the writer trying to do with his complex, contradictory and symbolic cow? Again Trinh provides one way to solve the riddle. She says "every discourse that breeds fault and guilt is a discourse of authority and arrogance" (1989, 11), and that the "language of Taoism and Zen . . . which is rife with paradox . . . is 'illogical' and 'nonsensical' " to Western readers expecting rhetoric, because "its intent lies outside the realm of persuasion" (16). Abbey's cow essay is rife with paradox. It is illogical, nonsensical, and his intent lies outside the realm of persuasion. In the introduction to *One Life at a Time, Please*, Abbey says the cow essay will "conclude its career as the nucleus of a book-length essay in mythology and meat" (1988, 3), which it did. As usual, he exercises his democracy-based freedom of speech to the limit, attacking several "sacred cows" as he attacks every authoritative and arrogant discourse that breeds fault and guilt. Under the rubric of mythology and meat, Abbey discusses world religions, world hunger, capitalism, feminism, art, and an author's heavy responsibility to his race, his gender, and the bigger picture. Learning to listen to the ED/ed voice, readers will find layer after layer of politics, religion, philosophy, and ecology.

Although readers examine Emerson, Dillard, and Thoreau for deep meaning, they often regard Edward Abbey's nonfiction as simple environmental journalism—similar to the position Trinh finds the minority writer struggling against (1989, 28). When a writer is labeled as a representative of some out-of-favor, angry group, readers look not for literature, but for rhetoric—and readers usually find what they are looking for. In the introduction to *Journey Home,* Abbey's voice booms, "I am not and never will be a goddamned two-bit sycophantic journalist for Christ's sake!" (1977, xxii). Wendell Berry more softly says, "Mr. Abbey is not an environmentalist" (1985, 19). And I say, more softly still, Mr. Abbey's cow is not just a cow.

Notes

This chapter was originally prepared for an independent study with distinguished Abbey scholar Ann Ronald while I was a Ph.D. candidate at the University of Nevada, Reno. I am indebted to Dr. Ronald for encouraging my rural ideas.

1. Edward Said posits that an outsider interpreting another culture usually exoticises and sometimes even reshapes that culture, blocking a more authentic understanding (*Orientalism* [1979]).

2. "Trinh" is considered her surname.

3. Abbey may also be making a similar complex statement when he implies in the essay "God's Plan for the Sate of Utah: A Revelation" that fictitious angelic representatives from God were "not familiar with" the Sahara Club, obviously a pun on the Sierra Club (1977, 105).

4. For excellent clarification between agribusiness and the family farm/ranch, see "Failure of the Agrarian Utopia" in Henry Nash Smith's *Virgin Land* (1970) or "Horse-Drawn Tools and the Doctrine of Labor Saving" in Wendell Berry's *The Gift of Good Land* (1981). Numerous perspectives and references also occur in Abbey's work: 1977, 163, 234–35; 1980; 1990, 131, 141; 1991a, 107, 137, 164, 196; 1991b, 43, 95; 1988, 63–66, 154–55; 1992a; 1992b; as well as in an interview by Solheim and Levin (1985, 90).

5. Paul Shepard, bashing agriculture in general, gives a good example of the heavily symbolic rhetoric surrounding food taboos when he argues, "The cereals are wind-pollinated annuals, shallow-rooted, ephemeral, without soil-forming virtues, and their association with flowering forms or pollinator insects is minimal. By supporting large, minimally nourished human populations and by their destructive effects on the environment when grown in cultivated uniformity, the cereals are truly the symbol and agent of agriculture's war against the planet" (1973, 25).

6. Abbey's numerous references to rocks with lips and teeth can be found in 1984, 156; 1991a, 119; 1991b, 45, 148; 1992, 112.

7. Edward Abbey wrote an introduction to a 1988 Penguin edition of Austin's *The Land of Little Rain* (1903), a book he says he "read for the first time forty years ago, during my own student days in the American Southwest."

8. For an excellent explanation of how horses are never "broken," see Tom Dorrance's *True Unity* (1987) or Ray Hunt's *Think Harmony With Horses* (1978), both from Give-it-a-Go-Enterprises, P.O. Box 288, Tuscarora, NV 89834.

9. For an excellent explanation of the practical reasons behind the Hindu sacred cow, see "Mother Cow" in Marvin Harris's *Cows, Pigs, Wars, and Witches: the Riddles of Culture* (1974).

Works Cited

Abbey, Edward. 1973. *Cactus Country.* New York: Time-Life Books.
———. 1976. *The Monkey Wrench Gang.* New York: Avon.
———. 1977. *The Journey Home.* New York: E. P. Dutton.
———. 1980. *Good News.* New York: E. P. Dutton.
———. [1971] 1982. *Black Sun.* Reprint, New York: Avon.
———. 1984. *Beyond the Wall.* New York: Henry Holt.
———. 1987. *Slickrock.* Layton, Utah: Peregrine Smith.
———. 1988. *One Life at a Time, Please.* New York: Henry Holt.
———. 1989. *A Voice Crying in the Wilderness.* New York: St. Martin's Press.
———. [1968] 1990. *Desert Solitaire: A Season in the Wilderness.* Reprint, New York: Ballantine.
———. [1979] 1991a. *Abbey's Road.* Reprint, New York: Plume.
———. [1981] 1991b. *Down the River.* Reprint, New York: Plume.
———. [1956] 1992a. *The Brave Cowboy.* Reprint, New York: Avon.
———. [1962] 1992b. *Fire on the Mountain.* Reprint, New York: Avon.
Austin, Mary. [1903] 1988. *The Land of Little Rain.* Introduction by Edward Abbey. Reprint, New York: Penguin.
Balian, Chairmaine. 1985. "The Carson Productions Interview." In Hepworth and McNamee.
Berry, Wendell. 1985. "A Few Words in Favor of Edward Abbey." In Hepworth and McNamee.
———. 1981. *The Gift of Good Land: Further Essays Cultural and Agricultural.* San Francisco: North Point Press.
Dillard, Annie. 1974. *Pilgrim at Tinker Creek.* New York: Harper and Row.
———. [1983] 1992. *Teaching a Stone To Talk.* Reprint, New York: Harper Perennial.
Dorrance, Tom. 1987. *True Unity: Willing Communication Between Horse and Human.* Tuscarora, Nev.: Give-it-a-Go Enterprises.
Eastlake, William. 1985. "A Note on Ed Abbey." In Hepworth and McNamee.
Harris, Marvin. 1974. *Cows, Pigs, Wars, and Witches; the Riddles of Culture.* New York: Random House.
Hepworth, James. 1985. "The Poetry Center Interview." In Hepworth and McNamee.

Hepworth, James, and Gregory McNamee. 1985. *Resist Much, Obey Little*. Salt Lake City: Dream Garden Press.

Hunt, Ray. 1978. *Think Harmony With Horses: An In-Depth Study of Horse/Man Relationship*. Tuscarora, Nev.: Give-it-a-Go Enterprises.

Mark, Peter. 1992. *The Wild Bull and the Sacred Forest: Form, Meaning, and Change in Senegambian Initiation Masks*. New York: Cambridge University Press.

Remley, David. 1985. "Fire on the Mountain." In Hepworth and McNamee.

Rifkin, Jeremy. 1992. *Beyond Beef: The Rise and Fall of the Cattle Culture*. New York: Dutton.

Ronald, Ann. 1982. *The New West of Edward Abbey*. Albuquerque: University of New Mexico Press.

Said, Edward W. 1979. *Orientalism*. New York: Vintage Books.

Shakespeare, William. 1975. *The History of Troilus and Cressida*. In *William Shakespeare: The Complete Works*, ed. Alfred Harbage. Baltimore: Penguin.

Shelton, Richard. 1985. "Creeping up on *Desert Solitaire*." In Hepworth and McNamee.

Shepard, Paul. 1973. *The Tender Carnivore and the Sacred Game*. New York: Scribner's.

Smith, Henry Nash. 1970. *Virgin Land: The American West as Symbol and Myth*. Cambridge: Harvard University Press.

Solheim, Dave, and Rob Levin. 1985. "The Bloomsbury Review: Interview." In Hepworth and McNamee.

Starrs, Paul F. 1994. "Cattle Free By '93 and the Imperatives of Environmental Radicalism." *Ubique: Notes from the American Geographical Society* 14 (1): 2–4.

Stegner, Wallace. 1993. *Where the Bluebird Sings to the Lemonade Springs: Living and Writing in the West*. New York: Penguin.

———. [1946] 1969. *The Sound of Mountain Water*. Reprint, New York: Doubleday.

Thoreau, Henry David. [1862] 1982. "Walking." In *The Portable Thoreau*, ed. Carl Bode. New York: Penguin.

———. [1862] 1980. "Wild Apples." *The Natural History Essays*. Salt Lake City, Utah: Peregrine Smith.

Trinh T. Minh-ha. 1989. *Woman Native Other: Writing Postcoloniality and Feminism*. Bloomington: Indiana University Press.

Tuan, Yi-Fu. 1984. *Dominance and Affection: The Making of Pets*. New Haven: Yale University Press.

Edward Abbey and Gender

PAUL T.

BRYANT

Edward Abbey and gender is, a feminist colleague has observed, a "rich subject." It also turns out to be a slippery one. Inevitably in reviewing criticism of Abbey, the question of sexism arises, but what is sexism? One finds implied or explicit definitions ranging over a wide diversity of human behavior. The tenth edition of *Merriam-Webster's Collegiate Dictionary* (1993) defines "sexism" as "prejudice or discrimination based on sex" or "behavior, conditions, or attitudes that foster stereotypes of social roles based on sex." This seems a useful definition, recognizing that prejudice, discrimination, and fostering of stereotypes can be subtle and insidious, but also granting that certain roles—childbearing is the obvious example—may be inevitably the realm of one gender. "Discrimination," to be sexist, might be restricted to those distinctions between genders that result in a disadvantage or implied superiority for one or the other.

Feminist theorists have developed far more intricate, nuanced, and sophisticated definitions and analyses of sexism. Useful as these are, they are quite variable and generally indeterminate. Epistemological speculations are interesting and sometimes enlightening, but they seldom lead to generally accepted conclusions.[1] It seems more productive to stay with the clearer, more direct—if more simple minded—dictionary definition.

Recognizing that it is peripheral to the central purpose of literary studies, particularly for an author no longer living, let us begin with

Abbey's personal behavior.

Personal Behavior

Edward Abbey had a strong sexual interest in women. There is no disagreement on that point. He acknowledges it in his journals, public pronouncements, and essays. He was married five times, losing three wives to divorce, one to illness, and leaving one a widow at his death. He also had several liaisons with other women, some while he was married. It seems likely, then, that in his interactions with women–at least young and handsome women–sexual attraction was part of his consciousness. The extent to which he showed such attraction, and how it was shown, has been difficult to determine, perhaps because it varied with circumstances.

Much of the difficulty arises from gossip about Abbey among literary scholars. Scholars male and female alike have offhandedly remarked that Ed Abbey was sexist, assuming that was an unquestioned fact. My problem has arisen when I have asked for specific instances of sexist behavior. I have *invariably* been told that the person making the remark had not witnessed it but has heard frequent accounts of such behavior by those who have. When I ask for names of witnesses, or victims, none are forthcoming. I am told instead to talk to "people" at the University of Arizona or "around Tucson" or "in the Southwest." Unsure how to address a query to "people" so vaguely located, I have yet to identify an actual witness or victim.

In lieu of finding such witnesses or victims, we may resort to published accounts by women who have actually known Abbey. James Bishop mentions two contrasting reactions to Abbey. Author Mary Sojourner, who took Abbey's writing course at the University of Arizona a year before he died, recalled,

> I came to his class to do battle. . . . I knew of him as a man who had a lot of judgments, who treated women as boobies, and who kept searching for younger and younger women as he grew older. I thought he stood for a lot of the qualities in men that make women so angry, all the macho bullshit. But he turned out to be a most compassionate man. We became comrades. He listened to me. He honored my writing. He never responded negatively and was very deferential to all the students. (qtd. in Bishop 1994, 24–25)

Another woman in one of Abbey's earlier writing classes was Nancy Mairs. She begins her account by objecting to being called

"Ms. Mairs": "I don't like titles, which reinforce distinctions and distances among people, thereby creating space for patterns of domination." She objects even more strongly to being called "Mrs. Mairs" by those who "still believe that some pigs are more equal than others" (1985, 44). I cite these comments to suggest that Mairs is not likely to overlook sexist behavior. By her account, Abbey at the beginning of the term was an awkward, shy, uncertain teacher, but "from the first a sure-handed editor, thorough, tough, and good-humored." He taught three different workshops each week, "no doubt editing all the submissions with the same painstaking attention he's given to mine" (47). Neither of these accounts gives any hint of sexist behavior. On the contrary, they suggest a shy, deferential, conscientious teacher.

A different view is presented by artist Cynthia Bennett, who knew Abbey when he was working a fire tower on the North Rim of Grand Canyon. "His heart was always breaking over some woman. He was the most romantic man. Yet he was patronizing toward women, not contemptuous exactly, but bored. He found them tedious" (qtd. in Bishop 1994, 116).

These disparate views seem hard to reconcile unless one hypothesizes that Abbey had different reactions to different women, just as he might to different men. Certainly Abbey did not find all women tedious or boring, and possibly he regarded visitors to his lookout as interruptions of his writing routine and desired solitude. Garth McCann follows the accepted view that Abbey was "obsessed by a love-hate relationship with women," stating that "he occasionally shows contempt for women," but McCann gives no source, support, or basis in experience for these damning statements (1977, 9). How do we know that he hated women? How did he show his contempt? We are not told.

Still, there is Abbey's undisputedly strong sexual interest, which he presumably showed to women who attracted him. How did he express such interest? At what point does the expression of sexual interest cross the line dividing acceptable from sexist behavior? Opinions vary, but there seems to be general agreement that lines exist.

Edward Abbey was born in 1927. Some of those who take Abbey's sexism for granted attribute it to his generation. Certainly Abbey did not follow the strictures, in his writing and speaking, of what has come to be called "political correctness. "Perhaps he did harbor views that recent thought has identified as sexist, without realizing he was doing so. Certainly, as Wendell Berry observes, he liked to attack sacred cows (1985, 14),[2] and anything he might be told he should not say was likely to be said, simply as an anarchist's defiance of formal taboos.

With witnesses that Abbey behaved in acceptable ways with women, and gossip to the contrary, we should look to Abbey's journal and other writings for evidence. In a "self-interview" in the *Whole Earth Review,* Abbey calls himself a radical sexist pig who believes "not only that women are radically different from men, as confirmed by my own personal researches over a period of forty years, but also that women are radically superior to men—far more loving, kind, gentle, generous, sensitive, loyal, and obviously much better looking" (1988, 17). But this was for public consumption late in Abbey's life, after he had felt some heat from charges of sexism, and still may leave him open to charges of stereotyping, however favorable. His private journal, including entries written before the height of the modern feminist movement, or even before Abbey had achieved a high level of public recognition, might be a better index of his feelings and beliefs.

Perhaps the most egregiously sexist entry in Abbey's journal was made in September 1966 in "A Modest Proposal" for state-sponsored, and socially accepted, prostitution. In his own defense, Abbey explains that he is simply proposing this as part of a program of free love that will release our society from the bonds of the hypocrisy that "poisons the spiritual atmosphere with a smog of cynicism, pornography, and commercialism" (1994, 207). However, the whole focus of the note is on female prostitution for the convenience of promiscuous males. Abbey tries to offer conditions that would not mean exploitation of the whores—everything is voluntary—but exploitation is what is involved. His concern is clearly male sexual pleasure. This is the sort of idea that would surely outrage feminists and should, at the least, make all of us uncomfortable. Does his heading the entry "A Modest Proposal" mean he was, as was Swift in his "Modest Proposal," being ironic? If so, he fails to carry the irony through in the entry itself. Did Abbey outgrow such ideas? No hint of them appears again in his journals or, to my knowledge, his other writing, private or public.

On July 3, 1973, Abbey wrote in his journal, "Women *are* better than men. I ought to know. Not only different—but better!" (234). However, this entry follows comments on the sexual response of the woman he was with at the time, which might invalidate it as being only based on sex. On the other hand, for September 14, 1966, the same month he made the entry on prostitution, we find a long note "On the Biological Basis of Female Beauty." This entry might raise objections from feminists for linking male ideals of feminine beauty, at the biological level, to the likelihood of a woman producing healthy children. Yet Abbey qualifies these observations with the comment that "it would be fallacious to assert that love consists of *nothing but* these biological compulsions." At the end of this speculation Abbey concludes,

> And only if we face the truth can we surmount, transcend and escape the menial role nature has assigned us, men and women both.
>
> Only by seeing and accepting the biological basis and limit of human life can we free ourselves from its animal bondage, cease struggling against it or denying it or lying to ourselves and to each other—and then, on that accomplishment, perhaps begin to realize the potential of mind, personality and spirit; and through sympathy, mutual aid, justice, creative work (the true forms of love), establish at last on earth a community and society where every man, every woman, will be free to fulfill the highest desires of the human soul. (203–5)

There will be disagreement on the best paths to these goals, but neither gender should object to the end result. The date of the entry and the fact that it is in his private journal suggest that it represents sincere sentiments.

Given the scant and contradictory evidence, and the pervasive but unspecific gossip, what are we to believe? Certainly, from his many acknowledged liaisons with women, we can assume that Abbey was at least some of the time the initiator of the relationship. It might also be reasonable to assume that he proposed more such relationships than were accepted. Thus to a woman offended by his manner in making such a proposal, or by the proposal itself, his behavior might have been called sexist. If heterosexual promiscuity is sexist behavior, Abbey was guilty.

What are we to make of the "macho" behavior mentioned by Mary Sojourner and often by others? For example, Lucinda Franks, in her review of *Abbey's Road*, speaks of his sexism but does not specify what she means other than that he is macho and proud of it. "We do not really take his sexism seriously," she concludes (1979, 8). Exactly what "macho" behavior includes is never specified. If "macho" refers to his interest in firearms and his accounts of drinking parties and beer-guzzling road trips, I would agree that these are often sophomoric, but hardly sexist. Deborah Slicer criticizes male "ecocentrists" "for positing a masculine 'self' " (1994, 37). To complain that a man writes from a male (androcentric) point of view seems excessively gynocentric. Most of us cannot help our gender, and each of us must write from our personal point of view if we are to write with integrity and authenticity.

In any case, I have found no evidence (beyond unsupported gossip) to show that Abbey was an egregious, blatant sexist, beyond his sexual promiscuity and the exploitive attitudes arising from it. That, with some justice, has been labeled sexist.

Having arrived at these conclusions, the appropriate question now is: So what? Abbey is no longer physically with us. There is no problem of preventing objectionable behavior by an influential member of society. We have only his works, and they deserve evaluation on their own terms. If we refuse to attend to artistic works because of the sexist behavior of the deceased artist, we will have to stop listening to Mozart's music, among others. In short, Abbey's personal behavior is now only marginally significant. His works, however, are still with us. They require evaluation regardless of their author's personal merits.

The Fiction

Women do not play a prominent role in Abbey's novels except for *The Monkey Wrench Gang* and its sequel, *Hayduke Lives!* Consequently, charges of sexism in his fiction focus on these two novels. Bishop speaks of "women who felt that Abbey was the classic male chauvinist in the way women were depicted in his books as often loopy, insultingly sexy caricatures" (1994, 45). No specific book or character is mentioned. McCann, writing before the sequel appeared, presents specifics. He says that Bonnie Abbzug of *The Monkey Wrench Gang* "has the mind of a teeny-bopper and the body of a goddess," and that she "remains a rather unreal figment of a semi-chauvinistic imagination" (1977, 39). Various responses to this charge are possible.

Must male writers of fiction only present female characters who are wise, heroic, and ugly? Further, to say that one female character represents denigration of an entire gender is to commit the kind of stereotyping sometimes charged against Abbey. On a more specific level, how can a character, male or female, be "insultingly sexy"? I suspect that few men or women in their twenties and thirties (the age range in Bonnie Abbzug's life in the two novels) would be insulted by being regarded as sexy. Do sexually attractive women exist only in the minds of male chauvinists? Concern over depicting men's sexual attraction to women suggests that we are returning to the times when frank discussion of sex was not allowed in literature. Perhaps Bishop and McCann, like William Dean Howells, feel that Bonnie Abbzug should only be described in terms that would not shock their adolescent daughters. If so, they may be surprised to learn what it takes to shock today's adolescents, male or female.

Abbey regarded these as comic novels, referring to *The Monkey Wrench Gang* in his journal as "sabotage and laughter and wild wild fun" (1994, 185). He presents comic images of himself as Ranger Abbott in *The Monkey Wrench Gang,* and as a timid and lecherous correspondent in *Hayduke Lives!* In the latter novel he presents environmentalist groups in a thoroughly comic light, yet he is not accused of being anti-environmental. Surely a writer of comic fiction can be allowed to present comic female as well as male figures. I have found no instance of critics condemning Jane Austin as sexist for some of the absurd male figures she created. To charge sexism on such a basis lacks credibility.

Second, the Monkey Wrench novels present male characters who are hardly ideal role models for young manhood. George Washington Hayduke is a borderline psychopath who frequently puts machismo in a bad light. Oral Hatch combines absurdity and pathos. Bishop Love is as absurd (and sexist) as he can be made. In short, there are comic, cartoonish male characters in both novels. If male novelists are allowed only to present comic male characters, such a restriction might be considered sexist in privileging one gender over the other.

Third, is Bonnie Abbzug as negatively presented as these critics maintain? Clearly she is least susceptible to the macho foolishness about firearms and explosives and beer guzzling. She is very much in control of her relationship with Sarvis and with Hayduke, and to a considerable extent in control of them when she wishes to be. She is consistently the most selfless of the group, concerning herself in particular with Doc Sarvis's welfare and that of her children. Some might react that this is simply what Abbey's macho mentality would expect of a woman, but we have already seen in Abbey's self-interview in *Whole Earth Review* (1988, 17) that he regards these very characteristics as conferring superiority, not from the insulation (and exclusion) of a pedestal but in full participation in the problems and challenges of life. The superiority is shown in how those challenges are met in the midst of life's dangers and ambiguities. Finally, Bonnie unhesitatingly gives herself up to arrest to help Dr. Sarvis care for Bishop Love when Love has a heart attack. These are not the actions of a loopy teeny-bopper.

In *Hayduke Lives!* Bonnie Abbzug becomes the stable center around whom much of the action turns. She has a son and is pregnant. For her children she seeks a stable world in which she can provide them security. In the chapter "Bonnie Abbzug-Sarvis Reviews Her Life," we see a series of reflections on her life and relationships that might not meet the requirements of any one feminist's "project," but which can hardly be regarded as shallow, trivial, or subordinate to male interests. Her reflections on men and masculine logocentrism are less than complimentary:

Men.
They all think they're so smart and they're all so dumb. Crude. Crude people, men. Dense as rocks. They think like rocks, in a straight line, nothing but gravity, straight down the hill, that's how they think. No feelings. They think they feel but they only feel with their skin, that's how they feel. Skin deep. Nothing makes sense to them unless you can explain it. Have to draw them pictures, diagrams, charts, formulas, equations, simple propositions with a subject and a verb and an object, that's it, that's all they, only way they, no sensitivity, no inner understanding, no empathy. Sympathy, sure, that's on the surface, only skin, they understand sympathy and can do a pretty good act with sympathy but empathy—? Wouldn't know what you were talking about.
I feel sorry for men. (1990a, 44)

This passage and the pages that follow might represent an effort on Abbey's part to suggest, in dramatized and hence simplified form, that he had some understanding of the feminist viewpoint and considerable sympathy.

Later in the novel, Abbey twice presents Abbzug-Sarvis as more than competent at what might be regarded as "macho" skills. That is, she outdoes the men in areas in which they are traditionally adept. In the chapter "The Last Poker Game," she dominates the play and out-bluffs Doc Sarvis, the master of the bluff and the poker face. When she finally agrees to participate in one last Monkey Wrench caper, she comes impressively prepared.

> She reached into her capacious Bedouin robes and drew forth, with both hands, a sleek elegant precision-tooled Uzi 9mm machine pistol. She unfolded the stock, snapped it in place. Aiming the Uzi's muzzle at the sky she reached inside her robe again, pulled out a full ammo magazine and slammed it firmly into the breech. With practiced ease she slid the carriage back then forward, loading the firing chamber, set the action on semi-automatic and locked the safety. "Jewish," she said proudly, smiling at Smith. "This here's a Jew-gun, men. Israeli made and Israeli deployed. The gun that won the West. West Bank, that is." Turning her head, she smirked at Doc. "Eat your heart out, Arafat. Today Israel—tomorrow the world!" She tucked it out of sight.
> Doc Sarvis and Seldom Seen stared at Bonnie. "Holy smoke," said Smith. Doc nodded sadly. (274)

Thus Abbey develops Bonnie Abbzug into a complex, competent, and often introspective woman with frequently stated feminist views.

Two other female characters have some prominence in *Hayduke Lives!*. Ranger Ginny Dick is not a totally positive figure, but she does show her superiority to Bishop Love. Erika, the young Swedish environmental activist, is presented as beautiful, sexually attractive (a characteristic apparently regarded by McCann as a flaw), but she is also given courage and dignity that can hardly be regarded as denigrating. Her stature as a significant human being is best summarized by Doc Sarvis during the last poker game.

> a healthy young woman like Erika whatshername—what is her last name by the way, anybody know?—is a whole, a being complete, intact and compact, with a personality—no, wrong word, trivialized word—is a vital spirit, by God, in a way that no amount of analysis psychoanalysis, chemical analysis, vivisectional analysis, tomographic analysis, computerized analysis could ever have predicted. A healthy active lively woman like your leader Erika is not

a mere clever assembly of intricate parts, like say a computer, but something more like a . . . like a composition: a poem; a symphony; a dance. Some humans can be reduced to robots, to slavery, given the proper training, torture, genetic breeding. (Some cannot.) But no amount of robot could ever manufacture a human being. Or make a human out of a slave. Or make any other vital, happy, healthy, defiant animal. That is my belief, my conviction, I couldn't prove it on paper or on a blackboard or on a printout but I can prove it by showing you somebody like Erika. Erika and her friends, those vital spirits we saw out there in the woods, on the edge of the yawning abyss. (232)

These are not descriptions of trivialized or subordinated characters, despite the fact that all three are sexually active. Thus it seems difficult to sustain a charge of sexism on the basis of Abbey's fictional female characters. In the two novels in which they play significant roles, they emerge as more complex and admirable than the best of the male characters.

The Nonfiction
Perhaps the crux of the problem lies in Abbey's nonfiction. In these works he purports to be speaking with his own voice, presenting actual events and his reaction to them. Here we should find ideas and attitudes for which Abbey was willing to take responsibility.

Again, however, matters are not so simple. To what extent was the voice of the essays truly the voice of Edward Abbey? Bishop reports that "Abbey was deeply introspective and did not want people to know just how sensitive he really was, so, as a cover, he developed a super-macho personality" (1994, 46). James Hepworth reports, "In conversation Abbey is extraordinarily quiet and shy, a disarming contrast to the public Abbey and the image he has himself helped to create as a boisterous iconoclast" (1985, 34). Hepworth quotes Abbey in the same vein:

It sometimes seems to me that the Edward Abbey who writes these articles and books and so on is just another fictional creation, not much resemblance to the real one. . . . The real Edward Abbey—whoever the hell that is—is a real shy, timid fellow, but the character I create in my journalism is perhaps a person I

would like to be: bold, brash, daring. I created this character, and
I gave him my name. I guess some people mistake the creation for
the author, but that's their problem. (42)

In the privacy of his journal, in 1976, Abbey echoed these distinctions between himself and the character he presents to his readers
in his "nonfiction": "The Edward Abbey of my books is largely a fictional creation: the true adventures of an imaginary person. The real
Edward Abbey? I think I hardly know him. A shy, retiring, very timid
fellow, obviously. Somewhat of a recluse, emerging rarely from his fictional den only when lured by money, vice, the prospect of applause"
(1994, 246–47). Barry Lopez uses similar terms, describing Abbey's
"ingenuous shyness, so at odds with the public image of a bold iconoclast" (1985, 64). My own single personal encounter with Abbey
left me with a similar impression, that Abbey "was not the sharp-
tongued, outrageous anarchist so many believe him to have been . . .
but rather a quiet, shy, thoughtful man who created a far different
persona for public consumption" (Bryant 1989, 37).

In effect, Abbey's nonfiction voice is at least partially a fictional
persona. While the careful reader should be aware of Abbey's mas-
querade, still, it is the persona's voice that will continue to be heard in
our literary tradition if Abbey's works endure.

The source of much of the sense that Abbey's writings are sexist
seems to lie in his tendency to be deliberately outrageous. "To challenge the taboo—that has always been a special delight of mine"
(1990b, xii). "Some people write to please, to soothe, to console.
Others to provoke, to challenge, to exasperate and infuriate. I've always found the second approach the more pleasing" (60). Those offended by this deliberate abrasiveness see it as childish contrariness.
Gesteland sees the generalized abrasiveness as sexism, although she
does not explain the connection (1993, 233). Those less disturbed by
it may consider it a way to provoke thought about too easily received
standard views. Wendell Berry acknowledges this by concluding that
"no reader can read much of Mr. Abbey without finding some insult
to something that he or she approves of. Mr. Abbey is very hard, for
instance, on 'movements'—the more solemn and sacred they are, the
more they tempt his ridicule" (1985, 14).

This tendency to set the reader's teeth on edge is almost always
supplemented by Abbey's (frequently self-effacing) irony. He often
makes an outrageous statement ironically to inject humor through

overstatement. A reader already reacting negatively, or one who holds a solemn and sacred view of the subject, may miss the irony and attribute views to Abbey that he does not hold. In a *New Republic* review of *Abbey's Road*, the reviewer completely misses Abbey's irony and interprets everything he says for its literal meaning (S.C. 1979, 37–38). In a letter to the magazine, Abbey protests that his "feeble attempts at irony, humor, self mockery were lost on your reviewer" (1979, 40–41).

Although Abbey's nonfiction would appear to be the best place to determine the nature of Abbey's sexist offenses, here again I have encountered difficulty in identifying a bill of particulars. Gesteland's objection to Abbey's use of language—such as when he speaks of the brown, silt-rich bosom of the Colorado River, or when he speaks of the unvegetated desert as nature in the nude—does not seem a valid instance of sexism. These references do not specify gender nor do they suggest sexual activity. In any case, if interest in sexual activity is in itself regarded as sexist, Pam Houston and Erica Jong are guilty, along with a great many other talented writers, unless we are prepared to say that female writers are privileged on this topic.

Both Gesteland (1993, 234) and SueEllen Campbell (1995, 6) object to Abbey's complaint in *Desert Solitaire* about "the same old wife every night" (1968, 155). This perhaps is an expression of sexual promiscuity or desire for promiscuity. Again, if that is sexist, then this might be evidence for such a charge. But is Abbey serious? The statement is part of a stream of consciousness in which he also mentions murdering his companion, killing officials of the government, and undergoing the tyranny of automatic washers, television, and telephones. Surely we are not to take all of these statements literally and seriously, and if not all of them, then why any of them?

Again, as does Gesteland, Campbell associates any imagery that suggests sexuality with sexist views, suggesting that anything associated with sex is somehow sexist. Further, images such as that of a bee approaching a "soft, lovely, sweet, desirable" cactus flower are presented as invoking sex. Does such an image necessarily invoke sex? For a cactus flower, the image might invoke thoughts of sexual activity if cactus flowers could think. They do depend upon the bee as a romantic intermediary. But I believe cactus flowers generally are both male and female, so it is hard to see how the image could be sexist. For the bee, the flower represents food and drink. Anyone who has experienced significant hunger and thirst in a desert environment would appreciate the desirability of food and drink without concern for sex. For humans, the image might merely invoke a sense of a beautiful cactus flower. Surely the invocation of natural beauty is not necessarily sexist.

It is also possible to suggest physical pleasure without invoking sex. And again, is the invocation of sex necessarily sexist? We seem to be reverting to nineteenth-century standards that consider sex a "dirty" topic not to be mentioned in polite literature. That is a censorship struggle many thought had been won years ago.

Campbell calls "laughably Freudian" Abbey's description of an area as "lovely and wild, with a virginal sweetness . . . [where] all is exposed and naked, dominated by the monolithic formations of sandstone which stand above the surface of the ground" (1995, 5). Why it is "laughable" is not explained, and why it is necessarily Freudian is not established, either, particularly in view of the rest of the passage, of which this is only a carefully selected part. It is taken from a description in *Desert Solitaire* of the desert in Arches National Monument (1968, 10). Anyone familiar with the area might agree that the passage is a fair, even eloquent description of the actual physical landscape. Nakedness of rock can mean only unvegetated, and virginal can mean untouched or unspoiled. Neither term requires sexual connections, and neither specifies gender. Even if—as happens, for example, with the paintings of Georgia O'Keefe—we persist in seeing sexual implications in images of natural objects, the connection still is not made between sexuality and sexism.

The pattern of complaints about sexism seems based primarily either on the mention of sex or the use of what is perceived as sexual metaphor, or on some mention of physical pleasure, such as Abbey's euphoria while floating down the warm, sediment-laden Colorado. If all mention of physical pleasure suggests sex, and if any suggestion of sex is automatically sexist and therefore proscribed, we may soon have a literature that would be acceptable to Cotton Mather in his sternest mood.

Conclusion

Ironically, the conventional wisdom that Abbey was sexist is correct, but generally the wrong reasons seem to be offered for that conclusion. Abbey's obsession with sex, and his relationships with his wives and numerous other women, apparently involved behavior that can be considered sexist to the extent that he ignored or sacrificed the wishes or feelings of others to the satisfaction of his own sexual desire. It is easy to find examples of such behavior, and of related attitudes, throughout Abbey's journals.

The curious aspect of all this, as I have tried to demonstrate, is that most of the criticism of Abbey's sexism is misdirected. The passages cited as examples of his sexism are sex, not sexism, or are simply descriptions of desert experience. Abbey's works are far less sexist than his personal life may have been or his journals suggest. It is as if the critics decided a priori that Abbey is sexist but don't know where to look to prove it.

This a priori conclusion may have been provoked by Abbey's fabled machismo, as if a male writer is not allowed to be too male. Obviously, not all feminists agree with Victoria Davion, who argues that "a truly feminist perspective cannot embrace either the feminine or the masculine uncritically, as a truly feminist perspective requires a critique of gender roles, and this critique must include masculinity and femininity" (1994, 9). Contributing to this tendency is what Gruen calls the development of "oppositional communities," communities of interest devoted to seeking out "oppression" in whatever form and combating it (1994, 128). An expectation of finding oppression everywhere may become a self-fulfilling prophecy. There is an old saying that if all you have is a hammer, everything looks like a nail.

In Abbey's defense, we might consider a principle generally held by eco-feminists that "the domination of nature by human beings comes from a patriarchal world view, the same world view that justifies the domination of women" (Davion 1994, 9; see also Gruen 1994, 120). Abbey acknowledges an occasional desire to "possess" the landscape much as he might desire to "possess" a woman, but the burden of his message is that he and the rest of us should *not* possess, dominate, or interfere with the desert. The whole thrust of the Monkey Wrench novels and Abbey's nonfiction is to *prevent* the domination of the landscape by humans where it has not yet occurred, and to reduce that domination where it has occurred. If Abbey lacked the "patriarchal world view" of the desert, he may not have had such a view of women, if the two are closely linked.

What is needed, then, is a careful, sensitive, open-minded reading of Abbey's work. Where he genuinely goes astray, we should note it and discount that work accordingly. At the same time, we should not casually issue broad condemnations. We should recognize that sexual activity is a normal part of human life and grant the artist the freedom to deal frankly with it. "Oppositional communities" can surely find enough clear-cut oppressions in this world without having to resort to gossip or innuendo or interpretation that finds "dirty sex" under every image such as bugs under rocks.

Perhaps the best advice comes from Barry Lopez: "You can point to the quirks and miscalculations of any writer exposed to the searing heat of public acclaim. Better to select what is admirable and encouraging" (1985, 65). Surely it is within the realm of responsible criticism to find not only the errors in a writer's life, but also, more importantly at last, the achievements in a writer's work.

Notes

1. Alison Assiter, in her introduction to *Enlightened Women* (1996), discusses some of the disagreements and reexaminations of assumptions among feminist thinkers, and some of the reevaluations of postmodernism and poststructuralism. Like most areas of philosophical study, feminism is not a single, monolithic set of ideas.

2. This is Wendell Berry's choice of words, and I am sure no pun was intended. "Cow" can refer to a bovine of either gender in this context. *Pace.*

Works Cited

Abbey, Edward. 1968. *Desert Solitaire: A Season in the Wilderness.* New York: McGraw-Hill.

———. 1975. *The Monkey Wrench Gang.* New York: J. B. Lippincott.

———. 1979. Letter to the editor. *New Republic* Sept. 29, 40–41.

———. 1988. Interview. *Whole Earth Review* 16:17.

———. 1990a. *Hayduke Lives!* Boston: Little, Brown and Co.

———. 1990b. *Vox Clamantis in Deserto: Notes from a Secret Journal.* New York: St. Martin's Press.

———. 1994. *Confessions of a Barbarian: Selections from the Journals of Edward Abbey, 1951–1989.* Ed. David Petersen. New York: Little, Brown.

Assiter, Alison. 1996. *Enlightened Women: Modernist Feminism in a Postmodern Age.* New York: Routledge.

Berry, Wendell. 1985. "A Few Words in Favor of Edward Abbey." In Hepworth and McNamee, 9–19.

Bishop, James, Jr. 1994. *Epitaph for a Desert Anarchist: The Life and Legacy of Edward Abbey.* New York: Atheneum.

Bryant, Paul T. 1989. "Edward Abbey and Environmental Quixoticism." *Western American Literature* 24:37–43.

———. 1994. Note to the editor. *Western American Literature* 29:143–45.

Campbell, SueEllen. 1995. "Magpie." Paper presented at the meeting of the Association for the Study of Literature and the Environment, Fort Collins, Colorado. Also published in this volume.

Davion, Victoria. 1994. "Is Ecofeminism Feminist?" In Warren, 8–28.

Franks, Lucinda. 1979. "Natural Involvement." Review of Edward Abbey's *Abbey's Road*. *New York Times Book Review*, Aug. 5, 8, 21.

Gesteland, Becky Jo. 1993. Note to the editor. *Western American Literature* 28:233–34.

Gruen, Lori. 1994. "Toward an Ecofeminist Moral Epistemology." In Warren, 120–38.

Hepworth, James. 1985. "The Poetry Center Interview." In Hepworth and McNamee, 33–42.

Hepworth, James, and Gregory McNamee, eds. 1985. *Resist Much, Obey Little: Some Notes on Edward Abbey*. Salt Lake City: Dream Garden Press.

Lopez, Barry. 1985. "Meeting Ed Abbey." In Hepworth and McNamee, 62–65.

Mairs, Nancy. 1985. "597ax." In Hepworth and McNamee, 43–49.

McCann, Garth. 1977. *Edward Abbey*. Boise State University Western Writers Series, no. 29. Boise, Idaho: Boise State University.

S. C. 1979. Review of Edward Abbey's *Abbey's Road*. *New Republic*, Aug. 25, 37–38.

Slicer, Deborah. 1994. "Wrongs of Passage: Three Challenges to the Maturing of Ecofeminism." In Warren, 29–41.

Warren, Karen J., ed. 1994. *Ecological Feminism*. New York: Routledge.

The Life of the Author

Emerson, Foucault, and the Reading of Edward Abbey's Journals

DAVID

COPLAND

MORRIS

Throughout his published journals, *Confessions of a Barbarian* (1994), Edward Abbey demonstrates an ability to register, in a brilliantly evoked intellectual and emotional drama, important tensions tearing at an individual life in late-twentieth-century America: how to experience a humble, worshipful stance toward the natural world while also preserving, nurturing, and expressing an authentically strong personality and mind; how to take effective, serious action while also being aware of one's smallness in the scheme of things; how, as a writer, to use honestly the formative texts of the past while speaking through, or constructing, one's own individual voice. He desires to be both heroic and humble, fiercely independent yet vitally connected. These somewhat personal preoccupations also lead to concerns over how the American West can retain the wildness and freedom he sees it as still possessing, while also serving as the home to some kind of modern society.

Abbey scorns the existentialists for their anthropocentrism, and yet he shares with them some sense of himself as heroically creating his own meaning. He wants to avoid abjectness, but he also wants to wholeheartedly praise, even worship, something outside of himself. He wants to be true to his talent and to be recognized for it while holding in his mind the vanity of human ambition. He strongly desires to be a self-reliant Emersonian nonconformist, yet he understands the ironic stance toward the possibility of such individualism imposed by his historical positioning in the late twentieth century.

All these tensions do not produce stasis—rather they produce language that David Petersen, the editor of *Confessions,* claims to be "some of the finest writing the prolific author ever put to paper" (1994, x). I agree, for the writing in the journals forcefully evokes strong conflicts in Abbey's life and in the larger culture, conflicts that cannot be avoided by any simple reverent piety or any simple nihilistic resignation. The tensions he felt are given freer rein in the journal format than in any other that he used, and therefore his journal, I would claim, is a central, not a marginal, element in his achievement as a writer despite his apparent lack of intention to ever publish it. His words in the journal force us to face the conflicts along with him and, in so doing, evoke a stronger sense of his extraordinary presence than we get even from the other nonfiction. This presence is the mark of what Petersen calls, with beautiful precision, Abbey's "great soulful intellect" (xii). It is an account of this powerful presence that I attempt to give in this essay.

I use the word "presence" above in keen awareness of its highly problematic connotations within the world of contemporary critical theory. However, as one reads *Confessions,* one does not say, with Foucault, that the author has disappeared; rather, Abbey's authority, in all the senses of that word, is almost too present for some readers. In "Self-Reliance," Emerson says, "I ought to go upright and vital, and speak the rude truth in all ways" (1903, 2:51). Abbey writes in the journals as if this motto were always in front of his eyes. In his quiet and appreciative essay on Emerson, Abbey singles out for approbation several lines from "Self-Reliance," among which are: "Trust thyself: every heart vibrates to that iron string," and "Whoso would be a man must be a nonconformist. . . . [Abbey's ellipsis] Nothing is at last sacred but the integrity of your own mind" (1988, 215). Abbey's own work calls these admonitions to mind more than almost any other writer I can think of, and he is not equivocal in citing his debt to Emerson: "Emerson was the first great American writer, 'the father of us all,' as Susan Sontag (of all people!) has said. Without Emerson there would have been only a lesser Thoreau and maybe no Walt Whitman at all. The concerns of Emerson are the concerns of most writers today, particularly American writers. The search for transcendence and integrity and truth goes on" (216). Quite clearly, it is implied, without Emerson there would have been no Edward Abbey either. Even if Emerson was not a direct influence on Abbey, there is no doubt that Thoreau and Whitman were crucial to him.

Abbey has indeed been assessed primarily in terms of Emersonian self-reliance. A sampling of review commentary printed on the back covers of his paperback nonfiction books reveals the typical terms in which he is described.

What entertains many and exasperates others is Abbey's unique prose voice. Alternately misanthropic and sentimental, enraged and hilarious, it is the voice of a full-blooded man airing his passions. (*One Life at a Time, Please*)

What has always made his work doubly interesting is the sense of a true maverick spirit at large within it—a kind of spirit not imitable. (*The Journey Home*)

Abbey's the original fly in the ointment. Give him money and prizes. Don't let anything happen to him. (*Abbey's Road*)

Abbey has always had a special authenticity and independence. (*Beyond the Wall*)

As much as one may wish to agree with these assessments and with Abbey's own description of his Emersonian goals, how can one, in a poststructuralist age, take seriously Abbey's overtly expressed desire to pursue "transcendence and integrity and truth" or the reviewers' notions of "independence" and "maverick spirit"? Or, rather, how can this desire be taken seriously if writing is examined under poststructuralist critical tenets? When Abbey mentions above the search of the writer for "transcendence and integrity and truth," he invokes terms which, of course, have been called into question by contemporary literary theory: all texts are said to be intertextual, and language is said to "construct" the "subject" rather than the other way around. From the standpoint of such theory, the author becomes merely a site for the operations of historically generated linguistic codes. The best that a writer can do is to self-reflexively play with and undermine the inherited codes, presumably—although this has always remained ambiguous—so that some unpredictable and undefinable liberation might somehow take place. How to meet the challenge of poststructuralism will occupy the middle portion of this essay.

Ironically, one of the sources of Abbey's self-reliant independent voice, and resultant authority as truth-teller, resides in a style that exhibits many of the playful, transgressive, multivalent traits that post-structuralism demands, a poststructuralism quite at odds with the notion of self-reliance or truth. One powerful way in which Abbey achieves his independence and pursues his truth is through a style that gives free play to his exploration of conflict and tension. Passage after passage from the journals shows Abbey giving voice to opposing notions and letting them clash in an intellectual and emotional drama.

To fully understand the accomplishment of the journals, one of Petersen's claims about what I would call their Emersonian aspect must be taken into account and defended, for this claim brings in its train a set of problems placed before by the juggernaut of contemporary literary theory. Petersen says that the journals—which I have just claimed to display a self-reflexive, postmodern surface—actually "compose an intimate record of this important and controversial figure's innermost thoughts and feelings" (1994, x). These two claims—that the journals exhibit a postmodern, self-reflexive surface or style, and that they reveal an "innermost" self—sit uneasily together, yet I assert them both. The fact that the journal supports both claims is what makes it, in my mind, such a compelling text.

The drama expressed through Abbey's complex postmodern style is more than just a flashy linguistic show. We have to see it as the way in which he can get closest to expressing his truth. The journals are a great achievement because they, more than any other of his work, reveal a self struggling with contradiction and against the temptation to accept easy answers. In one journal entry Abbey says, "I'm so complicated a person I don't know what role to effect, and I'm not clever enough to pass myself off as what I truly am, a complicated person" (1994, 116). This is a key passage, I believe, in understanding the journals and all of his work. It shows great self-knowledge. But the passage itself belies the complaint. The role he affected was, in fact, that of a complicated person because that is what he was—a person as complicated as the style and content of the quoted passage itself. The journals are replete with such passages.

The journals do, in fact, succeed in conveying memorably the sense of Abbey as a complicated person, and they do so in the very style in which he presents himself; the resulting complexity is then the actual substance of his "innermost thoughts and feelings." It is not the case that the reader discovers a static "essential" self, but rather the complicated, dynamic self that Abbey knew was at the center of his consciousness when he was thinking or feeling most honestly and urgently. And this self is a dramatist, not a dogmatist, as has sometimes been charged against him. Even when Abbey is unattractive and perhaps repellent in the journals, we experience what I think can best be described as a largeness of self, the sense of largeness being a product of the intensity of the drama that he submits himself to.

In reading the journals, one gathers an impression that culminates in a notion of "Abbeyesque," an example of what Charles Altieri calls a "one place predicate" (1994, 93). This is a predicate that expresses qualities so individual it becomes, in a sense, its own category. Let us look at a lengthy journal passage by way of example:

> Shakespeare: Certainly, he was a master poet—but his plays are archaic bores: the childish humor of his comedies; the farcical nonsense of his tragedies; the tedious sycophancy of his histories. One of the many things I dislike is the total absence of any real, free, independent men in his world—all we have are masters and slaves, bosses and the bossed, and the prevailing slime of servility by which the hierarchical machinery is lubricated; in short, no MEN. Therefore—no heroes, no tragedy.
>
> Shakespeare, the immortal bard—vastly overrated. Really belongs in the company of other distinguished hacks, such as S. N. Behrman, J. T. Racine, Ben Jonson, J. M. Barrie, Gilbert & Sullivan, etc. etc. . . . characters I admire most in Shakespeare are his villains: Jack Cade, Caliban, Edmund the Bastard, Macbeth, that chap who married Hamlet's mother, what's his name, etc. In all of Shakespeare, there is no Spartacus—not a single one.
>
> Ah, you say, but such a figure could not have been regarded as heroic in Shakespeare's time, and Shakespeare was very much a product of his time. To which I reply—Precisely. I think it unbecoming of a writer to submit, supinely, to evil institutions merely because they constitute the prevailing order of things. Raleigh serves as an example of a man who was able, unlike Shakespeare, to rise above and see beyond the narrow limitations of his own time. Marlowe was another.
>
> I'm a narrow-minded sonofabitch. I lack that generosity of spirit and easy tolerance of others I so much admire in a man like, well—who? Henry Miller? I suppose so. Yet he too is impatient with fools. He says. (1994, 242)

This is indeed a complicated passage; I can only hope my commentary will bring out some facets of the complexity while not committing a kind of crude reduction.

Here we see Abbey struggling for an independence of thought and dramatizing the conflicts he experiences. In a sense, he can be seen as attempting in 1975 the kind of revision of Shakespeare that was to become the focus much later of the New Historicist critics, yet Abbey does not share their unduly deterministic perspective; he sees Raleigh and Marlowe as models who have escaped, to some degree, the blinders of their age. And, of course, if there were no possibility of escaping one's age in some way, there would be no liberating potential in a study of the past. We can see the democrat in Abbey giving Shakespeare his due as poet but complaining about his political sycophancy. He attacks the way Shakespeare has been made ahistorical, timeless, when from another perspective "the immortal bard" can be seen as only too clearly a product of his time.

There is a bit of Twainian burlesque in the passage, with Abbey comparing Shakespeare to Gilbert and Sullivan and then lumping Racine in with the latter as well. There is also some high-handedness in referring to Claudius as "that chap" and "what's his name." And we find more comedy in Abbey's use of the word "unbecoming" (in the third paragraph); his real criticism of Shakespeare is much more deeply felt than is indicated by that word. The purpose of this low comedy, I think, is to express the very same leveling and democratic spirit Abbey sees as missing from Shakespeare. Shakespeare would never take the groundlings seriously, but democratic Abbey rejects that aristocratic attitude. He is all seriousness when he charges that in the whole Shakespeare canon there is no Spartacus, a truly damning accusation and one that led Whitman in *Democratic Vistas* to call Shakespeare the great poet of feudalism.

On the negative side, we can see two qualities in Abbey here that are (to me at least) unattractive, but which he freely reveals. The first is a sexism that implies that the only gender that really counts is the male; there is a strong sense that only men have personalities that matter. Second, Abbey's admiration for Macbeth, Edmund, and Claudius, while understandable from a certain anarchistic point of view, can nevertheless be seen as intellectually careless gangster worship. These characters weren't anarchists, they were murderers.

But to me, what especially enlarges my sense of Abbey as I read this passage is the conclusion, the humorous, touching, and partly accurate "I'm a narrow-minded sonofabitch." He knows that he has given an interesting and heartfelt but limited version of Shakespeare, a kind of extreme democratic and anarchistic view. And he knows that it is part of his character to be almost too much of an Emersonian nonconformist. The trait gives him force, but he is large enough to see it restricts him as well. He truly admires those who are more catholic and easygoing in their responses—like Henry Miller, one of his heroes. But he is also not quite positive about Miller: Is Miller as easygoing as he seems? Abbey notes that Miller claims, in fact, not to suffer fools gladly. Abbey wonders whether, in the end, it is possible for anyone with strong feelings to suffer those he perceives as fools with any gladness.

In "Self-Reliance," Emerson says of the individual, "Not for nothing one face, one character, one fact makes much impression on him [the individual] and another none. . . . The eye was placed where one ray might fall, that it might testify of that particular ray" (1903, 2:46). Abbey both believes in and exemplifies this notion. But he is also aware that we must be able to communicate our impressions to others if we are not to live in a solipsistic world, something he profoundly wants not to do.

Another, shorter passage from the journals shows how Abbey's complexity can display itself in a completely different tonal register.

> Transcendence. It is this which haunts me night and day. The desire to transcend my own limits, to exceed myself, to become more than I am. How? I don't know. To transcend this job, this work, this place, this kind of life—for the sake of something superlative, supreme, exalting. But where? Again, how? Don't know. It will come of itself . . . like lightning, like rain, like God's gift of grace, in its own good time. (If it comes at all.) (1994, 278)

Here Abbey meditates upon the desire for transcendence. The play of confidence and doubt, self-knowledge and mystery are quite moving. Abbey understands that he is a person for whom transcendence is a lure and a curse, for it enlivens the soul but also torments it. He knows that what he will have to do is wait. And in the final line he knows that he may be left there waiting, like a farmer in a drought-stricken field. This passage is neither a profession of faith nor an expression of doubt. It is a tough-minded description of the conditions of faith and grace. If one happens to be the kind of person who cannot help but desire transcendence, then part of what one must do is wait. This notion seems to me as resonant with meaning as any fervent or confident expression of either doubt or faith.

My readings of the above passages indicate my belief in the largeness of spirit inhabiting the text. I believe it is an exemplary "intimate record" of Emersonian independence and a complex rendering of "innermost thoughts and feelings." But from the standpoint of poststructuralist theory, certain red flags immediately go up upon reading Petersen's phrases: "intimate record" and "innermost thoughts and feelings" are, in the context of an theory, problematic at best, and possibly verboten. Michel Foucault, for example, has taught us not to look for an author in the sense of an animating spirit behind the text: "the writing of our day has freed itself from the necessity of 'expression'; it refers only to itself" (1977, 116). Such admonitions are familiar in contemporary theory, and one could even say, ironically, that they have achieved the status of "truth." That word is, of course, forbidden by "theory," but such statements as that of Foucault quoted above are often not part of contemporary critical debate, since they are simply assumed to require none. This silent acceptance would seem to me to be an operational equivalent of believing in a truth.

But one of my purposes here is to use Abbey to interrogate "theory" as much as it is to use theory to interrogate "Abbey." In the highly influential essay "What Is an Author?" Foucault approvingly quotes the following line from Samuel Beckett's *Texts for Nothing:* "What matter who's speaking, someone said, what matter who's speaking" (1977, 115). But most readers of Abbey have felt very strongly that it does matter. The remarks of the reviewers quoted earlier are rife with terms laughed out of court by poststructuralist theory: "unique prose voice," "the voice of a full-blooded man," "a true maverick spirit," "a kind of spirit not imitable," "authenticity," and "independence." "Voice" and "spirit" are considered nostalgic mystifications, as are notions of "unique" and "maverick," or "authenticity" and "independence." In addition, the idea that something is "not imitable" runs precisely counter to the poststructuralist notion that everything is imitable and nothing original. Moreover, the idea that the author himself is somehow precious in his person, as a creative being whom we should protect, could hardly be more opposed to Foucault's notion that in reading a text we should attend not to the author but to what he calls the "author-function" (124–31).

Despite poststructuralist objections, however, the notions expressed by Abbey's reviewers are quite understandable and defensible on some level, and it is an arguable point whether or not they are mystifications. Or, to put it another way, it is arguable whether or not they are any more mystifying than some of Foucault's own notions about how to read. For example, here is Foucault explaining the nature of contemporary writing: "Writing unfolds like a game that inevitably moves beyond its own rules and finally leaves them behind. Thus, the essential basis of this writing is not the exalted emotions related to the act of composition or the insertion of a subject into language. Rather, it is primarily concerned with creating an opening where the writing subject endlessly disappears" (116).

There are several difficulties here. First, while it is interesting of Foucault (or the author-function I am designating "Foucault") to assert that "writing unfolds" and to thereby suggest that language itself writes (or history or power through the medium of language) rather than any individual person, no text emerges unless someone engages in the existential act of putting pen to paper or finger to keyboard. Next, we must note Foucault's peculiar use of the phrase "the essential basis." It seems odd that in a poststructuralist text a phrase should be used that is so nakedly both essentialist and foundational. And it also seems odd for anyone at all—let alone a poststructuralist—to claim that there is an "essential basis" of writing that can be easily identified.

The last sentence of the Foucault quote above, in which he supposedly does identify the essential basis of writing, presents particularly knotty problems. He says, "it is primarily concerned with creating an opening where the writing subject endlessly disappears," but one has difficulty understanding what he might mean by "it." The antecedent of "it" is "writing." But how can "writing" be "concerned" with anything? Only someone endowed with agency can be "concerned," but Foucault, in his essay as a whole, specifically downplays the sense of a writer's agency. It is ironic that Foucault seems to be making the same mistake frequently found among a group of thinkers at opposite ends of the spectrum from him: the sociobiologists. They, too, unconsciously rely on the notion of agency in their arguments even as they attack it. However, instead of ascribing human emotions and motivations to "writing," as Foucault does, they ascribe them to genetic material. Thus one finds constant references to the genes "desiring" to reproduce themselves, or the genes "using" organisms in order to achieve the genes' "purposes." What unites both poststructuralism and sociobiology is the tendency to smuggle agency in through the back door.

I suggest that in saying "writing" is "concerned" with something, Foucault engages in a process of mystification at least as grievous as those "naive" critics above who refer to Abbey's "spirit." But the problems do not stop there, for what is it that "writing" is supposedly concerned with? It is concerned with "creating an opening where the writing subject endlessly disappears." I would suggest that this is largely opaque, but not because Foucault is a deficient writer. Rather, it is because he needs to elide his smuggling in of the notion of agency. We can imagine that Foucault has in mind in his opaque assertion the desire on the part of the writer (not so mysterious an entity after all—someone, indeed, like Foucault himself) to transgress conventional limits or restrictions in the interest of liberating people. One can, in fact, see this very motivation in Foucault's own work. And to the extent that this was Foucault's motivation in doing his own writing, he did have "exalted emotions related to the act of composition," and he did insert a sense of a "subject" (himself) into language. It is this "subject," this author, and finally the actual man who was the author, that fellow poststructuralist Edward Said honors in his essay "Michel Foucault, 1926–1984": "Even in this unprecedently exceptional company [his French contemporaries] Foucault stood out. For one, he was the most wide-ranging in his learning. . . . For another, he seemed the most committed to study for its own sake and hence the least Parisian, the least modish, fashionable or backbiting. . . . Even more interesting, he . . . seemed never to say routine or unoriginal things" (1988, 2).

One has to wonder about Said's unproblematized use of the word "unoriginal." Is he guilty of naiveté, possibly the gravest of all faults in poststructuralist eyes? Foucault wrote: "In short, the subject . . . must be stripped of its creative role and analyzed as a complex and variable function of discourse" (1988, 138), but that is not how the poststructuralist Said finally sees him. Said praises Foucault precisely for what Said sees as the latter's "creative role" in scholarship and in life. Should Said be faulted for weak-minded "nostalgia," another favorite poststructuralist bogeyman? A poststructuralist critic could, with consistency, so fault him, but I certainly would not. Said is praising and mourning a person—one might even with justice say a spirit—not an author-function.

In fact, Said writes about Foucault in nearly the same spirit (and I use the word deliberately) that Petersen writes about Abbey shortly after the latter's death: "I miss . . . his unassuming wisdom, his impassioned polemics, his towering . . . intellectual . . . presence, his ability to paint the West with an effortless brush of words. And most of all, I miss the moral courage and conviction Edward Abbey embodied" (1994, 356). At he end of "What Is an Author?" Foucault would seem to condemn such sentiments as those expressed by both Said and Petersen. He looks forward to a new culture of reading:

> No longer the tiresome repetitions:
> "Who is the real author?"
> "Have we proof of his authenticity and originality?"
> "What has he revealed of his profound self in his language?"
> (Foucault 1977, 138)

But it is to some of these very questions that both Said and Petersen turn, and their concern is not tiresome. Neither Said nor Petersen is engaged in naive and groveling genuflection before the "genius" of the writer; they are showing gratitude for what two different writers have been able to accomplish in a lifetime. Someone somewhere has said that one trouble with postmodernism is that it appears to be grateful for nothing. Perhaps it is this ingratitude, and not the things Foucault mentions, that is as of this date truly tiresome.

One last quarrel with Foucault needs to be articulated before going on to discuss how certain aspects of his theorizing might actually help us to appreciate Abbey's achievement in the journals. My objection is this: Although Foucault's project in "What Is an Author?" is to problematize the notions of subject, agency, the "I," intention, etc., these notions are used in a startlingly unproblematic way at the beginning of his essay itself. The first paragraph reads:

> In proposing this slightly odd question [What Is an Author?], I am conscious of the need for an explanation. To this day, the "author" remains an open question both with respect to its general function within discourse and in my own writings; that is, this question permits me to return to certain aspects of my own work which now appear ill-advised and misleading. In this regard, I wish to propose a necessary criticism and reevaluation. (113)

David Copland Morris   253

The use of "I" and "me" and "my own work" and "I wish to propose" in no sense suggests "an opening where the writing subject endlessly disappears." And four more paragraphs follow in which the subject is just as unproblematically presented to the reader. Again, I would say that an understandable and rather traditional notion of agency and intention is smuggled in. Perhaps "smuggled" is not the right word—they are carried rather nonchalantly in broad daylight. It seems to me a mystification in Foucault's essay that he relies in practice upon the very notions he philosophically attacks.

In a creative essay that I had not read when I wrote my comments on Foucault's opening paragraph, Daniel T. O'Hara sees Foucault's contradictions or apparent bad faith in that paragraph as a self-conscious hypertransgressive parody or self-parody, and he calls Foucault's essay a "revisionary parodic text of self-revision" (1988, 84). His arguments strike me as ingenious but unconvincing. Consider: Derrida, in his attack on the critics of Paul de Man after the latter's death, relentlessly accuses those critics of being, in many instances, simply wrong—this despite the fact that Derrida's whole philosophical project has as one of its ends the demolition of the true/false mode of thinking. Was Derrida being self-parodic? It is unlikely; he seemed all-too-humanly angry, unsettled, and desperate.

Also, consider that the poststructuralist refrain "everything is political" is made ad nauseum, despite its meaninglessness: if everything is political, nothing is political—the statement is useless in making actual distinctions. Furthermore, to the extent that "political" means something like "solely interested in power," the refrain is hopelessly entangled in Bertrand Russell's Cretan/liar paradox.[1] Are those who use the slogan "Everything is political" therefore simply being self-parodic? Given their vehemence, their earnestness, and their repetitiveness, the odds are against it. Recall Said's blandly unproblematic praise of Foucault's supposed inability to utter an "unoriginal" word. Is Said parodying himself? Is he really poking fun at bourgeois notions of originality? It would be an easier world than it is if every time we enmeshed ourselves in logical inconsistency someone like O'Hara would rush to our rescue claiming in our defense the notion of "self-parody." The recent hoax article by Alan Sokal in *Social Text* is an actual parody; the opening of Foucault's essay is not.

Foucault, however, can help us in reading the journals when he suggests that we do not reach through a text to an author as easily as might be supposed:

these aspects of an individual, which we designate as an author (or which comprise an individual as an author), are projections, in terms always more or less psychological, of our way of handling texts: in the comparisons we make, the traits we extract as pertinent, the continuities we assign, or the exclusions we practice. In addition, all these operations vary according to the period and the form of discourse concerned. A "philosopher" a "poet" are not constructed in the same manner; and the author of an eighteenth-century novel was formed differently from the modern novelist. (1977, 127)

Indeed, throughout the journals Abbey exhibits a keen awareness of the way in which "the author" has been constructed by readers of his writings. He is almost never entirely pleased and is frequently angry. But often he is as exasperated with friendly commentary as with hostile. Almost all his life as a published writer, he railed against what he saw as the unfair treatment, or simple neglect, by the so-called New York literary establishment.

Shortly before his death, Abbey talked about a problem more relevant to a current estimation of his stature: adoration from some environmentalists, and scorn from a variety of other sectarian readers.

> *One Life at a Time, Please* and *Best of Abbey* reviewed, sort of, in the NY Review of Books. That nice young man Bill Mckibben done it. Not bad, really, except like most other book reviewers I've had to endure now for the past twenty years, he seizes on one narrow aspect of my writing (the desert-loving, deep-ecology bit), and ignores the other ninety percent, thus misrepresenting my books and falsifying my life. Should I protest? What's the use? I haven't seen a review of any of my books that I couldn't have written much better myself. (1994, 350)

Clearly, near the end of his life Abbey was disturbed by the feeling that his writing and its author were being as inadequately read by admirers as by detractors. In fact, he has a palpably better time satirizing the latter than thanking the former. Here, just two weeks before his death, he takes a look at what he finds to be an irksome contemporary style of constructing the author:

Why book reviewers hate my books:
    Because they are really no good: Perhaps. But I think I have a
better explanation. Almost all reviewers, these days, are members
of and adherents to some anxious particular sect or faction. I.e.,
they are lesbians or New Agers or fem-libbers or (even worse)
male fem-libbers or tecnophiles or self-hating white liberals or
right-wing conservatives or Growth maniacs or Negroes or female
Negroes or Third-World lesbian militant Negro poetesses or
closet Marxists (Marxoids) or futurologists or academical specialists or Chicano ideologues or ballerinas or Kowboy Kultists or
Kerouac Kultists or Henry James Minimalist Perfectionists or one-
tenth Chippewa "Native American" Indians or at very least an all-
inclusive Official Chickenshit Correct-Thinking Liberals etc. etc.
    As such, any member of any one of those majority minorities
is going to find *for certain* a few remarks in any of *my* books that
will offend/outrage "s/he" to the marrow, leading inevitably in
turn, on the part of such sectarian reviewers, to a denunciation
not merely of the offending passage, but of the *entire book,* and
not merely of the book, but of the author too. (1994, 352–53)

Abbey here can be seen as echoing the Foucauldian point that
what we conceive of as the author reflects our way of handling texts,
and that how we handle texts is strongly influenced by how we are situated. But it is an Emersonian point, too, and Emerson anticipates
the side of this dilemma that so frustrates Abbey. Emerson doesn't
mince words: "If I know your sect, I anticipate your argument. . . .
Well, most men have bound their eyes with one or another handkerchief, and attached themselves to some one of these communities of
opinion. This conformity makes them not false in a few particulars,
but false in all particulars. . . . Meantime, nature is not slow to equip
us in the prison-uniform of the party to which we adhere" (2:54–55).
    Foucault and poststructuralism in general elaborate Emerson's
insight, but with some important differences. Poststructuralists almost entirely evade Emerson's issue of truth and falsity, and they emphasize the unconscious or deterministic aspect of how readers are
caught in the various codes. (They have achieved some powerful insights into the extent of this deterministic aspect, but as they approach a complete determinism, they themselves become caught in
the Cretan/liar paradox.)

The problem remains of how a writer might break through the codes, throw off the prison-uniform of the sect. Here, as suggested above, poststructuralists like Foucault provide an insight into how to read Abbey. Clearly the monocular methods of both the favorably disposed Mckibben and the unfavorably disposed sectarians do not satisfy Abbey in their ability to produce readings cognizant of what he feels is important in his writing.

I believe that what Abbey must have wanted most was an appreciation of two qualities in particular: the sheer vitality of his style and the willingness to resist the comfortable role of repeating received wisdom of whatever type. In his essay "A Writer's Credo," Abbey amplifies on this point as it relates to what he sees as the writer's duty:

> But the willingness to risk abuse for the sake of truth is one of the writer's obligatory chores.
> He who sticks out his neck may get his head chopped off. Quite so. Nevertheless it remains the writer's moral duty to stick out the neck, whether he lives in a totalitarian state or in a relatively open society such as our own. Speak out: or take up a different trade.
> Somebody has to do it. That somebody is the writer. If the independent author will not speak truth for us, who will? What will? Do we get truth from politicians? From the bureaucrats of big government? Or local government? Can we expect to hear truth from the U.S. Chamber of Commerce? . . . (1988, 164)

Abbey's notion of the "independent author" in pursuit of "truth" runs directly counter to Foucault, and yet, ironically, Foucault functions as a model for many people (as does Abbey himself) of precisely the truth-seeking independent author Abbey lauds.

Abbey is well aware of the troubled philosophical waters the notion of truth swims in: "What is truth? I don't know and I'm sorry I raised the point. I mean to dodge it if I can, for the question leads at once into a bog of epistemological problems too deep for me—or as I might say otherwise, beyond the scope of this essay" (1988, 165). It is beyond the scope of this essay as well, other than to say that the poststructuralist dismissal of the notion of truth is too often facile. But I can agree with and emphasize one other point that Abbey makes about the writer's duty to truth: "But the writer's duty, I am arguing, goes beyond the utterance and support of commonly agreed-upon truths" (166). If it is notoriously difficult to define the truth, it is perhaps less difficult to recognize the distinguishing marks of a writer who is in the pursuit of truth.

In the long quotation from the journals that satirizes sectarian criticism of his work, Abbey implies that the sectarians are too ready to accept and promulgate "agreed-upon truths" of any stripe. Another way of thinking about this issue is to suggest that Abbey faults the sectarians because they too easily (or smugly) accept their own situatedness—or are blind to it. He has earned, in my estimation, the right to criticize sectarian reading practices because in his own work, especially in the journals, he rarely settles for a group-sanctioned truth. He is difficult to peg as either left-wing or right-wing, classicist or romantic, individualist or commutarian, liberal or conservative, anarchist or reformer, egalitarian or elitist, patriot or subversive—in fact, his writing forces these dichotomies into question. And he is not simply mushy or comfortably in the middle of the road. No one has ever attacked him for the mildness of his beliefs or opinions.

Part of what I would claim for Abbey, and what I would presume to be an element he felt sectarian critics (favorable and unfavorable) often missed, is his ability to register the complexity of his life through his creative/innovative/inventive/imaginative/original— pick whichever forbidden word you want—use of language. His self-reflexive and self-questioning style allows him to get behind the received codes and use them for his own purposes. Or to put it another, perhaps less problematic way: what is so valuable about the style of Abbey's journal is precisely that it provides a powerful model for exploring the extent to which such a radical act is possible. In other words, we find out the extent to which the conventional determinations of language and culture can be transcended by reading such a writer as Abbey (or, for others, Foucault). The territory ahead is unknown until the boldest explorers push out into it. That writers such as Abbey (or Foucault) convey a sense of breakthrough is exactly what elicits such a feeling of gratitude on the part of their appreciative readers.

But Abbey's thrust is never simply negative (or deconstructionist, if you will). Abbey was an admirer of the ultra-postmodernist Donald Barthelme and recognized his significant accomplishment in making the detritus of cultural codes amusingly or disturbingly visible. But Abbey also thought there was no need for the legion of Barthelme imitators. He shares some of Barthelme's postmodern understanding that old codes are exhausted, but he is not content solely with a demolition exercise, as Barthelme seemed to be in his "fiction." On the other hand, Abbey never simply gave up and wrote anything as conventional and bland as Barthelme's film criticism in *The New Yorker*. Barthelme never seemed interested in integrating his wild postmodern side with his conventional one. But Abbey was always interested in such a wholeness and integration.

The two passages on Mckibben and the sectarians quoted above can serve as examples of Abbey's views on the subject of sectarian criticism and as models of his integrated style. All his writing life, Abbey had been craving attention from just such a magazine as *The New York Review of Books*, yet when he gets it he can't help feeling a certain irony. Mckibben does not attend to style in any significant way in his review. This omission provokes Abbey to ruthlessly parody one of his own deepest traits—his love of the natural world, particularly the desert—with the phrase "desert-loving, deep-ecology bit," because in Mckibben's hands Abbey feels that this is just what his writing has been reduced to. Abbey has been made a member of a sect, and he resents such a partial view. It is true that he doesn't want to jump on Mckibben because he genuinely appreciates the attention and the praise, but he ironizes his thanks. Mckibben becomes a "nice young man," a phrase which Abbey could simply not have meant in other than a partially ironic way. He calls the review "not bad, really" and in the word "really" conjures up a rueful comedy of his entire career vis-à-vis the critics. He finds himself wondering if he should protest the review, but this act would put him in the absurd situation of writing a major East Coast literary magazine to protest a favorable review. And then, in frustration, he spouts the narcissistic absurdity that probably every writer has both experienced and dismissed many times, namely that there has never been an adequate review and that only the author himself could remedy the sad situation.

As for the selection above, which comes close to a burlesque on sectarian criticism, it is not merely that. In the last part of the passage, Abbey is asking why the necessary situatedness of the reader seems to have led to some crude readings of his own work. Why, he asks, condemn the whole of the work and the character of the author because of some part given undue emphasis? Perhaps he wonders privately why he can't be read in the same manner as his own sensitive, tender, yet probing and sometimes skeptical treatment of *Walden* in *Down the River*. Again, in frustration, he throws out labels in crude, comical explosion to reflect back on the crudity of the names he himself has been called: racist, sexist, technophobe, elitist, criminal, etc.

I'll close with readings of two additional journal passages, one lengthy and one short, that illustrate what I see as the wrongheadedness of reading Abbey in a univocal way. The following short quotation was written in 1968 when he was forty-one, around the time of *Desert Solitaire:*

> Robert Kennedy was shot last night, as I toiled up the obscure mountain by moonlight.
> Alone on my mountain, feeling oh so lonely and desolate. I wish Judy would come. I wish Al would come, or Gus, or somebody, for Godsake. Even God. (1994, 220)

Abbey clearly valued solitude, as many passages in the journals and in *Desert Solitaire* make clear, but this passage movingly evokes an elemental need for human companionship in time of loss.

He much admired Robert Kennedy, yet he can't resist humor and wordplay even as he expresses his sorrow and loneliness. Nor can he pass up a chance for philosophical reflection on issues that had interested him all his life. In *Desert Solitaire* Abbey suggests that Occam's razor slices out God as a superfluous concept—what counts is the land and human companionship (1968, 208). In a moment of trial like that described above, one might expect him to soften his stance, to long for a kind of religious consolation. But he doesn't. Or, rather, he'd accept it if it came, but it ranks second in desirability to having some person he cares for show up to keep him company. He blasphemes partly for humorous effect, perhaps to keep his spirits up, but also partly to convey or crystallize his actual view of the relative importance of religious consolation when a genuine crisis occurs. It is through the complex rhetoric of the passage that feelings are adequately expressed. It is possible that someone of conventional religious beliefs could be offended by his writing here, but, ironically, he or she would miss the depth, honesty, intelligence, and character with which Abbey was exploring the phenomenon of religion.

Finally, a lengthier passage written when Abbey was twenty-five shows an independence of character, a willingness to listen to the inner Emersonian voice, even when it demanded a wrenching reconsideration of an idea Abbey thought he hated.

At the concert last night, listening to the orchestra open the affair with the British anthem ("God Save the Bloody Fucking King") but wordless see, no singing, and the simple tune also, that of my country, My country, 'tis of thee I sing, I was amazed and a little embarrassed as a strange emotion welled up from the heart, obstructing the larynx and troubling my eyes . . . a wave of homesickness and loneliness, yet more than that—an immense and inordinate and tearful tragic pride in my land, my country, America, sweet land of liberty; immense and inordinate with a profound and swelling love of the physical land, of the towns and farms, of the many folks I know—tragic with a sense of America as a promise yet far from complete, far from realization, and as a dream menaced by ugliness and by mean little enemies masquerading as defenders of that dream and armed now with the most awful POWER the world has ever known.

Conscious in heart and mind of all this, and of far more that only music can symbolically express and words cannot, I nearly cried, I nearly wept under that great burden of loneliness and alienation from my home, and with it the pride and joy and anger and sorrow which, combined, prove me to be a patriot of a most earnest kind and, I hope, a patriot of a most dangerous kind. Me, a patriot! It's true, my soul, it's true. (11)

Abbey, the avowed anarchist, discovers a feeling of patriotism in himself that he cannot disavow. What I find especially moving in these words is the way he acknowledges an emotion that intellectually he finds problematic at best. He analyzes the emotion, and he carefully refines and qualifies its implications and meaning, but he does not run from or try to convert it into something else. In the process, he defines a patriotism that could well serve as a model for those who feel their country is gravely flawed in many ways, but who also feel a need to love it. Moreover, he reveals a consciousness strong enough to hold patriotism and its critique in a resonant tension.

In this youthful passage one sees that at twenty-five, Abbey was already a master prose stylist, already capable of displaying that complicated sensibility he knew he possessed. American patriots of a more conventional stripe, together with those who would smugly condemn all American patriotism, might very well be offended by what Abbey has written. But that would be because they are not reading him as he can be read: they are only reading their woefully narrow constructions of him. If they are satisfied with such reading, it is their own loss.

In his introduction, David Petersen expresses concern that his "editorial carpentry" on *Confessions of a Barbarian* might somehow make Abbey appear less than the "great soulful intellect he in fact was" (xii). He need not have worried. The powerful fusion of disparate elements that Petersen's phrase suggests is indeed visible all over the book. But it is also true that the experience that one gets of Abbey in the quarter of his journal now in print makes one eager for the speedy publication of the three quarters not yet available. In the mountain of books published each year, room must be made for all of the work in which Abbey speaks in perhaps his freest and most vital voice.

Notes

1. The paradox that Russell discusses is of the form: " 'All Cretans are liars,' said the Cretan." The statement is self-contradictory and therefore meaningless. "Everything is political" is meaningless in an analogous way. To say that "everything is political" can mean one of two things: (1) "It is bad that something is political because being interested only in power is immoral." Yet if everything is political, there is no way out of the situation, for there is no alternative to being immoral; (2) "It is simply the case that everyone is always acting in the interest of gaining power and we should recognize this." But then everything becomes a war of all against all. The only way disputes can be settled is through violence, for there is no nonpolitical, objective realm of discourse in which disputes could be settled. "Everything is political" then becomes simply an invitation to a test of strength. The weak have no moral claim on the strong because there are no moral claims. All moral claims would have to be seen simply as disguised power grabs, and therefore the strong would have no reason to honor them.

It is possible that "Everything is political" is sometimes used only to mean that we should be on the lookout for hidden political motives in the actions of others. This is perfectly sensible, but it necessarily assumes that there is a distinction that can be made between political action and nonpolitical, or disinterested, action. If the capability of making that distinction is indeed assumed, then the statement "Everything is political" becomes an absurdity.

Works Cited
Abbey, Edward. 1968. *Desert Solitaire: A Season in the Wilderness.* New York: McGraw-Hill.
———. 1981. *Down the River.* New York: Dutton.
———. 1988. *One Life at a Time, Please.* New York: Henry Holt.

————. 1994. *Confessions of a Barbarian: Selections from the Journals of Edward Abbey, 1951–1989.* Ed. David Petersen. New York: Little, Brown and Co.

Altieri, Charles. 1994. *Subjective Agency: A Theory of First-Expressivity and Its Social Implications.* Cambridge, Mass.: Blackwell.

Emerson, Ralph Waldo. 1903. *The Complete Works of Ralph Waldo Emerson.* 2 vols. Ed. Edward Everett Emerson. Boston: Houghton, Mifflin.

Foucault, Michel. 1977. "What Is an Author?" In *Language, Counter-Memory, Practice: Selected Essays and Interviews by Michel Foucault,* ed. Donald Bouchard. Trans. Donald Bouchard and Sherry Simon. Ithaca, N.Y.: Cornell University Press.

O'Hara, Daniel T. 1988. "What Was Foucault?" In *After Foucault: Humanistic Knowledge, Postmodern Challenges,* ed. Jonathan Arac. New Brunswick, N.J.: Rutgers University Press.

Petersen, David. 1994. Introduction and postscript to *Confessions of a Barbarian: Selections from the Journals of Edward Abbey, 1951-1989.* Ed. Petersen. New York: Little, Brown and Co.

Said, Edward W. 1988. "Michel Foucault, 1926–1984." In *After Foucault: Humanistic Knowledge, Postmodern Challenges,* ed. Jonathan Arac. New Brunswick, N.J.: Rutgers University Press, 1988.

From the Banks of the Illisus to the Arches of Utah

Edward Abbey as Noble Rhetorician

BRYAN L.

MOORE

Edward Abbey has called himself, among other things, "a creator of fictions" (1979a, xxii), a writer of "personal history" (1977, xiii), an "agrarian anarchist" (1984b, 17), a "liberal" (1979a, 132), a "wild conservative" (1984b, 17), an "earthiest" (1984b, 19), and even a "curmudgeon" (1990, xiii), but clearly he did not think of himself as a "rhetorician." His few passing references to rhetoric are modified by adjectives that indicate his unfavorable view of the practice: "empty spaces of windy rhetoric," "skulking rhetoric," and "bloated rhetoric" (1982, 62, 221). These pejorative evaluations of rhetoric correspond with the most common, current usage of the word (i.e., "bombast"); but Abbey's choice of the adjectives "windy" and "skulking" also resonate back in time and place–fifth-century B.C.E. Athens–and find congruence with Plato's criticism in the *Gorgias* and *Phaedrus* of the Sophists' "neuter" and "base" rhetorics. Abbey writes that "The poets lie too much" (27) and attributes the quote to Robinson Jeffers. But this idea (also employed by Nietzsche) finds its origins in Plato, who would not allow artists, poets, and rhetoricians into his republic because they are concerned with appearances and not reality.

Despite Abbey's objections to rhetoric, which he apparently equates with verbal manipulation, he writes in a *conspicuously* rhetorical manner by attempting to show readers "better versions of themselves" (Weaver 1953, 25). For Abbey, as with Plato—who in *Phaedrus* paradoxically turns to a dramatization of Socrates as skilled   263 rhetorician—it is not persuasive discourse itself that is so sordid but rather discourse that is contrived to persuade an audience out of base motivation for untruthful ends.

In this chapter I appropriate Plato's writings on the ancient discipline as a means of positing the essential nobility of Edward Abbey's rhetoric. Some qualification of my methodology is warranted. Edwin Black writes that neo-Aristotelian critics "can only conjecture the extent to which, had Aristotle left any, his critical writing would adhere to the principles of [his treatise] the *Rhetoric*" (1965, 33). Black's statement applies even more so to neo-Platonic rhetoric; I thus employ *Phaedrus* and *Gorgias* in a manner that Plato may not have intended. Also, as demonstrated by writers from Aristotle to Derrida, Plato's absolutism is not beyond serious challenge, and it is not my intention to disregard that fact. Nor do I suggest that Abbey is a neo-Platonist; Abbey, unlike Plato, is a democrat, and in contrast to Plato, Abbey perceives truth through perceiving the external world: "What ideal, immutable Platonic cloud could equal the beauty and perfection of any ordinary everyday cloud floating over, say, Tuba City, Arizona, on a hot day in June?" (1990, 10). What I wish to show is that Plato's central ideas on rhetoric provide a still-fertile ground for testing the ethicality of Abbey's persistent, passionate critique on human encroachment of wilderness.

Before discussing Abbey's work, it might be useful to give a brief (and admittedly incomplete) overview of Plato's conception of rhetoric. Although Plato's *Gorgias* attacks the rhetoric of the Sophists as self-serving, "mere flattery," and a "knack" (and not an art), his *Phaedrus* takes up the discussion of three types of lovers/rhetoricians: neuter, base, and noble. The neuter form of discourse is represented in *Phaedrus* by a speech that a famous orator of the day, Lysias, has delivered "proving" that "the non-lover should be accepted rather than the lover" (1928, 227c). The non-lover becomes the incarnation of a gratifying speech that is noncommittal, objective, and merely referential—"nonrhetorical." Arguably, purely neuter discourse, completely void of inclination and subjectivity, is impossible. And yet the *intent* of Lysias's non-lover is the removal of inclination (or the illusion of it), which will enable him to "straddle the fence" on matters that are potentially volatile and, in so doing, maintain a favorable stance with his beloved.

Socrates's companion, Phaedrus, is impressed by Lysias's speech, and while the two sit on the banks of the Illisus, he reads a copy of it to Socrates. After the reading, Socrates facetiously responds, "Quite admirable; the effect on me was ravishing" (Plato 1928, 234d). Admonished by Phaedrus to "make another and better oration . . . on the same subject" (235d), Socrates invokes the Muses and launches into a speech in which the lover, "whose law of life is pleasure and not good," endeavors to keep his beloved utterly dependent and reduced to inferiority by fostering ignorance, dullness, and weakness. But the lover/persuader of Socrates's speech is base. He is not concerned with moving his beloved toward the good. On the contrary, he is diligent to remove any hindrance or reproof to "their most sweet converse" in maintaining his beloved as an "easy prey" (240a). The base lover is flattering and initially pleasant (240b), but his words are contrived, as twentieth-century rhetorician Richard Weaver writes, "to work against the true understanding of his followers" (1953, 11), and his motive is to subjugate the beloved's will to his own.

Feeling that he has "been guilty of impiety" in censuring the lover (albeit the base or "evil" lover), Socrates is moved to deliver a second speech in *praise* of the lover: "For if love be, as he surely is, a divinity, he cannot be evil" (242c). The noble lover, self-disciplined and thus exempt from his own base appetites, is given the divine gift of "the madness of love," which "is the greatest of heaven's blessings" (245c). This gift works in conjunction with his own innate knowledge of "true beauty" (of which every soul may potentially recollect, but only the noble lover clearly perceives in reality). On seeing his beloved, the lover beholds truth "in company with Modesty like an image placed upon a holy pedestal" (254b), and his reaction is not one of exploitation, but of "true and loyal service . . . not in pretense but in reality" (255b). The beloved is won over by the lover's humility and friendship, and "when he has received him into communion and intimacy, is quite amazed at the good-will of the lover; he recognizes that the inspired friend is worth all other friends or kinsmen." The beloved, whose rhetorical counterpart is the rhetor's audience, is "amazed" because he is convinced that the lover is in reality dedicated to his welfare. This is in direct opposition to the intent of the base lover (at his very best, "very pleasant" for an interval) which is the calculated concern for the mere appearance of good will. The noble lover's ethos is engaging because the lover *is* ethical.

Turning now to Abbey, we can easily eliminate any notions of his work being that of a neuter, non-lover. As a journalist, Abbey is unable—or unwilling—to disinterestedly describe that which he sees, and his anarchic message remains virtually unchanged over his almost forty years as a published writer. Abbey's personal histories are thoroughly subjective, as the author freely and often admits. Where the prudent non-lover holds to a verifiable "language of pure notation" that "distrusts any departure from the literal and prosaic" (Weaver 1953, 8), Abbey proves to be quite "imprudent." Lysias's speech states that the non-lover is desirable because he does not put the beloved in a position to be reproached by public opinion (Plato 1928, 231e–32a), and this, at least in part, explains the extreme (negative and positive) reactions that the passionate work of Abbey has generated. Weaver writes that "a 'style' in speech always causes one to be a marked man" (1953, 9), but for his part, Abbey would have it no other way. He writes that "too many American writers prefer to play safe, to avoid controversy, to stay out of trouble" in avoiding their obligation to speak out "boldly for their notion of the good and against the bad." Such "temporizing and trimming and equivocating," he continues, is "moral cowardice" (1988b, xi). Abbey suggests that even writers he admires and who hold similar commitments to environmental issues do not speak out boldly enough, and even approach neutrality. For example, in *Beyond the Wall,* when Abbey is asked what he thinks of the writer John McPhee, Abbey replies that he is "a first-rate reporter, but too mild, too nice, too cautious—no point of view" (1984a, 195). Other "neuter rhetoricians" in Abbey's nonfiction are represented by various writers, politicians, and employees of industry who sell and thus neutralize their abilities, not out of a love for democracy and the good of the people, but for moneyed interests. Never afraid to name names, in *Down the River* Abbey makes reference to the anti-environmental stance demonstrated by the "hired scribes (*Commentary, National Review, Time, Newsweek, Fortune, Wall Street Journal,* et al.)" of "the corporate sector" (1982, 6). Abbey's critique of such writers is reminiscent of Socrates's attack on the Sophists, whose rhetoric, in Plato's view,[1] served a purely pragmatic and not a philosophical function, and who were hired by wealthy Athenians to teach them (among other things) how to defend themselves and their property in the courts.

One of the recurring themes in Abbey's essay "The Second Rape of the West" (1977) is the contrasting motivations of the environmental activists and the promoters of development in various Western mining sites. The activists, the small staff of the *High Country News,* and the staff members of the Northern Plains Resource Council,

Abbey discovers, are paid $300 per month—"enough for rent and beans and shoes" (1977, 168). By contrast, the Montana Power Company has recently paid $100,000 for a TV commercial promoting strip mining, power plants, and EHV (extra-high-voltage) transmission lines. When Abbey asks upper management of the Western Energy Company his "unfair, irrelevant" question of what their salary is, he is told, "None of your business" (169). Abbey tours the bleak landscape of a Western Energy Company reclamation plot (a strip-mined area "returned" to its former state). Accompanied by a Western Energy employee, Abbey observes the surrounding flora: "The tumbleweeds are doing nicely, I commented, picking the stickers out of my shins, and my guide smiled and shrugged. She didn't give a damn one way or the other" (179). Abbey's neuter rhetoricians, then (to borrow from Yeats), at best "lack all conviction" and are employed by those who are "full of passionate intensity"—the exploitative, base lovers of industry and commerce.

Richard Weaver writes that the base lovers of Socrates's first speech are "not motivated by benevolence toward the beloved, but by selfish appetite" (1953, 10); they intermingle "a temporary pleasure and grace in their composition" (Plato 1928, 240a), but are "pleased if the beloved has intellectual limitations because they have the effect of making him manageable" (Weaver 1953, 10). As Abbey views the situation, this is one of the ways that base industry controls people and exploits their land. Continuing with "The Second Rape of the West," Abbey discusses the case of Black Mesa, where the Peabody Coal Company has strip-mined five thousand square miles of what had been the Navajos' home for centuries. Peabody Coal provides the Navajos with the temporary pleasure of three hundred jobs and an annual royalty of what amounts to "about $25 per Navajo." But the jobs and the royalty are short-lived: "thirty-five years, the estimated life of mine and power plant operations." Abbey's attack on the short-sightedness of Peabody Coal is centered around the notion of what constitutes *true* prudence with respect to the Navajos and their homeland. After the thirty-five years are up, Abbey asks, "Then what? No one knows for sure, but the fate of Appalachia provides a pretty good hint. Poverty, a blighted land, forced migration to the welfare slums: That has been the fate of Appalachians since King Coal moved into their homeland" (161).

Throughout his writings, Abbey calls into question the value and idea of "modern conveniences" (and this concern, of course, places

Abbey firmly in the tradition of American writers from Thoreau to Wendell Berry). Abbey believes that as an out-of-control consumer society, we have become too dependent on a dubious technology and industry that foster dullness, restrain individuality, and isolate consumers from their vital link with the natural world. "Junk, trash, rubbish—our lives are debauched, our natural resources squandered, our native land ravaged in this mad production of metal, plastic, glass and paper garbage" (1977, 186).[2] Convenience, which modern society has equated with "progress," is the notion under which industry has thrust intellectual limitations on the public to keep it manageable and dependent on an endless string of *new* conveniences. While Abbey's more concrete suggestions and agendas for breaking that string range from rational to highly polemical, his rhetorical and philosophical vision provides the attitudinal impetus to resist unquestioned compliance with consumerism.

Wilderness provides humans with an alternative to consumer society and serves as "a base for resistance to centralized domination" (Abbey 1968, 149). This explains Abbey's passionate stance toward keeping the interests of industry and commerce out of the national parks, where developers have fostered ignorance in visitors by building roads and retail businesses of all sorts in (once pristine) wilderness areas. The developers' intent to give a wilderness area "all the comforts of home" has the effect, Abbey argues, of keeping tourists (in the language of Plato's Socrates), "immature" and "weak." This is in contrast to the true wilderness experience, which for Abbey is a backdrop that fosters independence and the contemplation of philosophy: "Most of the formerly primitive road from Blanding west has now been improved beyond recognition. All of this, the engineers and bankers will tell you, makes the region now easily accessible to everybody, no matter how fat, feeble or flaccid. That is a lie. It is a lie. [They] will never be able to see what we saw. They will never feel what we felt. They will never learn what we know" (Abbey and Hyde 1971, 31).

In his first speech in *Phaedrus*, Socrates says that the (base) lover casts a "jealous eye" on the property (money, land, etc.) of the beloved "because they make him a less easy prey" and "less manageable" (Plato 1928, 240a). Abbey sees the industrialization of public wilderness areas and national parks as the final step in the governmental and commercial usurpation of individual freedom. After discussing the industrialization of Appalachia, Abbey steps back to generalize: "The final step in cultural breakdown is performed through commercial tourism, which diminishes the mountaineers like the Indians to the status of historical oddities, wax figures in labeled glass cases" (Abbey and Porter 1970, 85).

Like Thoreau, Abbey believes that wilderness corresponds with the wild, anarchic base of human nature (see Matthiessen 1941, 175); and like Leatherstocking (if not his creator, James Fenimore Cooper), Abbey realizes that this wildness is posited in diametrical (and dialectical) opposition to established order. While traveling through Great Smoky Mountains National Park, Abbey observes that "the encapsulated multitudes come, in their lemming-like masses, to follow one another's tail pipes along the asphalt trails" (Abbey and Porter 1970, 42). Against this loaded though undeniably valid image, Abbey sees the wilderness experience as a vital link to freedom, an alternative to the tyranny of consumer society. Floating with a friend down the Colorado River, through the pre-dam Glen Canyon, Abbey feels that he is "Cutting the bloody cord" and experiencing "the delirious exhilaration of independence" (1968, 177). Abbey's feelings in this wilderness setting parallel Socrates's conception of divine madness, "which is imputed to him who, when he sees the beauty of the earth, is transported with the recollection of the true beauty" (Plato 1928, *Phaedrus,* 249e). Abbey beholds the "true beauty" and "reality" of freedom, and is "rapt with amazement" (see Plato 1928, *Phaedrus,* 250a). On the river Abbey and his friend are "leaving behind for a while all that we most heartily and joyfully detest. That's what the first taste of the wild does to a man, after he has been too long penned up in the city. No wonder the Authorities are so anxious to smother the wilderness under asphalt and reservoirs. They know what they're doing; their lives depend on it, and all their rotten institutions. Play safe. Ski only in clockwise direction. Let's all have fun together" (1968, 178).

For Abbey the wilderness experience is a means of "a masculine exercise of imagination and will" (see Weaver 1953, 12). But since such an experience cannot be measured, appraised, or justified by the boorish wisdom of industry, the pristine wildness of a place like Glen Canyon is fair game for developers. If the damming of Glen Canyon has made the area more accessible and profitable, Abbey argues that the Glen Canyon Dam has created limitations, drawn regulations, and destroyed a paradisiacal ambience. With the erection of the dam, the visitor's pursuit of pleasure is channeled away from individual experience and into a fabricated process of mass consumption.

The argument against development for public access and regulations for public safety might open Abbey up to charges of elitism—one of the favorite topoi employed by such arch critics of environmentalism as Rush Limbaugh and, in previous decades, James Watt and Dixie Lee Ray. Nevertheless, Abbey may accurately be described as a proletarian writer. Socialist leanings were ingrained in Abbey as a child (his father was a socialist and Wobbly organizer), and he claims that his army experiences in Italy made him an anarchist (see Tuska and Piekarski 1983, 3). Abbey also has an extraordinary ability to turn the most mundane circumstance into a trope that promotes his populist rhetoric. For example, while walking alone in the desert, Abbey observes that his boots "are beginning to pinch my little toes. . . . As always, as everywhere in life, it is the little ones who suffer most" (1984a, 10). Abbey, unlike Limbaugh, Watt, or Ray, is a populist, though his desire—his demand—for individualism is at odds with the Marxian collectivism that, Marshall Berman writes, "seeks to submerge the self in a social role" (1982, 110).

Weaver writes that the "inspired madness" of Plato's noble lover is a metaphor for the kind of speech that goes beyond the bounds of the base lover's "reliable materiality" and consequently "subtly undermines the premise of his business" (1953, 14). With no pretensions to objectivity or flattery, the "passion" in the noble lover's speech "is revolutionary, and it has a practical end" (15). Proponents of development and industry can point to many tangible reasons for the precedence of wilderness exploitation over preservation: the generation of capital, the demand for raw materials, tourist accessibility, etc. But far too often, Abbey shows, the exploiters take into account the valuables and not the values of wilderness. The "nobility" of Abbey's work lies in its impulse to correct this institutionalized assumption by extolling wild (and in an etymological sense, "conservative") values, and by arguing that the "reliable materiality" of the developers is not in his audience's best interest. A question that Abbey is constantly asking (and prodding his audience to ask) is, with respect to wilderness and its offspring, freedom, what is the prudent action in this matter?

One of Abbey's strategies for questioning well-established beliefs (of which industrialism is his predominant target) is bare-faced facetiousness. Abbey, writes Wendell Berry, "is a great irreverencer of sacred cows. . . . This is one of his leitmotifs. He gets around to them all. These are glancing blows, mainly, delivered on the run, with a weapon no more lethal than his middle finger" (1985, 14). More than being merely humorous, Abbey's "blows" have the practical end of removing the well-established facades that, immunized from moral scrutiny, mask imprudent human behavior. Berry cites the example of Abbey's "corrective" epigram, "If guns are outlawed only the government will have guns", and writes that "what might appear to be an 'iconoclastic' joke at the expense of two public factions [the "gun lobby" and "the idea that the Second Amendment to the Bill of Rights confers a liberty that is merely personal"] becomes, on examination, the expression of a respectable political fear and an honorable political philosophy, a statement that the authors of our constitution would have recognized and welcomed" (1985, 16).

Granted, Plato's conception of a lover wooing his audience through a divine recollection of the Ideas seems a far cry from the facetious but confrontational stance of Abbey. But for all his idealistic high-mindedness, Plato's Socrates also employs facetiousness rhetorically in his dialogues. Socrates's bitterness toward the Sophists is intermingled with jocularity and a sense of "play": he deflates Polus's notion of rhetoric as a great art by equating it with "cookery" (Plato 1960, 463b), and Phaedrus (correctly) accuses Socrates of "making fun" of Lysias's speech (Plato 1928, 264e). And granted, it could be argued that Abbey often uses spurious arguments in presenting his case, or that by ignoring the necessity of a certain amount of industry and wilderness development, he eschews the common ground that is crucial for good rhetoric.

If Abbey's polemics are one-sided, they are delivered without flinching in the conviction that the *other* side, well-funded and thriving, is in reality overrepresented: "I say these things because too few others will, because far too many say the opposite" (1984, 39). A reader of Abbey quickly comes to be aware that his writings are presented subjectively and are to be interpreted by the reader in a like fashion.[3] Abbey would not expect a reader to agree with him on the hundreds of observations he offers on society and cultural phenomena. Some of his readers will not, for example, share Abbey's cranky appraisal of rock and roll as "music to hammer out fenders by" (1990, 72) or—more seriously—find his often callow attitude toward women acceptable. Though such peevish, sometimes irresponsible positions risk damaging or destroying the identification Abbey builds with his readers, they do serve to show that Abbey's persona—though described by the author as an "arrogant blustering macho fraud who counterfeits his name" (1979a, xv)—is believable, critical of the things that he believes are hindrances to freedom, and open to the reader's objections. Wendell Berry's defense of Abbey "begins with the fact that I want him to argue with, as I want to argue with Thoreau, another writer full of cranky opinions and strong feelings" (1985, 14).

A complex persona that refuses to embrace any official party line, Abbey has the potential to appeal to—and repulse—a wide audience. His open statements in support of the National Rifle Association (NRA) (and the group's interpretation of the Second Amendment) (1979a, 130–32) and his anti-immigration stance (1988a, 41–44)— not to mention his criticism of the women's movement and his general hatred of government—put his claim "I'm a liberal—and proud of it" (1979a, 132) into question. There is something for everyone in Abbey's work—to love and to hate. The majority of Abbey's readers (receptive or otherwise) will not, as a direct result of reading his work, be compelled to burn down billboards, pull up survey stakes, and the like (even as monkeywrenching has come to be seen by many as a viable alternative to conventional political channels). Kenneth Burke writes that rhetoric sometimes works through persuasion " 'to attitude' rather than persuasion to out-and-out action" (1950, 50).

His sabotage tactics notwithstanding, Abbey's main appeal and value, in my view, is his ability to change attitudes through self-dramatization. Al Fick, in his review of *Abbey's Road,* notes Abbey's "rare talent for making the profound sound simple" (1980, 44). Abbey's rhetoric is a first-person demonstration that: (1) freedom is the most important quality for human happiness and self-awareness, and (2) the wilderness is the crucial component in one's realization of that freedom. Indeed, for Abbey, freedom and wilderness are equivalent terms. (One of the essays in *The Journey Home* [1977] is entitled "Freedom and Wilderness, Wilderness and Freedom.") If a reader accepts this premise as a common value, she or he may choose to overlook Abbey's occasional lapses into spurious reasoning and logical fallacy. As Wayne Booth writes, an audience will "excuse gaps in argumentative cogency if we believe that the speaker or writer is essentially reliable in sharing values we share" (1974, 157).

Abbey respected the "Calm, reasonable, gentle persuasion" of Joseph Wood Krutch, his mentor in defending the Southwest, even while acknowledging his own "self-defeating tendencies as a pro-pagandist" (1988a, 181). Walker Gibson would have categorized Abbey as a "tough talker," a writer who tends to browbeat his audience into submission (1966, 40). But there is a dichotomy present in the "passion" of Abbey's nonfiction, and this is a characteristic to which many of Abbey's reviewers and critics have frequently pointed. Richard Shelton writes that, with Desert Solitaire, perhaps the author "was trying to hide his love letters behind a smoke screen of abrasive rhetoric" (1985, 67). Similarly, Tim Cahill writes that Abbey "writes lyrically about the things he loves . . . and with contempt about the things he hates" (1982, 6). *Audubon*'s obituary on Abbey states that like "any good hater, he fumed in hyperbole. And like any ardent lover, he could murmur the most tender nonsense" ("Edward Abbey," 1989, 16). These quotes characterize Abbey as a lover in the literal sense of the word (i.e., as one whose passion is directed toward the things that he loves and hates). But can Abbey be characterized as a lover in the Platonic sense of the word?

While Abbey's persona is forthright, even cantankerous, it also possesses a (Platonic) lover's intent of, first, entertaining, then of educating, and, finally, of moving his audience. Ann Ronald writes that Abbey "makes the reader laugh, and then think" (1982, 125). Abbey's rhetorical stance begins with a deep reverence for the sacredness of the wild, the realm of being that is untouched and unexploited by culture. For Abbey, environmentalism is "the conscience of our race" (1979b, xix) and is Abbey's touchstone—the basic, indivisible "first principle" that is required of a rhetor who wishes to "handle arguments according to the rules of art" (Plato 1928, *Phaedrus*, 277c).

In his reading of *Phaedrus*, Weaver states that "There is, then, no true rhetoric without dialectic" (1953, 17). Abbey's nonfiction makes constant use of dialectical argument through epigrammatic bursts of irony. One of many instances of this operation occurs in *Cactus Country*, in which Abbey refers to Phoenix as "a city dying from too much gluttonous success" (1973, 43). Underlying the ironic juxtaposition of "dying" and "success" is Abbey's analogical valuation of industrial culture in contrast to a more conventional usage of "success" (i.e., the term as employed, Abbey projects, by Phoenix's proponents of industry and growth). In espousing his contrary definition, Abbey wishes to move his audience to a questioning attitude of what constitutes success—namely, moderation and sensitivity as opposed to excess or "gluttony." In typical Abbey fashion, his appraisal of a "dying"

Phoenix is delivered almost in passing, in the midst of a description of a trip into the nearby Superstition Mountains. After noting some of the surrounding area's flora ("the scarlet hedgehog and the brilliant yellow cups of the prickly pear"), Abbey shifts his tone with the next paragraph: "Flowers; also garbage . . ." And here Abbey briefly considers Phoenix, whose "50-mile-wide pall across the sky" he can see from forty miles away (43). In the context of the surrounding descriptive discourse, which works to evoke the beauty of the desert, the "dying" Phoenix sentence espouses Abbey's contrary position and functions dialectically as "a small analogue of all justice" (Weaver 1953, 18). In this case, Phoenix is for Abbey a small representation of all industrial/cultural intrusion on wilderness. Throughout his nonfiction, Abbey, as Weaver writes of skilled rhetoricians in general, "makes extensive use of synecdoche" (18).

In spite of his belief in the manipulative function of rhetoric, Abbey is a skilled rhetorician whose central concerns are, I believe, noble, and whose moral character is established *because of,* and not despite, his unminced, opinionated voice. Abbey's highly personalized rhetorical response to contemporary American society, which he sees as overly impersonal, mechanized, and industrialized, is fitting in its noncompliance. Reviewers have characterized his persona as "irritating" and "ornery" (Baumel 1984), "acerbic" (Stuttuford 1987), and "cantankerous" (Hoffman 1984), but these (quite accurate) adjectives are by no means strikes against Abbey's relationship with his audience. On the contrary, he is a conspicuous "non-flatterer," a cranky lover who woos his audience by, in Weaver's words, "showing them better versions of themselves" (1953, 25)—not by suggesting that the audience emulate his life or character (even if that were possible or desirable), but through helping us realize our own means for confronting "the bare bones of existence, the elemental and fundamental, the bedrock which sustains us" (1968, 6). The *unity* of Abbey's crankiness, which is inseparable from his desire to subvert and redefine the too easily accepted public notions of freedom, results in a realness of voice, an ethos, and a noble rhetoric that, in the words of Peter Elbow, gives "the sense of coming to the reader, of doing the work for the reader, and of producing genuine and direct contact with the reader" (1989, 233).

Notes

1. Plato's criticism of the Sophists' tendency to favor opinion (*doxa*) over truth (*episteme*) has in turn been repeatedly attacked throughout history. For some contemporary views, see Susan Jarratt, *Rereading the Sophists: Classical Rhetoric Refigured* (Carbondale: Southern Illinois University Press, 1991); Renato Barilli, *Rhetoric,* trans. Giuliana Menozzi (Minneapolis: University of Minnesota Press, 1989); and Samuel Ijsseling, *Rhetoric and Philosophy in Conflict: An Historical Survey* (The Hague: Martinus Nijhoff, 1976).

2. This concern is also addressed in Abbey's fiction. Jack Burns, the anarchic antihero of Abbey's novel *The Brave Cowboy* (1956), is knocked off his horse and left moribund on an interstate highway by a diesel truck transporting "bathroom fixtures."

3. Such phrases as "authorial intrusion" or "editorializing" are not helpful in discussing Abbey's nonfiction voice. Abbey himself, or at least the "implied" or "fictive" Abbey, is the bread and butter, the substance, of his nonfiction books. Montaigne's "authorial position," established in his short, prefatory "To the Reader," could easily be applied to Abbey: "I want to be seen here in my simple, natural, ordinary fashion, without straining or artifice; for it is myself that I portray" (1957); and yet Abbey acknowledges the artifice: "The writer puts the best of himself, not the whole, into the work" (1979). See Ronald 1982.

Works Cited

Abbey, Edward. 1956. *The Brave Cowboy.* New York: Avon.

———. 1968. *Desert Solitaire: A Season in the Wilderness.* New York: McGraw-Hill.

———. 1973. *Cactus Country.* Alexandria, Va.: Time-Life Books.

———. 1977. *The Journey Home: Some Words in Defense of the American West.* New York: Dutton.

———. 1979a. *Abbey's Road.* New York: Dutton.

———. 1979b. Introduction to *Pioneer Conservationists of Western America,* by Peter Wild. Missoula, Mont.: Mountain Press.

———. 1982. *Down the River.* New York: Dutton.

———. 1984a. *Beyond the Wall.* New York: Henry Holt.

———. 1984b. "Edward Abbey: Slowing the Industrialization of Planet Earth." Interview by David Petersen. *Mother Earth News* (May–June): 17–20, 22, 24.

———. 1988a. *One Life at a Time, Please.* New York: Henry Holt.

———. 1988b. Preface to *Desert Solitaire.* Tucson: University of Arizona Press.

———. 1990. *A Voice Crying in the Wilderness (Vox Clamantis in Deserto).* New York: St. Martin's Press.

Abbey, Edward, and Philip Hyde (photographs). 1971. *Slickrock.* San Francisco: Sierra Club Books.

Abbey, Edward, and Eliot Porter (photographs). 1970. *Appalachian Wilderness.* New York: Dutton.

Baumel, Judith. 1984. Review of *Slumgullion Stew,* by Edward Abbey. *New York Times Book Review,* Dec. 16, 27.

Berman, Marshall. 1982. *All That is Solid Melts into Air: The Experience of Modernity.* New York: Penguin.

Berry, Wendell. 1985. "A Few Words in Favor of Edward Abbey." In *Resist Much, Obey Little,* ed. James Hepworth and Gregory McNamee. Salt Lake City: Dream Garden Press.

Black, Edwin. 1965. *Rhetorical Criticism: A Study in Method.* New York: Macmillan.

Booth, Wayne. 1974. *Modern Dogma and the Rhetoric of Assent.* Chicago: University of Chicago Press.

Burke, Kenneth. 1950. *A Rhetoric of Motives.* Berkeley: University of California Press.

Cahill, Tim. 1982. Review of *Down the River,* by Edward Abbey. *New York Times Book Review,* May 30, 6.

"Edward Abbey." 1989. Obituary. *Audubon* (July): 14, 16.

Elbow, Peter. 1989. "The Pleasures of Voice." In *Literary Nonfiction: Theory, Criticism, Pedagogy,* ed. Chris Anderson. Carbondale: Southern Illinois University Press.

Fick, Al. 1980. Review of *Abbey's Road. Conservationist* (Jan.–Feb.): 44.

Gibson, Walker. 1966. *Tough, Sweet, and Stuffy: An Essay on Modern American Prose Styles.* Bloomington: Indiana University Press.

Hoffman, Alice. 1984. Review of *Beyond the Wall. New York Times Book Review,* Apr. 15, 34.

Matthiessen, F. O. 1941. *American Renaissance: Art and Experience in the Age of Emerson and Whitman.* New York: Oxford University Press.

Montaigne, Michel de. 1957. *The Complete Essays.* Trans. Donald Frame. Stanford, Calif.: Stanford University Press.

Plato. 1928. *Phaedrus.* Trans. Benjamin Jowett. In *The Works of Plato,* ed. Irwin Edman. New York: Random House.

———. 1960. *Gorgias.* Trans. Walter Hamilton. New York: Penguin.

Ronald, Ann. 1982. *The New West of Edward Abbey.* Albuquerque: University of New Mexico Press.

Shelton, Richard. 1985. "Creeping Up on *Desert Solitaire.*" In *Resist Much, Obey Little,* ed. James Hepworth and Gregory McNamee. Salt Lake City: Dream Garden Press.

Stuttaford, Genevieve. 1987. Review of *One Life at a Time, Please. Publisher's Weekly,* Nov. 27, 73.

Tuska, Jon, and Vicki Piekarski, eds. 1983. "Edward Abbey." *Encyclopedia of Frontier and Western Fiction.* New York: McGraw-Hill.

Weaver, Richard M. 1953. *The Ethics of Rhetoric.* Davis, Calif.: Hermagoras Press.

Biocentrism and Green Existentialism

Edward Abbey's Conflicting Conceptualizations of Nature

WERNER

BIGELL

Because Edward Abbey's fictional depictions of ecological sabotage inspired the founding of the activist group Earth First!, he is often seen as part of the radical environmental movement. Paul Watson claims that Abbey "drafted" him into radical environmentalism and sees his Sea Shepherds as "the navy of mother Earth and Earth First! the army" (Manes 1990, 111). Abbey's critics also often see him as a macho-style eco-warrior, a "crusty, take-no-guff curmudgeon" (Saeger 1993, 226). In spite of the fact that Abbey was indeed "one of the crowd" (Manes 1990, 4), it can be argued that his relationship to radical environmentalism is an uneasy one. On one hand, he uses the militancy and visibility of such organizations, while on the other he is aware of their conceptual and ideological limitations. I will first analyze some of these limitations and then demonstrate that Abbey's texts often exceed the scope of radical environmentalism as he simultaneously battles anthropocentrism and asks questions about the meaning of existence.

The ideological force behind radical environmentalism is the philosophy of deep ecology, a term coined by Arne Naess. The main elements of Naess's philosophy are the notions of inherent rights of nature (which implies an intrinsic morality) and the concept of an "enlarged self," where the individual identifies with a meaningful whole, the ecosystem.[1] Deep ecology sees itself as a nonanthropocentric philosophy and operates with the notion of equality among all living entities: biocentrism.

Biocentrism and Green Existentialism

Deep ecology, however, has problematic conceptual implications. Biocentrism presents itself as nonanthropocentric, yet conceptualizes a nature that is passive and vulnerable, needing a strong environmentalist to defend her. Patrick Murphy points out that "designating a female entity in a patriarchal culture guarantees its subservient status" (1988, 157). When a radical environmentalist sets out to protect his mother, he reinforces the sexual stereotypes that have led to the marginalization of both women and nature. The rhetoric of care and protection is related to the rhetoric of serving and dominating. Saeger points at the fact that the majority of the radical environmental movement is male and uses a macho-style rhetoric. According to Greta Gaard, "Abbey's solution of the problem involves a reconnection with nature . . . a return to the womb," and he "continues to feminize the earth" (1996, 162). Perhaps the problem of sexism that feminist critics identify in Abbey is linked to the deep ecology concept of nature as a weak, passive, and caring entity.

In an attempt to fit the notion of intrinsic value or "rights of nature" into the political context of American liberalism, Roderick Nash presents a model of an enlarging ethical circle, an extension of ethics to animals, plants, and ecosystems. For the ethical future, he even predicts rights for the universe (1989, 5). Often "nature" in Abbey is an entity that does not need protection, but that he has to protect himself against. Abbey is influenced by Robinson Jeffers, whose universe is not an entity that can be protected: "Guard yourself from the terrible empty light of / space, the bottomless / pool of stars. (Expose yourself to it: you might learn / something.)" (1977, 118). For Abbey "there has been, over everything, the great starry universe included, the hint of tragedy" (1994, 17). Emptiness and tragedy are aspects of nature that exceed the discourse of deep ecology.

Ecology confers, according to James McClintock, "new validity and authority" on romantic ideas, and writers can find a "measure of hope, a common thread of meaning and significance" in it (1994, 129); Abbey and other nature writers have integrated Thoreauvian veneration of nature and post-Darwinian ecology, which "describes a more benign nature kept stable through complex networks of interdependent organisms" (3). Jack Loeffler also sees Abbey as an exclusively biocentric writer:

Abbey loved the natural world or wilderness. . . . His refined sense of egalitarianism extended far beyond the realm of man to include all species of fauna and flora. . . . He perceived everything to be part of the whole. . . . He came to fully realize that as the wilderness is reduced by the hand of man . . . biotic diversity is threatened . . . and that Nature is seen simplistically as a reservoir of natural resources and not what it really is—a planetary biotic community. (1993, 47-48)

Radical environmentalism operates with notions of a destructive human culture and a life-generating nature, a "biotic community." Peter Quigley criticizes radical environmentalism for merely inverting existing binary oppositions (nature-culture, male-female) and deriving a new hierarchical system from the resulting "better metaphor" (299): "By fetishizing or giving permanent ontological status to what has been attacked by logocentric power, one runs the risk of repeating the transgressions of power" (297).

Deep ecology sees nature as an outer-cultural referent that provides "a measure of hope" for a troubled culture. In the biocentric/romantic view, what is not nature is a mere supplement, not a parallel signification. Jacques Derrida identifies conceptual marginalization in Rousseau where "the negativity of evil will always have the form of supplementarity. Evil is exterior to nature, to what is by nature innocent and good" (1995, 145). In the romantic narrative of nature writing, the powerful and violent aspects of nature (such as natural catastrophes) are often excluded. Placing a benign nature at the center of a new paradigm inevitably creates a new margin of both culture and the aspects of nature that are not desirable. William Cronon points out that the idea of nature as a moral imperative is the product of monotheistic Western culture. The spiritual qualities that were once ascribed to God are now transferred to a capitalized "Nature" (1996, 36). For people with a non-monotheistic cultural background, the romantic veneration of nature often remains incomprehensible (35). When McClintock states that biocentrism is "Abbey's brand of religious feeling" (1994, 74), he places him into the context of a Western metaphysical tradition, a tradition that Abbey questions and partially rejects, and makes him vulnerable to a nonessentialist criticism.

Abbey is often seen as a late-romantic antimodernist who offers a "positive vision" of biocentrism in an increasingly technocratic world (McClintock 1994, xvi). Since this positive vision is grounded in the sexist and logocentric rhetoric of deep ecology, Abbey has become a target for feminist critics. I will argue that the characterization of Abbey as an antimodernist is wrong, and that, in fact, his texts are marked by postmodern elements. He is a myth broker who plays and experiments with different mythologies, one of them being the macho defender of Mother Earth.

An exclusively romantic conceptualization of nature narrows the range of possible meanings of the term and makes literary effects of ambiguity or paradox appear antithetical to the politics of environmentalism. The texts of Abbey are rich in these often contradicting significations; he is an author of many poses. His texts constantly construct and deconstruct these poses as that of the eco-warrior. This fact, however, does not fit into an environmental discourse that made Abbey into the prototype of the defender of Mother Nature. Daniel G. Payne, depicting the environmentalist position that would like more clarity and consistency, explains how Abbey's ambiguity in signification conflicts with the politics of radical environmentalism: "[it is a paradox that] some of the same things that help to make [Abbey's] work so rich in a literary sense often serve to diminish its effectiveness as environmental rhetoric. While paradox and textual ambiguity certainly have their virtues, particularly where *academicians and literary critics* are concerned, in a rhetorical context they are usually counterproductive" (1996, 153, my emphasis).

Many of Abbey's texts, such as *The Monkey Wrench Gang*, indeed depict the prototypical eco-warrior. Other texts evoke a more indifferent and existential nature. The texts where Abbey conceptualizes nature as weak and passive have received the major part of critical attention, while other texts are virtually ignored. In the course of making Abbey an environmental hero, the reception of his texts had to undergo a narrowing, as in McClintock: "The essentials of Abbey's spiritual insight are that love, light, and joy are possible, despite the seductions of despair" (1994, 67). By calling elements of existential despair "seductive," McClintock marginalizes these textual elements, although he admits that Abbey has a "darker side" (1994, xviii): "[Abbey and other nature writers] acknowledge dramatic conversions in their thinking, feeling, and behavior that turned them from modernist alienation characteristics of mainstream American literary *intellectuals* to affirmations based upon experiences in nature" (1994, 17, my emphasis). In this narrative of environmental conversion and salvation from modernistic seductions, there is little space for doubt and paradox. The intellectual straitjacket that limits Abbey to an affirmative biocentric position makes an appreciation of his more questioning texts impossible.

The environmentalist favoring of one metaphor over the other forces a narrow reading upon an author for the sake of political effectiveness. Radical environmentalism ignores the potential that lies within a more open play of significations and renders itself to dogmatism and a paradoxical salvation of the androcentric and anthropocentric cultural paradigms. The dogmatism and anti-intellectualism peaks in Christopher Manes, who denounces the problem of signification of nature as "philosophical speculation [for] critics [who] have remained in an academic wasteland still debating whether nature is a meaningful concept." He states that "[t]his epistemological conundrum may be of great interest to traditional philosophy in search of ultimate grounds for knowledge, but it is irrelevant to dealing with the environmental crisis as a social reality" (1990, 157–58). The better metaphor has already resulted in totalitarian and anti-intellectual rhetoric. Only philosophers, academicians, and intellectuals question the Mother Earth metaphor. Placing Abbey into this conceptual context removes him from the readers who do not believe in "Nature."

Abbey's biocentric stance of radical environmentalism has been acknowledged. His "darker side," however, is a less explored aspect of his writing. Whereas some texts are dominated by ambivalent and paradoxical elements, other more monologic narratives are only occasionally punctured by such elements. It is not surprising that the more straightforward, monologic texts (e.g., *The Brave Cowboy, The Monkey Wrench Gang,* and *Hayduke Lives!*) have received most of the critical attention. Other texts (e.g., *Jonathan Troy, Black Sun,* and *Fool's Progress*) have been largely ignored or treated apologetically. Throughout his literary career, Abbey shifted between "darker," ambivalent texts and monologic narratives. His early novels (with the exception of *Jonathan Troy,* which feature narratives of Jeffersonian heroes fighting the industrial megamachine) are paralleled by introspective journal entries.

A major part of Abbey's literary production is essays, and here also he alternates between a straightforward romantic/biocentric narrative and a questioning and ambivalent stance. The following quotations describing mountain lions are from different essays but are only a few pages apart in the same collection: "About fifty yards behind me . . . stood this big cat, looking straight at me. I could see the gleam of the twilight in his eyes. . . . I felt what I always feel when I meet a large animal face to face in the wild: I felt a kind of affection and the crazy desire to communicate, to make some kind of emotional, even physical contact with the animal" (1991b, 237). This passage fits into the romantic master narrative of "reentering the womb" of nature, of enlarging the self by reintegrating into the ecosystem. The second passage features a nature that is different from romantic identification.

> Slowly, deliberately, the lion turns its head and stares with burning yellow eyes directly into the camera. The camera zooms in close, the eyes fill the screen, and we see in their golden depths the reflection of the sunrise, the soaring birds, the cliffs, the clouds, the sky, the earth, the human mind, the world beyond this world we love and hardly know at all . . . dissolve. This film goes on, it has no end . . . dissolve . . . dissolve . . . dissolve. . . . (1991b, 242)

In this excerpt showing Abbeys' "darker side," a romantic identification of the human individual with nature is impossible. Identification here means identification with death. Transitoriness, not ecology, unites the elements of the picture, the birds, the human mind, and the Earth.

In European existentialism the environment of the individual often represents the forces of an absurd universe. Abbey finds this type of existentialism "completely homocentric egocentric anthropocentric" (1994, 351). Abbey's critique of existentialism may be justified,[2] but he develops its main theme in a different direction. In contrast to European existentialists, Abbey highlights the fact that all living and nonhuman entities share a fate of death, from which he develops a lifeboat ethic. As in Stephen Crane's short story "The Open Boat," about a handful of men who discover their communality in the face of an indifferent ocean, in Abbey all natural entities share a common fate and sit, metaphorically speaking, in the same boat. In contrast to the European existentialist view that sees the human mind confronting an absurd world, in Abbey the world of existence (the totality of living and nonliving entities) confronts nonexistence, the nature of the void. The resulting sense of interconnectedness does not stem from common cooperation in a meaningful ecosystem, or from common "natural rights," but from common transitoriness. Since all entities share this fate, human beings do not have a privileged position in the existential drama.

Whereas the biocentric narrative of deep ecology and parts of Abbey's texts are rooted in Naess's philosophy, Abbey's existential conceptualization of nature is paralleled in another Norwegian eco-philosopher, Peter Wessel Zapffe. In both Abbey and Zapffe the search for meaning in a meaningless cosmos is the main theme.[3] Abbey explains to the reader why he goes into the desert and what he finds there:

> Near the summit I found an arrow sign. . . . The arrow pointed into the north. But what was it pointing *at?* I looked at the sign closely and saw that those dark, desert-varnished stones had been in place for a long, long time. . . . I studied the scene with care, looking for an ancient Indian ruin, a significant cairn, perhaps an abandoned mine, a hidden treasure of some inconceivable wealth, the mother of all mother lodes. . . . But there was nothing out there. Nothing at all. Nothing but the desert. Nothing but the silent world. *That's why.* (1991b, 22–23)

Although Zapffe was a mountaineer and not a desert rat, both writers describe the same sense of emptiness in a natural space that has no in-trinsic meaning: "Mountaineering is, by the way, not a sport. It is a dionysic affirmation of life"; "But the purpose, people ask, what is the meaning, the aim? There is no meaning and no aim. Mountaineering is meaningless as life itself" (1993a, 89, 92, my translation).

The emptiness does not have the same negative connotations as the Puritan wilderness or the hostile nature of naturalism; it is, to the contrary, the element that the two writers actively seek. The relativity of meaning both writers experience in a natural space becomes mean-ingful in a cultural context. Zapffe visualizes the transfer of natural meaninglessness into a cultural context, the finding of meaning in the absence of meaning, when the mountaineer returns to society: "And what they grasp there, what happens in them when they stand at a point beyond life, in a world of spiritual rock-bottom, where the law of the stones is the only and eternal one, they carry back with them to the hothouses as a new dimension, a freedom over duty, a power in powerlessness, a new knowledge about what it means to be human" (1977, 55, my translation). The "power in powerlessness" indicates that the existential position, although it questions the individual, also provides a tool for the individual to question his or her cultural environment. Existential meaninglessness, translated into a cultural context, becomes meaningful. Existential nature has two aspects, existence and non-existence; the nature of the void questions cultural constructs, whereas the shared nature of existence contains an element of interconnectedness with a transitory world. Zapffe sees the existential void as a negative reference for culture, which he defines as a collective meaning-creating system. Things have meaning in relation to other things, but not in themselves. For Zapffe, the human brain that seeks meaning in existence is but a freak product of evolution (1993b). Existential nature allows Abbey and Zapffe to question culture without referring to better metaphors or reference to metaphysical grounds. In Abbey's journals, there is an example of how the existential, meaning-corroding concept of nature can function as cultural criticism. Writing about Peter Matthiesen's *Snow Leopard,* Abbey says, "Good writing, but—there's something ludicrous and pathetic in the spectacle of these rich Americans going all the way to Nepal, trekking through the Himalaya, followed by a string of porters bearing the white man's burden, spending thousands of dollars, in order to—"find themselves"! . . . The colossal egoism of these soul-searchers. What makes them think their useless pitiful souls are so godawful important?" (1994, 282–83).

The invocation of existential nature serves two purposes in the texts of Abbey. On one hand, it suggests heroic struggle against the unavoidable: not only biological death, but also the transitoriness of meaning. On the other hand, the absence of intrinsic meaning and importance suggests a position of humility, as seen in the example above. Abbey does not criticize Matthiesen's Americans for their unethical treatment of bio-nature, their negative impact on the Himalayan ecosystem, but for their lack of humility in the face of existential nature, their unreflected affirmation of individual meaning and significance. The conceptual limitation to a favorable nature impoverishes experience; it makes the feeling of limitation of the human existence difficult. In an environmental context, the notion of a powerful nature is often thought to be counterproductive; there are no groups that want to protect natural catastrophes. Environmentalists often highlight the weak and battered side of nature; this appeal may institute a feeling of guilt, but it will hardly evoke respect for the outer world.

Bio-nature and existential nature are not two aspects of the same concept but represent two distinct strategies. "Nature knows best" and "Mother Earth" metaphors have no common ground with a nature of cosmic indifference. Note the conceptual difference of nature in the following examples of Abbey's writing on the one hand, and McClintock's "common thread of meaning and significance" and Loeffler's "planetary biotic community" on the other:

> Always looking and listening, these deer. Even the fawns have that wary look. Danger everywhere. . . . Always hard times for the deer. The struggle for existence. All their energy goes into survival—and reproduction. The only point of it all—to go on. On and on and on. What else is there? Sometimes I am appalled by the brutality, the horror of this planetary spawning and scheming and striving and dying. One no longer searches for any ulterior significance in all this, as in the finest music, the meaning is in the music itself, not in anything beyond it. (1991b, 57)

In contrast to Loeffler and McClintock, Abbey does not see a "measure of hope" in nature, no intrinsic meaning. Nature is neither a "better metaphor," nor can it function as point of reference in a political context; it merely exists. The biologist Richard Dawkins warns against the derivation of ethics from an assumed natural order: "if you wish, as I do, to build a society in which individuals cooperate generously and unselfishly towards a common good, you can expect little help from biological nature" (1989, 3). All grounding of an ethical system in a concept of nature is problematic: "Human suffering has been caused because too many of us cannot grasp that words are only tools for use, and that the mere presence in the dictionary of a word like 'living' does not mean it necessarily has to refer to something definite in the real world" (Dawkins 1989, 18). Abbey's nature is meaningless and is incompatible with the meaning-creating systems of culture. It is an ontological question mark, not a moral ground.

By intermingling and alternating the two strategies, biocentrism and existential nature, Abbey constantly deconstructs his own narrative. The biocentrist perspective is corroded with a cosmic outlook, and the bleakness of the existential outlook is counteracted by an affirmation of the importance of life. In the essay "Cape Solitude" there is a juxtaposition between life and death as Abbey seeks a place overlooking the Grand Canyon.

I come to the edge. The verge of the abyss. . . . One step further would take me into another world, the next world, the ultimate world. But I pause, hesitate . . . as always. Not out of fear . . . but again from respect. Respect for my obligation to others . . . respect for myself. The despair that haunts the background of our lives, sometimes obtruding itself into consciousness, can still be modulated . . . into a comfortable melancholia and from there to defiance, delight, a roaring affirmation of our existence. . . . I . . . take my flute from the pack . . . and play a little desert music: . . . a song for any coyotes that may be listening, a song for the river and the great canyon, a song for the sky. . . . I stop; we listen to the echoes floating back: I write "we" because, in the company of other nearby living things—lizards, ravens, snakes, bushes, grass, weeds—I do not feel myself to be alone. (1991a, 194)

Here the suicidal temptation of an existential outlook is relativized by a life-affirming position, where Abbey shares his existence with other beings. The element of sharing a common fate, existence, is highlighted here, not identification with nature. Life—his own and that of other humans and other beings—is contrasted to the abyss. In the natural space, both strategies—questioning the meaning by highlighting transitoriness and affirming the communality of all life—are possible. Abbey's novel *Black Sun* functions the other way round: life-affirming cultural strategies are constantly destabilized by an existential nature.

Although it seems to be paradoxical, Zapffe's and Abbey's existential positions have an environmental rationale. Both authors do not want to protect nature as such, but spaces where the experience of nature is possible. In contrast to the biocentric notion of "rights of nature," these spaces do not mean anything in themselves but represent spaces of open signification, spaces that acquire meaning in a cultural context. For Zapffe, the white spots on the map are sacred not because nature represents a value in itself but because "they represent spaces for contemplation" (Kvaløy 1992, 275).

Michel Foucault calls these spaces of contemplation "heterotopias": spaces that have a special function inside a culture. Foucault thought mainly about spaces like prisons and psychiatric hospitals, but the term can be applied to natural spaces, as William Chaloupka and R. McGreggor Cawley (1993) have suggested. Heterotopias can have different functions: "Either their role is to create a space of illusion that exposes every real space, all the sites into which human life is partitioned, as still more illusory . . . [o]r else, on the contrary, their role is to create a space that is other, another real space, as perfect, as meticulous, as well arranged as ours is messy, ill constructed, and jumbled" (Foucault 1986, 27).

The space of illusion corresponds to existential nature where the absence of meaning questions all cultural constructs; the perfect space, on the other hand, corresponds to biocentric/romantic imagery where a nurturing nature exposes the destructiveness of Western culture. An identical space can be experienced as a harmonious ecosystem or an existential question mark. Neither experience is "natural"; instead, both are culturally determined experiences. Without heterotopian spaces, culture would become intolerable, with no alternative way to define meaning. Foucault pleads for the heterotopia of the ship: "The ship is the heterotopia par excellence. In civilizations without boats dreams dry up, espionage takes the place of adventure, and the police takes the place of pirates" (1986, 27). Abbey expresses the same idea: "What makes life in our cities at once still tolerable, exciting, and stimulating is the existence of an alternative option . . . a radically different mode of being out there, in the forests, on the lakes and rivers, in the desert, up in the mountains" (1991b, 229). Protecting heterotopias such as wilderness areas does not mean protecting "nature," but protecting a cultural openness, both in space and signification.

Abbey most clearly conceptualizes nature as space with conflicting meanings (as perfect romantic space and space of existential terror) in *Black Sun*. In this novel the two functions of a psychiatric ward—treating a crisis (in a perfect space) or providing space for living through a crisis (by exposing the illusory character of all spaces)—can be equally fulfilled by natural spaces such as forests and deserts. For environmentalism, Foucault's concept of heterotopia provides the possibility of linking the necessity of cultural crisis, of different perspectives that compete inside a cultural discourse, with the protection of existing natural spaces. The concept represents a way beyond the nature/culture opposition without denying nature its particularity. Natural spaces play a special role in cultural discourse and are open to signification. Roland Barthes calls the system in which existing objects become cultural signifiers a "second order semiological system" (1993, 114).

In the opening of *Black Sun*, well-arranged and perfect nature has a meaning-confirming quality depicted in romantic hyperbole:

Each day begins like any other. Gently. Cautiously. The way he likes it. A dawn wind through the forest, the questioning calls of obscure birds. He hears the flutelike song, cool as silver, of a hermit thrush. . . . The sun is close but not yet up. A few dim stars still hang blinking on the west. Deer are grazing at the far side of the clearing near the foot of the fire tower—dim figures in pearl-gray light: The dark and somber forest surrounds them all with its heavy stillness. (1982, 13)

Gatlin, the protagonist, seeks shelter from an existential crisis, a divorce, and becomes a fire lookout. Green and friendly nature insulates him for the time being from an intolerable reality in the city, and his crisis is temporarily alleviated in the heterotopian space of the forest. The forest, like a psychiatric ward, has the function of treating Gatlin's instability and of insulating him against the outside world.[4]

The cultural creation of meaning is directed against meaninglessness, the amoral character of daily experience against which culture must insulate itself. Zapffe speaks about "the thousand comforting fictions" (Kvaløy 1992, 155) that insulate the individual from an intolerable reality. The cultural defense mechanisms are, in the terminology of Zapffe and in analogy to Freudian thought, isolation, distraction, attachment, and sublimation (1993b, 40–52). Heterotopias play a special role in the enactment of these mechanisms that create meaning. Consolation and questioning can be experienced in both wilderness areas and psychiatric wards, giving the visitor/patient either relief from existential angst or a chance to live through the crisis.

Gatlin uses the defense mechanism of isolation in a secluded natural space. Art Ballantine, his friend, represents another defense mechanism, diversion. Gatlin's isolation, the eventless world of romantic nature, gives Ballantine a negative point of reference. With his life of incessant entertainment, he is also in need of a heterotopia. Gatlin and the forest demonstrate for Ballantine how boring the life in the woods is, thus confirming his own lifestyle. On the other hand, the forest represents a space where Ballantine can express his existential doubts; for example, his problems with aging. Taking up the analogy of a psychiatric hospital, Ballantine is an outpatient who experiences his moments of crisis at a safe distance from his everyday life. For Gatlin, Ballantine's letters and visits are a constant reminder to keep up his isolation. Their friendship is essential for both men:

they each need the other's life as a point of reference outside their own experienced reality in order to maintain a certain degree of stability.

The central narrative in *Black Sun* is the Dionysian love story between Gatlin and Sandy. Nature is benevolent for both; the desert provides a heterotopian space where they can live their "plutonic" love (1982, 75). The life-affirming passion of this relationship is juxtaposed to life-negating natural forces. The desert, at this stage, functions as a double metaphor. It provides space for their passion but also reminds them that life is transitory. Making love is contrasted to "deserts of vast eternity." The joyful swimming in a river almost ends in a lethal contact with the rapids. In his journals, Abbey also uses the mutual amplification of life-affirming and life-negating forces: "Paris—the city of light and light-hearted laughter . . . of all that is brightest and most lyrical in men. Exactly. That's why it is so tragic. The sweeter the more poignant; the more beautiful, the more pathetic. There is more tragedy in the kiss of young lovers than in all the murders of all the royal clowns who ever lived" (1994, 95).

For Sandy, the natural spaces and the affair with Gatlin allow her to gain a vantage point over her future and her planned marriage. For all three characters, nature provides a different perspective and outlook on life that all three use in different ways. Turner, Sandy's fiancé, is the only character whose defense mechanism, an attachment to a military code of conduct, is functioning well, and who is not plagued by doubt and crisis. He is, however, depicted as almost inhuman. When Sandy disappears, nature can no longer provide isolation and treatment for Gatlin; it is now a space where he can experience the breakdown of his defense mechanisms, the collapse of his meaning-creating systems: "The idiot. Alone on tower. Walking around the catwalk. Again. And again. And again. . . . Anything, anything to smash his idleness and reverie, to drag him into the midst of trouble and terror. . . . Tower and forest and world—ship without stars, in a boundless sea—sail into night" (1982, 128–29).

What Gatlin now finds in the forest is something different: a space to live through the crisis, a psychiatric ward that keeps him at safe distance from more controlled cultural spaces. In the desert he can enact the final destruction of meaning: "The sun rose out of the desert far beyond and glared through an unclouded sky into the canyon. The heat intensified immediately. . . . His descent into this inferno was itself an act of insanity. . . . Searching for a shred of cloth, the imprint of a girl's foot, a sign of meaning, he found only the maze made of feral burros among the brush and rocks, and the winding trail of reptiles in the dust" (1982, 140–46). Heterotopia is no longer the green idyllic cabin in the forest, but a space of existential terror in the desert. The end of the novel is positive: Although he has gained neither stability nor meaning during his time in the forest, Gatlin survives his crisis and closes the road to his old life.

The circumstances of Sandy's disappearance suggest that she had used the desert as a space for reflection in which to question her relationships with Gatlin and Turner. In the end she rejects both Gatlin's instability, self-centeredness, and inability to commit, and Turner's stability, which allows no existential doubt. It is rather revealing that neither man even considers the possibility that Sandy has deliberately left them; it seems that their lover's death is easier to grasp for the men than a possible rejection.

Nature exists in the form of heterotopian space, as a second-order signifier. Its signification is completely dependent upon the protagonist's state of interest. Abbey demonstrates in *Black Sun* that several significations, serving different needs, are possible. All conceptualizations are unstable, but inevitably so; there is no original or unified meaning of nature. *Black Sun* demonstrates both the arbitrariness of the signification of nature and the cultural need for the signifier, because it makes cultural crisis possible and forms, itself, a part of a cultural discourse. This is why Abbey can say: "Who needs wilderness? Civilization needs wilderness" (1991b, 229). Although there is a need for natural spaces as signifier (as there is for language) in order to make discourse possible, there is no need for a fixed signification.

The typescript of Abbey's *Jonathan Troy* contains a synopsis of the novel that demonstrates its thematic parallel to *Black Sun*:

What is wrong with Jonathan Troy? Several things; first of all, he is too intelligent . . . to accept and live by any available and particular system of ethics and ideals. . . . He has the unfortunate talent for seeing not merely *into* but also *through* things and so naturally imagines that he sees nothing at all. The world of appearance is for him an obvious lie and a fake, without any certain or intrinsic value, and behind the appearance he sees only the appalling void. . . . [H]e lacks the moral and intellectual courage necessary to cope with his valueless world; he cannot accept it as it seems to be, so he spends his days seeking better illusions. (1950, 1)

The inability to find essences behind natural appearances connects both Gatlin and Troy, although Gatlin, in the beginning of *Black Sun*, manages to insulate himself against the void. The conceptualization of nature that is most prevalent in both novels is nature as the "totality of all things," and in this respect Abbey is, indeed, a nature writer. In both novels, natural spaces such as deserts and forests play a central role because questioning and crisis take place there.

The time has come to reconsider the scope of Abbey's work. Although he is a central figure in radical environmentalism, many of his texts go beyond advocacy of monkeywrenching and the shallow-versus-deep debate in environmentalism to ask questions about the meaning of life. The conflicting conceptualizations are the key to making sense of Abbey's texts. It is not the protection of a unified notion of nature that is central, but the necessity of crisis and opposition. This is why he so vehemently opposes the centralist tendencies of industrialism. Environmentalism is today losing influence due to the globalization of power structures, and the protection of romantic nature is either being appropriated by the system or criminalized. The existential concept of nature is a possibility of maintaining the crisis, even if there are fewer and fewer uncontrolled spaces. Even if these spaces, as well as biological nature, are subdued, existential nature remains unaffected. The possibility of experiencing existential nature, however—of gaining a different perspective on culture—may be lost through the development of natural spaces.

Abbey sees nature as an open space. Zapffe's existential nature already contains conflicting elements of nature (existence and nonexistence), and Abbey further adds the biocentric conceptualization to this narrative, allowing him to pose as either an eco-warrior or an introspective existentialist, and to muse about Mother Nature or the abyss. The meaning of nature is in all cases determined by culture.[5] With the concept of heterotopia, nature reenters language, not only as a concept with a "myriad of meanings" (Winner 1994, 137) but as a material entity, a second-order signifier. In the process of reentering the linguistic stage as concept, as second-order signifier, or as heterotopia, nature loses its quality as an outer-cultural referent. If nature is seen as a linguistic construct, its ambivalent and conflicting conceptualizations are a means to explore the cultural significance of a nonhuman entity without appropriating it.

Paradoxically, it is the process of making nature cultural that makes it possible for nature to maintain its otherness, to keep conflicting meanings that exceed a monologic conceptualization. Abbey does not try to unify these conflicting meanings but plays with them. According to J. Hillis Miller, "[t]he linguistic play is necessary to break up or destabilise the ways of thinking, speaking, and writing that are already programmed and in place in order to give a chance to the secret other that is hidden in . . . places where language shimmers with contradictory meanings. . . . [T]he other never comes except in multiple voices" (1996, 169). The problem of most Abbey criticism is that it tries to either ignore the conflicting conceptualizations or to marginalize them (for example, as his "darker side").[6] If nature is seen as a open signifier, the biocentric and existential conceptualizations might conflict, but they do not exclude each other. Abbey feels both romantic kinship with nature and existential meaninglessness. Existential nature is not the "real" nature; neither is the romantic/biocentric one. In order to stay natural, nature must keep its conflicting meanings.

Since the world "out there" always exceeds the meanings that are ascribed to it by language, the only way to write about nature without appropriating it is in a voice that points at its own limitations by using paradoxes and polyphony. The bedrock of Abbey's writing is paradox.[7] Seeing Abbey as an author of postmodern relativity who plays with conflicting meanings does not deny the ethical dimension of his writings, because the absence of a fixed system of moral reference makes a constant ethical reevaluation necessary. Abbey's major achievement is not that he provided a rationale for the militant protection of Mother Nature but that he transformed the often monologic genre of nature writing into a postmodern form of environmental literature—from a nature of conceptual appropriation to a nature of open signification.

Notes

1. The idea that different species cooperate in an ecological web has found its most extreme form in the Gaia hypothesis, which defines the Earth as a caring organism. It should be noted that deep ecology's biological assumptions are not generally shared by biologists. Richard Dawkins states that the elements of an ecological system interact but do not cooperate: "A network of relation-

ships there may be, but it is made up of small, self-interested components" (1983, 237).

2. In his study on existentialism, John Macquarry points out that existentialism gives us "an unduly anthropomorphic understanding of reality" where the universe is simply seen as a setting for humanity, and that existentialism has not provided a philosophy that "could encourage a respect for non-human realities" (1972, 281).

3. Abbey mentions Naess, but he could not have known Zapffe since his texts remained untranslated until after Abbey's death (a few were translated in Rothenberg and Reed, 1993). The reason for the parallel development of a nonanthropocentric existentialism is a comparable historical situation. Whereas European existentialism was a reaction against the dehumanizing social forces in this century, the situation is different both in Abbey's Southwest and Zapffe's northern Norway. Nature is still perceived as a powerful and often threatening force in these remote parts of the planet, and industrialization has reached these parts of the world as late as the 1950s and 1960s. Here humanity is not primarily seen as a victim of social forces but as a victimizer of nature. The two main symbols of destruction in the respective areas were dams, Glen Canyon and Alta. The changes in the land were seen as lack of respect for nature. The focus of existential meaninglessness in the two authors is not directed against nature but against the massive changes of the environment. Although nature in the meaning of "totality of all things" cannot be destroyed, it is possible to demonstrate arrogance and a lack of respect for this nature by defacing natural spaces.

Both authors' reactions to the changes in their environment are not romantic notions of harmony and identification (which is difficult in such extreme environments) but stress the powerful aspect of nature and the relativity of human importance. In both authors this relativity can be experienced in either a tragic or a playful way, because both nature and the human spectator are freed from the cultural ballast of meaning and importance.

4. Gatlin's position as a fire lookout has nothing to do with the protection of nature. For Abbey, forest fires are part of a natural cycle, and fire lookouts serve the interests of the lumber industry more than those of the forest. In *Black Sun* this contradiction is exposed when Gatlin cannot report what at first glance looks like smoke but turns out to be dust from a construction site (1982, 19).

5. Karen J. Winkler observes that eco-criticism is often reluctant to use modern literary theory because theory is supposed to negate the importance, even the existence, of the natural world. This perception is due to a misinterpretation of, for example, Derrida's statement that there is nothing outside the text; critics such as Lawrence Buell often interpret text as "a world of words" (Winkler 1996, 3), not in the more general meaning of cultural context. Buell's statement that "a stone is a stone" had long been answered (in 1957) by Roland Barthes: "A tree is a tree. Yes, of course. But a tree expressed by Minou Drouet is no longer quite a tree, it is a tree which . . . is adapted to a certain type of consumption, laden with literary self-indulgence, revolt, images, in short with a type of social usage which is added to pure matter" (1993, 109). Poststructuralism and deconstruction do not deny the existence of a stone or nature, but they do deny the existence of entities "as such" in a cultural context.

Seeing a thing "as such" means, as Derrida points out, removing the subject from the scene, seeing a thing "as if you were dead" (1996, 216). Deconstruction does not deny the existence of a stone, but Buell denies his own existence (subjectivity) in his statement.

6. Scott Slovic acknowledges that there are textual tensions in Abbey. He ascribes them to the conflict between thematic elements, the "moral stratum" of the text, and aesthetic elements such as wordplay (1992, 90–91). I would argue that conflicts in Abbey's texts mainly exist on the conceptual and thematic level and have aesthetic effects.

7. I refer here to the last chapter in *Desert Solitaire*, "Bedrock and Paradox."

Works Cited

Abbey, Edward. 1950. "Jonathan Troy." Manuscript. University of New Mexico General Library, Special Collection.

———. 1982. *Black Sun*. New York: Avon.

———. 1991a. *Abbey's Road*. New York: Plume.

———. 1991b. *The Journey Home*. New York: Plume.

———. [1968] 1991c. *Desert Solitaire: A Season in the Wilderness*. Reprint, New York: Ballantine.

———. 1994. *Confessions of a Barbarian: Selections from the Journals of Edward Abbey, 1951-1989*. Boston: Little, Brown and Co.

Barthes, Roland. 1993. *Mythologies*. London: Vintage.

Chaloupka, William, and R. McGreggor Cawley. 1993. "The Great Wild Hope: Nature, Environmentalism, and the Open Secret." In *In the Nature of Things*, ed. Jane Bennett and William Chaloupka. Minneapolis: University of Minnesota Press.

Cronon, William. 1996. *Uncommon Ground: Rethinking the Human Place in Nature*. New York: Norton.

Dawkins, Richard. 1983. *The Extended Phenotype*. Oxford: Oxford University Press.

———.1989. *The Selfish Gene*. Oxford: Oxford University Press.

Derrida, Jacques. 1995. *Of Grammatology*. Baltimore: Johns Hopkins University Press.

———. 1996. "As If I Were Dead: An Interview with Jacques Derrida." In *Applying to: Derrida*, ed. John Brannigan, Ruth Robbins, and Julian Wolfreys. London: Macmillan.

Foucault, Michel. 1986. "Of Other Spaces." *Diacritics* 16:22–27.

Gaard, Greta. 1996. "Hiking without a Map: Reflections on Teaching Ecofeminist Literary Criticism." *Interdisciplinary Studies in Literature and the Environment* 31 (summer 1996).

Hillis Miller, J. 1996. "Derrida's Others." In *Applying to: Derrida*, ed. John Brannigan, Ruth Robbins, and Julian Wolfreys. London: Macmillan.

Jeffers, Robinson. 1977. *The Double Axe*. New York: Liveright.

Kvaløy, Sigmund. 1992. Etterord (epilogue) to *Essays*, by Peter Wessel Zapffe. Oslo: Aventura.

Loeffler, Jack. 1993. "Edward Abbey, Anarchism, and the Environment." *Western American Literature* 28:1, 43–49.

Macquarrie, John. 1991. *Existentialism*. London: Penguin.

Manes, Christopher. 1990. *Green Rage: Radical Environmentalism and the Unmaking of Civilization*. Boston: Little, Brown and Co.

McClintock, James. 1994. *Nature's Kindred Spirits*. Madison: University of Wisconsin Press.

Murphy, Patrick. 1988. "Sex-Typing the Planet: Gaia Imagery and the Problem of Subverting Patriarchy." *Environmental Ethics* 10:155–67.

Nash, Roderick. 1989. *The Rights of Nature*. Madison: University of Wisconsin Press.

Payne, Daniel. 1996. *Voices in the Wilderness: American Nature Writing and Environmental Politics*. Hanover, N.H.: University of New England Press.

Quigley, Peter. 1992. "Rethinking Resistance: Environmentalism, Literature, and Poststructural Theory." *Environmental Ethics* 14 (4): 291–306.

Rothenberg, David, and Peter Reed, eds. 1993. *Wisdom in the Open Air: The Norwegian Roots of Deep Ecology*. Minneapolis: University of Minnesota Press.

Saeger, Joni. 1993. *Earth Follies: Feminism, Politics, and the Environment*. London: Earthscan.

Slovic, Scott. 1992. *Seeking Awareness in American Nature Writing*. Salt Lake City: University of Utah Press.

Winkler, Karen J. 1996. "Scholars Embark on Study of Literature About the Environment." *Chronicle of Higher Education*, Aug. 9, 8–9.

Winner, Langdon. 1994. *The Whale and the Reactor: A Search for Limits in an Age of High Technology*. Chicago: University of Chicago Press.

Zapffe, Peter Wessel. 1977. *Sprøk og Alvor*. Oslo: Gyldendal.

———. 1992. *Essays*. Oslo: Aventura.

———. 1993a. *Barske Glæder*. Oslo: Aventura.

———. 1993. "The Last Messiah." In Rothenberg and Reed, 40–52.

The Politics and Aesthetics of a Hopeful Anarchism

Edward Abbey's Postmodern
"Angelic Demonology"

PETER

QUIGLEY

"You're dead."
"Not yet I ain't."
—Abbey, *Hayduke Lives!*

This exchange of words suggests the spirit of rebellion, born in the sixties, that is the center of all of Abbey's work. Hayduke's surprise return is part of a cycle of rebellious characters that keep coming back into novels after their previous apparent demise. These two lines are particularly poignant since they refer not only to Abbey's essential theme of resistance, but also to the fact that Abbey was indeed dying (and resisting) as he wrote. What one sees here is the determination and commitment in Abbey that was clearly more than a literary theme or public posture. Abbey never wavered in his oppositional positioning; and he did not "go gently into that good night." Hope, determination, and humor emerge as incredibly genuine sentiments, fire tested, one might say, under these conditions.

As early as *The Brave Cowboy,* written in the '50s, Abbey's early Hayduke prototype exhibits this spirit: "I'm like water: boil me away and I come back in the next thunderhead" (1992, 26–27). In this image of the magic of water and its rejuvenating qualities is Abbey's most salient theme: joyous and eternal resistance to power. This oppositional profile is not utopian, final, or authoritarian, but it is in the best spirit of postmodern and anarchist resistance. Abbey's politics of

eternal opposition is what Ursula Le Guin has called "the permanent revolution" (1974, 267). The permanent revolution assumes that there is no one truth, and that the health of the human brain, the political structure, and the ecosystem depends on process and movement. As Abbey put it, "Society is like a stew. If you don't keep it stirred up, you get a lot of scum on top" (1989, 21). When my students complain that all politicians do is talk, I suggest that democracy depends upon an uninterrupted continuous conversation (and the more conversation, the more radical the democracy). If the issue is ever settled, if the conversation stops, fascism has won.

It is the purpose of this chapter to clarify this unique form of opposition and to suggest how understanding its quality will allow a fuller appreciation of Abbey's fiction. By so doing, I will want to address the perception of critics that Abbey is a cynically didactic writer who also possesses a "mindless pride in lack of consistency" (in Bishop 1994, 191). I will further want to suggest that *Hayduke Lives!* is a much better book than even sympathetic critics have suggested. Specifically, I make the claim that the voice of *Hayduke Lives!* is highly ironic and floats in and about the various speech zones of the characters. Finally, I will discuss the nature of anarchist aesthetics and the hope for a future embedded in anarchist politics.

Like Robinson Jeffers, Abbey is often seen as a didactic writer who leans to the right and who doesn't make enough use of ambiguity. But as Cary Nelson says in *Repression and Recovery,* the political nature of a text changes depending on political contexts (1989, 10–11). Abbey's railing against the FBI combined with his populist position defending rugged, rural individualism easily places him, given recent events, in a right-wing category; however, one can object to this in a number of ways. Populist politics, as Duncan Webster has pointed out in *Looka Yonder!: The Imaginary America of Populist Culture,* is not politically monolithic, and in the 1890s it advocated "state regulation of the emergent corporate capitalism" (1988, 18). The issue is actually more complex in that there are no pure positions, and overlap between positions occurs more than we commonly admit. Although rural populism can go left or right, and overlapping occurs, I would like to suggest that Abbey's text contains many elements that can distinguish him from right-wing trajectories and point strongly to a progressive left wing.

In addition to complicating Abbey's position by disputing textual meanings, it is instructive to recall that Abbey drew FBI attention because of an antiwar letter proclaiming his pacifism (Bishop 1994, 93).

This is hardly the behavior of a Tim McVeigh or the mindset of today's militia groups. Additional evidence of Abbey's left-wing sympathies is his interest in the International Workers of the World (IWW), which before being broken into the AFL-CIO was a powerful socialist-anarchist threat to property-based capitalism. In *Hayduke Lives!*, Abbey connects the environmental movement historically with the IWW and its fight against industry. In this way Abbey advances his anarchistic critique of culture via the environmental movement. In the novel, the intelligence community sees environmentalists as " 'worse than terrorists' " because " 'These people attack property. *Property,* Oral' " (1990, 148). This is a Marxist or socialist critique, not a right-wing position.[1]

As most readers will know, Marxism sees property ownership (the base) as the principle that informs all other structures (superstructure) in a society: legal, educational, spiritual, and artistic. The worst thing one can threaten in a capitalist society is property. Abbey continues by having the FBI describe the degree of political threat posed by Earth First!: " 'we haven't had to deal with anything like this since the A.G. [Attorney General] wiped out the IWW back in the twenties' " (148). Abbey claims that Joe Hill would have been a member of Earth First! and Hill, Abbey claims, would have approved of "the evolution of the IWW into the EF!" (208).[2] What seems clear is that although Abbey often rebuffed claims that he was an environmentalist, he enjoyed the emergence of Earth First! because it carries on a tradition of opposing centralized power.

In *Hayduke Lives!*, Abbey also targets the Mormon influence in Utah to criticize the way commercial, patriarchal, restrictive, and hierarchical forces govern America. Bishop Love, an Archie Bunker with money and a plan, is the specific target. In a county commission meeting to determine whether a uranium mine will be approved, Bishop Love announces that the mine smells like jobs and money. He is not afraid of cancer, he bellows, and claims that "radiation is good for you." Echoing the old cliché about General Motors ("What is good for GM is good for the country"), Love goes on to say, "Uranium is good for Utah and Arizona! The nuclear industry is good for America!" (24).

This character is also seen virtually raping his wife, trying to fulfill the Mormon commandment to bring twelve children into the world. Abbey is graphically critical of sexuality conditioned by patriarchy, as it is in this scene, which is also heavily ironic. While Love tells his wife that it is their duty to be fruitful, his insect exterminator zaps all the winging nature drawn to its blue humming light. This obvious anthropocentric thinking allows Abbey to link his critique of religion, and finally power, with his interest in environmental issues. Love owns all the major businesses in town and has the county commission in his pocket. He represents all of the forces Abbey sees as responsible for the destruction of the West: timber cutting supervised by the Forest Service, cattle ranching on public land, damming of rivers, industrial tourism, general development to make enormous profit at the expense of the arid Western land.

In a general way, Abbey's critique is focused against capitalism and patriarchy. Again, these hardly seem the material for right-wing interests. Nonetheless, Abbey was never doctrinaire enough to please committed Marxists (or environmentalists, or any other group). As James Bishop reminds us, Alexander Cockburn (a noted Marxist journalist) called Abbey "reactionary slime" (qtd. in Bishop 1994, 164). In a sympathetic 1990 review of *Hayduke Lives!* in *The Nation,* Erik Ness reacts with characteristic left-wing ambivalence: "Abbey is something of a sore spot for the ecoleft. His writing has emboldened countless individuals to act courageously in defense of our planet, and anyone . . . must appreciate the power of his language to incite and to inspire. . . . His infamy lies in his insensitivity to feminist issues and language, not to mention isolationist views on immigration and a passing scorn for homosexuality" (1990, 458).

This writer for the radical and progressive *The Nation* goes on to complain that with "no compromise," Abbey's last novel makes no apologies but "contains a full volley of objectionable language" (458). Not satisfied yet with this priggish display, the critic goes on to have us ask ourselves this probing question: "What, after all, is one to think of a man who called himself a pervert?" (458). Does Ness assume that Abbey believed he was a pervert, that this was a moment of confession? Does the use of the term itself disturb him, suggesting, as it might, that the user subscribes to a normalized view of sexuality? In either case, Ness shows he lacks the ability to read playfully and with the ironic wit Abbey expected from his readers. With all due respect to Cockburn and other ideologues, I submit that they just missed the point. Like comedian George Carlin, Abbey will thrill you with criticism of your opponents, but sooner or later he will get around to you.

As a means of advancing this discussion of Abbey's politics, it may do well to discuss his use of Norway in *Hayduke Lives!* In the novel,

Abbey passes the torch from one generation to another, using Norway as an ideological foundation for environmental and social critique. First, it is interesting to note that Abbey makes use of Norway at all. Why, one might ask? Not only does Norway get used at length in *Hayduke*, but in *A Fool's Progress*, he specifically mentions Bergen, Norway's second largest city; he also mentions Uppsala, Sweden. Now that selections from his journals (1994) have been published, we have a record of his trip to Norway and Sweden in 1952. It is clear from his journals that Abbey was taken by the beautiful landscapes and hearty people of Norway. And having just returned after living in Norway for three years, I concur. Given the complete sacrifice our culture has made to buying and having (we have no architecture, or, I should say, the strip mall is our architecture; our towns are endless highways; we have no use for a wooden bench with wrought-iron arm rests, nor does a flower garden need to be planted in a downtown where no one walks by), Norwegians find our indictment of their environmental behavior (Greenpeace has criticized them for whaling) a little problematic. Norway's recent "Nei" vote on European unity (Mastricht) reflects the fact they do not want to become part of the increasing commercialization of Europe—what they refer to as the "United States" of Europe. Abbey's journal entries never tire of describing the simple, cultured lifestyle; the beautiful, athletic men and women; and the landscape of Norway. This trip clearly made a deep impression on him.

In addition to asking why Abbey used Norway and how it functions in *Hayduke*, I want to ask why Abbey waited so long to draw on his experience. The trip to Norway was in 1952, and *Hayduke Lives!* was the last thing he wrote before his death in 1989.

Abbey's use of Norway suggests how this image has recently gained cultural purchase in the political imagination of American environmentalism. Publications such as *Wisdom in the Open Air: The Roots of Norwegian Deep Ecology* (Rottenberg and Reed 1993) are evidence of continuing interest among Americans in Norwegian theory. The popular book *Deep Ecology* is dedicated by its authors, Sessions and Duvall, to Arne Naess, the Norwegian eco-philosopher, along with Gary Snyder. Norway returns in Abbey's art because of its powerful presence in his imagination and because it is active in the imagination of American environmental politics, especially in the '70s and '80s.

Clearly there is the sense that Norway represents a rugged and pristine alternative to the American life of cars, fast food, and lack of contact or understanding of nature.[3] One of my Norwegian students came back from a trip to the States and said, "It is a drive-through country." About Norwegians, Abbey says in *Hayduke Lives!*, that "they are a wild and hearty breed" (1990, 192). And, in fact, it is true. Norwegians will instinctively use stairs instead of an elevator;[4] they walk religiously in town and in the mountains (and cannot imagine not having "nature" nearby); and they have many downhill ski villages, although most Norwegians prefer the less mechanical cross-country skiing. Older folks—women, for instance, in their seventies and even eighties—can be seen sparking down the snow-covered streets at breakneck speeds.[5] Everyone uses backpacks, which typically contain a simple but hearty *matpaken* (lunch pack), books, and whatever else they will need for the day: a car is not usually used.[6] But for all of this vigor, Norwegians are remarkably shy and quiet as a people. For example, during the winter Olympics of 1993, which they hosted, my Norwegian friends became concerned that they were winning too many medals; they like to win, but not at the total expense of others. This mixture of vigor, constraint, and fairness certainly seems like something Abbey would have been drawn to.

I should add a couple of examples that suggest Norway's slow-paced, reading culture. There are few restaurants because meals are eaten at home with family (nothing is open for breakfast), so the time spent at home (without TV) instead of "out" is part of life there. Also, in the Bergen airport, the book selection shocked me. Instead of "trash" novels with some version of Clark Gable leaning over a fainting Scarlet with torn sleeve and Tara burning in the background, the rack was filled with mostly Victorian and modern English novels: George Eliot in the book rack! In addition, as opposed to the world Bonnie worries about—a world of "child molesters," a world where one senses "There is danger everywhere," where she asks, "How could a little boy only three years old have bad dreams?" (1990, 43)—children are a major priority in Norway, and it is a conscious goal to make them part of Norwegian society.[7] Playgrounds abound, as do puppet shows. On the train between Bergen and Oslo (a trip Abbey took in 1952), a whole car is given up for children. Inside is a slide, a pretend train big enough to stand up in, and numerous other toys.

So, as I have been trying to suggest, there is small wonder that Abbey chose Norway as a counter image to the world being brought into being by Bishop Love, defender of uranium mining, "people and industry and jobs and unlimited opportunity" (1990, 260), symbol of bloated personalities totally shaped by the profit motive, tourism, jobs at the expense of the environment, and corporate expansion. A taxi driver once told me, "You Americans live to work; we work to live." The fact that Norway is a socialist state presents more evidence of Abbey's left-leaning, not reactionary, political sympathies.

It is clear right from the early part of *Hayduke* that Abbey intends to use Norway as an oppositional force in the novel. It is also clear in what particular ways he finds it a significant image. Norway becomes a sign of fierce environmentalism, eco-feminist spirituality and independence, sexual energy, and a pagan, anti-Christian world. Norway allows Abbey to attack the absolutist position of Christianity as well as the greed of capitalism. In the early moments of the novel a scene occurs that reinforces the tension between the world of Bishop Love and the counterculture movement. Nordic, feminine, environmental power overwhelms male, Western, Christian dominance. Oral Hatch, a young Mormon missionary, has been busy making Norwegian converts. However, he wakes one night to find that with two of the converts, the spell has worn off. "Appointed to the slender pendant barely tumescent damned Gentile nation of Norway, he awoke one night to find himself nude" (1990, 49). Poor Oral is strapped to a table being "handled" by Birgit and Erika. He had, unsuccessfully it would appear, "converted them both to Mormonism only a month before" (50). As it happens, Norway is crawling with American Mormon missionaries (the first person I met in Norway was an American Mormon missionary), along with an assortment of other American fundamentalists. This scene in the novel appealed to many Norwegian students who object to yet another form of American cultural persuasion. Abbey clearly relished producing this scene, which suggests a usurpation by female sexual energy of patriarchal and religious domination.

One can never forget that in the period when Abbey was politicized—the 1950s through 1970s—outward demonstrations of sexual desire were considered subversive acts, especially if done by a woman. The way Abbey approaches this topic often feels inappropriate, especially in *The Monkey Wrench Gang*, but this is very much a matter of context. All imagery suffers from the problems associated with context: context in the writer's mind; context in a social, historical, or linguistic sense; context in relationship to other texts that were circulating at the time the writer wrote. And so I was surprised to find while teaching in Norway, a land of strong and largely uncontested feminist politics, a less hostile reaction to Abbey than I would expect (and sympathize with) in the States. Before starting to teach *Hayduke Lives!* in a graduate seminar on environmental writers, I launched into an apologia for a writer and a novel that I was sure were going to be troublesome. To my surprise, I was politely interrupted by a young woman who had been exchanging glances with another classmate. She said, "Quigley, we can see quite clearly his interest in the female body. Can we get on with the novel? We like it very much. It is wild."

We overdo everything it seems: our violence, our commercialism, and our sense of textual injustice. This isn't to say they didn't have their complaints (I certainly have mine) about Abbey: Norwegians, in general, are quite direct. But this textual issue of gender seemed, not unimportant, but different in scale, without desperation. Their textual interests were broadly focused: on resistance communities and possibilities within American culture, on contradiction, on nature, on humor, on the depiction of Native Americans, on American energy, on American views of Norwegians, on the alleged "American-ness" of the writing. Nevertheless, now that I am back in the States, it seems appropriate and necessary to engage the issue of gender on the textual level. Foreground and background are extremely contextual and determined by culture. My sense about all of this now is that Norwegians have addressed many issues regarding gender in the public sphere, in the shape of their lives. Americans, perhaps feeling cut off from the ability to seriously engage with the material culture, work these issues out at the textual level. Perhaps Terry Eagleton was right when he stated that poststructuralism seems to be a jaded reaction to the failure of the movements of the sixties; the revolution was simply taken indoors, from the street to the text (1983, 141–42).

It is clear that Abbey finds in Norway an alternative to, and a critique of, Christian culture. Even the novel's title signals its attack on Christianity. In addition to resembling the name of the environmental group Earth First!, "Hayduke Lives!" also strikes me as a direct reference to the irritating and ubiquitous bumper sticker popular in the '70s, "Jesus Lives!"[8] In this way, Pan is reborn in the works of Abbey, overwhelming the abstract, earth-destroying, transcendent religion of Christianity. Hayduke is a mythic, Pan-like figure who represents unbridled disregard for inhibition. He is Bacchus and Orc mixed into one. One recalls that in *The Monkey Wrench Gang*, Hayduke lives in a cave with a rattlesnake at the entrance; the image has the air of a classic mythic figure of the unconscious, of death-daring defiance. Hayduke, in this last novel, is an irrepressible, smiling, hairy, lusty iconoclast. As a means of reinforcing the theme, Abbey gives the reader a softer version of Hayduke in the person of one of the EF! members, whom Abbey describes as "the goat-bearded young man with the curly horns and fipple-fingered wood recorder" (1990, 84). Hayduke is a more formidable and threatening version of this pagan figure: Pan pissed off!

Norway is also used to suggest a counter to modern life. Modern life is where we find "Passion sublimated to the love and pursuit of intellectual titillation. Honest anger perverted into benign tolerance, joy degraded to mere pleasure, rebellion channeled into legal procedures, genteel letters to the editor, the political process" (168). Norway, the land of Vikings, has a history of being a vital and relentless conquering nation and one of the last to be Christianized.[9] Abbey seems to valorize this when he states that "they are a wild and hearty breed . . . untainted by cynical affectation" (192). Erika is a powerful, Earth-loving goddess, representing Abbey's anti-anthropocentric attraction to the beauties and duties of this world. Her presence in the United States suggests her conquering power as environmentalism sweeps the culture. It is important to remember that she represents a kind of counter raid. She now tracks Oral, the symbol of American cultural imperialism, narrowness, and rigidity, who before was in her land attempting to convert her to Mormonism. It is the mind and soul of Norway that Erika possesses, we are told. This Nordic ecofeminist who has come to America to save the land, represents "the song of Norway, the mind of Arne Naess, the spirit of Grieg, Nielsen, Sibelius" (1990, 187). Abbey, with Erika, exhibits the qualities of carnival. By combining her sexual and physical qualities with the loftier elements of classical music and philosophy, we see, as Bakhtin states, that "Carnival brings together . . . the sacred and the profane, the lofty with the low, the great with the insignificant" (1994, 123).

To all that Bishop Love stands for, Erika emerges as a dynamic counter. Although Abbey seems more connected to his aging rebels left over from *The Monkey Wrench Gang,* and although he paints the young generation of Earth First! eco-anarchists with irony,[10] Erika, a member of this younger crowd, nevertheless shares center stage with Hayduke in Abbey's pantheon. If Hayduke, in his cave guarded by a rattlesnake, is the god of uncompromising rebellion, Erika from Norway is Gaia,[11] the Earth personified as Goddess. Abbey describes the scene of Erika's ascension to power as she mouths the Earth First! battle cry:

Libertié mounting the barricades. . . . Taking the mike, raising it a foot, she thrust her right fist *ad astra*. "Zee Eart' She First!" . . . The battle cry . . . echoed from a thousand hoarse throats. . . . They wouldn't do it for the others, but who would not do anything for Erika? . . . so beautiful that she existed somewhere beyond the envy of other women, safe from the animal lust of even the simplest young men. All loved her, all looked upon her as a work of natural art rather than (as simply) an object of sexual inspiration. Erika her self,

> Princess of Moon Power. . . . "Down wiss empire up wiss spring!" (1990, 205)

Although Erika functions well as symbol of a pagan icon of Earth worship and political inspiration, her depiction had serious flaws for Norwegians. First, "Erika" is a common Swedish name for a woman but seldom used in Norway.[12] In addition, Abbey refers to her as "Erika the Svenska Maid" (205). How can she be from Norway and be a Swedish maid as well? Also, Norwegians took special exception to Erika's dialect, which is German. A Norwegian, for instance, would not say "wiss" for the English "with." With dialect interference, she would say "widt." Another example is "Zank you" instead of the Norwegian interference, which would be "Tank you." It could be said that Abbey was just creating a Nordic composite and had no intention of creating an accurate ethnic portrayal. But such an issue as dialect becomes a particularly touchy error in Norway, a country occupied by the Germans during World War II and still harboring a good deal of mistrust.

Nevertheless, despite her rather flat character construction, overly drawn feminine features,[13] and sloppy ethnic depiction, she functions well as the power of the Earth calling the square, young, white, male, Mormon Oral Hatch away from the service of the CIA and the American value system, and toward the enchantment of the Maypole, "the lurid fifty-foot pole" (208), and all that it suggests. Suggesting Norway's role in the political imagination of America, one recalls that Erika comes seeking Oral as though the principles of ecology and socialism come in the form of a beautiful woman. Oral abandons and betrays the CIA and moves to Norway with Erika, suggesting Abbey's hope for political movement to the left on the American scene.[14]

Most people associate Abbey's anarchism with dynamite-throwing opposition to buildings and any organized government.

Worse yet, it is typical to associate Abbey's anarchism with a kind of juvenile freedom, a rejection of any constraints. As Graham Purchase has pointed out in *Anarchism and Environmental Survival* (1994), anarchism, as opposed to American assumptions about chaos and violence, presents an orderly alternative and a "plan" to live by. The central point is the realization that truth is a human concept subject to contextual sociohistorical desires: truth is power. In addition, this tradition of thought recognizes that there is always an attempt to erase the human element and allow truth to appear *natural*. As John Carlos Rowe paraphrases Derrida, "the coin of the realm erases its figure. Social convention works to obliterate its figurative origins" (1987, 134). Pascal questions the naturalness of culture and points to the culture of nature: "Custom is a second nature, which destroys the first one. But what is nature? Why is custom not natural? I greatly fear that nature may in itself be but a first custom, as custom is a second nature" (qtd. in Evernden 1994, 1).

Both Derrida and Pascal point to the fact that human knowledge systems have tended to arrange themselves by establishing some unassailable point of authority that all else is structured with. This understanding has made poststructuralists utter phrases such as "all is text" or "all is figure." Admitting that all knowledge is mediated exposes human interest in all imagery, and it suggests our limited perspective. In many places Abbey demonstrates that he was well aware of this issue: "Something in our human consciousnesses seems to make us forever spectators of the world we live in" (qtd. in Bishop 1994, 181). In *Desert Solitaire*, Abbey sounds more like a French poststructuralist than a Thoreauvian metaphysician when he admits that his book "fails to engage and reveal the patterns of unifying relationships which form the true underlying reality of existence. Here I must confess that I know nothing whatever about a true underlying reality, having never met any. . . . For my part *I am pleased enough with surfaces*" (1992, xi, my emphasis). The point is to see that human interest is always implicated, that there is no innocent position, that power is pervasive, and that even positions of opposition partake of such commanding points of authority. The art of living and writing becomes the ability to evade settling into a one-sided position of power. The strategy of opposition that emerges is to attack all authoritative formulations that wish to pass as truth or "the way things are." As Abbey states, "I write to oppose injustice, to defy power, and to speak for the voiceless" (1988, 178).

This strategy, interestingly enough, does not lead to despair or nihilism; on the contrary, it brings on a youthful energy, what poststructuralists call "play." In all these cases there seems to be an interest in the process of change instead of settling things in some permanent shape. In philosophy, one sees this argument between permanence and fluidity at the very opening of the Western tradition.[15] In environmentalism, Marxism, and anarchism, there is the belief that process is the whole point and the supreme value. In ecology, it is diversity that exudes health; a clear-cut, then, is imperial domination and death. Bakhtin discusses this dynamic as the tension between centrifugal and centripetal forces. Like Foucault, Bakhtin builds fluidity and movement into the history of ideas: not teleology or historical determinism, but synchronic junctures, Kuhnian paradigm shifts that, for an instant, stabilize and authorize the natural and the normal for a culture. Bakhtin uses the terms "centripetal" and "centrifugal" to describe how alongside "centralization and unification, the uninterrupted processes of decentralization and disunification go forward" (1986, 668).

Abbey refuses definition because, as an anarchist, it is not this or that position that he is aiming for but the abandonment of static positions that disallow democratic multiplicity. It is crucial to recall that it is not freedom from any responsibility that is the goal. As Abbey states, "*Anarchy is democracy taken seriously*" (1988, 26, my emphasis). The dream is to live together in a community of mutual aid and mutual consent. In *Desert Solitaire,* the qualities Abbey lists as being important for human survival are "mutual aid, cooperation, and sharing" (1991, 266). Therefore, the undermining of positions is not merely dissonance or the aesthetic stimulation that Scott Slovic suggests (1992, 99–114). Contradictions are not canceling each other out, but they point to the validity of all voices. This explains the importance for writing in the comic mode.

Comedy—carnivalistic comedy, that is—allows for a jettisoning/ including of all positions. Bakhtin clarifies the importance of comedy and laughter:

Carnivalistic laughter . . . is directed toward something higher— toward a shift of authorities and truths, a shift of world orders. Laughter embraces both poles of change, it deals with the very *process of change,* with crisis itself. Combined in the act of carnival laughter are death and rebirth, negation (a smirk) and affirmation (rejoicing laughter). This is a profoundly universal laughter, a laughter that contains a whole outlook on the world. Such is the specific quality of *ambivalent carnival laughter*. (1994, 127, my emphasis)

The first complaint that politically oriented readers voice when encountering poststructural or anarchistic theory is the following: without a basis in truth, without a knowledge system that refers to reality in an unmediated fashion, there is no basis for resistance, action, or any other activity. A response by Leo Marx in 1990 is typical. Generally sympathetic with emerging skeptical theories, Marx nevertheless finds that "it is difficult to imagine what form such a positive alternative, compatible with the spirit of post-modernist skepticism, might take" (14). I am claiming that abandoning an absolutist position allows for an energetic and youthful resistance as well as an egalitarian social structure based on mutual aid and consent.

James Bishop, author of the Abbey biography *Epitaph for a Desert Anarchist,* sensed the nature of Abbey's joyousness: "Although Abbey was physically unwell when most of these essays were written, suffering bleeding attacks at irregular intervals, remarkably they are not drenched in despair, but punctuated instead with flashes of iconoclastic humor—and hope" (1994, 190). This hope, optimism, and complexity is embedded in *Hayduke Lives!* This complexity and joy is seen throughout the novel, as when Abbey describes the outpouring at an EF! meeting as sounding like "angelic demonology" (1990, 190). Abbey finds wonder in any force, natural or social, that disrupts the tyranny of the accepted, the sense that reality is just so. In this case, it is the nature cult that undermines and defamiliarizes. He admires the youthful energy at the rally, and "Even the cops and rangers were impressed by this mass outburst of *angelic demonology . . .* and they remembered, under the thin imposed film of cultural consciousness, something older, deeper, richer, warmer, lovelier, and finer than anything they'd ever been taught in school. . . . What was it? . . . It was the message of the wolf's cry, the lion's roar, the whispering of the forest. . . . The drumming of the heart. The beating of drums" (1990, 190, my emphasis). Notice the conflation of polar opposites in the phrase "angelic demonology" and the sense of a wickedly holy energy; notice, also, the implication that there is creation in destruction. As Doc Sarvis witnesses an environmental rally, he notes the joyous play, what French poststructuralists have referred to as "jouissance," that is inseparable from oppositional politics: "Why yes, gay. You don't think so? Look at them out there, prancing around and around like red savages, beating drums, laughing like idiots, howling at the moon, wrapping themselves in one fantastic tangle around that maypole. If these are revolutionists, they're the happiest, jolliest craziest ones I've ever heard of. Wasn't it Emma Goldman who said, If there's no dancing at the revolution I won't come?" (208).

There is no question that others have commented on Abbey's use of irony, ambiguity, and contradiction before. Abbey's writing, Scott Slovic says, "calls into question the very notion of a static ideology, whether pro-environment or pro-development. . . . Abbey, it seems, delights in luring us to make a commitment to one ideology or another, to one mode of reading or another, only to pull the rug out from under our feet suddenly" (1992, 101). Slovic is one of the best critics on Abbey's use of language, and he does a fine job at suggesting that there is a connection between Abbey's aesthetics and ideology. He is also instinctively aware that Abbey eschews the real, the comfortable, and the intimate. However, Slovic conflates Abbey's aesthetic and contradictory elements in his argument. Slovic suggests that Abbey's use of language is purposely self-indulgent. Abbey luxuriates in the aesthetic dimension, and the result is that we are awakened. Failing to distinguish imagery, puns, and "beautiful objects and beautiful language" (106) from the use of contradiction forces Slovic to say that Abbey employed contradiction, as well as these other elements, as a "stimulation" that was "an end in itself" (112), or a means to higher attentiveness.

Slovic wants to say that Abbey's aesthetics and ideology merge. True enough, but what are we to do with this "giddy aestheticism" (114)? It seems we are to be "free" and "attentive," according to Slovic. I think Slovic is on to Abbey here; I think he is right that Abbey wants to shake us up, that he wants to introduce something wild, but Slovic leaves the purpose of contradiction and ambiguity at an undeveloped level of "stimulation" and "freedom." This pushes Slovic toward uttering a typical comment concerning Abbey's politics: "It is difficult, if not impossible, to distill a coherent moral argument . . . an argument which could translate into new attitudes and new behavior" (99). Like Leo Marx, Slovic seems to play into a conventional notion of anarchism, a view that sees anarchism as simply free of system and responsibility. In addition, the focus on "heightened sensitivity" seems to echo values associated with the aesthetics and morality of New Criticism. He seems also to have borrowed from Ann Ronald, who complains that Abbey's earlier work fails because it offers no answers, no option, no final vision; the contradictions are seen as simply "negated options" (1982, 36–37). Only later, according to Ronald, did Abbey get to the point where the negations made sense, since they canceled human knowledge and left only solid rock. Slovic treats Abbey similarly since his method "tends to stimulate the reader's attentiveness to specific natural phenomena" (1992, 100). As I have been arguing, contradiction is a way to break down human-constructed systems, a way of letting the laughter and the vastness of the cosmos sweep in. *But one cannot rush too quickly by the contradictions to the answer.* In comedy, the main point is to relish the noise. In the end, I think Slovic, Ronald, and I are headed in the same direction. I tend to see the contradictory style being used in a more positive and content-filled manner than either of these two fine critics.

Daniel Payne seems to recognize the central issue at stake when he states that Abbey was moving beyond what was immediately possible within this system (1996, 164). Payne is also quite good at elucidating the connections between Abbey's essays and environmental policy, but he too desperately looks for a pattern of environmental doctrine. In his generally fine book, *Voices in the Wilderness,* Payne, like so many critics, feels he must sidestep Abbey's use of contradiction. Like Slovic, Payne sees no positive, position-taking quality in the contradictions. In the end, Payne seems to find the contradictions and the ambiguity rhetorically lacking. They are tossed off as being successful "in a literary sense" but ineffective as "environmental rhetoric" (153), and again, although this behavior makes him "interesting as a writer," it "works against him as a polemicist" (163). He "goes out in front of his audience" (163) flouting his views and therefore falls short at being a more effective spokesperson for the environment. Ignoring the radical multivocality of *Hayduke Lives!,* Payne goes on to suggest that Abbey had no intention of trying to achieve "environmental reform through the democratic political system" (163). My point has been, of course, that stirring the stew of the political process is exactly Abbey's goal and the point is to enhance democracy. "*Anarchy is democracy taken seriously*" (1988, 26, my emphasis), Abbey states. He accomplishes this in his narrative by removing authority from any one voice. Wanting to be sympathetic to Abbey, however, Payne suggests that the contradictions were used as a way to avoid participating in a system that Abbey saw as an entrapment. Once again the contradictions and ambiguity have no "positive" qualities but are either failures, stimulants, or evasive techniques.

Bishop comments again and again on the irony, but he never even hints as to Abbey's purpose in employing it. It is as though using it is an end in itself. Bishop states that Abbey recognized that "paradox was to be embraced" (1994, 97); that "*perhaps*" Bakunin "was one of the sources" of Abbey's reliance on "irony, paradox, and contradiction" (109, my emphasis); that Abbey knew that the "only bedrock solid enough to stand on is paradox" (143); that "Lopez senses paradox everywhere" in Abbey (151); that "the quintessential paradox of Abbey's work" is that he lives in the desert and the city (153). Bishop recognizes well enough this strong feature but does not take the time to look at the language, to probe beyond the recognition of this feature. Bishop states that Abbey understood that it was not a matter of dismissing the city for nature, "that escaping from one to the other would not resolve the conflict" (97). But he takes it no further; he doesn't suggest what would resolve the conflict or the importance of the tension in the conflict. In fact, he finds it necessary to trot out Walt Whitman's overused "Do I contradict myself?" This approach to Abbey's usage serves as a means for dismissing critics (by proving he is not didactic) as well as mystifying the motivation for contradiction, irony, or paradox in Abbey's work.

Actually, Bishop himself begins to back away from Abbey's use of "contradictions," suggesting that *Hayduke Lives!* contains an act of violence that Abbey supposedly is opposed to. Abbey's apparent doctrine of nonviolence is broken because Abbey "introduces gratuitous violence for the first time" (120) in *Hayduke Lives!* This is an odd analysis, but repeated by others such as Payne and Ness. The casualties in the shooting are more than prepared for by the plot. The CIA man who commits suicide does so for complex psychological and political reasons not out of Abbey's indulgence in "senseless violence" (1994, 120). Bishop fails to account for Abbey's use of language, and therefore he fails to adequately account for the intellectual issues in Abbey's work.

Perhaps the Norwegian eco-feminist Erika in *Hayduke Lives!* best sums up this in-between positioning I am discussing, a position Bakhtin called the loophole or the penultimate word (1984, 233). Erika represents the Earth and, therefore, the vitality that goes beyond resting on absolute positioning. She takes a position between the developers and the Earth First! people. When she is asked whether she feels that a desert turtle is more important than people, she states that they are equally important. This position disengages the dialectical tension of polarization and advances a dialogical dynamic: A *and* B instead of A *or* B. The old journalist in the novel, Abbey's self-caricature, thinks this is a point of brilliance: "Hah! thought the old buzzard . . . she's hit it, square on the head. While those young punks . . . funneling emery powder into the crankcase via the dipstick pipe, missed the whole thing" (1990, 84). Abbey, too, positions himself between.

In addition to Erika's "middle path," and Abbey's tendency to abandon any position soon after embracing it, the other piece of strong evidence of anarchist aesthetics is the character of the journalist. The narrative voice cannot help but be connected with a self-effacing self-portrait of an "old graybearded rednosed corespondent" who, while Erika was speaking, "gaped up with wonder in his bleary eyes" (206). This character is linked with the author, who chastises himself for his indulgence in describing Erika with unfashionable zest: "She wore—but who cares except the author?—faded Levi britches. . . . " (81). He is a "seedy old buzzard from nowhere who called himself a 'literary journalist' " (82). It is essential to note that the journalist distances himself from the action, neither fully apart nor fully involved, like the narrative voice in general. This "old buzzard" was always "hovering near, making his mental notes, groaning with lust, *observing with his usual ambivalent interests*" (83, my emphasis). It is this refusal to give into standing by an absolute that provides for hope. If power never settles, it can never get a hold; it can never build a police force, an intelligence unit, a black budget. Bakhtin's centrifugal force and carnival laughter keep power right where it belongs: on its way to the margins and seriously undermined.

In *Hayduke Lives!* Abbey has written a more playful and ironic novel than he has been given credit for. It has experienced the same kind of muffled neglect as Melville's *The Confidence Man*, another ironic, position-switching narrative. Yet even though Abbey's narrative voice is undermined, it is not finally unreliable. And although committed to the beauty and strength of Norway, Gaia, Erika, young revolutionaries, and the Earth, he also makes it clear, with a playful Buddhist detachment reminiscent of Gary Snyder, that "Saving the world was only a hobby" (169). Nevertheless, Norway, although a bit flawed in its conception, does serve as a kind of feminist, unconscious rebellion in Abbey. Norway remains a world of earthly dreams for Abbey, a world of physical beauty and social justice. It is remarkable that such a novel, written with death approaching swiftly in 1989, is given to so much adoration of the living, a celebration of fallible and infinitely vain youth, and an ending where old man turtle, buried by Goliath in the first chapter, emerges in a miraculous, impossible resurrection. On such a note, Abbey finds it irresistible not to include his favorite image, present at least as far back as the '50s, in his last novel: "a certain half-dead half-alive juniper tree that lifts a twisted silvergray limb toward the sky, a gesture of static assertion, the affirmation of an embattled but undefeated existence" (307). With this gesture, Abbey passed out of our lives; with this, he deserves full entrance into the arena of serious study and appreciation.

Notes

1. As opposed to popular conception, which assumes anarchism by definition has no method or theory, anarchism borrowed from Marxism a theory of materialism. Anarchism, for thinkers like Emma Goldman, combines a liberal view of individual freedom coupled with a socialist critique of the distribution of wealth.

2. Originally Joel Emmanuel Hagglund, b. Sweden, c. 1879, d. Nov. 19, 1915. He was an American labor organizer for the IWW and he wrote songs such as "Casey Jones" and "The Union Scab." He gained world-wide attention after being sentenced to death and then executed by firing squad in Utah. He was accused of murder. President Woodrow Wilson and the Swedish government asked for a new trial. On the eve of his execution, he telegraphed Big Bill Haywood, the head of the IWW, and said, "Don't waste time mourning. Organize." During the 1960s Joan Baez frequently sang "The Ballad of Joe Hill," which was popular after his execution.

3. In Bergen, a town of 250,000 people, people expect to be able to walk ten to fifteen minutes and be in the woods.

4. There were only two people in the English department who used the elevator religiously: myself and a Brit.

5. A "spark" is a sled, but instead of lying down, one stands straight up holding onto handles that come up from the frame. Feet are placed on the runners that extend two meters out the back of the sled.

6. I am sad to see that the car is becoming more and more prominent in Norway. The consequences are depressing. The obvious pollution issues need no explaining, but the health effects of not walking will be felt. Also, because of the car, the wonderful ferries are disappearing. Norway has a broken coastline made up of thousands of islands. This island life is one of the ways Norway has preserved quiet rural living. The ferry has been the major means of connecting this water-divided country. The growing popularity of cars has brought the demand for bridges, especially in the bigger cities such as Bergen and Oslo, and consequently the ferries are disappearing. Ferries provide the morning

commuter precious quiet minutes to reflect or to socialize; the world of the car reflects the goal of mechanization: total, nonstop automation.

7. Norwegians, from an American perspective, could appear undemocratic when it comes to child protection. When a child hurt another child on the playground while imitating the Power Rangers, the show was off the air the next week. Done.

8. The other seventies bumper sticker seen everywhere was "I Found It."

9. This reputation needs to be balanced by the fact that Norway is also a nation of frequent occupations as well. Between the Middle Ages and 1905, Norway was ruled by either Sweden or Denmark. It was also, of course, occupied by the Germans during World War II. The nineteenth century saw a romantic and nationalist revival producing major figures such as Ibsen, Grieg, and Munch. Abbey mentions Grieg several times, as well as contemporary legendary figures such as Arne Naess, the founder of deep ecology.

10. He basically sees them as naive, bumbling, self-indulgent, well-meaning but finally ineffective—and wonderfully youthful.

11. Abbey comments on Gaia in language similar to his descriptions of Erika: "Gaia, green-bosomed, brown-thighed, rosy-bellied Earth" (1990, 223).

12. "Erik," however, is a common Norwegian name for a male.

13. It must be said that Abbey balances things out on this score, as he does all through the novel. The character of Virginia Dick—with her intelligence, sensitivity, strength, and round form—serves as an interesting juxtaposition to Erika.

14. Strangely enough, the scene Abbey narrates comes oddly close to what actually happened between the FBI and Earth First! "You say she likes you, we know you like her, make the most of it" (1990, 197). This is the advice given to Oral by his FBI boss. It is also what happened when an FBI agent infiltrated Earth First!, all of which ended in a federal conspiracy trial in Prescott, Arizona.

15. See my "Rethinking Resistance: Poststructuralism, Environmentalism, and Literature," in *Postmodern Environmental Ethics,* ed. Max Oelschlager (New York: SUNY Press, 1995) for a discussion of this issue.

Works Cited

Abbey, Edward. 1988. *One Life at a Time, Please.* New York: Henry Holt.

———. 1989. *A Voice Crying in the Wilderness.* New York: St. Martin's Press.

———. 1990. *Hayduke Lives!* New York: Little, Brown, and Co.

———. [1968] 1991. *Desert Solitaire: A Season in the Wilderness.* Reprint, New York: Ballantine.

———. [1956] 1992. *The Brave Cowboy.* Reprint, New York: Avon.

———. 1994. *Confessions of a Barbarian: Selections from the Journals of Edward Abbey, 1951–1989.* Ed. David Petersen. New York: Little, Brown and Co.

Bakhtin, Mikhail. [1981] 1986. "Discourse in the Novel." In *Critical Theory Since 1965,* ed. H. Adams and L. Searle. Reprint, Tallahassee: Florida State University Press.

———. [1984] 1994. *Problems of Dostoevsky's Poetics.* Reprint, Minneapolis: University of Minnesota Press.

Bishop, James. 1994. *Epitaph for a Desert Anarchist.* New York: Atheneum.

Eagleton, Terry. 1983. *Literary Theory*. Minneapolis: University of Minnesota Press.

Evernden, Neil. 1992. *The Social Creation of Nature*. Baltimore: Johns Hopkins University Press.

Le Guin, Ursula. 1974. *The Dispossessed*. New York: Avon.

Marx, Leo. 1990. "Post-Modernism and the Environmental Crisis." In *Report From the Institute for Philosophy and Public Policy*, 13–15. College Park: University of Maryland.

Nelson, Cary. 1989. *Repression and Recovery: Modern American Poetry and the Politics of Cultural Memory*. Madison: University of Wisconsin Press.

Ness, Erik. 1990. "Abbey Lode." *The Nation*, Apr. 2, 458–60.

Payne, Daniel. 1996. *Voices in the Wilderness*. Hanover, N.H.: University Press of New England.

Purchase, Graham. 1994. *Anarchism and Environmental Survival*. Tucson, Ariz.: See Sharp Press.

Ronald, Ann. 1982. *The New West of Edward Abbey*. Reno: University of Nevada Press.

Rothenberg, David, and Peter Reed, eds. 1993. *The Norwegian Roots of Deep Ecology: Wisdom in the Open Air*. Minneapolis: University of Minnesota Press.

Rowe, John Carlos. 1987. "Surplus Economies: Deconstruction, Ideology and the Humanities." In *The Aims of Representation: Subject/Text/History*, ed. Murray Krieger. New York: Columbia University Press.

Sessions, George, and Bill Duvall. 1985. *Deep Ecology: Living as if Nature Mattered*. Salt Lake City: Peregrine Smith.

Slovic, Scott. 1992. *Seeking Awareness in American Nature Writing: Henry Thoreau, Annie Dillard, Edward Abbey, Wendell Berry, Barry Lopez*. Salt Lake City: University of Utah Press.

Webster, Duncan. 1988. *Looka Yonder!: The Imaginary America of Populist Culture*. London/New York: Routledge.

The Politics of Leisure

"Industrial Tourism" in Edward Abbey's Desert Solitaire

JAMES A.

PAPA, JR.

Since the latter half of the nineteenth century, America's national parks and wilderness areas have played an important role in American culture.[1] There is, perhaps, no greater symbol of American leisure than the national park system.[2] When Yellowstone, America's first national park, was established in 1872, "it was as 'a public park or pleasuring ground for the benefit and enjoyment of the people'" (Tilden 1968, 20). The creation of a good number of other well-known parks, including Yosemite (1890), Grand Canyon (1908), Zion (1909), and Glacier (1910), in the decades surrounding the turn of the century only strengthened the nation's belief in the redemptive value of such places.[3] Today, in an increasingly crowded and hectic world where the individual is ever more reined in by bureaucratic, social, and governmental restrictions, the parks, despite the pressures and injuries of overuse, continue to offer "the average person . . . the feeling of elbowroom, bigness, far horizon, freedom" (Tilden 1968, 7).[4] Such feelings help to maintain not only the psychological health of individual visitors, but to keep alive some semblance of the original frontier conditions that shaped the mythical American identity in our arts and popular culture.[5] The parks also provide the possibility for a sense of communion or kinship with nature (Tilden 1968, 15). Unfortunately, what seem like good enough reasons for the public's love affair with America's national parks are also the cause of some of the greatest threats to the park system— overuse and misuse.[6] This last point is at the heart of Edward Abbey's pugnacious critique of American society's relationship to nature in *Desert Solitaire* (1968).

Edward Abbey (1927–89)—novelist, radical environmentalist, and author of numerous books and articles on the wilderness and the American Southwest—is best known as the author of *Desert Solitaire: A Season in the Wilderness* and *The Monkey Wrench Gang* (1975), the latter a novel promoting militant environmentalism in defense of nature and the wilderness. *Desert Solitaire*, Abbey's fourth book, is a *Walden*-like account of his time spent living alone in the Utah desert while working as a National Park Service ranger at Arches National Monument. *Desert Solitaire*, like Thoreau's *Walden* (1854), relies on example and experience as much as argument to illustrate and defend its philosophy. Most of the themes that were to preoccupy Abbey throughout his career as a writer—the moral responsibility and integrity of the individual; the intrinsic value of nature and wilderness; and the environmental, social, and spiritual damage wrought by blind faith in technological advancement and capitalist consumption—find their first clear articulation in *Desert Solitaire*. While these concerns are obviously echoes of Thoreau's thought in *Walden,* calling Abbey a disciple of Thoreau, as many are inclined to do, is not without problems. Like all disciples, Abbey might be said to borrow liberally from Thoreau and even to find his roots in Thoreau's work, but Abbey's message is his own, directed toward and derivative of his own time, and tempered by the consequences and circumstances of his own existence.

Abbey's love of the American desert can be traced back to his first acquaintance with the canyon country at the age of seventeen, when he hitchhiked across the country to California before going off to serve in the army during World War II. On his return to the family farm in the Appalachian Mountains of Pennsylvania, his route took him through the desert regions of the Southwest, where he was taken by the wonder and beauty of the landscape. Like the scholar and nature writer Joseph Wood Krutch (author of *The Desert Year* and *The Voice of the Desert,* and a favorite of Abbey's), Abbey recognized in the desert something akin to a spiritual home. After the war, with the help of the G.I. Bill, Abbey enrolled at the University of New Mexico in 1947. There he studied philosophy and took up what was to be a lifetime residence in the Southwest, punctuated by a few brief stints in the East. His best work chronicles and explores the relationship between the desert landscape and his inner being. Believing as he does that wild places are "vital" to the health of the "human spirit," as well as to "the principle of civilization itself" (1968, 192), much of Abbey's work is directed toward preserving the desert and other wilderness areas. Ironically, Abbey would keep man out of the wilderness in order that he might be able to enter and be saved by it.

Before going further, it must be noted that while *Desert Solitaire* is commonly categorized as nonfiction (it is an autobiographical work), the structure of the book in terms of its time frame is a literary invention. As in *Walden,* the events of several years are collapsed into one, with the exception of obvious digressions in the text referring to past happenings. Because of this, both the narration and the narrator may, strictly considered, be thought of as fictional fabrications. For this reason, conflating the author of the text with the narrator might raise epistemological objections on the part of some contemporary critics whose theoretical paradigms do not allow for such readings. In the case of this study, however, which is concerned primarily with Abbey's views on public use of wilderness areas and national parks, the author and the narrator of *Desert Solitaire* will be considered one and the same. Given the understanding that the text's autobiographical nature has been restructured in order to accommodate the narrative's aesthetic considerations, and that the ideas expressed find frequent reiteration in Abbey's later essay collections, such a reading should not raise any significant problems in terms of the issues under discussion here.

Desert Solitaire opens with Abbey's arrival in Arches National Monument as a ranger. The park is still relatively undeveloped.[7] It lacks many of the amenities present in the more popular and better-known parks at that time—amenities that in the backcountry might be characterized as luxuries, such as flush toilets and showers. Arches is also under-utilized by the public as far as those in the park system's bureaucracy are concerned, especially those in the upper echelons. The park system bureaucrats favor further improvements in order to encourage, as well as meet rising demands for, use of the parks (and, one might suspect, to protect their jobs and whatever possible opportunities for advancement development of the parks might provide). As Abbey explains it: "To all accusations of excessive development the administrators can reply, as they will if pressed hard enough, that they are giving the public what it wants, that their primary duty is to serve the public not preserve the wilds. 'Parks are for People' is the public relation slogan, which decoded means that parks are for people in automobiles" (1968, 58). But at the moment the park is still unimproved, and this suits Abbey just fine, since the "under-utilization" of the park and its lack of any real infrastructure are responsible for the relative ease and freedom of his job: "it's a good job. On the rare occasions when I peer into the future for more than a few days I can foresee myself returning here for season after season, year after year, indefinitely. And why not? What better sinecure could a man with small needs, infinite desires, and philosophical pretensions ask for?" (45).

Yet Abbey knows that things will inevitably change for the worse due to "progress," the inevitable transformation of the park in order to accommodate not just people, but people in automobiles:

> . . . there is a cloud on my horizon. A small dark cloud no bigger than my hand. Its name is progress.
>
> The ease and relative freedom of this lovely job at Arches follow from the comparative absence of the motorized tourists, who stay away by the millions. And they stay away because of the unpaved entrance road, the unflushable toilets in the campgrounds, and the fact that most of them have never even heard of Arches National Monument. (Could there be a more genuine testimonial to its beauty and integrity?) All this must change. (48)

Those in the Park Service above Abbey, and even many close to his own level, do not share his fondness for Thoreau's observation in *Walden* that "a man is rich in proportion to the number of things which he can afford to let alone" (1966, 55). They are determined to transform the backwards park into a future commercial success. The engineers that come to survey the route of a new road through the park, and who lay the groundwork for its eventual destruction by doing so, cannot fathom Abbey's inability to grasp the ultimate benefit of what they are doing. The conversation that occurs between Abbey and the chief of the engineering party underscores the inability of each to understand the other's position:

> Look, the party chief explained, you *need* this road. He was a pleasant-mannered, soft-spoken civil engineer with an unquestioning dedication to his work. A very dangerous man. Who needs it? I said; we get very few tourists in this park. That's why you need it, the engineer explained patiently; look, he said, when

this road is built you'll get ten, twenty, thirty times as many tourists in here as you get now. His men nodded in solemn agreement, and he stared at me intently, waiting to see what possible answer I could have to that.

. . . I had an answer all right but I was saving it for later. I knew that I was dealing with a madman. (50)

What Abbey is "dealing with" here is the same kind of men that horrified Thoreau in *Walden*—men who "think it essential that the *Nation* have commerce, and export ice, and talk through a telegraph, and ride thirty miles an hour, without a doubt, whether they do or not" (1966, 62). These are men who believe in the traditional Western notion of progress,[8] and who are particularly fond of building roads. But "thirty miles an hour" has become sixty-five miles an hour by the time Abbey takes up residence in Arches National Monument, and Abbey is more than a little justified in his grim predictions regarding the park's future, informing us that what he feared has in fact come true: "As I type these words, several years after the little episode of the gray jeep and the thirsty engineers, all that was foretold has come to pass. Arches National Monument has been developed" (1968, 51).[9]

Other parks that had already succumbed to traditional American notions of progress were hardly the better for it in Abbey's eyes. Like many preservationists, Abbey believes that "motors" and other products of industrial society "don't belong in . . . remote and wild place[s]; that they betray the idea of man immersed in nature and bring industrialization to a place whose meaning inheres in its isolation from, and contrast to, life in society" (Sax 1980, 12–13). Abbey's feeling in *Desert Solitaire* is that the parks are decidedly *not* "for people," at least not for people in automobiles who must bring into the parks with them every modern convenience.

The sad and sobering truth is that by the time of *Desert Solitaire*'s publication, and for several years preceding it, a number of the most spectacular and once wild parks had been transformed, at least in the immediate areas surrounding their most popular attractions, into nothing less than disorderly carnivals of people who seemed unable to appreciate the wilderness except as a backdrop to a congested campground.[10] The same fate ultimately befalls Abbey's beloved Arches some years after his final departure. "[T]he little campground where [he] used to putter around reading three-day-old newspapers full of lies and watermelon seeds" is eventually transformed into "one master campground that looks, during the busy season, like a suburban village," complete with the "blue glow of television" and "the studio laughter of Los Angeles" (1968, 51). Still, Abbey's love for Arches National Monument leads him to do whatever he can to save the desert from the onslaught of civilization. And so, following the departure of the engineering crew, "for about five miles [he] followed the course of their survey back toward headquarters, and as [he] went. . .pulled up each little stake and threw it away, and cut all the bright ribbons from the bushes and hid them under a rock" (67).

If the act is a "futile" but "feel good" gesture (67), it is also a symbolic and inspiring, if not wholly efficacious, example of what Terrel Dixon (1991) refers to as "ecotage (that is, sabotage in the service of ecological values" (35). More important, what Abbey does, however futile, goes beyond anything ever thought or done by Thoreau, who many consider Abbey's spiritual mentor. Thoreau's fervent opposition to society's mad thirst for material wealth and comfort never developed into anything beyond literary rhetoric or a somewhat eccentric lifestyle. In all of *Walden* there is not one instance even vaguely comparable to Abbey's sabotaging the survey route. Such a distinction illustrates a critical juncture between Abbey and Thoreau. By engaging in behavior meant to slow the expansion of the technocratic military-industrial complex into the remaining wilderness areas, Abbey steps outside the bounds of his individual existence to act in defense of something besides his own idealized notions of how life should be lived. In pulling up the survey stakes, he becomes the militant guardian of a natural world that appears defenseless against the onslaught of industrial civilization. More than that, Abbey's "futile" gesture is a supremely eloquent example of an existential act on the part of a solitary individual. It offers Abbey, and the reader as well, both meaning and the momentary illusion of hope in a world ruled by disassociated bureaucracies.

If Thoreau was incapable of such an act, it may be in part because his time did not demand one. His failure to take an active and subversive role against man's intrusions into the wilderness is understandable, if still lamentable, given the fact that wilderness may have yet seemed an inexhaustible commodity in mid-nineteenth-century America. However, Thoreau also suffered from a preoccupation with his own self and life, which may have prevented him from identifying with the natural world to the extent that Abbey does. Abbey's passionate love of the desert leads to a possessiveness not seen in Thoreau, whose fondness for Walden Pond never seems to go beyond mere affection. Thoreau feels no need to derail the train that runs by Walden Pond because he does not perceive the railroad as a threat to the pond's beauty and wonder. Nor does he see the defilement of nature as a danger to his own psyche or being in the way that Abbey does. On the contrary, Thoreau's inability to foresee the future implications of the developments of his own time allows him to celebrate the locomotive's strength, power, and nobility: "when I hear the iron horse make the hills echo with his snort like thunder, shaking the earth with his feet, and breathing fire and smoke from his nostrils . . . it seems as if the earth had got a race now worthy to inhabit it" (1966, 78).

Abbey, on the other hand, living as he does in the nuclear/space age, must suffer the despair and frustration that come with knowing that time and distance are no longer adequate defenses against the exponential nature of industrial growth. He cannot afford the kind of romantic sentiment Thoreau sometimes exhibits in his musing about the railroad. Thoreau, living in the relatively stable period of the mid-nineteenth century, lacked the ability to see ahead of his age—a gift of prophecy denied humankind until the invention of the atomic bomb, which forced humanity to confront the possible, and perhaps instantaneous, destruction of the world. The railroad, like most everything in *Walden,* is simply grist for tropes. The deeper implications of the railroad as a technological assault on the landscape and the culture of nineteenth-century America are lost on Thoreau.

This much being understood, the exhortation in *Desert Solitaire*'s introduction to "throw [the text] at something big and glassy" (Abbey 1968, xii) (the image suggests a modern corporate structure) encourages the reader to pull up some survey stakes of his own, so to speak, and provides a founding rationale for the more radical ecological warfare celebrated in *The Monkey Wrench Gang* (1975), a slight hint of which is foreshadowed in *Desert Solitaire* when Abbey imagines "some unknown hero with a rucksack full of dynamite" blowing up the future Glen Canyon Dam (188). Whereas *Walden* might be considered a retreat from society's assault upon (human) nature, *Desert Solitaire* is anything but. The fact that as a ranger Abbey is dutifully employed to "protect, preserve, and defend all living things within the park boundaries" (20) reinforces the text's confrontational tone, albeit in a subversive manner, since as a ranger Abbey also represents the Park Service itself, which is behind the proposed development of Arches.

While Abbey's removal of survey stakes may appear nothing more than a symbolic protest, the act's relevance is magnified given the time-worn controversy concerning the issue of public access in the national park system, as well as in other remaining wilderness areas in America. The question of access is at the core of Abbey's "Polemic" in chapter 5, since it relates directly to questions of use and conservation, and "[a]lmost every decision affecting the parks involves the balancing of preservation and use values" (Everhart 1983, 47).

Abbey's actions are in direct opposition to the dominant cultural forces concerning economic issues related to the national park system, ranging from the securement of funds to create and maintain the parks, to the need for—and the profitability of—private concessions operating within the parks. Suffice it to say, the position of Congress, independent of shifts in Park Service philosophy at various times, has consistently been one of securing for the people what we might call a practical return on their investment. Perhaps nowhere is this sentiment so clearly expressed as in an account of the passage of the Wilderness Act of 1964:

> According to the record, those who voted for the legislation did so with the understanding that wilderness would be open to extensive use. Frank Church, floor manager of the bill when it passed the Senate, later explained: " . . . it was not the intent of Congress that wilderness be administered in so pure a fashion as to needlessly restrict their customary public use and enjoyment. Quite to the contrary, Congress fully intended that wilderness should be managed to allow its use by a wide spectrum of Americans." (Everhart 1983, 99)

Such a stance on the part of Congress echoes rather clearly the philosophy of Stephen T. Mather, the first director of the Park Service.[11] Mather saw "growth," in terms of recreational use by the public, as necessary to the "ultimate security of the parks" in their early days, when their future existence was seriously challenged by " 'exploitive' enemies" such as timber and mining interests. For Mather, the survival and growth of the national parks was dependent on "a swelling, grass-roots popularity . . . among the American people," who upon coming to "understand and appreciate the parks . . . would . . . rise to protect and cherish them" (see Demars 1991, 85). The fifty years or so following Mather's administration of the parks saw a rather enthusiastic effort on the part of the Park Service to accomplish this goal. It was not until the 1970s and the growing awareness of ecological and environmental concerns that the Park Service began to abandon Mather's vision in favor of formulating a new policy that would actually set about to reverse what had, in many cases, become crises of overdevelopment.[12]

At the time of Abbey's tenure in Arches National Monument, a number of national parks in the immediate vicinity had, ironically, already fallen victim to overdevelopment and so-called improvement while under the protective wing of the Park Service.

> Lee's Ferry. Until a few years ago a simple, quiet, primitive place on the shore's of the Colorado, Lee's Ferry has now fallen under the protection of the Park Service. And who can protect it against the Park Service? Powerlines now bisect the scene; a 100-foot pink water tower looms against the red cliffs; tract-style houses are built to house the "protectors"; natural campsites along the river are closed off while all campers are now herded into an artificial steel-and-asphalt "campground" in the hottest, windiest spot in the area; historic buildings are razed by bulldozers to save the expense of maintaining them while at the same time hundreds of thousands of dollars are spent on an unneeded paved entrance road. And the administrators complain of vandalism. (Abbey 1968, 53–54)

Because of such profane assaults on national parks and wilderness areas, Abbey proposes his own designs regarding the public's use of them, designs diametrically opposed to those of Congress and the average armchair American partial to such niceties of life as air-conditioning and Winnebagos—people Abbey refers to with disdain as "Industrial Tourists" (58). At the core of Abbey's "Polemic" in *Desert Solitaire* is a policy restricting motor vehicles of all kinds from entering the parks.[13] Abbey, vehemently opposed in principle to the internal-combustion engine as an emblem of progress, believes it a grave threat to the parks: "The developers insist that the parks must be made fully accessible not only to the people but also to their machines . . . automobiles, motorboats, etc. The preservers argue, in principle at least, that wilderness and motors are incompatible, and that the former can best be experienced, understood, and enjoyed when the machines are left behind where they belong" (55).

Most preservationists would agree with Abbey that the internal combustion engine is a threat to the flora and fauna, as well as the actual physical topography, of the national parks and wilderness areas. They also consider it a threat to the subjective enjoyment of these places by those who seek to experience the original atmosphere of the land. In some cases, such an appreciation of the parks has already been severely impacted, even by automobiles and industrial forces operating far outside their boundaries.[14] In a land where the only thing one should smell is "juniper smoke, [which] like the perfume of sagebrush after rain, evokes in magical catalysis, like certain music, the space and light and clarity and piercing strangeness of the American West" (13), the desert visitor instead is forced to breathe air that at times smells curiously like the rush-hour smog of Los Angeles, Denver, or any other Western city.[15] Like Thoreau, who in his more reflective moments would not have his "eyes put out" and his "ears spoiled" by the locomotive's "smoke and steam and hissing" (1966, 83), Abbey could do well enough without such a disturbance.

Thoreau urged his readers to "simplify" their wants (62). Abbey, up against a society squarely entrenched in its material ways, would have people do the same. The average park visitor, unwilling to give up his modern conveniences, remains estranged from the natural world, no matter how close he may come to it:

> The motorized tourists, reluctant to give up the old ways, will complain that they can't see enough without their automobiles to bear them swiftly (traffic permitting) through the parks. But this is nonsense. A man on foot, a man on horseback or on a bicycle will see more, feel more, enjoy more in one mile than the motorized tourists can in a hundred miles. Better to idle through one park in two weeks than try to race through a dozen in the same amount of time. Those who are familiar with both modes of travel know from experience that this is true; the rest have only to make the experiment to discover the same truth for themselves. (1968, 61–62)

But that which appears at first glance to be a more efficient and economical means of travel is, on second glance, seen in a very different manner. The perceived rewards of industrial progress are nothing but illusions, which rather than enriching our lives actually impoverish them. In *Walden,* Thoreau defines the economic cost of a railroad ticket not in terms of dollars and cents but in terms of the time necessary to earn the money to purchase one. For him, time is the only commodity of any real worth, and its value is determined by the way in which it is used. Building and riding upon the railroad, as well as laboring to earn the money for a ticket, are poor uses of a man's time if they do not improve that portion of a man's life that they take up: "As with our colleges, so with a hundred 'modern improvements'; there is an illusion about them; there is not always a positive advance. The devil goes on extracting compound interest to the last for his early share and numerous succeeding investments in them. Our inventions are wont to be pretty toys, which distract our attention from serious things. They are but improved means to an unimproved end" (1966, 35).

Thoreau was not so foolish as the better number of his contemporaries as to be taken in by the supposed advantages of the railway. Declaring himself "wiser than that," he "learned that the swiftest traveler is he that goes afoot" (35). It isn't just that traveling by foot will bring him to a given destination sooner—all things taken into consideration—but that he will arrive at a different destination altogether. This is the whole point behind the "experiment" at Walden Pond. The "experiment" is not so much to find a way, for instance, to secure the particular necessities of life, material or otherwise, but to determine what those necessities are: "I went to the woods because I wished to live deliberately, to front only the essential facts of life, and see if I could not learn what it had to teach" (61). Thoreau's contemporaries in their railway cars, speeding through the woods on their way to and from Boston—catching only fragmentary glimpses of the world as they go, and hearing, smelling, and touching none of it—are no better off than the tourists in America's national parks a hundred years later who cannot be "pry[ed] . . . out of their . . . backbreaking upholstered mechanized wheelchairs and onto their feet, onto the strange warmth and solidity of Mother Earth" (Abbey 1968, 59). They have no sense of the true worth of the world or of their lives as gifts of time.

Abbey would have the industrial tourists abandon their vehicles if they are to get any real return on their travels through the desert. The park system, however, is designed to encourage the use of the automobile. Its very existence, as well as its growth and success, stems from and is ultimately dependent upon the popularity and the continued affordability of the automobile in America, especially as concerns the middle class (see Demars 1991, 112). In their automobiles, industrial tourists can retire to lands far from their backyards for little more than the cost of gas and time behind the wheel (Abbey 1968, 58). But this new freedom, and the whole infrastructure set up to make it possible—the creation of interstate highways, as well as concessions within the parks, including gas stations, that cater to automobiles—are in the end nothing more than a transference to the wilderness of just those things the industrial tourist would declare that he wishes to escape: "But the chief victims of the [industrial tourism] system are the motorized tourists. They are being robbed and robbing themselves. So long as they are unwilling to crawl out of their cars they will not discover the treasures of the national parks and will never escape the stress and turmoil of the urban-suburban complexes which they had hoped, presumably, to leave behind for a while" (59). All those things Abbey considers most valuable about the desert—those physical phenomena that render such an impact on human spiritual nature—remain inaccessible for the tourist in an automobile. Thus Abbey's call to redesign the parks to preclude the need for automobiles: "[w]hatever the cost, however financed, the benefits for park visitors in health and happiness—virtues unknown to the statisticians—would be immeasurable" (65).

The problem is that Abbey is up against a cultural legacy in which there is nothing out there in the parks of any real value except what can be *seen,* and much of that easily and from a distance. "Monumentalism, not environmentalism, was the driving force" behind the creation of most national parks, and remained the predominant rationale for setting aside large portions of the public trust at the time of Abbey's employment at Arches National Monument (Runte 1979, 29). Even those topographical areas deemed to have some sort of value as landscapes had to be proven economically "worthless" before they could be set aside as parks. The charters of most national parks continue to allow for economic development (mining, forestry, or agricultural use) within the parks if and when such development is found to be feasible or in the natural interest (48–64).

For Abbey, the value of the land goes far beyond visual or aesthetic qualities. Though these matter greatly to him, the more important point is that the desert allows individuals the opportunity to explore various aesthetic and sensual experiences as a direct result of a physical, and often solitary, confrontation with the natural world. Any true understanding of the desert's treasures can only be achieved—purchased, if you will—through physical endeavor. This is, of course, a modification of the observation made by Thoreau in *Walden* that by cutting his own logs for firewood they "warmed [him] twice, once while [he] was splitting them, and again when they were on the fire" (1966, 167).[16] For Abbey, the ultimate aesthetic payoff of the desert is inversely related to the difficulty involved in achieving it. Abbey's reflection on a long and arduous trek up a side canyon in pursuit of Rainbow Bridge while on a raft trip down soon to be dammed Glen Canyon makes this clear:

> Those who see it after [the canyon is dammed] will not understand that half the beauty of Rainbow Bridge lay in its remoteness, its relative difficulty of access, and in the wilderness surrounding it, of which it was an integral part. When these aspects are removed the Bridge will be no more than an isolated geological oddity, an extension of that museum-like diorama to which industrial tourism tends to reduce the world. 'All things excellent are as difficult as they are rare,' said a wise man. . . . (1968, 217)

The "wise man" referred to here is, of course, Thoreau, who understood that experience is all, and that what we seek is often less important than the manner in which we seek it. Abbey is not a pure ascetic; he does not deny himself what he wants, and he is in the last analysis a sensualist. The same might be said of Thoreau, who is after all in pursuit of "treasures," albeit not purely material ones, as his reference to Matthew 6:19 attests (1966, 3). Thoreau's admonishment that "a man is rich in proportion to the number of things he can afford to let alone" (55) is not a call to poverty, if that poverty be of the spirit. Nor is Thoreau calling for material poverty. Consummation of one's desires is the goal, and not the bane, of life if those desires be wise ones springing from our true nature.[17] What Abbey and Thoreau would have us shun is the easy pursuit of false treasures whose attainment demands nothing of us and leaves us no better off than we were in terms of our humanity or spiritual development.

In our contemporary consumer society, the pecuniary cost of a thing is more often than not the primary factor in determining its worth. We shy away from and discount ascetic endeavors that might reveal something to us about who we really are and where we are going; for the most part, denial and sacrifice have no cultural appeal. How something is attained is infinitely less important than what is acquired. For most Americans, means and ends no longer have any relation to each other, while for Abbey and Thoreau, the relationship between the two is obviously grist for spiritual growth.

For Abbey, the ultimate challenge of the desert is physical and several chapters in *Desert Solitaire* relate in great detail a number of quests that depend ultimately on both physical courage and ability: Abbey's harrowing escape from a side canyon in Havasu, his solitary ascent of Mt. Tukuhnikvats, and his descent into the Maze, a no-man's land of unexplored canyons, with Robert Waterman. Even his quest for the moon-eyed Horse centers on the varying abilities of horse and man to endure the desert heat. Man does not belong in the desert. It is, Abbey writes, "a land of surprises, some of them terrible surprises. Terrible as derived from terror" (1968, 132). The absence of water in any great quantity is a continual reminder of the alien nature of the desert, and yet there are solitary and driven individuals willing to risk their lives in pursuit of its spiritual appeal. It is this potentially high cost, the actual risk to one's own life, that invests so much value in what one finds.[18] Even the Western writer Zane Grey—a popular writer whom Abbey, in a quick aside, knocks for throwing up "dust clouds" that obscured the desert's "baffling reality"—shared his deeper sentiments, believing also that the beauty and uniqueness of such curiosities as Rainbow Bridge were greatly enhanced by their remote location and the physical challenge presented to those who wished to see them. Said Grey, "[t]he tourist, the leisurely traveler, the comfort loving motorist would never behold it. Only by toil, sweat, endurance, and pain could any man ever look at [Rainbow Bridge]. It seemed well to realize that the great things of life had to be earned" (qtd. in Everhart 1983, 48).

It is a matter of supply and demand. Those things that few can or will see because of the actual physical difficulties involved in reaching them, or a suitable observation point, are inherently more valuable. To do away with the physical obstacles, or reduce in any substantial way the capabilities or time needed to reach places such as Rainbow Bridge so that "what was formerly an adventure" is turned "into a routine motorboat excursion" (1968, 217) is to devalue both the object and the experience.[19] The object, once a wonder of the wilderness, will lose whatever true aesthetic or spiritual value it may have held the minute it is overrun by industrial tourists and left awash in "gum wrappers, cigarette butts, and bottlecaps" (214). Like any commodity put into mass production, the value of Rainbow Bridge will decline, though in the case of industrial tourism, it isn't the object per se that is mass produced (there is, after all, only one Rainbow Bridge) but the opportunity to experience the object. Abbey, the "14,467th" visitor to Rainbow Bridge "since the first white men . . . in 1909" (217), knows that when the canyon is flooded and easily accessible by boat, that many more will come in a day, and one more "veil of mystery" will be stripped forever from the face of the desert.[20] There will be no difference in value between the real Rainbow Bridge and the one available on a postcard.

The same holds true for the desert wilderness as a whole. Development and access mean the destruction of those intangible qualities that make wilderness what it is and that, once lost, lie beyond reclamation. Without the wilderness as "medium," even the idea of wilderness and the qualities it engenders may lie beyond "evocation" (Abbey 1968, x). The true cost of a thing is not always known at first. It often isn't revealed until we've taken full possession of the thing we thought we wanted and cannot divest ourselves of it. In Abbey's eyes, Americans have traded the possibility of a deep encounter with the desert, the ancient and traditional home of spiritual mystics, for a more superficial meeting contained by the comfort and convenience of modern existence. We have traded foot trails and deep solitude for paved roads and panoramic views through the windshields of air-conditioned automobiles. The bargain is a bad one.

Notes

1. "The national park idea set forth in the legislation establishing Yellowstone National Park in 1872 decreed that some of our natural inheritance should be preserved in perpetuity for other than material gain and riches. This novel idea in public land policy is a unique contribution of the United States to world culture. It has inspired more than one hundred nations around the world to set aside national parks and similar preserves" (Hartzog 1988, 10–11). As Dyan Zaslowsky also notes, "the creation of natural national parks ranks among the few thoroughly American contributions to world culture." The importance of America's remaining wilderness areas and open spaces to foreigners as well as to Americans must not be underestimated (Zaslowsky 1986, 9). America's attempt to afford citizens access to nature is not limited to national parks and wilderness areas alone. For a historical overview of the creation of the city park in America, see Barth 1990, 123–80.

2. Unfortunately, America's national parks have historically been under-utilized by ethnic minorities and continue to be so (Goldsmith 1994, 20–21).

3. See Zaslowsky 1986, 18–19.

4. While the first parks may have been set aside for their "spectacular land-scapes" and their wildness, the system today embraces a number of parks that celebrate human accomplishments as well as nature (Zaslowsky 1996, 10). Horace Albright, the second director of the Park Service, following Stephen T. Mather, had much to do with the early Park Service's decision to acquire and preserve historical and cultural sites (Zaslowsky 1996, 28; Albright 1985, 30, 188, 243–44).

5. See Clough 1964, 143–52. Seen in this sense, one can understand Free-man Tilden's view of the national parks as "national museums" whose "purpose is to *preserve* . . . the wilderness that greeted the eyes of the first white men who challenged and conquered it" (1968, 22). There is a present absence, however, of a number of dangers central to any true conception of wilderness as carried over to America from Europe (notwithstanding, for instance, the presence of grizzly bears in Western parks)—those things that would reduce man to a "brutish existence" (Zaslowsky 1996, 3). For a fuller discussion of the Western concept of wilderness as it relates to the American pioneers, see Nash 1982, 1–43.

6. Only a decade or so after *Desert Solitaire*'s publication 1968, the explo-sive popularity of the national parks, and the government's refusal to allocate adequate funds for their administration (despite its penchant for the improve-ment of existing parks), had reduced the national parks to a state of "near col-lapse" (Soucie 1976, 123–28). The government's continual failure to provide enough financial support for the national parks has been a problem from the very beginning, when "[w]ith the easy establishment of Yellowstone, Congress inaugurated the dubious tradition of creating a park without appropriating money for its protection" (Zaslowsky 1996, 15). The National Park Service it-self was not created until 1916.

7. In chronicling his seasonal career with the Park Service, Edward Abbey refers to Arches National Park as "then quite a primitive place" (1979, 153).

8. Abbey defines "progress" not as the continual invention and implemen-tation of new and improved technology but as "the tortuous advance toward the idea of civilization," with civilization understood to be "a form of human society in which the primary values are openness, diversity, tolerance, personal liberty, reason," and where "the natural world must be treated as an equal part-ner" (1988, 179–80).

9. In his later work Abbey bemoans the fact that "Arches National Monu-ment . . . has become a travesty called Arches National Park—a static diorama seen through [windshield] glass" (1984, xv–xvi).

10. Yosemite, one of the most famous of the national parks, had as early as 1966 been reduced to little more than a large suburban backyard party, "heavy with a pall of eye-watering smoke . . . cut by the blare of transistor radios, the clatter of pots and pans, the roar [of motorcycles], and the squeals of teenagers" (Everhart 1983, 61).

11. Mather's efforts in helping to establish the National Park Service, and his success in increasing the number of parks during his directorship,

cannot be praised enough. However, his views on the necessity of commercial development within the parks by private concessionaires as well as his decision "to allow automobiles into the parks" paved the way for the kind of "improvements" so distasteful to Abbey (see Zaslowsky 1996, 24).

12. For a fuller discussion of the Park Service's reevaluation of Mather's philosophy, see Demars 1991, chap. 6.

13. An exception would be Ansel Adams's favorable comments regarding the automobile's introduction into Yosemite Valley in the early 1900s. Adams remarked in an interview that the introduction of the automobile into Yosemite was a blessing, not a curse, and declared that after sixty years of observing and photographing the park, it was "more beautiful than it's ever been," despite the incredible increase in the number of visitors over the years (see Everhart 1983, 71). For a brief discussion of the less pristine condition of Yosemite Valley prior to its creation as a national park, when it served as an agricultural resource for the state of California, which then administered the valley, and on its later restoration, on which the above quote bears, see Everhart 1983, 71–72, as well as Demars 1991, 48–51.

14. "For one hundred days a year the view from the rim of the Grand Canyon is obscured by haze from nearby power plants and smelters and by pollutants from urban centers. 'We thought we were leaving smog in Denver,' wrote one visitor in the Arches complaint register. 'What's that chemical smell in the air?' asked another" (Everhart 1983, 80). An in-depth account of the legislative history concerning the specific problem of impaired visibility in the national parks can be found in Freemuth 1991, 85–130. For a discussion of external threats to the national parks in general, see Zaslowsky 1996, 42–46.

15. For an interesting discussion of how preservationist forces have actually worsened the damaging effects of air pollution stemming from power plants on several national parks, due to their efforts to keep hydroelectric plants out of the canyons, see Runte 1979, 184–85.

16. Thoreau makes a similar statement in his *Journal:* "What I obtain with the most labor—the most water-logged and heaviest wood which I fish up from the bottom and split and dry—warms the most. The greater, too, the distance from which I have conveyed it, the more I am warmed by it in my thought" (1975, 24).

17. Joan Burbick (1986) argues that the work of Emily Dickinson betrays a nineteenth-century preoccupation with the constraint of desire and, in particular, sexual desire, where the denial of immediate pleasure or satisfaction in love is actually a source of spiritual enrichment or wealth. Of a particular voice in Dickinson's work, Burbick writes: "The consumption of what is desired is continually deferred and the activity of striving acquires value over the satisfaction of obtaining the goal" (368). "The activity of not-having can . . . gain such importance that it begins to rival consumption. Each denial builds the prize to such proportions that actual possession pales in relation to the struggle to acquire" (369). Thoreau shows no penchant for denial; acquisition is all. What matters to Thoreau is the means for discovering what one truly wants or needs and how to set about getting it. His paring away of the nonessential is not denial, though it is often misunderstood as such. The same may be said of Abbey.

18. Sax sees this value in terms of experiential intensity: "The kind of encounter [with the wilderness] that routinely takes place in the modern motor-

ized vehicle, or in the managed, prepackaged resort, is calculated to diminish such intensity of experience. Nothing distinctive about us as individuals is crucial. The margin of error permitted is great enough to neutralize the importance of what we know. If we roar off in the wrong direction, we can easily roar back again, for none of our energy is expended. It isn't important to pay close attention to the weather; we are insulated from it. We need not notice a small spring; we are not at the margin where water counts. The opportunity for intensity of experience is drained away" (1980, 31).

19. For a fuller discussion by Abbey of the eventual environmental and economic outcomes resulting from construction of the Glen Canyon Dam, see Abbey 1984, 95–103.

20. For a brief illustration of the ways in which Abbey's prophecy has come to pass, see Reiger 1977, 114–24.

Works Cited

Abbey, Edward. 1968. *Desert Solitaire: A Season in the Wilderness*. New York: McGraw-Hill.

———. 1975. *The Monkey Wrench Gang*. New York: Avon.

———. 1977. *The Journey Home: Some Words in Defense of the American West*. New York: E. P. Dutton.

———. 1979. *Abbey's Road*. New York: E. P. Dutton.

———. 1984. *Beyond the Wall: Essays from the Outside*. New York: Holt, Rinehart and Winston.

———. 1988. *One Life at a Time, Please*. New York: Henry Holt.

Albright, Horace. 1985. *The Birth of the National Park Service: The Founding Years, 1913–33*. Salt Lake City and Chicago: Howe Bros.

Barth, Gunther. 1990. *Fleeting Moments: Nature and Culture in American History*. New York: Oxford University Press.

Burbick, Joan. 1986. "Emily Dickinson and the Economics of Desire." *American Literature* 58:361–78.

Clough, Wilson O. 1964. *The Necessary Earth: Nature and Solitude in American Literature*. Austin: University of Texas Press.

Demars, Stanford E. 1991. *The Tourist in Yosemite*. Salt Lake City: University of Utah Press.

Dixon, Terrel. 1991. "Abbey's Biocentric Epiphany: *Desert Solitaire* and the Teaching of Environmental Literature." *Critic* 54 (1): 35–42.

Everhart, William C. 1983. *The National Park Service*. Boulder, Colo.: Westview.

Freemuth, John C. 1991. *Islands under Siege: National Parks and the Politics of External Threats*. Lawrence: University Press of Kansas.

Hartzog, George B., Jr. 1988. *Battling for the National Parks*. Mt. Kisco, N.Y.: Moyer Bell.

Lee, David. 1994. "Breaking the Sound Barrier." *National Parks* (July–Aug.): 25–29.

Marx, Leo. 1988. *The Pilot and the Passenger: Essays on Literature, Technology, and Culture in the United States*. New York: Oxford University Press.

Milstein, Michael. 1993. "Roads to Ruin." *National Parks* (Sept.–Oct.): 29–33.

Nash, Roderick. 1982. *Wilderness and the American Mind.* 3d ed. New Haven, Conn.: Yale University Press.

Paul, Sherman. 1962. *Thoreau: A Collection of Critical Essays.* Englewood Cliffs, N.J.: Prentice-Hall.

Reiger, George. 1977. "The Trammeling of Rainbow Bridge." *Audubon* (Nov.): 114–24.

Ruess, Everett. 1983. *A Vagabond for Beauty.* Ed. W. L. Rusko. Salt Lake City, Utah: Peregrine Smith.

Runte, Alfred. 1979. *National Parks: The American Experience.* Lincoln: University of Nebraska Press.

Sax, Joseph L. 1980. *Mountains without Handrails.* Ann Arbor: University of Michigan Press.

"Snowmobiles and the National Parks." 1972. *American Forests* (Apr.): 28–31.

Soucie, Gary. 1976. "More People, Less Priority, National Parks Near Collapse." *Audubon* (July): 123–28.

Thoreau, Henry David. 1966. *Walden and Civil Disobedience.* Ed. Owen Thomas. Reprint, New York: Norton.

———. 1975. *The Selected Works of Henry Thoreau.* Ed. Walter Harding. Boston: Houghton Mifflin.

Tilden, Freeman. 1968. *The National Parks.* New York: Knopf.

Whitman, Walt. 1973. *Leaves of Grass.* Ed. Scully Bradley and Harold W. Blodgett. New York: Norton.

Zaslowsky, Dyan. 1986. *These American Lands.* New York: Holt.

CONTRIBUTORS

Harold Alderman is a Professor of Philosophy at Sonoma State University in California. He is the author of a book on Nietzsche, a former member of the executive committee for SPEP, an editor of *The Encyclopedia of Ethics*, and the author of more than thirty articles on a variety of philosophical topics. His novel *Death First!* is now under consideration by a major publisher.

Werner Bigell started his professional career as a nurse in Germany. Later he studied English and Spanish in Germersheim, Germany; El Paso, Texas; and Bergen, Norway. Currently he teaches American studies at Nesna Teacher's College, close to the Arctic Circle in Norway. He is writing his doctoral thesis on the concept of nature in Edward Abbey; his other literary interests include travel writing and the poetry of Robinson Jeffers. His favorite outdoor activities are hiking, fishing, and mushroom picking.

Paul T. Bryant is Professor Emeritus at Colorado State University. He has variously published on nature writing, teaching and research in composition, the teaching of Western American literature, graduate study in American universities, and the writings of Edward Abbey, H. L. Davis, A. B. Guthrie, Jr., and Benton McKaye.

SueEllen Campbell is a Professor at Colorado State University. She has written essays about twentieth-century literature and American 335 nature and wilderness writing, a book about Wyndham Lewis, and a book of personal narratives about being in wild places, *Bringing the Mountain Home* (University of Arizona Press, 1996).

William Chaloupka is a Professor of Environmental Studies at the University of Montana, Missoula, where he teaches courses in social theory, policy, and environmental politics. His recent books include *Knowing Nukes: The Politics and Culture of the Atom,* and he coedited, with Jane Bennett, *In the Nature of Things: Language, Politics, and the Environment.* He is currently writing a book on cynicism in American politics and culture.

Claire Lawrence teaches environmental and multicultural literature in the Scholars Community program at the University of Houston. She has written on landscape, the pastoral, and gender. Her current research interests are focused on the intersection of architecture, literature, and environment. She identifies this research area as theorizing place and space. She has published criticism and creative work in *ISLE, Terra Nova,* and *Western Humanities Review.* Lawrence is currently at work on a novel and a collection of short stories.

Paul Lindholdt teaches writing and literature at Eastern Washington University. His areas of specialization are early American literature and environmental literature. He edited *John Josselyn, Colonial Traveler* and *Cascadia Wild: Protecting an International Ecosystem.*

Tom Lynch, a poet, freelance writer, and adjunct professor of Southwestern literature at New Mexico State University, resides in the Chihuahuan Desert of Las Cruces with his wife and two small boys. Between tramps in the desert and excursions in the mountains, he is pursuing research on cross-cultural eco-regional literature and pondering reinhabitory strategies for the Southwestern bioregions.

Bryan L. Moore received a Ph.D. in English from Texas Christian University in 1996 and is now an Assistant Professor of English at Arkansas State University. His articles have appeared in the *Journal of the American Studies Association of Texas, Composition Studies,* and *Publications of the Arkansas Philological Association,* and he is currently writing on personification in American literature. Moore lives in Jonesboro, Arkansas, with his wife and two children.

David Copland Morris is Associate Professor of American Literature and Environmental Studies at the University of Washington, Tacoma. He has published essays on the canon of American environmental literature and on Robinson Jeffers, John Muir, and Edward Abbey.

Barbara Barney Nelson has a Ph.D. from the University of Nevada, Reno, and she is an Assistant Professor of English in the Languages and Literature Department at Sul Ross State University in Alpine, Texas. Her research interests are eco-criticism, rural culture, rural women, animals, ranching, and agriculture. Nelson has published three books on cowboys: *The Last Campfire, Voices and Visions of the American West,* and a collection of cowboy poetry called *Here's to the Vinegarroon.*

Steve Norwick is Professor of Geology in the Department of Environmental Studies and Planning, Sonoma State University. He holds a Ph.D. from the University of Montana. He teaches courses on environmental physical science, soil science, water quality, computer modeling, and environmental literature. He is on the California North Coast Water Quality Control Board and has recently written on geomorphology of vernal pools and on techniques for identifying obscure but earthquake-prone faults. He has just finished the first draft of "The Verbal Image of Nature," which recounts the three-thousand-year history of the words that Western cultures have used to depict nature.

James A. Papa, Jr., received his Ph.D. in English from the State University of New York at Stony Brook in 1995. He has critical articles on Jack London, Henry Thoreau, and Annie Dillard forthcoming in the *Midwest Quarterly* and *Weaver Studies.* His poems have appeared most recently in the *Long Island Quarterly.*

Peter Quigley received a Ph.D. from Indiana University of Pennsylvania in 1990. He is an editor of the journal *Jeffers Studies* and the chair of the Humanities and Social Science Department at Embry Riddle University in Prescott, Arizona, where he teaches courses in literature and environmental studies in the Science, Technology, and Globalization program. He has published articles on Herman Melville, environmental ethics, Gary Snyder, Robinson Jeffers, T. S. Eliot, and technology and culture.

Rebecca Raglon received her Ph.D. from Queen's University, Canada. Her articles have appeared in *Women's Studies, Weber Studies,* and *Critique;* she has also written chapters for *Scribner's Book of Nature Writing and Natural Eloquence* (Wisconsin University Press, 1997), a collection dealing with women and science. A book of her short stories, *The Gridlock Mechanism,* was published by Oberon Press in 1992. She teaches at Simon Fraser University and lives on Bowen Island, British Columbia.

David Rothenberg has a Ph.D. from Boston University and currently teaches environmental ethics and philosophy of technology in the Environmental Policy program at New Jersey Institute of Technology. He is the editor of the new journal *Terra Nova,* and he previously edited *Wisdom in the Open Air: The Norwegian Roots of Deep Ecology.* He is the author of *Is It Painful to Think? Conversations with Arne Naess.* His most recent book is *Hands End,* which examines technology's influence on the concept of nature. Rothenberg also is a composer and jazz clarinetist.

David J. Rothman received a Ph.D. in English from New York University in 1992. He has published a book of poems, *Dominion of the Shadow* (Gardner Lithographs) in collaboration with photographer Allen Brown, and *Hollywood's America: Social and Political Themes in Motion Pictures* (Westview), coauthored with his father, Stanley Rothman, and Steven Powers. His poetry appears in journals such as *Agni, Atlantic, Kenyon Review, Literary Review, Poetry, Poetry Northwest,* and others. He has taught English at the University of Utah, Zhejiang University (People's Republic of China), New York University, and Western State College of Colorado. Rothman lives in the small town of Crested Butte, Colorado, with his wife, Emily, and son, Jacob.

Edward S. Twining taught British and American literature for thirty years at the University of Denver, including courses in Western American literature. He is currently working on a full-length study of Abbey.

INDEX

339

ACKNOWLEDGMENTS

"Carmel Point" and "November Surf," excerpted from *The Collected Poetry of Robinson Jeffers*, Three volumes, edited by Tim Hunt, with the permission of the publishers, Stanford University Press.
Copyright © 1995 by the Board of Trustees of the Leland Stanford Junior University.

Excerpts from Edward Abbey, *Desert Solitaire*, reprinted by permission of Don Congdon Associates, Inc.
Copyright © 1968 by Edward Abbey, renewed 1996 by Clarke Abbey.

"Just Past Shiprock" and "The Motion of Songs Rising," excerpted from Luci Tapahonso, *Sáanii Dahataal: The Women are Singing*, with the permission of the publishers, The University of Arizona Press.
Copyright © 1993 The University of Arizona Press.

"It Was the Third Day, July 12, 1971" and "To Insure Survival," excerpted from Simon Ortiz, *Woven Stone*, The University of Arizona Press (1992), with the permission of the author.

"Storyteller" and "Slim Man Canyon" excerpted from Leslie Marmon Silko, *Storyteller* and *Laguna Woman*, reprinted with the permission of The Wylie Agency, Inc.
Copyright © 1981 and 1974 by Leslie Marmon Silko.